BLACK BEHIND THE EARS

Black behind the Ears

DOMINICAN RACIAL IDENTITY FROM

MUSEUMS TO BEAUTY SHOPS

Ginetta E. B. Candelario

DUKE UNIVERSITY PRESS

DURHAM & LONDON 2007

© 2007 Duke University Press

All rights reserved

Printed in the United States of America on acid-free paper

Designed by C. H. Westmoreland

Typeset in Scala and Verdana by Tseng Information Systems, Inc.

Library of Congress Cataloging-in-Publication Data appear on the last printed

page of this book.

En honor de Elena

In memory of Dr. Robert Alford

Contents

Figures and Tables

TABLES

Acknowledgments

In the process of undertaking this project, I have relied on the good graces and generosity of very many people.

The late Dr. Robert Alford of the Ph.D. Program in Sociology at the City University of New York (CUNY) Graduate School and University Center chaired my dissertation committee and shared his unflagging pedagogical dedication and intellectual rigor, both of which were foundational to the early stages of this project. The depth and breadth of his mentoring offer a sterling example most scholars can only hope to approximate. My sincere gratitude and appreciation extend as well to the Graduate Center's Dr. Gail Smith, Dr. Juan Flores, and Dr. Ella Shohat, each of whom provided invaluable institutional and scholarly support. My classmates at the CUNY Graduate Program in Sociology, Dr. Nancy López and Dr. Belkis Suazo-García, offered cherished companionship, collaboration, cheerleading, and support throughout graduate school, but especially during the early research stages of this project. Por eso y por mucho más, mil gracias comais.

Dr. Ramona Hernández, Dr. Silvio Torres-Sallaint, and Ms. Sara Aponte of the Dominican Studies Institute (DSI) have consistently provided intellectual and financial support for this work. Through the DSI, I was granted a 1998 Rockefeller Fellowship for research on the Dominican salon and the subsequent article and presentation that resulted. Chapters 4 and 5 of this work are fuller manifestations of that research.

I am equally grateful to Smith College and to Five Colleges, Inc., for providing various grants, course releases, and forums for this work from 1998 to 2003. At Smith, many students have provided invaluable research assistance, kept me organized, and challenged me to hone my ideas. Layla Rivera '00, Janira Bonilla '02, Luz Henao '02, Erica Starks '02, Nora Grais-Clements '03, Diana Noyes '04, Emily Arnold '05, Mary Burford '07, and Jessica Netto '07 deserve my special thanks for all the traveling, photocopying, filing, indexing, copy editing, and data inputting they did without complaint. My colleagues in Sociology and

Latin American and Latina/o Studies have been supportive of the project overall, but Marc Steinberg was particularly generous with his time. He read the entire manuscript several times and offered many insightful and helpful suggestions for revision, which have undeniably contributed to the sociological value of this study. Likewise, I had the good fortune to participate in a writing group with four wonderful Smith colleagues and friends: Lisa Armstrong, Adriane Lentz-Smith, Jennifer Guglielmo, and Daphne Lamothe. Together they provided much needed moral support, insightful critiques, and intellectual collaboration that enriched this project enormously.

In addition, while I was revising this manuscript I was fortunate enough to be teaching a seminar on Dominican Identity Formations in the Latino Studies Program at Cornell University. The students in that seminar were among the brightest, most disciplined, and most dedicated group of young thinkers I have had the pleasure to engage with. Each reminded me why I love teaching, research, and writing so much. Their curious and fresh approaches to the subject of Dominican identity challenged my own thinking in important ways, which I hope they will recognize here.

The Inter-University Program in Latino Research and the Smithsonian Institution provided the first research assistance in the form of the 1997 Latino Graduate Training Seminar in Qualitative Methodology, "Interpreting Latino Cultures: Research and Museums." This was followed in 1998 by a Latino Studies Fellowship through the Office of Fellowships and Grants at the Smithsonian, which allowed me to be in residence at the Anacostia Museum for two months and to conduct research at Museo del Hombre Dominicano. The late Dr. Dato Pagán-Perdomo, director of the Museo del Hombre Dominicano from 1996 to 2002, shared his vast knowledge of Dominican historiography and was a most gracious host during my visits to the Museo. At the Anacostia, the assistance and guidance of Portia James proved invaluable, as did the administrative generosity of the entire Anacostia staff. I owe a special debt to Mr. Héctor Corporán, who was employed by the Anacostia as a community scholar with the Black Mosaic Exhibit, who first made me aware of the Dominican presence in Washington, D.C.; who introduced me to the community; and who continues to share his insight and historical knowledge of that community with passion and grace.

The researchers and staff at the Facultad Latino Americana de Ciencias Sociales (FLACSO) in Santo Domingo provided a welcoming space in which to undertake revisions to this text while I was there as a Fulbright

Scholar during the spring of 2003. María Filomena González, Rubén Silié, Pilar Corporán, Adribel Ruíz, and Dania Correa Fortuna were particularly helpful. Karin Weyland of Fundación Melassa read several drafts of this work and was generous with both her friendship and her insights into Dominican blackness.

There are countless librarians, researchers, and community members who contributed their expertise and knowledge, and to whom I send a collective "thank you." In particular, however, I must mention the generous assistance of Roland Roebuck of the Washington, D.C., Department of Human Services and Dr. Gladys Martínez of the U.S. Census Bureau and her husband, Horacio Badia, of *La Nación* newspaper, all in Washington, D.C.

I am grateful to Dr. Wambui Mwangi for her many years of friendship and political and intellectual inspiration, and for her willingness to read and discuss this work endlessly. Likewise, I imposed far too often on the good graces of my childhood friend, Maritza Rodríguez, for her unflagging support and humor. Though not herself an academic, she influenced some of the most valuable insights contained here. My sister friend Amy Gilliam and her daughter Jordan Copeland gave my son and me a home and hearth during my months of research at the Anacostia. Without their support, I could not have completed this work.

A warm thank you to Reynolds Smith and Sharon Torian of Duke University Press, who saw this project through to its completion with gracious and good-humored patience. I express my sincere appreciation also to the anonymous readers who reviewed the manuscript and offered wonderfully helpful advice for its improvement. Any remaining flaws in the text are attributable to me alone.

Finally, I am indebted to my mother, Elena María Candelario Cáceres, for her courage, tenacity, laughter, and love. She was the first to ask me the questions that drive this project. I hope I've answered well. My children, Marlena Candelario Romero and Christian Candelario Romero, have given meaning and richness to my life and all my endeavors, and my former stepdaughter Krystal Romero has been present in our hearts despite the miles that have separated us. More than anyone else, these children helped to define the evolution, contours, and fruition of this project.

BLACK BEHIND THE EARS

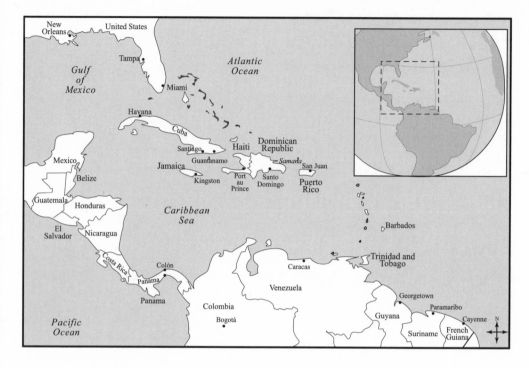

1. Map of the Caribbean

"We Declare That We Are Indians"

DOMINICAN IDENTITY DISPLAYS AND DISCOURSES IN TRAVEL WRITING, MUSEUMS, BEAUTY SHOPS, AND BODIES

> We declare that we are Indians so as not to recognize ourselves as mulattos, to deny the black we have behind the ears, in our aspiration to whiten the race.[1]

> In 1613, after many decades of research and travel in Peru, Huamán Poma (a Quecheua Indian) wrote: "When mulattoes—a mixture of negro and Indian—produce quadroon children, these children lose all physical trace of their negro origin except for the ear, which still gives them away by its shape and size."
> —Jack Forbes[2]

Dominicans will often say "Tenemos el negro detrás de las orejas [We have the black behind the ears]" when speaking to matters of blackness and Dominican identity. In doing so, they echo and affirm the most famous line of a Dominican *décima* (ten-line poem) written by Juan Antonio Alix in 1883.[3] In the décima, "El negro tras de la oreja," Dominicans are humorously chastised for their "overwhelming" desire to whiten:

Como hoy la preocupación	Since nowadays there are so many
A más de una gente abruma,	Whom this dismays
Emplearé mi débil pluma	I will employ my weak pen
Para darle una lección;	To offer all a lesson;

Pues esto en nuestra Nación	For in our Nation
Ni buen resultado deja,	This will not do,
Eso era en la España vieja	*That was then in old Spain*
Según desde chico escucho	Or so I heard as a youngster
Pero hoy abunda mucho	But nowadays what abounds
"El negro tras de la oreja."	Is "the black behind the ear."[4]

Alix tells his listeners that their preoccupation with whiteness may have been appropriate in "old Spain" but it "will not do" in the Dominican Republic. He implies that the obsessive referencing of a white heritage only highlights the blackness of the speaker, for the "black behind the ears" may be hidden, but it is hidden just behind the face of Dominican national and individual bodies.

For much of Dominican history, the national body has been defined as not-black, even as black ancestry has been grudgingly acknowledged. In the place of blackness, officially identity discourses and displays have held that Dominicans are racially Indian and culturally Hispanic. In light of this history, the Dominican body "is simultaneously a referent of individual continuity, an index of collective similarity and differentiation, and a canvas upon which identification can play,"[5] as the identity theorist Richard Jenkins put it. The continuity, collectivity, and particularity of blackness in the Dominican Republic and its contrapuntal relationship to Haiti are aptly expressed by Alix's poetic chastisement, which has been fully incorporated into the Dominican racial vernacular.

Juan Antonio Alix was born and experienced his childhood under the Haitian Unification government of 1822 to 1844.[6] Perhaps that is why simultaneous to his recognition and affirmation of African ancestry among Dominicans, several of Alix's décimas reflect the anti-Haitianist foundations of Dominican identity. For example, in "February 27th," written in 1884 to commemorate the fortieth anniversary of Dominican separation from Haiti, Alix's depiction of Haitians and the atrocities of "the Occupation" are nothing short of racist:

Los cafres de grande boca	The big-mouthed Kaffirs
Y de bembas de soleta,	With their thick leather lips
Cogían los niños de teta	Would take children from the tit
Y al aire los arrojaban	And fling them into the air
Y al caer los aparaban	And on falling they would be pricked
En aguda bayoneta.	On sharpened bayonet.

Esos diablos infernales	Those infernal devils
El año cinco quemaron	In the fifth year burned
A Santiago, y degollaron	Santiago, and slaughtered
Miles seres racionales.	Thousands of Christians.
Todos fueron ahorcados,	All were hung
Y otros asesinados	And others were assassinated
De la Iglesia en el altar,	At the Church altar,
Sin dejarlos terminar	Not letting them finish
La misa, esos condenados!	The mass, those damned ones!
Los infames degollaban	These infamous men slaughtered
A los de familia padres,	Fathers of families,
Y en presencia de las madres	And before the mothers,
A sus hijas las violaban;	They raped the daughters;
A nadie pues, respetaban,	So they respected not one
En estos pueblos cristianos	Of these Christian peoples,
Pero hoy, dominicanos	But today, Dominicans
Debemos todos decir:	Should all say:
¡Morir, cien veces morir!	Death, a thousand times Death!
¡Antes que ser haitianos!	Rather than Haitian be!

In this text, Haitians are textually depicted in gross caricature as embodying evil and uncivilized hypermasculinity: savage, animalistic, sexually violent, and devilish. Dominicans are implicitly contrasted to the "big-mouthed Kaffirs" as respectable fathers and mothers, virginal daughters,[7] Hispanic, Catholic, and white. Written just a few months after "Black behind the Ears," this décima contains all the ideological markings of official Dominicanidad: Negrophobia, white supremacy, and anti-Haitianism.

Dominican scholars such as Frank Moya Pons, Juan Bosch, and Silvio Torres-Sallaint attribute this identity formation to the historically distinctive material conditions of the colonists, their slaves, and their descendants in the Spanish colony of Santo Domingo. They argue that a series of regionally anomalous events in the political-economic history of Santo Domingo account for this distinctive socio-racial formation. Chief among those anomalies are (1) the relatively short duration and limited importance of plantation slavery; (2) the massive depopulations caused by white emigration; (3) the impoverishment of the remaining Spanish and Creole colonials during the "Devastations"; and (4) the concomitantly heavy reliance on blacks and mulattos in the armed forces and religious infrastructure.

Plantation-based African slavery in the Spanish colony of Santo Domingo began in earnest in 1516 when the colonist Gonzalo de Vellosa developed a successful method for processing sugar cane.[8] However, the Spanish crown's imposition of trade restrictions made the industry far less lucrative than it would become in Haiti. As a result, the Spanish colonists engaged in contraband trading with smugglers and pirates who frequented and ultimately established outposts on the island's shores. The Spanish Crown responded from 1605 to 1606 by forcibly depopulating the northern coastal zone towns of Monti Cristi, Puerto Plata, and Yaguana, an event known as *Las Devastaciones*, or "The Devastations." Colonists' homes and crops were burned; towns were razed; and the Creoles, the enslaved, and the freedmen and women alike were forced to reside in cities more easily controlled by the crown. The Devastations, taken together with the English privateer Sir Francis Drake's 1585 sacking and plunder of the Santo Domingo, led to a sharp drop in the Spanish colony's European and Creole population. The African and Afro-Creole population, however, remained and outnumbered the remaining colonials by as many as nine to one. Those colonials who stayed found themselves increasingly impoverished and therefore unable to sustain either the slave trade or the sugar industry that relied on it.

The seventeenth century came to be known as "The Century of Misery" on Hispaniola. Epidemic illnesses such as smallpox combined with economic misfortunes to completely transform the colony's social organization. The material distance between slave and master was so small as to be negligible. At the same time, the number of Africans and their descendants in the Spanish colony was increased by runaways from the neighboring French San Domingüe, established by the Treaty of Ryswick in 1697. Spanish Santo Domingo guaranteed enslaved runaways from the French San Domingüe their freedom and did not honor French fugitive-slave laws.

By the eighteenth century, the two colonies had articulated their respective sugar- and cattle-based slave economies serving European consumer markets. French San Domingüe established itself as a major producer of sugar using plantation-based slavery. Likewise, Spanish Santo Domingo's cattle industry grew in response to the growing demand in Europe for leather goods.[9] At the same time, Spanish Santo Domingo's cattle industry supported French San Domingüe's sugar industry in that it was Santo Domingo's cattle that fed San Domingüe's slaves.

Although the cattle-ranching economy was reliant on slave labor, it relied on a far less labor intensive and much more autonomous mode of production than the sugar plantations. "The uniqueness of the eighteenth-century cattle ranch (*hato ganadero*) lay in the peculiar combination of labor forces: a strikingly unconventional blend of labor performed by free property owners alongside slaves. What evolved was a kind of socio-economic unit that was both patriarchal and feudal."[10] Moreover, by the time cattle ranching surfaced as Santo Domingo's principal economic and social base, a large group of freedmen and women existed, many of whom either lived daily lives that were somewhat autonomous from the government and the ruling classes because they were geographically dispersed, resided far from the urban center, and were economically self-sufficient. For those freedmen and women who were in the urban centers, the key governing institutions—the colonial administration, the military, and the church—relied on them as soldiers, petty administrators, and religious leaders. According to Moya Pons, this meant that "despite their color," these freedmen and women not only considered themselves "different from the slaves whom they saw as the only blacks of the island," but as the "whites of the land."[11] In other words, Dominican whiteness was an explicitly achieved (and achievable) status with connotations of social, political, and economic privilege, and blackness signaled foreignness, socioeconomic subordination, and inferiority.

Thus, rather than use the discourses of negritude to understand and represent themselves, Dominicans use language that affirms their "Indian" heritage—*Indio, Indio oscuro, Indio claro, trigüeño*—and signals their resistance to foreign authority, whether Spanish or Haitian, and their autochthonous claims to sovereignty while accounting for the preponderance of medium to dark skin tones and complexions in the population. Currently, this discourse is buttressed by educational literature from primary school onward, by print and electronic media, by proto-Indo-Hispanic models of female beauty; by commercialization of indigenous words, images, and icons; and by the public-history venues in the Dominican Republic.

Observers of Dominican racial self-identifications have long implied that rejection of negritude is absurd in that it flies in the face of what is visible: dark skin color, "African" facial features, and coarse and tightly curled hair. As this book went to press, the *Miami Herald* published "Black Denial."[12] This article on race in the Dominican Republic was widely circulated on the Internet and generated great debate. Among academics, the general response was that it again represented Dominicans as uniformly negrophobic, and did little to engage the long history of anti-racist Dominican research, writing, and activism.[13] Readers commented online that the article confirmed a general sense that Domini-cans are self-loathing and deluded people who are "really" black yet in "denial."[14] Yet as the cultural studies scholar Ella Shohat insists, "Identity and looks . . . are negotiated differently in different contexts."[15] For me the issue is not whether or not Dominicans are "in fact" black; whatever one concludes when engaging in racial categorization inevitably draws on presumptions that derive from colonial histories and racist ideolo-gies. Rather, I am interested in mapping the multiple strategies Domini-cans marshal as they daily confront those histories and ideologies. How do Dominicans face the "black behind the ears" when confronted with both Haiti's and the United States' expansionist agendas and racial ide-ologies that would define them as black so as to legitimate Dominicans' subordination to their respective states and social orders?

This book is about Dominican identity discourses that negotiate black-ness and Hispanicity in four related and mutually referential cultural sites of identity display—travel narratives, the museum, the beauty shop, and the female body—in three historically connected geographic locations (Santo Domingo, New York City, and Washington, D.C.). More broadly, the book is about how ethno-racial discourses are narrated, in-ternalized, and displayed by actors and institutions negotiating identity in transnational social fields.[16] By "identity displays" I mean material representations of a sense of self that is manifested in various ways: dis-cursively, symbolically, and bodily. By choosing "identity display" as a key conceptual device in the analysis, I am signaling both the purposeful nature of conveying identity and the equivocal nature of how those con-veyances are received, interpreted, and responded to.

To this end, I utilize discourse analysis, content analysis, a local ethnography, open-ended in-depth interviewing, and photo elicitation.[17] Together, this bricolage approach to methodology offers a complex, in-depth ethnographic understanding of Dominican identity and blackness and offers a model for similar studies of ethno-racial identity forma-tion.[18] To cohere that bricolage, in this introductory chapter I undertake a literature review, theoretical and methodological discussion, and sum-mary of the book's structure.

Identifying the Self in Society

Theories of identity abound in psychology, social psychology, philoso-phy, folklore studies, communications, and, of course, sociology.[19] Although each of these disciplines offers important insights into identity formation, my interest in the relationship between institutions and individuals, and between official discourse and everyday life practices, lead me to draw on sociological theories of identity and group formation. In particular, I am influenced by the tenets of symbolic interactionism in which the self is produced through interactions with others,[20] interactions that are mediated and structured through multiple social groups and institutions and that are enacted through multiple role identities. Thus, particular identities of a given individual will be more or less salient in different circumstances and contexts.[21]

Further, the salience of a given identity depends on an individual's commitment to the role-conferring identity. Commitment can be interactive or affective; one refers to the number of relationships tied to the identity, the other to the importance of those relationships.[22] Drawing on the insights offered by Erving Goffman on the presentation of self, I view identity as being enacted through staged practices and interactions.[23] I diverge from the dramaturgical model, however, in that I do not view roles as monolingually scripted and as always mutually intelligible for performer and audience. Successful impression management relies on shared symbols and codes for proper interpretation of the displayed identity. When those symbols are not shared, when the codes are not intelligible or are rapidly switched, identities can be mis-taken. Thus, while skin color and any African heritage are the phenotypical symbol and genealogical and ideological codes for determining racial identity in the United States, for Dominicans the phenotypical symbol is hair, and the ideological code is anti-Haitianism. Here I am drawing on Dorothy Smith's formulation of ideological codes as "order[ing] and organiz[ing] texts across discursive sites, concerting discourse focused on divergent topics and sites, often having divergent audiences, and variously hooked into policy or political practice."[24] The Dominican case illustrates that identities can be situational, equivocal, and ambiguous, but the fact that they are also structured by power relations as self-perception is perforce mediated by the perception of others and our structured relation to them.

Benedict Anderson instructs us that imagined communities are produced through cultural media and institutions such as the newspaper, the novel, the map, and the museum. Imagined communities foster a sense of belonging, according to Anderson, "because, regardless of the actual inequality and exploitation that may prevail in each, the nation is always conceived as a deep, horizontal comradeship."[25] The value of

Anderson's conceptualization to this project is the attention it asks us to pay to the links between institutions and texts. However, it does not go far enough in explaining how and why members of the nation reconcile the notion of "deep horizontal comradeship" with the fact of social stratification. Further, the link between the imagined community and social identity—that is, sense of self as member of a particular social grouping—is also undertheorized.

Reflecting on Anderson's insights alongside Smith's, I wondered how individual members of an imagined community narrate, display, or enact their belonging to the imagined community in everyday life. Put another way: In what ways are the representations of Dominican identity offered by influential interlocutors such as travel writers, journalists, scholars, national museums, and various agents of socialization into identity norms internalized and reflected in Dominicans' conceptualizations and presentation of self? These questions echo the longstanding sociological concern with the relationship between self and society, between individual and structure. In the contexts of this project, I have found Richard Jenkins's argument that there is an "internal–external dialectic of identification" through which both individual and collective identities are constituted to be particularly useful in creating a link between institutions' and individuals' identity narratives and displays.[26]

Following Charles Cooley, George Mead, and Erving Goffman, Jenkins argues that identity is a "dialectical synthesis of internal and external definitions" and, important for my argument here, that identity is embodied.[27] Thus, identity is a process of both internationalization and externalization; it is at once structured through institutions and left open to interpretive practices of its subjects; and it relies on the expressive and perceptive practices and paradigms of both the self and the other who reflects back the existence of the identified self. To consider issues of blackness and ambiguity in Dominican identity displays, then, is to consider the relationship between self and society. But that is not all.

Because Dominicans are a transnational community, one that has historically existed in dynamic dialectic between the United States and Haiti, Dominican identities must be understood in relation to that triangular dialectic (see figure 1, above). That is, while I agree that identities are internally cohesive, paying attention to the complexity of identity discourses and displays forces me to argue that Dominican identities are also embodied, displayed, enacted, and perceived according to their context. This study, then, is driven by a desire to understand how institutionally normative identity displays and discourses are embodied in everyday life, and how ideological codes "switch" depending on the discursive field.

Approaching Dominican Identity

Santo Domingo is the capital of the Dominican Republic and currently is home to nearly a third of the national population of 8 million. In addition to housing the national government, Santo Domingo holds the cultural and historical institutions defined by the state as fundamental to the national patrimony, principally in the colonial district and the Plaza de la Cultura. These areas and institutions are routinely visited by national residents and tourists. Thus, while there are arguably other important sites of Dominican identity displays throughout the country, Santo Domingo's state-sanctioned cultural institutions continue to exert hegemonic influence over the country and its social-identity norms.[28]

Narratives indicating the non-black identity of the inhabitants of the Spanish part of Santo Domingo began circulating between the island and the United States in the late eighteenth century. By the twentieth century, narratives that framed Dominicans as non-blacks became institutionalized in the country's academic and public-history venues. Although members of the small elite had traveled abroad throughout the nineteenth century, it was not until the second half of the twentieth century that large numbers of non-elite Dominicans began to travel to the United States as political exiles, immigrants, migrants, and, most recently, transmigrants.[29] Whether in Santo Domingo, New York City, or Washington, D.C., Dominicans have been forced to contend with blackness—their own and others.' Each geographic site is uniquely situated in relation to the larger Dominican population yet reflective of broader issues in Dominican identity displays. Both travel narratives of the Dominican Republic and Dominican traveler's narratives of their identity draw on ambiguous and equivocal displays of their relationship to blackness to situate Dominicans in local ethno-racial regimes.

David Howard's study of Dominican race ideology and anti-Haitianism, *Coloring the Nation: Race and Ethnicity in the Dominican Republic,* has offered evidence of the hegemonic nature of negrophobic identity norms among Dominicans of various classes. Surveying over three hundred Dominicans in the capital and in a rural town, Howard found that Dominican identity incorporates anti-Haitianism and "insidious" racism in its everyday expressions. Likewise, a more recent comparative study of attitudes toward whiteness and blackness in the Dominican Republic, Cuba, Puerto Rico, and the U.S. mainland found that Hispanic Caribbean respondents—including those with visible black ancestry—were even more likely than Latina and Latino respondents in the United States to attribute negative qualities to blacks.[30] In my research, I asked whether negrophobic identity norms held in the United States, and if they did, how Dominican norms interacted with norms in the host society.

Traveling with Dominican Identity

Dominican identity in the United States must be understood as simultaneously ethnic and racial, or "ethno-racial." By ethno-racial I mean that Dominicans are negotiating their status as racialized minorities operating in the context of histories and structures beyond their control, but they do so with a degree of agency and self-determination. They bring to the local context, in other words, their own histories and understanding of their identities and they display them accordingly. The degree to which they are successful in securing others' acceptance of their self-perceptions depends on their receiving context and the relative salience of gender, class, citizenship, and place in their lives. As home to the oldest and still the largest Dominican community outside the Dominican Republic, New York City's Washington Heights was a logical place to explore that question.

In his 1994 monograph *Quisqueya on the Hudson: The Transnational Identity of Dominicans in Washington Heights*, the anthropologist Jorge Duany undertook a groundbreaking study of Dominican transnational identity in Washington Heights. In that work, Duany and a team of local researchers undertook an intensive ethnographic study of a city block in Washington Heights based on participant observation and in-depth interviewing of over 350 Dominicans. Duany concluded that everyday cultural practices showed the formation and maintenance of a transnational identity among Dominicans, who at the same time affirmed their national distinctiveness from other Latino communities in the United States. Interestingly, although the report notes that Dominicans are perceived to be and are positioned "as a racial minority," after posing one of the study's fundamental questions—"How have the migrants reshaped their traditional values and practices in response to an alien environment?"—Dominican racial identity ideologies and practices were not systematically examined. Instead, the study focused on national identity issues, and researchers "classified" their respondents as black, white, or mulatto in consultation with the subjects themselves but primarily derived from the researchers' own observations of their phenotypes.[31] A footnote to this single reference to racial identity called for further investigation of how racial terminology and perception change on migration.[32] My work here picks up that call.

There has been an ongoing debate within Dominican Studies about whether and how the racial perceptions and ideologies of Dominicans change on migration. Some argue that the migration process and the experience of a racial system different from the one they were socialized into causes a shift in Dominican perceptions of self and other—and, therefore, of Dominican identity. Others argue that Dominicans' perceptions do not change, or that they change only in that their ideological commitment to anti-Haitianism and Negrophobia is hardened. Still others argue that even if there is a shift or a reorientation of Dominican identity outside the Dominican Republic, migrants who return to the Republic reassume local identity norms, often with increased vigor.

The historian Frank Moya Pons, for example, has argued that during the 1970s, return migrants had "discovered their black roots as a result of their contact with blacks and other minorities in the United States."[33] Yet in the early 1970s, the social psychologist Antonio de Moya examined how living in New York affected Dominican children's perceptions of Haitians and found that anti-Haitianist sentiments remained quite strong among Dominican emigrants, even while they were living in New York City.[34] Similarly, residential proximity and sharing of institutions such as George Washington High School with African Americans did not lead to increased black self-identification among Dominican immigrant youth in the 1970s. The historian Jesse Hoffnang found that, although responses ranged from outright rejection of black identities to political affirmation of solidarity with blacks as racialized minorities, evidently the 1970s did not see an overall shift in the racial self-perception of Dominicans in New York City.[35] Nor does it seem to have influenced those who return to the Dominican Republic.

In his mid-1990s study, David Howard examined the racial perceptions of return migrants among his respondents. He found that, although while residing in New York most had been recategorized into or closer to black categories, they did not necessarily adopt or internalize those ascriptions. Indeed, when they returned to Santo Domingo, many re-embraced local racial perceptions and ideologies, and some even hardened their anti-Haitianist stances. Likewise, the sociologist

Peggy Levitt found that, even though they had experienced racialized discrimination and prejudice in Boston, return migrants to Miraflores "did not bring or send back ideas or behaviors that seriously challenged the racial hierarchy."[36] According to Levitt, Dominicans in Massachusetts classified themselves as "other" nearly twice as often as they did "black" in the 1990 Census.[37] Similarly, a 1995 Gallup Poll conducted in the Dominican Republic found that few people favored black identities.[38] Thus, return migrants such as the feminist writer Chiqui Vicioso, whose experiences as a student at George Washington High School and, later, at Brooklyn College led to a revised consciousness of herself as a mulatto who identified as black "as a gesture of solidarity," are evidently not representative of return migrants overall.[39] Yet those return migrants who claim a black identity are important, precisely because they might lead to insights into the conditions that foster shifts in the racial self-perception of Dominican immigrants, if not of return migrants, toward blackness.

The sociologist Mary Waters has argued that the maintenance of ethnic distinctiveness has been a strategy of upward mobility and assimilation for black West Indian, especially Jamaican, immigrants to New York City. This is so "because when West Indians lose their distinctiveness as immigrants or ethnics, they become not just Americans, but black Americans."[40] Waters argues that as immigrants, black West Indians bring with them a combination of high ambitions, expectation of equal treatment based on their individual attributes, and strong antidiscrimination stances. This set of values articulates with the "color-blind" and individualistic values of their white co-workers and employers in New York City, who in turn reward the immigrants for not being like Anglo-American blacks. For their children, however, the situation is different. Because they are not immigrants but second-generation Americans, they are more likely to be treated like native blacks in the public sphere, school system, workplace, and in relations with state authorities. They are also more likely to "use American, not Caribbean, yardsticks to measure" their opportunities and their place in the social structure.[41] Racial discrimination in their everyday lives pushes the second generation into a black identity.

Although Dominicans often share the experience of being Caribbean immigrants who are perceived to be black, unlike British West Indians Dominicans are also Hispanic. Hispanicity in both the United States and the Dominican Republic offers an alternative to blackness. Although "Hispanic" is a racialized non-white category in the United States, it is also a non-black one. Thus, for example, in his work the linguist

Benjamin Bailey has found that second-generation Dominican youth in Providence, Rhode Island, use purposeful linguistic strategies to mark themselves as Hispanic rather than black:

> The many second-generation Dominican high school students who are phenotypically indistinguishable from African Americans regularly show that they can "speak Spanish" in order to counter others' assumptions—in both intra- and inter-ethnic contexts—that they are "black." Many of their peers, including non-Hispanics, accept this Spanish speaking as evidence of non-black identity. In many contexts, Dominican Americans are thus reversing the historical precedence of African descent of ethnolinguistic identity for social classification.[42]

That is, although they routinely are mistaken for African American or black, they mark themselves as Hispanic as a preferred alternative to blackness. This discursive display may be recently evident in the United States, but it has a long history dating back to the island.

Narrating Haitian Blackness, Displaying Dominican Negrophobia

Chapter 1, "'It Is Said That Haiti Is Getting Blacker and Blacker': Traveling Narratives of Dominican Identity," offers an extended examination of the leading travel narratives' renditions of the island's people. These narratives were written by foreign visitors to the island who reported on their experiences on their return to their homes. Although the primary audiences for the narratives were the travelers' countrymen and -women, most of the travel narratives themselves "traveled" back to the Dominican Republic. That is, the Dominican intelligentsia, politicos, and socially dominant classes read the accounts as well, often incorporating those texts into their own narrations of Dominican identity.

For over one hundred years spanning the colonial, revolutionary, and national periods, observers compared and contrasted the residents of the western (French and later Haitian) and eastern (Spanish and later Dominican) parts of the island. The comparison rarely favored Haiti or the Haitians. Instead, as revealed by the evocative words of U.S. Navy Rear Admiral Colby M. Chester, quoted in the chapter's title, Haiti was narrated repeatedly as increasingly blacker while the Dominican Republic was simultaneously narrated as whiter. Writing from geopolitically framed vantage points, observers with varied political agendas such as

M. L. Moreau de Saint-Méry (1796), Charles Mackenzie (1830), David Dixon Porter (1846), and Consul Maxime Raybaud (1856), W. S. Courtney (1860), Joseph W. Fabens (1863), De Bonneville Randolph Keim (1870), Samuel Hazard (1873), Frederic Albion Ober (1904), William D. Boyce (1914), A. Hyatt Verrill (1914, 1926), Harry A. Frank (1920), Samuel Guy Inman (1920, 1930), Harry L. Foster (1929), and Arthur J. Burkes (1932) colluded in the representation of Dominicans and the Dominican Republic as a nation with a minimal degree of "pure blackness."

I argue that this should be understood as part of a geopolitically framed racial project of U.S. imperialism that intersected unevenly but importantly with Dominican nation-building projects through anti-Haitianist discourses and ideologies. Those projects coalesced during the regime of Rafael Trujillo, when the Dominican state fully institutionalized anti-Haitianist national-identity formations and began to circulate in the United States its own travel-narrative accounts of Dominicans' racial identity. Largely organized and distributed through the regime's propaganda machine, these narratives legitimized both the Trujilloist states' policies—in particular its 1937 massacre of tens of thousands of Haitians—and the United States' policies toward Trujillo. Simultaneous with the foreign propaganda circuits was the increasing attention paid by the Dominican state to preserving and protecting the national patrimony through public-history projects. After all, a national patrimony reliant on pre-Columbian artifacts and Spanish colonial architecture and ruins together offered evidence for the nation's claims to Indo-Hispanicity.

Chapter 2, "'The Africans Have No [Public] History': The Museo del Hombre Dominicano and Indigenous Displays of Dominican Identity," examines Dominican historiography and public history—both of which have drawn consistently on U.S. travel narratives as primary materials—as a case study of how foreign representations both reflect and responded to Dominican identities and racial ideologies. The permanent exhibit at the Museo del Hombre Dominicano is dedicated largely to the island's pre-Columbian archeological history and culture and has changed little over the past twenty years. The pre-Columbian artifacts constitute the entirety of the archeological collection, research agenda, and displays. The ethnological collection focuses on the nature of pre-Columbian life; provides brief histories of Spanish conquest and colonization, African slavery, and creolization; and offers a celebration of contemporary folk life and culture. Through each of these collections and displays, the foundational—indeed, fundamental—Indo-Hispanicity of contemporary Dominicans is emphasized.

Interestingly, close examination of the display strategies of the Museo offers evidence of the geopolitical situatedness of Dominican identity. In particular, the extensive use of travel narratives as primary materials for the ethnological collection offers evidence of the linkages between foreign ethnography and local auto-ethnographic displays of Dominican identity. Rather than viewing travel narratives simply as foreign perspectival and ideological impositions on Dominicans, or considering the incorporation of those narratives into the national historiography and museography as simple appropriation, I will suggest that those narratives served the ideological agendas of Dominican political, social, and intellectual elites, and they have come to form part of Dominican official identity displays and discourses.

Travel writings have had ethnographic purposes historically akin to those of the metropolitan museum and the World's Fairs: They were meant to offer an account of "foreign" others to audiences in the metropolis.[43] The ideological and institutional linkage between travel writing and museum representations, however, extended beyond the metropolitan centers that produced both forms of display. The linkage between travel writing and museum representations was also present within auto-ethnographies of the "contact zone." As Mary Louise Pratt explains, the contact zone is

> the space in which peoples geographically and historically separated come into contact with each other and establish ongoing relations, usually involving conditions of coercion, radical inequality, and intractable conflict. [Auto-ethnography is used] to refer to instances in which colonized subjects undertake to represent themselves in ways that engage with the colonizer's own terms. If ethnographic texts are a means by which Europeans represent to themselves their (usually subjugated) others, autoethnographic texts are those the others construct in response to or in dialogue with those metropolitan representations. . . . Auto-ethnographic texts are not, then, what are usually thought of as "authentic" or autochthonous forms of self-representation. . . . Rather auto-ethnography involves partial collaboration with and appropriation of the idioms of the conqueror. . . . Often . . . the idioms appropriate and transformed are those of travel and exploration writing, merged with or infiltrated to varying degrees with indigenous modes.[44]

Extending Pratt's insights, I am reading the Museo del Hombre Dominicano's permanent exhibit as a sort of "auto-ethnographic expression" of the contact zone created by the Dominican Republic's geopolitical negotiations with the United States and Haiti from the nineteenth century onward. This is exemplified in the Museo's use of both travel-narrative text and illustrations in the display.

Dominicans' ability to assert their dominant status as *los blancos de la tierra viz a viz* Haitians in the Dominican Republic was mediated by consciousness of their being perceived, at best, as the whites of the land and, at worst, as lighter blacks by U.S. observers. As Richard Harvey Brown argues, "Efforts to resist domination can readily re-enforce it, if such resistance is cast in the code of the dominator."[45] Although this discourse-analysis approach offers wonderful insights into the official ideology, it does not explain the relationship of those traveling narratives on the self- and other-perceptions of Dominicans in their everyday lives. For that task, ethnographic research strategies and interviewing are more appropriate.

"*Negro*" Negation in Everyday Life: Hair Is at the Root of Race

One of the few studies of racial perception in everyday life within the Dominican Republic is the linguist Daysi Josefina Guzmán's "Raza y lenguaje en el Cibao."[46] Guzmán conducted interviews with forty-eight adults who had resided for twenty-five years or more in Santiago de los Caballeros and who were from a range of social classes to determine the racial classifications currently in use, as well as the meaning of words used to signal racial classifications. According to her study, twenty-two categorical race terms were currently in use: *rubio, blanco, pelirrojo, blanco "jipato," blanco jojoto, Indio lavado, Indio claro, trigüeño claro, trigüeño, pinto, pinto jovero, jabao, Indio canelo, trigüeño oscuro, Indio quemao, Moreno, mulatto, prieto, negro, cenizo, cocolo,* and *albino.* These words were then categorized into five major racial groupings: white; white–mulatto range; mulatto; mulatto–black range; black (table 1).

Operating in tandem with those categories are the six "variables" used to denote racialized physical features: skin color, hair color, eye color, hair texture, facial features, and other bodily features such as ears and buttocks. Respondents were asked to provide terms and descriptions relative to each of these variables. They were then asked to explain which variables characterized each of the twenty-two racial categories. The variable that most often appeared in a given category was considered "fundamental" to that category. In the mulatto, mulatto–black border, and black categories, hair texture was the fundamental determinant. That

Table 1 Dominican Racial Categories

Racial Category	Racial Types Included
White	*Rubio*
	Blanco
	Pelirrojo
	Blanco jipato
White–mulatto range	*Blanco jojoto*
	Indio lavado
	Indio claro
	Trigüeño claro
	Trigüeño
Mulatto	*Pinto*
	Pinto jovero
	Jabao
	Indio canelo
Mulatto–black range	*Trigüeño oscuro*
	Indio quemao
Black	*Moreno*
	Mulato
	Prieto
	Negro
	Cenizo
	Cocolo

Source: Guzmán, "Raza y lenguaje en el Cibao," 41.

is, coarser hair textures placed one increasingly further away from the white and white–mulatto border groups. Whites and those in the white–mulatto border group were fundamentally defined by skin color, eye color, hair color, and hair texture combined. The hair texture for whites and the white–mulatto border group was "good" and "loose" or "straight" (*lacio*).

An overarching tendency among those interviewed in Guzmán's study was to "blacken the white category" and "whiten the black category."[47] I take this as indicative of a generalized effort to fit self and others into the "prototypically" Dominican middle: the *Indio* category. The rise of the

"*Indio*" category as a rejection of, and replacement for, black categories is historically rooted in a simultaneous recognition of dark(er) skin color and disavowal of Dominican affinities with both Haiti and Spain. Unlike mulatto, which historically had connotations of illegitimacy and the stigma of slavery in colonial and early national discourses of race, Indio "identity was an 'internal' identity with historicity, as opposed to 'white/Spanish' or 'black/African,' identities which had their roots elsewhere."[48]

I argue that hair is of preeminent importance in the project of managing "the black behind the ears" because of this emphasis on indigeneity as the basis for Dominican identity. The British sociologist Anthony Synnott noted nearly two decades ago that

> Hair is perhaps our most powerful symbol of individual and group identity—powerful first because it is physical and therefore extremely personal, and second because although personal, it is also public rather than private. Furthermore, hair symbolism is usually voluntary rather than imposed or "given." Finally, hair is malleable, in various ways, and therefore singularly apt to symbolize both differentiations between and changes in, individual and group identities.[49]

Yet despite its important symbolic role as a marker of group boundaries and individual membership status, hair has received relatively little attention in the sociological literature on the embodiment of identity.[50] The dynamic interplay between internal and external definitions of Dominican identities is routinely enacted in the everyday practices of Dominican hair culture. Analyzing Dominican hair culture also reminds us to pay attention to the intersectionality of stratification systems such as gender, class, race, and sexuality.

Given this early scholarly recognition of the role of hair in marking group boundaries, its particularly salient role in the achievement of gender statuses, and the predominance of women in hair culture work, I was curious about the gendered nature of racialized identities and identifications among Dominicans. In light of the visible role women play as symbols, icons, producers, and reproducers of Dominican identity, I decided to focus on women. Moreover, taking seriously the literatures on the socially constructed nature of gender, on the mutual referentiality of race and gender identities, and on women's central roles in social reproduction required a gendered analytic.

At the same time, I wanted an entry point that would allow me to develop sustained and trusting relationships with Dominican women.

The Dominican salon, a ubiquitous women's institution in Washington Heights (and, indeed, wherever Dominican women are found), offered the ideal site for exploring issues of gendered racial identity in a sustained, in-depth way. Although my focus and methods were different, and my research took place three decades later among Dominican women in New York City, my results were similar to Guzmán's to the extent that I found that hair was a fundamental marker for Dominican women's racial ascription discourses and identity displays.[51] This suggests to me that Dominican indigenism is reliant on bodily as well as discursive practices.

The institutionalization of the Indio designation found its apogee during the Trujillato through mechanisms such as the *cédula de identidad nacional*, a national identification card that citizens became legally required to secure and carry beginning in 1947. A decade after the 1937 massacre of tens of thousands of Haitians, Dominicans of Haitian descent and black Dominicans, through the *cédula de identidad nacional*, were further disappeared by fiat under the state's official classificatory system. Carlos Dore-Cabral has argued that during the Trujillo era and its aftermath, "Indio" has come to be an affirmation of Dominican whiteness as well as of non-blackness.[52] Meindert Fennema and Troetje Loewenthal have further argued that "Indio" is a neutral, "un-marked" term that excludes blackness as it affirms Hispanicity of a different hue and (hair) texture.[53] As Peter Roberts put it, "Officially there are no native-born *'negros'* in the Dominican Republic."[54]

This *"negro"* negation appears to hold for Dominicans in the United States, as well. In a study of the racial self-perception of approximately four hundred Dominican immigrants, conducted through survey-based interviews in 1995–96 in New York City and Providence, Rhode Island, the sociologist José Itzigsohn found that, when allowed to choose their racial self-descriptors, Dominicans overwhelmingly chose "Indio," either alone or with the usual qualifiers of *claro* (light), *quemado* (toasted), or *oscuro* (dark). When asked to select a descriptor from a limited list (black, Hispanic, Latino, white) they favored "Hispanic" over black, white, and Latino. Finally, when asked how Americans perceived them, over a third answered "black," a much larger percentage than those who identified themselves in that way. Itzigsohn concludes that Dominican racial categories continue to hold as "their interpretative frame of reference" and that identifying as "Indio" and Hispanic in the United States reflects a continued preference for intermediate racial categories and a rejection of blackness.[55] It is, in other words, a response to the mainstream racial classification system of the United States that draws on both Dominican and U.S. racial ideologies and settles on a term common to both countries—Hispanic—but with very different histories, symbolic uses, and meanings in each.[56] This is an example of ideological code switching that highlights the need to consider not simply the discursive practices and strategies Dominicans are using in regard to race, but also the meaning-making frameworks they employ to make sense of race, including ideology and culture.

In his extensive writing on Dominican transnationalism and identity formation, Duany has argued that the experience of migration has led to a "profound ideological transformation [as] the so-called Indios suddenly become black, Hispanic, or 'other.'"[57] He notes that the local contexts of New York and San Juan each exert distinctly local pressures on Dominicans residing in those societies to identify as black—or, at least, to recognize that they are identified as blacks by those in the host society. He argues that external pressure leads to a reactive nationalist identity that is displayed through the use of symbols such as the Dominican flag and practices such as playing and dancing merengue, eating typical Dominican food, and retaining, perhaps even exaggerating, linguistic Dominicanisms.

Although I agree with Duany about the increasing recognition of and nationalist reaction to others' perceiving them as black, I want to argue that a profound ideological transformation has not in fact occurred for Dominicans—at least, not among the first generation in New York City. Rather, the transformation has been in Dominicans' *consciousness* of the fragility of their claims to Indo-Hispanic identities and, for some, their consciousness of the ideological irony of Dominican identity's reliance on anti-Haitianism and Negrophobia as identity boundary markers. There is an important difference between being *aware* of the inconsistencies between one's racist beliefs about others and one's own experiences of racism, and actually *rejecting* racist ideas and practices. An extensive ideological transformation would require a reconsideration of negrophobic and anti-Haitianist ideologies, and there is little evidence that that has occurred. For example, a Census 2000 Report found that only 9.4 percent of Dominicans in the United States identified themselves as black; 23.1 percent said they were white; 51.6 percent said they were "some other race"; and 12.4 percent did not answer the question at all.[58]

The last population census to collect data on race in the Dominican Republic was taken in 1960, and it was based on the observations of census takers who were "instructed to record as white all Dominicans who were not obviously black."[59] Accordingly, in addition to encouraging the diminution of the "obviously black" category—for it was better officially to err on the side of whiteness—the 1960 Dominican census did not measure the population's own understanding of its racial status or color. Further, even if it had been based on self-definition, the 1960 census, in the context of the fully entrenched hegemony of the Trujillato, is unlikely to have yielded large numbers who self-identified as black. Four decades later, the situation might have been different, but it is not.

Although the Trujillo era officially ended with the dictator's assassination in 1961, Trujillist ideology continued to be dominant because of the work of Trujillo's leading ideologue, Joaquín Balaguer. Balaguer rose to power in 1966, and during both of his now infamous periods of rule—1966–78 and 1988–96—he worked to institutionalize anti-Haitianism, Negrophobia, and Hispanophilia more fully.[60] Despite Balaguer's final expulsion from office and his death in 2002, the official racial-composition percentages of the Dominican Republic are evidently still based on that 1960 census. Thus, that a substantially larger share of the Dominican population in New York City self-identifies as black in U.S. census statistics than in Dominican census statistics does not necessarily reflect an increase in black self-identification post-migration. In fact, according to Census 2000 data, "Dominicans most identified with general Hispanic responses" to the ethnic and racial identity questions.[61] This point will be taken up more fully in chapters 2 and 3.

Displaying Blackness in Washington, D.C.

While I was participating in a graduate student seminar on qualitative methods sponsored by the Inter-University Program on Latino Research and the Smithsonian Institution's Center for Museum Studies, Héctor Corporán, the lead community scholar of the Anacostia Museum, spoke to our seminar group about the *Black Mosaic* exhibition. The Anacostia is the Smithsonian Institution's only museum dedicated to the research and exhibition of African American history and culture in the United States. It is located in the predominantly African American neighborhood of Anacostia and is staffed primarily by African Americans. Thus, when Corporán mentioned in passing that the majority of the participants in the exhibition were Dominican, like him, I wondered whether the participants were illustrative of general patterns in Washington,

D.C., or anomalous in terms of their willingness to identify as black. I searched the census data and found that 40 percent of the Dominican population in the Washington, D.C., metropolitan area likewise identified as black. In New York City, by contrast, only 26 percent of Dominicans identified as black. Intrigued, I decided to explore why more Dominicans in D.C. identified as black. The *Black Mosaic* exhibition and its participants seemed a logical entry point to those inquiries because they offered ready access to some of those black-identified Dominicans.

The *Black Mosaic* exhibition ran from August 1994 to November 1995. It focused on Afro-descended immigrants and Afro-Latinos in Washington, D.C. *Black Mosaic* "examined migration, issues of race and ethnicity, music, and community history in Washington, D.C. *Black Mosaic* programs included films, family days, gallery talks, teachers' workshops, and a conference on Latino music in the District of Columbia."[62] In preparation for *Black Mosaic*, and as part of twenty life-history interviews of other Afro-Latinos in Washington, D.C., Anacostia staff collected eight extensive life-history interviews with D.C. Dominicans. Throughout, the central effort was recovery and recognition of Latin America's African diaspora and its immigrants to Washington, D.C. Included in the exhibition were photographs and videotaped interviews of Dominicans who identified as black. Indeed, much of the publicity literature for the exhibit features images of Dominican immigrants. In light of the fact that Dominicans have been officially constructed as "not black," their participation in this exhibit represents a substantial departure from hegemonic Dominican identity displays and discourses.

The earliest contingent of Dominicans in the U.S. capital arrived in the 1940s as domestics for the Dominican Embassy and its diplomatic families. This fairly small group expanded as a result of the 1965 Immigration and Naturalization Act's family-preference provision. Corporán has noted that a central mission of the exhibition was to determine how immigrants such as these had "negotiated U.S. racial ideologies and institutions" across various decades of racial flux.[63] As Steven Newsome, director of the Anacostia Museum, put it, "Exhibits define civic culture, they tell the public what is important to know, they act as definers of culture and validators of exhibit."[64] At the same time that the exhibition represented Dominicans, therefore, it also represented African American perceptions of Dominicans.

As chapter 3, "'I Could Go the African American Route': Dominicans in the Black Mosaic of Washington, D.C.," describes, my examination of *The Black Mosaic: Community, Race and Ethnicity among Black Immigrants*

Table 2 Percentage of Dominicans Identifying as Black
in 1990 Census, Selected States

State	Identifying as Black (%)
Washington, D.C.	40
New York	27
Massachusetts	23
California	12
Texas	12

Source: Levitt and Gómez, "The Intersection of Race and Gender
among Dominicans in the U.S."

in Washington, D.C., offers important insights into the context-sensitive
nature of Dominican identity displays and discourses. First, the exhibition represented an important departure from the Dominican state's
officially sanctioned racial imaginary, akin to Silvio Torres-Saillant's oft-
cited claim that 90 percent of the Dominican population is black and
mulatto.[65] Second, *Black Mosaic* represented the outcome of negotiated
interactions between Dominican immigrants and African Americans
charged with representing communities. Third, it offers the possibility
of examining a larger social fact—the self-identification as black of 40
percent of Dominicans in the Washington, D.C., area—and the influence
of residential and socioeconomic context on that racial identity. Finally,
it provides rich community-formation data via the oral histories, family
photos, and slides already collected by the museum, as well as those I
collected subsequently.[66] All of the participants in *Black Mosaic* belonged
to either the second or the 1.5 generation of Dominican immigrations
to Washington, D.C. Having been born or arrived in the United States
approximately four decades ago, this was largely a middle-aged group.
I wanted to understand why these Dominicans affirmed their African
ancestry more often and more extensively than the Dominicans in New
York City and in the Dominican Republic itself, because I thought that
might offer further insights into the factors that influence social identity
formation.

In 1990, Levitt and Christina Gómez found that, on average, about 25
percent of Dominicans in the United States identified as black, though
there was substantial variability by region, as table 2 shows. Noticeably,
there seemed to be a relationship between black self-identification and
residential context. Dominicans in the West and Southwest were the least

likely to identity as black, while Dominicans in Washington, D.C., were the most likely, and those in the Northeast fell in the middle ranges.

Levitt and Gómez also found that, "as socioeconomic status increases and English language proficiency increases, both foreign-born and native-born Dominicans were more likely to classify themselves as white."[67] My ethnographic findings in Washington, D.C., however, indicate the exact opposite: Greater degrees of educational attainment and socioeconomic status were related to an affirmative black identity. Unlike their New York City counterparts, this group of adult Dominicans incorporated into the local economic opportunity structure fairly successfully because they were too few and far between to make up a "visible" minority that could make claims competing with those of African Americans. According to José Itzigsohn, Silvio Giorguli, and Obed Vázquez, "Self-identification as black is also the result of the internationalization of the external gaze that sees Dominicans as blacks, in other words, the result of reflective appraisals produced by the acculturation process."[68] This argument was echoed in the accounts of the Dominicans who came of age in Washington, D.C., during the heyday of the Civil Rights Movement and Black Power Movement, and away from the sustained influence of Dominican educational systems and cultural institutions that favor indigenist identity formation.

Ideology, Consciousness, and Identity

To what degree, then, does local context matter in terms of how Dominicans in the United States identify? And if it does matter, how does it matter? Does Dominicans' sense of self change in some stable, fundamental way? Does how they think about themselves and others change as they become aware of differences between the histories, ideologies, and cultural presuppositions that background their identities and those of the local population? Some Dominicans have reported anecdotally undergoing some sort of racial-identity reevaluation experience upon contact with U.S. racial paradigms.[69] The sociologist and poet Chiqui Vicioso elaborates:

> I was also racially classified at Brooklyn College, which was an interesting experience for me. In Santo Domingo, the popular classes have a pretty clear grasp of racial divisions, but the middle and upper-middle classes are very deluded on this point. People straighten their hair and marry "in order

to improve the race," etc., etc., and don't realize the racist connotations of their language or their attitude. In the United States, there is no space for fine distinctions of race, and one goes from being "trigüeño" or "Indio" to being "mulatto" or "black" or "Hispanic." This was an excellent experience for me. From that point on, I discovered myself as a Caribbean *mulata* and adopted the black identity as a gesture of solidarity.[70]

That Vicioso feels able to "adopt" a racialized identity as a "gesture of solidarity" highlights the unique position in which Dominicans in the United States find themselves. They can apparently choose to identify for political purposes, but it is a voluntary gesture rather than a structural imposition. If this is so, then Dominicans, unlike other West Indian immigrants perceived to be of African heritage in the United States,[71] are able to impose their own understandings of blackness in their host societies. They can choose likewise to assimilate into blackness and reject their sending society's Indo-Hispanic ethno-racial ascriptions.

However, it is not clear to me that Dominicans can universally impose their own understandings of themselves, or that Dominicans generally are eschewing "Indio" identities in favor of black ones in New York. They can, and apparently do, however, exert a measure of self-ascription within Dominican transnational spaces. To Dominicans, Dominicanness and Hispanicity are by definition *not black*, both in the United States and on the island. Indeed, ethnographic research suggests that Dominicans continue to favor "Indio" or "Hispanic"—or as one Dominican put it to a team of researchers, "Indo-Hispanic"[72]—identities in New York, Providence, Boston, and Miami; to reject black identities; to be highly endogamous and when exogamous, primarily with other Latinos; and to engage in anti-Haitianist rhetoric. Moreover, the very recourse both to reactive national identity displays and to affirmations of Hispanic identity indicates a rejection of local racial ideologies that would shift Dominicans downward on the racial hierarchy. Indeed, migration can even be said to whiten returnees, particularly those whose greater access to income and capital has allowed them to increase their consumption of consumer goods and the formation of various forms of social, cultural, political, and economic capital which are marked as white in the Dominican Republic.[73]

If there has been a shift in racial identity, it is likely to have occurred among the 1.5 and second generation, which Duany indicates is already occurring, perhaps because they have been socialized at least in part in an entirely different ideological system and social order.[74] Although more generalizable research is sure to yield an invaluable contribution to the debates, ethnographic evidence indicates that residential and institutional proximity to African American communities lead to a shift in Caribbean immigrants' reference orientation away from their first-generation kin and toward their generational peers in the host society. My findings in Washington, D.C., indicate that the generation of immigration is indeed among the constellation of factors that contribute to historic black self-identification for Dominicans in D.C.

In the Dominican Republic, class status affects racial identification. If, for example, in the United States race is largely an ascribed status regardless of class status, in the Dominican context class can have a "whitening" or a "darkening effect." Thus, a member of the upper classes who would be "black" in the United States is perceived, and perceives himself or herself, to be "white" or "whiter" with much more ease than she or he might were she or he to occupy a lower socioeconomic status. Indeed, it is now a truism of studies of race in Latin America and the Caribbean that—at least, to some extent—race is as much an achieved status as it is an ascribed one.[75] In the United States, by contrast, race is largely an ascribed status that often determines socioeconomic status; race is considered a pre-existing, fixed reality. Thus, the "fact of blackness," as Fanon calls it, might be covertly denied and hidden through "passing" but is never changed by circumstance.

In the Dominican case, the notion of "passing" seems not to exist, because one's race is as *contingent* on one's class position as it is *determinative* of it.[76] Nonetheless, although class can supersede race as a mechanism of social stratification, the fact remains that while "acceptability to the highest social class in Santo Domingo is based on a variety of factors . . . persons exhibiting a distinct Negroid appearance are excluded" from the upper echelons of the social hierarchy.[77] Moreover, as Harry Hoetink has pointed out, features that are considered "white" or "European" seem to be more highly valued than those that are not.[78]

Looking Dominican

Another key question guiding my research was how—rather than simply why—Dominicans with facial and bodily features that show African ancestry see themselves as "not black." Although I am interested in briefly tracing why "the black behind the ears" is kept there, I am equally intrigued by the process through which perception is trained to make that blackness visible or not. Ethnographic research fleshes out how members of social groups construct their sense of social identity in the context of larger historical, political, economic, and cultural structures. By analyzing the accounts group members provide of given social phenomena, the researcher is able to understand how those phenomena are constructed in everyday life practices. In the context of this study, how Dominicans construct and display their identities in their everyday life experiences and practices were approached through a beauty-shop ethnography and through extended, open-ended interviews with respondents culled from that ethnography. Those findings are presented in chapter 4, "'They Are Taken into Account for Their Opinions': Making Community and Displaying Identity at a Dominican Beauty Shop in New York City."

The sociologist Luís Guarnizo has undertaken an important study of Dominican entrepreneurship in which he argues that structural and social rejection by both U.S. and Dominican society has forced migrants to New York City to form a distinctive bi-national social world that accommodates both but does not assimilate either.[79] That bi-national society is a heterogeneous yet cohesive one that operates in a transnational space and selectively activates elements of "both U.S. and Dominican cultural influences."[80] Consequently, migrants are foreigners in both spaces and at home only in their bi-national society. Guarnizo's primary focus is the degree to which migrants are able to assimilate socioeconomically into their home and host societies, defined primarily in terms of how they are received by the economic and political elites and where they fit in the local class structure.[81]

Accordingly, Guarnizo only briefly notes the important role of Dominican firms in the production and sustenance of Dominican identity in the United States.[82] Presumably some of these firms reproduce a central component of Dominican culture—the embracing and display of Indo-Hispanic identity—both internally and externally in their daily practices. In this, the Dominican salon is exemplary. To get a sense of the import and visibility of Dominican beauty culture in Washington Heights, I undertook quantitative and spatial analysis of the Dominican beauty-shop industry in New York and an ethnography of a particular beauty shop.

In seeking a particular shop to enter, I confronted several challenges. Although I am a member of the transnational Dominican community with family ties in Washington Heights, I was loath to use kinship connections to gain entry into a field site, largely due to concerns about the effects of relationships between my kin and shop owners, workers, and clients on my own interactions with them. At the same time, because I was going to enter the shop as an explicitly named observer/researcher, I needed to be introduced into the shop by a trusted member of that shop's community. This was so both due to cultural norms of appropriate sociality and in response to the shop community's potential distrust of my investigative intentions in the context of recent welfare reforms, the "War on Drugs," and increased deportations of Dominicans. As a stranger, I could easily be mistaken for a government agent rather than a researcher.

These factors, taken together, led me to ask another Dominican woman who was my classmate in the City University of New York (CUNY) Ph.D. Program in Sociology and who lived and used a salon in Washington Heights to introduce me to her shop, Salon Lamadas.[83] She was an irregular customer at Salon Lamadas and so was familiar enough to be trusted by the shop's owner and staff, but not so familiar as to be enmeshed in the shop's idiosyncratic culture and politics. She took me to the shop in March 1998 for my first visit. The shop owner was not there, so we waited for about an hour for her to arrive. During that time I took note of the shop's location, layout, activity, and personnel. It took two more visits over the next several weeks to meet with the owner, explain the research project, complete consent forms,[84] and establish the shop as the research site. During that time, I visited half a dozen other shops in the area to gauge the typicalness of the shop I was interested in based on physical plant, size of space, number of personnel, presence of an owner-operator, and flow of clients. Based on those indicators, Salon Lamadas seemed typical and well suited as an entry point.

I began my participant observation at Salon Lamadas in May 1998. I attended Salon Lamadas four to five days of the week, for five to eight hours at a time, over a period of six months. During that time I also conducted extended, in-depth interviews with the six salon staff, the two owners, and one vendor of hair-care products. In addition, I established preliminary contacts with thirty regular salon clients whom I would later approach for interviews. I interviewed each of the staff members at least once, usually twice. In addition to establishing a life history regarding the respondent's migrations, labor-market experience, educational experience, and family life, I wanted to understand how the stylists came to their profession and how they viewed their role in the larger community. I found that the shop was an important socializing agent that facilitated immigrant and transmigrant adaptation to New York City and helped to sustain Dominican women's ethno-racial identities as Indo-

Hispanic. If the absence of specifically Dominican institutions of acculturation allowed Dominicans in Washington, D.C., to develop black identities, the proliferation of those Dominican cultural institutions in New York City limit the development of black identities and promote Indo-Hispanicity.

The Ethnographer's Body in the Field

The Dominican anthropologist Casandra Badillo and the researchers at Oné Respé have noted that, given the history of repression, despotism, and dictatorship in the Dominican Republic, successful research on matters of race among Dominicans requires the establishment of a relationship between the researcher and the respondent. She writes: "Our experience with interviewing indicates that in delicate maters that imply and trigger sensitivity and identity issues, the responses obtained in a first interview tend to be evasive, general, attempts to satisfy the interviewer's agenda. It takes time, patience and a relatively long process of mutual 'recognition' for the real opinions of a given population to appear."[85] Certainly, my experiences at Salon Lamadas supported these claims, as shall be seen.

In the context of the beauty parlor, my being perceived as a white-skinned and lank-haired *rubia*[86] certainly could have influenced the participants' responses to my questions, at least initially and during particular moments in the interview process. My lifelong experiences inside various Dominican communities, both on the island and in the United States, prepared me for those moments. On countless occasions the revelation that I identify as Dominican was met with initial disbelief, which then generally evolved into celebration of my membership because of my appearance. My body has often been displayed to other Dominicans as an example of the outer limits of Dominicanidad: *"¡Mira! ¡Mira! ¡Una Dominicana rubia!* [Look! Look! A blonde/white Dominican!"]. I was often reminded of the popular Dominican joke that "the eighth wonder of the world would be a white Dominican," which, as the anthropologist Nancie González pointed out, recognizes the black ancestry of most Dominicans while "poking fun at the upper classes who often consider themselves to be pure Caucasoid [*sic*]."[87]

A related concern was whether my appearance would influence the identity discourses of informants. The sociologist Clara Rodríguez has found that "the relation of the referent to the speaker and context are important to 'racial classification.'"[88] Might they be more likely to describe themselves differently than they would if they perceived me to be more similar to them in appearance? Did my very corporeality construct a "Hawthorne Effect" on racial perception?[89] I believe that my experience with the informants in a variety of locales—the beauty salon, neighborhood, and their homes—mediated against some of those researcher effects. In addition, these methodological concerns led me to choose photo elicitation as a method for understanding Dominican women's perceptive practices. As the visual sociologist Douglas Harper has strongly argued, photos and images "evoke deeper elements of human consciousness than do words" and therefore elicit information untapped by interviewing.[90] Given that among Dominicans labeling someone black is often considered offensive and denigrating, and that it was therefore possible that respondents would attempt to avoid this "gaffe," photo elicitation allowed me to explore how race is marked and perceived by Dominicans in a way that did not ask respondents to racially assess people we both know or are acquainted with.

In addition to my phenotype, my status as a mother to a newborn son influenced my entry into the salon, my ethnographic experiences, and my interviews. When I first approached Salon Lamadas's owner and staff, I was in my last trimester of pregnancy. I began my fieldwork when my son was six weeks old. My son accompanied me to the beauty salon every day for six weeks, several times a week for another six weeks, about once a week for six more weeks, and occasionally through the remainder of my time in the field. As might be imagined, his presence influenced my experience in and of the field in several salient ways.

Two members of the salon staff were in advanced stages of pregnancy when I entered the field, and they gave birth during the time I was there. Their experiences, choices, and constraints regarding pregnancy, labor, birthing, nursing, and child care were often juxtaposed with my own. Our very different experiences of giving birth and of mothering highlighted the fact that class, color, and citizenship status affects Dominican women's identities and mothering cultures in the United States.[91] My experiences in the health-care system and of pregnancy, and my ability to care for my children unhampered by geographical distance and immigration laws that force many mothers to emigrate without their children, marked the boundaries between myself as native and privileged ethnographer and my co-ethnics.

First, because I nursed my son while he was with me, and expressed milk for him when he was not, conversations were often initiated on the subject of Dominican gender roles and mothering practices, as well as on the nature of Dominican women's employment and domestic labor. These not only offered increased levels of intimacy between myself and the women I was working with, but increased insight into how class and social context influence Dominican gender norms and practices. Second, my son's physical appearance occasionally provoked comments that were revealing of ethno-racial perceptions and ideologies. Third, my public mothering role made me a trustworthy participant observer. Indeed, toward the end of my fieldwork I was even asked and agreed to wet nurse one staff member's newborn who was not thriving because she had been rejecting the formula offered to her by a caretaker while her mother was working in the salon. I took that request and my response as indicative of my success in establishing authentic and reciprocal relationships with the women of the salon. That authenticity and reciprocity was not only personally heartening; it was appropriate to my role as researcher in that context.[92]

At the Root of It All: Black Hair and Indo-Hispanicity

Chapter 5, "'Black Women Are Confusing, but the Hair Lets You Know': Perceiving the Boundaries of Dominicanidad," examines how Dominican Indo-Hispanic identity is constructed, represented, and contested through women's bodies. It is based on extended interviewing and photo elicitation with the salon's regular clientele, using versions of methods employed by other researchers of racial perception in Latin American.[93] For example, in his study of race in Brazil, Conrad Kottak presented one hundred Bahians with photographs of three sisters who were considered physically "representative" of various "racial types."[94] Each respondent was asked to categorize or describe racially each of the sisters. Kottak found no uniformity in how each sister was identified. Indeed, the answers reflected the "idiosyncratic" nature of perceived racial types. Another sample of one hundred people was shown nine drawings of people with diverse combinations of hair textures and shades, nose and lip shapes, and skin tones. In all, respondents offered forty different "racial types."

In addition to the variety of racial designations for any one individual, Kottak discovered no consensus on the "abstract meaning of the racial terms" assigned. Finally, there was variability across time in how a given respondent racially characterized the same person. I have drawn on Kottak's methodological model, but my research question extends beyond merely documenting Dominican racial descriptors. I am also concerned to determine *how* Dominican race ideology frames everyday practices of perception, as well as to analyze how identity is displayed through what Marcel Mauss has termed "techniques of the body." This refers to the ways bodies are trained to perform certain tasks or to appear in certain ways. Though Mauss called for the adoption of a "triple viewpoint" of these techniques (biological, psychological, and sociological), I am most interested in the sociological viewpoint—that is, how body techniques are "developed, stored, and transmitted through social organization and social relationships."[95] Thus, the intersubjectivities of Dominicans are of central importance.

This elicitation was meant to tease out the relationship between how respondents characterized others ethno-racially and their perceptions of those others' suitability for activities that conceivably could be racially circumscribed—reproduction, capital accumulation, political legitimacy, and child rearing. Overall, I found that although there was a marked rhetorical preference of Indo-Hispanic looks and rejection of "black" looks, this preference did not translate perfectly to practices. Thus, for example, the prettiest, smartest, and most likely to succeed girls were those perceived to have browner skin; coarser and curlier hair arranged in braids, buns, and twists; and fuller features, while the girls perceived to have white skin, straight loose hair, and thin features were considered bland, dull, and superficial. It would appear that even as these Dominican women endeavor to meet the prescribed ethno-racial model of Dominicanidad, they are able to view their unaltered daughters as beautiful, smart, and upwardly bound. It is not until girls become women of reproductive age that they are expected to transform and conform to the normative ethno-racial model of Dominicanidad. That is to say, once girls become women, they become embodiments of the Indo-Hispanic nation.

Thus, in the course of a single interview a Spanish monolingual Dominican woman in New York described herself as *dominicana* (Dominican), *blanca* (white), *hispana* (Hispanic), *latina* (Latina), *ordinaria* (ordinary; i.e., black featured), *elegante* (elegant; i.e., upper class), and *mezclada* (mixed). Her niece, a fluent bilingual, similarly deployed various referents to locate herself in the ethno-racial landscape: *dominicana* (Dominican), *trigueña* (lit., wheat-skinned; fig., brown-skinned), *india* (Indian), *fina* (fine featured), *hispana* (Hispanic), black, light-skinned, and Latina. Each of these terms operates in a complex semantic field to create a more complete picture of the selves understood by my respondents to constitute their gendered ethno-racial identities.

Isar Pilar Godreau has noted that Puerto Ricans engage in what she has termed "slippery semantics" in their simultaneous reproduction of and challenges to "Hispanophile and nationalistic preferences for *blanqueamiento*." Godreau defines slippery semantics as "a process whereby people constantly shift racial terms when they are lauding people they consider black, using one term in one sentence, another term in another sentence, and so forth."[96] Rather than being merely euphemisms or synonyms, the slippage between the terms "contain the problematic racial nuances of Hispanofilia as a nation-building strategy."[97] Among the Dominicans I interviewed, it was not so much slippery semantics as strategic ambiguity that obtained.

Strategic ambiguity allowed simultaneously for purposeful self-presentation strategies and for equivocation in dynamic interplay between the internalization and externalization of official identity discourses. Identity is situationally bound. A given individual, group, or community can experience and understand itself in complex, complementary, or contradictory ways at any particular historical or biographical moment. This work maps the ways in which Dominicans have negotiated identity displays and discourses individually and collectively, institutionally and culturally across time and place in such a way as to simultaneously negotiate multiple social and symbolic orders. The conclusion, "Black behind the Ears, and Up Front, Too: Ideological Code Switching and Ambiguity in Dominican Identity," summarizes my argument and points the way to future research.

CHAPTER 1

"It Is Said That Haiti Is Getting Blacker and Blacker"

TRAVELING NARRATIVES OF DOMINICAN IDENTITY

> In much of Latin America, the official and unofficial policies of the state are played out on the bodies of its citizens, thus becoming the intimate personal experience and shaping the unique vision of the individual that gets expressed in what we recognize as the writer's particular voice.—Amy K. Kaminsky[1]

> On October 12 of every year, the entire country celebrates different cultural, religious, sports, and social events organized by both public and private institutions to commemorate the "Discovery of America," subsequently baptized "The Day of the Race" and today labeled more subtly, but still maliciously, "The Day of Hispanicity."—Dagoberto Tejada Ortíz[2]

In her important book *Imperial Eyes: Travel Writing and Transculturation*, Mary Louise Pratt convincingly argues that Spanish American independence movements were of such great interest to the French and British empires that an entirely new literary genre, the travel narrative, was developed to offer information about these new nations to the European metropolis. Acting as "advance scouts for European capital,"[3] these writers rewrote and reinvented the Americas in ways that suited the ideological, economic, and political projects of their empires. At the same time, American Creole intellectuals and elites engaged these narratives and offered their own transcultural visions of independent America. That transcultural vision positioned Creoles as legitimately hegemonic in the Americas because they were "Europeanizing" yet American, indigenous yet white, and republican yet patriarchal.[4] Thus, European travel writing offered a narrative against which Creole counter-narratives of national identity and political legitimacy were elaborated.

In Santo Domingo and later in the Dominican Republic, travel writing played a similar role in the development of a discourse of *Dominicanidad* generated in dynamic dialogue with foreign interlocutors. However, the foreign narratives and narrators of the republic who inspired a Dominican counter-narrative were not so much European as North American. Moreover, as a people emerging from an island divided between two different colonial powers and, later, two different nations, Dominicans faced a geopolitical context to their identities unique in the Americas. The Dominican Republic came into existence through separation not so much from Spain, as was the case for the other emergent Latin American nation-states, as from French San Domingüe and later Haiti. In addition, the Dominican Republic was seriously considered for U.S. annexation and territorial incorporation in the nineteenth century and was occupied and governed by U.S. Marines twice in the twentieth century. Accordingly, an examination of leading travel accounts of the island's landscape and people offers us insight into the ideological and political contexts in which Dominican identity was being formed, narrated, and displayed. In large measure, that context was defined by a triangle of relations between Haiti, the United States, and the Dominican Republic.

This chapter will offer a critique of travel narratives about the Dominican Republic and Haiti, paying special attention to the relationship between the travelers' racial projects and Dominican nation-building projects. "A racial project is simultaneously an interpretation, representation, or explanation of racial dynamics, and an effort to reorganize and redistribute resources along particular racial lines."[5] Following Michael Omi's and Howard Winant's helpful conceptualization, I am arguing that travel narratives formed part of an evolving geopolitical racial project that did the "ideological 'work'" of both U.S. imperialism and Dominican nation building through anti-Haitianist discourses. As Rear Admiral Colby M. Chester put it in his address to the National Geographic Society as part of that ideological work, "It [was] said that Haiti [was] getting blacker and blacker" as the Dominican Republic was getting whiter.

The Birth of a Dominican Nation:
The Black Republic and the Whites of the Land

As the first black republic in the Americas, Haiti posed a great ideological and political challenge to white-supremacist, slaveholding states in the Western Hemisphere. Repeatedly threatened by the French empire and shunned by slaveowning states throughout the Americas, Haitian leaders justified their expansion into the Spanish part of Santo Domingo as beneficial to both parts of the colonially divided island. In 1822, Jean-Pierre Boyer invaded and unified the eastern two-thirds of the island to Haiti's western third. Just weeks prior to Boyer's unification of the island, Santo Domingo had declared itself to be independent of Spain and newly constituted as Haití Español, or Spanish Haiti, under the leadership of José Nuñez de Cáceres, whose original plan to participate in Bolivar's Gran Colombia project was easily reoriented toward Haitian unification. During the twenty-two-year period of unified Haitian rule, many Creoles in the former Spanish part chaffed under Haitian rule, even as others collaborated with the Unification government. Meanwhile many in the impoverished mulatto and black masses supported the Haitian revolutionaries who had ended their enslavement and institutionalized policies intended to prevent black subordination and white supremacy in the future.[6]

Independence-minded Creoles—most notably, the "Father of the Republic," Juan Pablo Duarte—fashioned a liberal vision of the emergent Dominican nation-state that integrated the "colored" masses while differentiating them from Haitians by extolling their Hispanicity, their allegiance to Catholicism, and their (relative) whiteness. At various moments throughout the nineteenth century and into the first half of the twentieth century, U.S. government agents and North American capitalists colluded with this Dominican elite in presenting the Dominican Republic as the most "Hispanic, Catholic, and white" of (Latin) American nations against the Haitian Other. Expansionists to a one, they saw enormous potential for capitalist investment and military positioning in the Dominican Republic.

These North American expansionists argued that the Dominican Republic, although superior to Haiti, could only benefit from further infusions of Yankee industriousness, whether in the form of individual colonists, military governance, customs receivership, or, later, tourism and multinational corporations. Thus, despite the country's African heritage, Dominican identity formations negotiated the fraught space between U.S.-dominant notions of white supremacy that defined mixture as degeneration and the geopolitical positioning of Dominicans as "*los blancos de la tierra* [the whites of the land]" relative to Haitians. However, the end of Spanish colonial rule, coupled with contemporary theories of "ecological contamination" that claimed that the tropics transformed Spanish Creoles into indigenes in the Americas and the rise of indigenist ideologies of national identity throughout the former Spanish colonies, led to Dominicans' embracing racially indigenous monikers even as cultural Hispanicity was being affirmed.

Rather than calling themselves "black," as the Haitians had, Dominicans would be *Indios*, or Indians. Frank Moya Pons argues:

> By calling themselves Indians, Dominicans have been able to provisionally resolve the profound drama that filled most their history: that of being a colored nation ruled by a quasi-white elite that did not want to accept the reality of its color and the history of their race. Somehow Dominicans assimilated the romantic discourse of the "*indigenista*" writers of the 19th century, and found it instrumental in accommodating their racial self-perception to the prejudices of the elite, by accepting their "color" while denying their "race."[7]

Responding to the unasked question in Moya Pons's provocative "somehow," I will argue here that *indigenista* discourses and narratives were assimilated in the twentieth century through the work of key socialization institutions such as the national school system, the national museum, the national media, and, more recently, the beauty shop. An important precursor to this *indigenista* discourse were the travel narratives of Dominicans as "not black" and as "the whites of the land" that were created and circulated by foreign observers and assimilated into nationalist discourses from the late nineteenth century into the twentieth century. These narratives were legitimated through their absorption by Dominican scholars into the national historiography and public history. In particular, nineteenth-century French colonial and North American narratives of the Dominican Republic and its people are used either directly in displays of Dominican history and peoples or in the historiography that forms the background of the exhibits.

"They Give Great Importance to That Ancestry": Indo-Hispanicity and Whiteness

Among the first accounts of Santo Domingo to circulate in the Americas is M. L. Moreau de Saint-Méry's *A Topographical and Political Description of the Spanish Part of Santo Domingo* (1796).[8] Moreau de Saint-Méry was a Martinique-born mulatto Creole. Educated in Paris and subsequently appointed as a lawyer in French San Domingüe, Moreau de Saint-Méry collected and codified French West Indian laws. In the course of his research, he traveled to Santo Domingo, Martinique, Guadeloupe, and St. Lucia. He returned to Paris, became a member of the Musée de Paris, published a six-volume collection of laws from 1784 to 1790, and became an accepted member of the intellectual elite. Moreau de Saint-Méry's fortunes rose and fell with his ardent support for the French Revolution, and he subsequently was forced to immigrate to Philadelphia. There he opened a small bookstore and print shop, from which he published his two-volume travelogue.[9]

After presenting a brief history of the island from the point at which the French presence became relevant to Santo Domingo's political future (1630–1777, in his estimation), Moreau de Saint-Méry described the island's topography and people. He claimed that the population of the Spanish part when he visited in 1783 was composed of whites, free men and women of color, and slaves. In his estimation, whites outnumbered free people of color, who in turn outnumbered the enslaved. He attributed the large population of free people of color to the liberal manumission policies encoded in Spanish law and to the proclivity of Spanish masters to mate with slave concubines. It was that weakness, he argued, that led free women of color into "infamous commerce," or prostitution. Immediately following his commentary on prostitution, he wrote: "Color prejudice, so powerful in other nations where barriers between whites and freedmen or their descendents have been established hardly exists in the Spanish part. That is why the Spanish laws in the Indies regarding freedmen have absolutely fallen into disuse."[10] Having stated this, he then listed the many legally codified limitations to free men's and women's freedom: proscriptions against participation in certain professions; prohibitions against the use of bodily adornment; barring of intermarriage; and barriers to civil and military employment if "the color of [an individual's] skin still indicates his origin." Still, he asserted that because Spaniards themselves were of mixed racial heritage and because material conditions created a situation in which a slave's "luck will always be analogous to his master's, as a result of which they are more companions than slaves," racial animosity was far more limited in the Spanish part of Santo Domingo than in other slaveholding societies.[11]

Interestingly, Moreau de Saint-Méry was suspicious of the claims to indigenous ancestry made by residents of the Spanish part of the island. He wrote:

> If we could believe some individuals of the Spanish part, we would have to add to the three classes into which this population is divided a fourth class that would be very interesting due to the long series of misfortunes which it recalls. I refer to certain Creoles (really a small number) who have hair similar to that of the Indians, that is, long, straight, and very black, who claim to be descendants of the primitive natives of the island. They give great importance to that ancestry, although it is denied by the historical facts that prove that that race of men was completely exterminated.[12]

This paragraph is informative on several levels. First, it is informative as a historical document, because we learn that residents of the Spanish part of Santo Domingo made claims to indigenous ancestry in the 1790s. Thus, subsequent nineteenth-century indigenism had earlier antecedents on which to draw. Second, the Creole colonial-era reference to hair as a bodily sign of indigenous ancestry signals its importance in the construction of racial identity in Santo Domingo and, later, in the Dominican Republic, to which I will return in chapter 4. And finally, the tone of incredulousness—"if we could believe"—indicates that Moreau de Saint-Méry could not, in fact, believe that people in the Spanish part had indigenous ancestry.

Moreau de Saint-Méry's overall characterization of the Spanish part of the island and its people was strongly influenced by his anti-Spanish colonial politics. Moreau de Saint-Méry spent a fair amount of text describing Spanish women, usually negatively. In his account, they were fat, ugly, poorly coifed, lacking in fashion sense, uninspired cooks, tobacco-chewing, falsely modest, promiscuous, and prolific breeders. Likewise, Spanish men were portrayed as lazy, siesta-loving, syphilitic braggarts who were ill-suited to the proper husbanding that Santo Domingo's land and women require, as both the land's and the women's state of near-abandonment reflected. In short, the entire condition of the Spanish part of Santo Domingo was one of backwardness and decay, thanks to Spanish Creole neglect.[13]

Accordingly, the emphasis in his analysis of the island's condition was the untapped potential of the Spanish colony. This is unsurprising given that he advocated French dominion over the entire island, which was subsequently secured in 1795 under the Treaty of Basel, when the Spanish crown conceded its first colony in the Americas to France. Though three times as large as the French part, the Spanish part, he claimed, was barely one-tenth as productive. He felt that untapped productivity was due in large measure to Spanish deism, laziness, and misguidedly liberal Creole social and sexual intercourse with slaves and freed people.

Although it was researched and written from 1783–87, well before the Haitian Revolution (1791–1804) and the 1795 Treaty of Basel, Moreau de Saint-Méry's text was published after these events. Thus, he wrote in his prologue that his narrative was written "in a manner as distant as possible from all that the French Revolution could have produced."[14] That is, as his "six reasons for France to possess the entire island" illustrate,[15] Moreau de Saint-Méry's critique was intended to support French expansionist designs rather than the Haitian Revolution, which was in full swing at the time of his account's publication.[16] Therefore, he had no vested political interest in portraying the population of the Spanish part in anything other than negative terms. Indeed, ideologically and politically, he had a vested interest in portraying that population as inferior to the French in manners and custom.

Despite Napoleon Bonaparte's best efforts to re-colonize San Domingüe and to circumscribe Toussaint Louverture's growing power on the island—including having him taken to France, where he was jailed and died—however, the revolution successfully ended in establishment of the Republic of Haiti in 1804 by Jean-Jacques Dessalines. Following nearly two decades of shifting balances of power between the country's northern and southern rulers, Jean-Pierre Boyer consolidated national rule in Port au Prince in 1818.[17] Immediately after, he extended that consolidation over the island as a whole, and in a bloodless transfer of power he established Unified Haiti in 1822. Under Boyer's rule, diplomatic and commercial relations began to normalize. As a result, France and Britain each sent agents to the island. Among these, was Charles Mackenzie, Britain's consul-general in Haiti in 1826–27.

Mackenzie spent fourteen months traveling throughout the island and in 1830 published *Notes on Haiti: Made during a Residence in That Republic*, a two-volume account. It is distinguished not only by being written by a British government representative but also by being the only published English-language account of the former Spanish part during the Unification period. Traveling throughout the east, Mackenzie noted that the residents of the former Spanish part considered themselves not only distinct from the Haitians, but superior to them. "I was not a little amused," he wrote, "with the contemptuous mode in which even the blacks speak of their western neighbours as 'aquellos negros.'"[18] In other words, even during the early years of the Unification, before the rise of Dominican nationalism, people in the former Spanish part of Santo Domingo understood themselves to be ethnically and racially distinct from their Haitian neighbors.

Thirty years later, Maxime Raybaud, the French consul-general in Haiti, wrote after Dominican separation from Haiti in support of expanding the role of France in Hispaniola. Raybaud claimed that the people of the Spanish part of Santo Domingo were obviously of mixed African and Spanish descent yet considered themselves not mulattos or colored, as the Haitians did, but *"blancos de la tierra* [whites of the land]." He explained:

> The double layers of free blood that the conquering race and the last nucleus of the indigenous race were mixing with African blood was so little distinguished after the second generation—the bronzed complexion of the Spaniard, the copper complexion of the Indian, and the bistre complexion of the mulatto tended to be confused to such an extent under the influence of a common hygiene and climate—that interested observers, if there had been any, would have often found themselves with a problem in discovering in the faces the secret of a genealogy lost in the savannas and forests. This labor of fusion, which was retarded by neither European immigration, from a moral point of view, nor African immigration, from a physiological point of view, was summed up at the time of the [Haitian] revolution in the following figures: 25,000 whites of pure Spanish stock; 15,000 Africans, who, by being scattered, were not victims of any insurrectionist propaganda and who moreover, felt too proud of the social superiority that daily contact with their masters imparted them over the slaves in the French section to consent to imitate the latter, whom they haughtily called *"los negros"*; finally, 73,000 mestizos who said they were white and who, as they gave no cause for injurious objections regarding themselves, had ended up being considered just that. The separatist element of the French colony [the mulattoes] had thus become the conservative element of the Spanish colony. The vanity that had dug an abyss of hatred between the three classes there had operated for their cohesion here.[19]

Raybaud argued that both demographics (small Spanish and African populations and a large "mestizo" population) and social structure (small social distances between castes, low population density, an independent rural population of color, and "mestizos" structurally and ideologically allowed to assume white status) account for the ethno-racial differences between Haiti and Santo Domingo. In particular, he was struck by the "conservative" role played by mulattos who had been allowed to become white rather than a race apart, as had been the case in Haiti. Because they were socially white, they became politically white as well. Moreover, even the enslaved Africans understood themselves to be "socially" superior to their peers in Haiti because slavery was primarily based in the household and the cattle ranch rather than through sugar plantations, and they accordingly operated in a more paternalistic social structure.[20]

Acting as part of a multilateral effort by England, France, and the United States to contain Emperor Faustin Soulouque's aggressive military policy toward the Dominican Republic, Raybaud was politically sympathetic to the Dominicans.[21] Soulouque threatened repeatedly to invade the Dominican Republic and reunify the island under Haitian rule to once again gain access to the land and labor of the eastern part of the island. This not only would have undermined Dominican sovereignty; it also would have undermined European commercial and diplomatic interests on the island. Thus, although he was technically representing the Haitian Soulouque in his negotiations with the Dominicans, Raybaud was vociferously critical of Haiti and of the emperor. At the same time, Raybaud was vehemently opposed to U.S. annexation and was working actively against the expansionist machinations of William and Jane Cazneau, Texan colonists residing in Santo Domingo at the time of his mission. His description of the racial composition of the Dominican people, therefore, contested the Cazneaus' claims that the country would be as amenable to slaveholding colonists as Mexico had been originally to Anglos in Texas.

Though it was the second slaveholding state in the Americas to seek its independence from European colonizers, Haiti was the first American nation to abolish slavery and to establish itself as a black republic. As Mimi Sheller argues, the "Black Republic" struck "the Haytian Fear" throughout the Americas and influenced European colonial and U.S. policy toward the region throughout the nineteenth century.[22] Word of the Haitian Revolution did in fact reach and inspire Africans throughout the diaspora to revolt and pursue emancipation, including those in the neighboring islands of the Caribbean and in the United States.[23] In this geopolitical context, the Dominican Republic was a useful and willing "non-black" antithesis to Haiti and its black-liberation agenda. European and U.S. travel writers and observers of the nascent Dominican nation represented Haiti as the Dominican Republic's "Other" as much because of their own racial ideologies as because of Dominican self-perception. Haitians were repeatedly depicted as barbaric, savage, violent, apelike buffoons who contrasted sharply to cultured, refined, progressive, and near-white Dominicans.

Montague argues that sensational, distorted, and racist depictions of Haiti and of Haitians in travel writings and newspapers during the late eighteenth century and throughout the nineteenth century supported the Manifest Destiny ideologies of U.S. government expansionists and emergent capitalist imperialists. The rise of an independent black re-public in the Caribbean threatened U.S. interests because the economy of the northeastern United States relied on continued access to the in-expensive molasses produced in the French colonies. The Southern U.S. economy relied on enslaved black labor. As Montague explains it, mo-lasses circulated together with hard currency, rum, and slaves in New England, the British West Indies, and the French West Indies and on the European circuit. The Haitian Revolution and the abolition of slavery interfered with that triangular trade and jeopardized incipient U.S. and European economic and political interests in the hemisphere.[24]

From the Continental Empire to the Black and Colored Republics: A Triangle of Relations Emerges

In the late eighteenth century and throughout the nineteenth century, a chief concern of the newly founded United States was to limit the Euro-pean sphere of influence in the Americas, primarily by undermining and removing European colonial rule while expanding the United States' sphere of influence under the aegis of the Monroe Doctrine and the im-petus of what William Earl Weeks has called the "building [of] the con-tinental empire."[25] Ironically, it was precisely the contentions between Spain, France, England, and the United States over Santo Domingo's territory and governance that repeatedly forced the Dominican Repub-lic's independence, despite the desires of certain pro-annexation sectors within the nation. "The designs of one nation were neutralized by those of others, producing a stalemate."[26] Following the end of island-wide Haitian governance (1822–44), the short-lived re-colonization by Spain (1861–65), and the War of Restoration (1863–65), the imbrications of the

Dominican Republic in the geopolitical and ideological web of the Caribbean region influenced its identity formations and displays.

Between 1844 and 1871, the U.S. government sent several commercial agents and one Senate investigating commission to explore the possibility of expanding U.S. economic and military presence in the Dominican territory. The earliest inquiries took place to determine whether recognition of the new state should be granted. As U.S. government directives to their agents made explicit, diplomatic recognition was contingent on the racial composition of the Dominican Republic. During this period, the republic was in a constant state of political contestation and upheaval as two rival *caudillos*—Buenaventura Báez in the south and Pedro Santana in the north—struggled for power in the aftermath of the 1844 separation of the Dominican Republic from Unified Haiti. Each caudillo became president several times: Santana presided in 1844–48, 1853–56, 1858–61, and Báez presided in 1849–53, 1856–57, 1865–66, 1868–74, and 1876–78. Each also courted the re-colonization or the annexation of the Dominican Republic to France, Spain, and the United States by turn.[27]

In the United States, presidential responses to annexation varied according to the president's party membership. In general, Whigs "favored restraint in expanding the nation's territorial holdings" while Democrats favored "expansion in order to provide an ever-expanding frontier for migration-minded Americans."[28] Thus, presidents John Tyler (1841–45), James Polk (1845–49), Zachary Taylor (1849–50), Franklin Pierce (1853–57), and Ulysses S. Grant (1869–77) each seriously entertained the possibility of annexing some or all of the Dominican Republic. The debates in favor and against annexation hinged on a complex set of interests ranging from the appropriate balance of federal and state powers to the future of slavery to the status of people already present in newly acquired territories.[29]

Throughout the debates, however, the question of race was of fundamental and often determining importance:

> That Dominican statesmen were fully aware of the importance of race and color in the recognition policy of the United States is evident from their attempt to minimize the proportion of the Negro element in their republic. Dr. José María Caminero, the Dominican agent to the United States, declared in his note of January 8, 1845, to President Tyler that it had been the "white Dominicans" who had led the uprising against the "oppression and vexations of the negroes of Hayti."[30]

It appears that Caminero's assurances were insufficient for the slaveholding United States, as President Tyler's Secretary of State John C. Calhoun sent the commercial agent John Hogan to assess "the proportions of European, African, and mixed races" in the Dominican Republic.[31] In his only report on the matter, Hogan emphasized the whiteness of the Dominican Republic *relative to* Haiti. He assessed the Dominican Republic's population as composed "of about two hundred and thirty thousand of who forty thousand are blacks and over one hundred thousand are whites," the rest being mixed.[32] In Hogan's report, Haitian rapacity was responsible for whatever blackness did exist in the Dominican Republic, as Caminero had argued in his communication with President Tyler. That is to say, if Dominicans were less than white, it was due not to affinities between Haitians and Dominicans but to sexual violence on the part of Haitians. In his own report to President Tyler, Calhoun suggested that "the new Republic [be recognized] as a means of preventing the further spread of negro influence in the West Indies."[33]

A few months after Hogan's 1846 visit, since the matter of Dominican recognition was not yet resolved and Tyler had lost the presidential elections, Navy Commander David Dixon Porter was sent by newly elected President Polk to once again assess the island's resources, political situation, social order, and people, both to determine whether diplomatic recognition would be granted and as part of discussions of the possibility of annexing all or part of the Dominican territory. Porter was a career Navy man who published several books, including his memoirs, a history of the Civil War Navy, and two novels. The son of a commodore, Porter had lived in Mexico for several years as a child. Later, when he enlisted in the U.S. Navy and became a prisoner in Cuba, his Spanish acquired native fluency. According to the Dominican historian Juan Tomás Tavares K., it is likely that his family pedigree, together with his fluency in Spanish, familiarity with the Caribbean, and physical hardiness, accounted for his selection for the secret mission.

Like Hogan, Porter held the Dominicans to be racially superior to the Haitians, although he was less willing than Hogan to assign whiteness to Dominicans. According to Porter, there were few "pure whites" in Santo Domingo, "but almost two thirds of the population is composed of mestizo whites and mulattos, or near-whites, and they are considered as such. They varied in color from dark brown to white, with intermediate shades, but I think it would be difficult to find twenty women of pure white blood."[34] Nonetheless, Porter indicated his support for the young republic explicitly because it was whiter than Haiti, despite the large number of blacks in the border regions. Porter's report to the president, which he filed with U.S. State Department and Navy Department, was subsequently lost sometime before the outbreak of the Civil War.

Later, a copy of Porter's original 1846 report to the president was subsequently discovered at the Duke University Library by the leading U.S. historian of Dominican politics, Charles Tansill.[35] Porter's report was translated by Father Gustavo Amigó Jansen and published as *Diario de una mission secreta a Santo Domingo (1846)* in 1978 by the Dominican Society of Bibliophiles, with an introductory biographic essay by Juan Tomás Tavares K.[36] As Tavares notes in his introductory essay, "During his brief visit, [Porter] saw more of the country and got to know its landscape better than the majority of Dominicans of that time," and he offered the most extensive account available of the country in the immediate aftermath of its separation from Haiti.[37]

Almost immediately in his account, Porter noted that men he perceived as whites, mulattos, and blacks "mixed indiscriminately." At the same time, "They all considered it an insult to be called anything other than white; black refers solely to the Haitians in the far east" of the island.[38] Porter himself considered the Haitians "a barbaric and indomitable race of Negroes," while the Dominicans under their rule were an "oppressed nation of whites."[39] According to Porter, these "Spaniards" were forced to submit to a tyrannical and unnatural rule by rapacious and inferior blacks because they had been abandoned to their fate by the civilized nations and, having witnessed Haitian brutality against their former French masters, were unable to resist Haitian rule. Ultimately, however, Haitian excesses were such that the Dominicans were forced to liberate themselves.

Throughout his account, Porter contrasted the Dominican Republic and Dominicans to Haiti and Haitians. One was white, Spanish, and Catholic; the other was black, French, and irreligious. One was "civilized" because it courted the United States and Americans; the other was "barbaric" because it jealously defended its political and economic sovereignty. That being the case, Porter concluded, the U.S. government should take advantage of Dominican independence and support the country because, despite the fact that some Dominicans were black, power resided in the hands of whites and mulattos who were far more welcoming of foreigners and foreign industry than the Haitians. In other words, the social and political supremacy of whites in the Dominican Republic made that nation worthy of U.S. recognition.

Porter's depiction of Haitians and Haitian history was virulently

Negrophobic and violently hostile to black emancipation; his view of Dominicans, by contrast, was as the civilized antinomy of Haitians. He wrote:

> It is a well known fact that "the free Haitian nation, at work or in revolution, even when viewed in the best possible light, is nothing more than a horde of merciless savages," covered by the crimes and gluttony of its liberty; and even though it may appear to a passing observer that there is little difference between *them* and the people of the eastern part, it should not be forgotten that all the elements of disorder are simply dormant within them, ready to burst at the slightest provocation; and since the time of its first revolution to the present, it has been a scourge upon the inhabitants of this beautiful island and they have fallen upon it like a perfect plague, a curse to themselves and to their superiors, destroying everything that was beauty in art and nature and raising in this place of God the altars of betrayal. What else could the Spanish do besides throw off the yoke that became increasingly bitter and which probably would reduce them even lower in the scale of civilization than the brutish people who called themselves their masters? They arrived at revolution because of a universal explosion of indignation, and their oppressors were forced to flee from a poorly armed mob, one which deserves all the sympathy in the world, if only for the *moderation* with which they treated their enemies. Neither acknowledged nor aided when they raised their voices to ask for recognition of their independence by the leading nations, they have kept to themselves to the present time, in the face of opposing forces ten times larger than they and with a patriotism unsurpassed by other countries.[40]

Porter dismissed outright any possibility that Haitian sovereignty was at par with Dominican sovereignty, claiming that "a nation of Negroes has yet to prove its capacity for self governance, much less for the governance of others."[41] He argued that, given the oppressive rule of "a horde of merciless savages" who thought themselves "masters" over "Spanish," the temperateness of Dominican separation from Haiti should be admired and the Dominicans' sovereignty recognized by the United States. That recognition, in turn, would support white supremacy in the Dominican Republic, would justly undermine and contain Haiti's Black Republic, and would serve U.S. economic and political interests.

Despite Porter's 1846 recommendation to President Polk, three years later diplomatic recognition of the Dominican Republic still had not been granted. This time, the new Taylor administration dispatched Benjamin Green as special agent to the Dominican Republic to once again assess the racial state of the republic. Green wrote that, while "most Dominicans were of mixed blood," they understood themselves to be white and to share a "white interest." As he recounted with a degree of awe, "Some Negroes even called themselves 'white Negroes' or 'Negroes with a white heart.'"[42]

The historian Luís Martínez-Fernández argues that "the more ardently expansionist the reporter, the lighter the racial portrayal of the Dominican people. Significantly, several of these envoys were northern entrepreneurs who established exploitative ventures in the island."[43] The most prominent of these were General William L. Cazneau and Colonel Joseph W. Fabens. Together with Cazneau's wife, the author Jane MacManus Cazneau, they spent the better part of three decades after Dominican separation from Haiti accumulating land and resource concessions from the Dominican government, developing investment schemes with New York financiers, and lobbying in both the media and U.S. government circles in favor of either total or partial annexation.[44]

Jane MacManus Cazneau, who was recently credited with having coined the term "Manifest Destiny" before John L. O'Sullivan's now famous editorial, was a prolific writer of national renown. MacManus Cazneau was also a public proponent of Texas annexation and a facilitator of German immigrant colonization projects in Mexican Texas. She encouraged U.S. territorial and commercial expansion westward and south through her prolific writings published in the *New Yorker, New York Sun, Democratic Review, New York Tribune,* and *Union,* as well as in dozens of books and pamphlets. MacManus Cazneau was known as a "terror with her pen" and, as Linda Hudson has recently argued, was an influential figure in expansionist U.S. circles.[45]

Together, Cazneau's, MacManus Cazneau's, and Fabens's principal agendas were either Anglo-American colonization of the Samaná Bay or annexation of the entire country, as much for the expansion of the U.S. South's slave economy as for resource extraction and military outposts. Samaná was considered a strategic location for a naval coaling station and military outpost, located as it is at the midway point of the Caribbean. Fabens wrote one of the earliest travel accounts of Santo Domingo by a North American, *In the Tropics: By a Settler in Santo Domingo*, published in 1863 and republished in 1873 under a new title, *Life in Santo Domingo*.[46] In addition, Fabens delivered and published half a dozen addresses on Santo Domingo to the American Geographical and Statistical Society of New York, all intended to sway public opinion in favor of annexation.[47]

Both Southern slaveholders and Northern abolitionists who opposed annexation did so because they perceived the country to be predominantly black. For the Southern slaveholders, the issue was the inconceivability of admitting blacks and mulattos as citizens of the United States. "White southerners' perception of the Dominican Republic as a struggling nation comprising a lawless, free, dark-skinned population made it difficult for any administration to establish solid diplomatic relations, or even to grant recognition, which was deemed by many the first step toward acquisition."[48] Annexationists therefore argued forcefully that the Dominican population was not, in fact, predominantly black. Rather, they claimed that the country was principally white—racially, culturally, and ideologically. The claim could only be made, however, with Haiti as counterpoint. This is evident not only in that the comparison is usually made explicitly, but also in that the comparison was exclusively with Haiti.

Northern abolitionists such as Senator Charles Sumner, an ardent supporter of recognition of Haiti and of black emancipation in the United States and chair of the Senate Foreign Relations Committee, claimed that efforts to represent Dominicans as white or nearly white were not only inaccurate, but also pro-slavery and imperialist. "An abolitionist paper declared on April 8, 1847, that a 'white' Dominican Republic was 'a convenient fiction . . . fabricated for the purpose of securing some of our destiny-folk a foot-hold in Hayti, that they might play the same game there that has been enacted on a larger theater in Texas.'"[49] The Texas game, of course, was expansion, annexation, and ultimately incorporation into the Union of a former Mexican territory already populated by a racially suspect people.

What is especially interesting about this state of affairs is the political paradox created by these competing representations of Dominican racial identity. Either Dominicans were white or nearly white and thus could be annexed to the United States, or they were not white and therefore could remain sovereign—at least, officially. The Dominican case is curious because of how its relationship to Haiti was perceived and represented by Dominican and U.S. elites alike. Thus, Dominican pro-annexationists would warn of the threat of Haitian invasion in a suasive attempt to have the United States protect the young republic. For example, Manuel María Guatier, the minister for foreign affairs under Báez, wrote to U.S. Secretary of State Hamilton Fish:

> The enemies of peace and progress of the country, fearful lest a change be made from this provisional state of affairs which favors so highly their shady projects, have made every effort to overthrow this Government in which they see a menace and a bar to their iniquitous plans. General Gregorio Luperón, a voluntary exile, a man of vindictive spirit and very backward ideas, has declared that the African race shall dominate this Island and that that race should unite in order to exterminate the other races. . . . In this situation, overcoming natural reluctance brought about by the idea of asking too much, my Government has decided to ask most urgently of Your Excellency's Government that like a powerful and philanthropic sister it may be good enough to assist the Dominican Government in its difficulties.[50]

Guatier's claims that black invaders would "exterminate the other races" frame Dominicans as the white victims of Haitians and their allies, such as Luperón. As a "powerful and philanthropic sister" nation, the United States must intervene "to assist" the Dominicans in preventing this assault. Framed this way, Dominican annexationists' call for U.S. intervention was a call for racial and patriarchal solidarity.

Santana, Báez's predecessor and long-time nemesis, had made the same charge of allowing race suicide against Báez a decade earlier when he was seeking the protection of a foreign government. William Cazneau had claimed that, with Santana in charge of the Dominican Republic, "the Cabinet, Congress, and the Courts are filled by white men," in contrast to the manner of a Báez whose party "aims at placing the supreme control in the hands of the negroes."[51] And indeed, given that Báez had been a member of the Haitian Unification government for over a decade, the charge was believable, if inaccurate.

Not long after Cazneau's missive, W. S. Courtney's *The Gold Fields of Santo Domingo* (1860) was published. Courtney had been commissioned by the *New York Herald*'s editor, James Gordon Bennet, who was in favor of annexation and had frequently published the pro-annexationist editorials and propaganda penned by Jane MacManus Cazneau.[52] Following the model offered by MacManus Cazneau's letters to the *New York Herald*, Courtney described the island as fecund, virginal, and passively awaiting U.S. husbanding and fertilization. Santo Domingo was a new "El Dorado," unexploited and ripe for U.S. expansion. Dominicans themselves were portrayed as docile, polite, and utterly unmotivated to exploit their land's rich resources. Courtney found it "scarcely credible that such vast wealth, and especially mineral wealth, should have lain there so easily attainable, for so many years and almost within the suburbs of our great commercial cities, without exciting at least the cupidity, if not the enterprise of the Yankee."[53]

The timing of Courtney's panegyric, however, was unfortunate for enterprising Anglo colonizers and annexationists such as Cazneau and Fabens because the U.S. Civil War broke out in 1861. Even if it had wanted to apply the Monroe Doctrine, with the outbreak of Civil War, the United States' eyes were fully focused on matters at home. Nonetheless, President Santana's efforts to place the country under the protective tutelage of some (white) foreign power to prevent Haitian reunification finally succeeded. A year after *The Gold Fields of Santo Domingo* was published, in 1861, Santo Domingo was reannexed by Spain at Santana's invitation. Almost immediately, however, anti-annexationists fought to "restore" Dominican independence. By 1865, the Dominican War of Restoration had been won and Dominican sovereignty evidently secured. However, with the U.S. Civil War over in 1865 as well, U.S. proponents of expansion and annexation turned their "imperial eyes" to the Caribbean, with a renewed focus on the Dominican Republic.

Twenty years after his first visit to the country, David Dixon Porter was again sent to the country, this time by President Grant's Secretary of State William H. Seward on a diplomatic mission to negotiate the purchase of the Samaná Bay isthmus. Despite Porter's tenacity and diplomatic skill, the offer was turned down by the Dominican government, which, as he noted, "had just emerged from a revolution" in which it had recovered its sovereignty from Spain for once and for all in 1865. That did not dissuade the U.S. government, however, as five years later President Grant again attempted to negotiate by treaty the annexation of the Dominican Republic to the United States.[54]

Once again, travel narratives offered support to expansionists' efforts. And once again, the editor at the *New York Herald* commissioned a writer to gather information "to create a public sentiment friendly to U.S. expansion in the Caribbean" in keeping with President Grant's annexationist agenda.[55] De Bonneville Randolph Keim's narrative, *Santo Domingo, Pen Pictures and Leaves of Travel, Romance and History, from the Portfolio of a Correspondent in the American Tropics*, was published in 1870 and included "large chunks of romanticized history, among those the figure of Anacaona, based largely on Washington Irving's depiction [as the archetypical victim of Spanish brutality]."[56] Irving, of course, wrote the leading nineteenth-century biography of Christopher Columbus and the early history of Spanish conquest.[57]

In Keim's account, the Dominican Republic was ripe for U.S. colonization because, relative to Haiti, Dominicans could be considered honorary whites. For example, Keim informed his readers that Dominican President Báez, who was the son of a white merchant and a black slave woman, had an "off color" complexion, a "brunette face," and a "very agreeable expression."[58] Unfortunately for the annexationists, Senator Charles Sumner's staunch abolitionism and his ability to marshal substantial public and congressional opinion against the annexationist project forced President Grant to appoint a Commission of Inquiry to visit Santo Domingo early in 1871 to look into the matter. The commission was composed of five men, among them Senator Benjamin F. Wade, Cornell University president Andrew D. White, and philanthropist minister Samuel G. Howe, together with former U.S. envoy to Colombia A. A. Burton and the renowned abolitionist Frederick Douglass as secretaries.[59] It arrived in Santo Domingo on January 16, 1871, along with a cadre of scientists led by the geologist William M. Gabb. They were charged with ascertaining popular support for annexation and assessing the physical, moral, and intellectual conditions of the people and the quality of the land and its resources. As with previous U.S. government agents, part of the commissions' task was to assess the racial composition of the country and the power of the white elite, both of which were central to any viable colonization or annexation scheme. After spending two months in the country, and several weeks in Haiti, the commissioners concluded that "the interests of our country and of San Domingo alike invite the annexation of that republic," as President Grant informed Congress.[60]

Ten journalists accompanied the commission, including J. E. Taylor, an artist-reporter for *Frank Leslie's Illustrated Newspaper*, and Samuel Hazard, a pro-annexation journalist.[61] Taylor produced at least eleven drawings of the Dominican Republic while traveling with the commission; though it is not clear whether any of those were ever published in the United States, they certainly offered an important complement to the commission's report. Moreover, they were published a century later in the Dominican Republic by Bernardo Vega, director of the Museo del Hombre Dominicano, as part of a collection of rare images of turn-of-the-century Santo Domingo.[62] Samuel Hazard's narrative, by contrast,

2. Pen-and-ink portrait of Báez by Samuel Hazard

was not only published in the United States but became an almost canonical account of the Dominican Republic and its people in the Dominican Republic.

Hazard had traveled for free on the steamer *Tybee*, which was owned by Spofford, Tileston, and Company, a New York investment company that sponsored junkets to the Dominican Republic and had a vested economic interest in annexation.[63] In *Santo Domingo, Past and Present: With a Glance at Hayti*, which he published in 1873, Hazard wrote that he "freely" used the commission's report as a reference source, "At times even quoting their very language." And indeed, Hazard quoted entire sections of the commission's report without citation. For example, Hazard quoted verbatim the report's sections on "The Conditions of the People," "Population," and "Agricultural Products," among others. He also provided anecdotes illustrating the commissioners' findings that "the Dominican people are not averse to work when certain of reasonable reward"; that they were supportive of annexation; and that insurrections and anti-annexation feelings were the work of foreign Jews and exiled political leaders.[64] Given that the commission's report concluded that annexation was favorable, the propagandist nature of Hazard's account, particularly because it was written in travelogue form and without citations, is evident. Because of the vast popularity and influence of this genre, however, it was an oversight likely to be ignored or forgiven by the general public.[65]

Following Keim's example, Hazard described Báez (figure 2) this way:

President Báez is a courtly, pleasant man, of medium height and agreeable appearance. He is just fifty-seven years of age, and would never be taken for other than a Spaniard were it not that his hair, as he turns his head, shows just a little of the character of the African. He speaks French as well as he does Spanish, but English only tolerably well. He seems perfectly frank. With the easy air and manner of a thorough man of the world, he impresses me as a perfectly upright man, and that seems to be generally the impression made. . . . The portraits circulated representing him as a black man are utterly false.[66]

Interestingly, although he noted that his hair showed Báez's African ancestry, Keim denied Báez's blackness, even as he admitted that "in some parts of the South [Báez] would have been placed on a par with the field labourer of the plantation."[67] Pro-annexation Dominicans, it seems, were exempted from the one-drop-of-blood rule operative in the United States. Although Hazard made several references to black or colored Dominicans, he devoted equal attention and more emphasis to white Dominicans. The Dominican people in general were depicted as "of a mixed race, much nearer white than black."

Haitians, conversely, Hazard described as "piccaninnies," "uncles and mammies," at once "quiet, docile, and peaceful" and "brutish." Hazard lamented the loss of French colonial rule, for "now, with these semibarbarians, [Haiti] has been for years retrograding in civilisation and improvement."[68] Haiti's land was underdeveloped and overgrown; the houses were "of the most ordinary kind"; and the nation was overcrowded. Of course, references to "the sound of the tum-tum" and to "Vaudoux" were made, as well.[69] The comparative, and at times anxious, glance at Haiti is in fact sustained throughout the text, both explicitly and implicitly. Hazard writes:

The great majority [of Dominicans], especially along the coast, are neither pure black nor pure white; they are mixed in every conceivable degree. In some parts of the interior considerable numbers of the white race are to be found, and generally in the mixed race the white blood predominates. The Dominican people differ widely in this particular from the Haytians, among whom the black race is in complete ascendancy. The cultivated and educated, such as the President, members of his Cabinet, senators, judges, and local magistrates, compare well with the same classes in other countries, and the uneducated appear to equal to the same class in any country with which we are acquainted. They seem to be practically destitute of prejudice of class, race, or colour. In their intercourse with each other and with strangers, they are courteous in manner, respectful and polite. In all their relations with them the Commissioners found them kind and hospitable.[70]

Compared with Haitians, then, Dominicans were progressive, civilized, capable of political maturity, and supportive of white supremacy.

Throughout Hazard's narrative, the leitmotif is that of untapped potential expressed in racialized and gendered metaphors:

> As regards the future, this question of population is a very satisfactory one, if St. Domingo should become allied to any strong Government; for five years' emigration would entirely change its character, as has been the case in California.
>
> It has been the fashion among some of our politicians to urge the purchase of Cuba, even at the price of one hundred millions of dollars, and it has a large and extensively mixed population, with all their habits, ideas, and customs fully established, with still a larger number of slaves and coolies.
>
> But here [in Santo Domingo] there is an almost virgin island, more desirable in every way, with a free, limited, and simple people, who have no particularly fixed ideas, or customs, that would not readily assimilate to those of the new-comers. One-tenth of the above-named sum, expended in improving the means of communication, in exploring and seeking information of its resources, with the change that American machinery and enterprise, accompanying emigration into the island, would bring, would in a few years give us an island equally valuable as Cuba, and aptly illustrate the fact that our institutions and civilization are adapted to any climate and to any people.[71]

That the project is Anglo-American colonization justified by the ideology of Manifest Destiny is clear by the reference to California, which was made a state in 1850 via extensive Anglo-American colonization during the Mexican-American War of 1846–48 and the California Gold Rush of 1849.[72] The role of military and vigilante violence in the expulsion and subjugation of Mexican *californios* in the establishment of California underscored Hazard's emphasis on the passive, congenial, and hospitable nature of Dominicans.[73] Unlike the Mexicans, the implication was, Dominicans are malleable and open to the invaders, who will "cultivate" them as well as the land with "intelligence, industry, and enterprise." The emphasis on the "depopulated" nature of the land highlighted the call to Anglo-American colonization.

Here again, the contrast to Haiti was seminal. Haiti was black, overpopulated, and ugly in land and people. Dominicans were *not black*, underpopulated, and attractive, if "dusky." Several anecdotes serve to assure readers that there are established pockets of "pure white people . . . of a superior nature" that would easily prove hospitable to Anglo immigration, particularly in the Cibao region. The "unmistakable" whiteness of Moca, for example, was proved both by the town's Spanish colonial architecture and by the presence of "the first really beautiful women encountered by the commissioners," and before whom some of Hazard's party prostrated themselves. The presence of white women was key, for U.S. antimiscegenation ideology ran deeper than its people's practices. The land was "fertile" and "virgin," awaiting the technologically advanced (that is, racially superior) husbanding of Anglo-American emigrants: "Though to-day impoverished and a beggar, yet she will prove, under proper care, such a precious jewel to the power that may be induced to take her under its protection, as many kings would be glad to place in their crowns."[74]

Despite Hazard's openly annexationist politics and the fact that his travelogue was produced in support of those politics, *Santo Domingo, Past and Present*, has long been considered a sound primary document that is heavily relied on by Dominican historians and historiography. Indeed, Hazard's work was one of the first to be published in Spanish translation by the Dominican Society of Bibliophiles. And his illustrations are prominently displayed in the Museo del Hombre Dominicano's exhibit on the early national period, a curatorial strategy that I will examine more carefully in the next chapter.

"These Destinies Are Manifest":
Narrating Dominican Indo-Hispanicity

Nineteenth-century Dominicans were well aware of the United States' Manifest Destiny ideologies. They responded by assimilating Manifest Destiny and adapting it to their own sociopolitical exigencies. For example, Pedro Franciso Bonó, a prominent late-nineteenth-century thinker and, according to Franklin Franco, the first Dominican social scientist, wrote in an 1884 letter to Gregorio Luperón:

> It is good that the government . . . begin to think seriously about the destinies that Providence is setting aside for blacks and mulattoes in America. From this point on these destinies are manifest, given the current numbers of this race; and I believe the island of Santo Domingo is called upon to be the nucleus, the model of its exaltation, and its embodiment in this hemisphere. And who better than you will be able to begin to place the first stones, to establish the bases of this grandeur? Who better than you can

know just how necessary the white race is for attaining it, but at the same time know the superiority of combinations of this so superior race; and who better than you will be able to fuse, amalgamate, and shape a homogeneous whole out of the wisdom and the ignorance of both families so that, model of tolerance and contention, we might place ourselves in an enviable position in the Universe.[75]

Predating Pedro Henríquez Ureña's and José Vasconcelos's *la raza cósmica* formulation by several decades, Bonó articulated an explicitly white-supremacist model of *mestizaje* that reflected the internal logic of the attempt at post-Haitian Unification racial and political liberalism. If for nineteenth-century North Americans "amalgamation was an abomination," for their contemporaries among Dominican elites, amalgamation was salvation. It was the Dominican elites' version of a manifest destiny.

The tension in the Dominican context, therefore, was how to sustain white supremacy while encouraging publically sanctioned intimate relations between whites, near-whites, and people of color. The rhetorical solution was the displacement of blackness onto Haitians and the aesthetic exultation of *lo Indio*, the indigenous. *Lo Indio* is the middle term, the central point of the racial continuum, the "native" alternative to foreign blackness and whiteness alike. In this project, literary and expressive forms were both illustrative and supportive of ideological indigenism. "*Lo Indio's*" role in the formation of Dominican racial identity, therefore, must be understood in that context as much as in relationship to Haiti and the larger indigenist movement throughout Latin America.

The first Dominican text to articulate that vision fully was *Enriquillo* (1882), written by Manuel de Jesus Galván. Galván was minister of foreign affairs under the dictatorial government of Ulises (Lilís) Heureaux, the country's first and last openly Haitian-descended ruler. Yet the only blacks in Galván's narrative were the slaves on Diego Columbus's plantation who engaged in the colony's first rebellion and were quickly suppressed. Indeed, it was precisely in response to the presence of blackness—at the pinnacle of national power and in the country's midst, at the borders with Haiti and to the north—and the "absence" of Native Americans that *Enriquillo* resonated. Lilís's predecessor, Luperón, even pointed to the supposedly scientific link between men of color and the Dominican Indians: "the mulattos, through the law of climates, [tend] to return to the primitive race of the island."[76] Dominicans would be neither Africanized Haitians nor peninsular Spaniards, whom the War of

Restoration had proven rejected Dominicans as racially inferior. Instead, they would be like Enriquillo: Hispanicized natives with a legitimate claim to sovereignty.

Enriquillo is a romantic novel that has functioned in the service of what Homi Bhabha has called pedagogical national identity formation, acting as both historiographic and historic text.[77] Doris Sommer argues, "The Dominican Republic was virtually constituted as a modern nation with the publication of [*Enriquillo*]."[78] Indeed, she considers *Enriquillo* the country's "foundational fiction." Franklin Franco informs us that *Enriquillo* became required reading in Dominican public schools shortly after it was published and quickly "fulfilled its roles as an ideological bridge that allowed for the rehabilitation of Hispanophilia." At present, the typical Dominican public high school graduate will have been required to read *Enriquillo* at least four times in the curriculum.[79]

Galván's *Enriquillo* dramatized and romanticized the story of the sixteenth-century Taíno *cacique* named in the title. *Enriquillo* the text made a metaphor of the noble, masculine, and indigenous origins of the Dominican nation through the person of Enriquillo the man. In so doing, the romance undertook egregious erasures and revisions. As Sommer critiques:

> By pushing this story so far back that blacks seem not to figure in Dominican origins, by squinting at the Dominican crowd to create an optical illusion of racial simplicity, Galván manages to write a national identity by erasing. . . . By shifting the historical emphasis from the mass of black slaves to Enriquillo's remnant of a tribe, he offered a conciliating fiction that such distinguished readers as José Martí and Pedro Henríquez Ureña enthusiastically claimed as a model of American writing. From the time Galván published *Enriquillo* . . . Dominicans are Indians or mestizos, descendant of Enriquillo's valiant tribesmen and of the Spaniards to whom they were bound by love and respect, whereas the blacks are considered foreigners, Haitians.[80]

Galván, in other words, was a "political storyteller" who fashioned a cohesive, telluric national identity out of a racially heterogeneous, complex, and contradictory past through the model of romantic love textually embodied in the figure of Enriquillo.

Thus, Enriquillo represented Dominicanidad's new ethno-racial archetype: the culturally Hispanic and Catholic Indio who bested the Spanish Catholics and Taínos alike, for he was more cultured, more pious, and nobler than they. The rise and early institutionalization of this archetype occurred precisely during the country's first stable government: Lilís's dictatorship. Under Lilís's rule, the Dominican Republic began to expand its diplomatic and commercial relations not only with the United States, but also with Europe. It also began to foster international relations through participation in World Fairs, such as the 1889 Paris Universal Exposition, the 1892 Exposición histórico-americana de Madrid, and the 1907 Jamestown Tercentennial Exposition.[81] Although this was done mostly for commercial purposes (the Dominican Republic's pavilions in these fairs showcased the country's agricultural products and mineral resources), it also served as a vehicle for showcasing Dominican national identity.

The country had ambassadors in Washington, D.C., New York City, various cities of Puerto Rico, and in France, Germany, Holland, and Belgium who were charged with encouraging not only commercial relations but immigration.[82] To that end, the country's Hispanic heritage was actively publicized. The best example of this was Lilís's attempt to sell Christopher Columbus's remains to the 1892 Columbian World's Fair representative, Frederic Albion Ober. Ober related in his 1904 travelogue, *Our West Indian Neighbors*, that the exchange was never realized, but the Dominican state's seeming willingness to display Dominican-ness via the proxy of the nation's most iconographic "Hispanic" figure is instructive.

Writing about the willingness of the descendants of Santiago de los Caballeros's conquistador-founders to sell their family heirlooms to him, Ober highlights the racial irony of the Dominican Republic's late-nineteenth-century situation:

> The degradation to which the Sons of Somebody have descended, and the poverty that would induce the parting with such precious heirlooms, are suggestive, to say the least. But what can you expect from a people who have been under the iron heel of oppression for many generations, who have been accustomed to look up to, and not down upon, the African sons of nobody? . . . To-day we find the remote descendants of Africans who were torn from their homes by the Spaniards, and who wore their lives out beneath the lash of Spanish task-masters, exhibiting as the most precious of their treasures the remains of the man who laid the foundations of that slavery![83]

Unlike other observers, Ober was not quick to cast the Dominicans as "near whites" and instead wrote openly of the political predominance of men of color. Nonetheless, he considered Dominicans "the remote descendants of Africans," in contrast to Haitians who were "the African sons of nobody." The Dominicans' remote ancestors may have once been subjected to "the lash of Spanish task-masters," but ultimately they identified with those Spaniards and considered that heritage "precious." Unlike the Haitians, they knew whose children they were.

One might infer that the difference was due at least in part to the fact that at the time of Ober's writing and the book's publication, Haiti was steadfastly resisting foreign investments and limiting whites' property rights. The Dominican Republic, by contrast, was busily courting foreign investment and would soon be under the U.S. Customs Receivership. As Ober put it, "Haiti never grants any concession to the white man, of whatever kind, having had one bitter experience at least, which has sufficed her for more than a century. The black man knows when he has enough; but the colored citizen of the Dominican half of the island has yet to learn."[84] If that was so at the turn of the century, it certainly changed a decade later with the initiation of the U.S. occupation.

"The Courtesy of the Latin": Blackness, Backwardness, and U.S. Occupation

William D. Boyce's United States Colonies and Dependencies, Illustrated, was published in 1914. Boyce, the publisher of the Saturday Blade, Chicago Ledger, Farming Business, and Indiana Daily Times, was a well-traveled exponent of Manifest Destiny and of the U.S. imperial project. He was a proponent of ecological theories of race and was openly white supremacist in his assessment and depiction of Filipinos, Puerto Ricans, Alaskans, Hawaiians, and sundry other colonial and neocolonial "natives." Yet he was almost salutary in his description of Dominicans. Indeed, the Dominican Republic is depicted as both kin and akin to the United States: "The 'black and tan' Dominican Republic has a Spanish-speaking population and its metropolis, Santo Domingo City, is grandmother of the Americas."[85] Boyce made only limited references to the African origins of Dominicans, claiming that "[indigenous] blood flows today in the veins of many a Dominican, mixed with that of the Spanish conquerors and the American slaves."[86]

The depiction of Haiti that follows the chapter on the Dominican Republic is strikingly different. Boyce, like others before and after him, drew on existing Negrophobic U.S. tropes:

As far as we are aware, Haiti's story has never been really staged in a literary sense. There is so much action that it would require three rings and a several sideshows to do it justice. It certainly lends itself to black-face tragedy or a melodrama of blood and thunder in every scene. There would be enough material left over for a first-class minstrel show and a gorgeous costume piece. But, as a motion-picture film, it would hardly get by the censor. . . . This fertile country, where the white man is not allowed to own land, is an interesting study. Its childlike people have been bullied, ridiculed, exploited and maligned in turn, through the years. . . . Born in Africa, or the offspring of savages captured in the jungles of the Dark Continent, the Haitians were ill-fitted for self-government and have been left to work out their own salvation. . . . When roused by the fear of recurrent white domination, these happy-go-lucky children of nature revert to savagery, fighting to preserve for their own this one little isle of the earth where they are working out their destiny.[87]

Drawing on familiar racist caricatures of blacks, Boyce scorned Haitian sovereignty as "a melodrama of blood and thunder" suited for a minstrel show. Since minstrel shows were public spectacles staged by white men in blackface anxious to deny black men's humanity, political aims, and intellectual aspirations, Boyce's claim that Haitian history was "first-class" minstrel-show material indicated the anxiety Haiti provoked for him. The source of that anxiety becomes clear when Boyce complains about the Haitian constitutional abrogation of whites' property rights in Haiti. For Boyce, this legislative barrier to white power in Haiti meant that the Haitians were "childlike . . . savages" who would have "to work out their own salvation" without the guidance of white patriarchs like him. Dominicans appeared more amenable to the likes of Boyce.

The contrast Boyce drew between Dominicans and Haitians extended beyond racialized bodies to racialized social settings such as the marketplace and to government bodies such as the military. If Boyce perceived only cleanliness and order in the Dominican markets and military, the converse was true in Haiti. Of the Dominicans he wrote: "The country folk, with their wares, are bound for the marketplace, undoubtedly the most 'colorful' spot in town, where beasts of burden form a patient line, relieved finally of the ill-fitting straw saddles and huge panniers woven from banana and plantain fiber."[88] Similarly, the multiple revolutions, caudillos, and sundry political imbroglios in Santo Domingo were glossed over. A photograph of neatly attired and orderly "soldier-policemen" was included, and the picture of Dominican market women showed them well dressed and standing or sitting at their vending tables.

Haitians, conversely, were represented as undisciplined, dirty, and disorderly:

"Generals are thicker than flies down here," the steamer captain told us, and on the very first street back of the waterfront we met a batch of officers, dazzling beyond description, their multi-colored uniforms heavily incrusted with gilt. We followed some tattered soldiers to a public square. They did not seem in the least belligerent. Some sprawled in the shade chewing sugar cane; others accosted us with the one scrap of English on the tongue of every Haitian private, "Give me five cents."

There are over 20,000 of these ragamuffins under arms and probably 6,000 bedecked officers. . . .

If you want to see the people of Haiti at their liveliest, take your smelling salts and sally forth to the marketplace. You will find one market well housed, where the food is shaded from the fierce tropic sun, and another, more popular, in an open square. Here the glistening white cathedral with its stately spires seems out of tune with the surroundings, as it towers above over laden donkeys, sun-spoiled products and a chattering, perspiring crowd of blacks.[89]

The accompanying photographs show ragtag Haitian soldiers and squatting women sifting through coffee beans in the street. If the Dominican Republic was underpopulated in Boyce's narrative, then Haiti, "the Ebony Land," was "like a pail overflowing with Blackberries."

That same year, in 1914, A. Hyatt Verrill (1871–1954) published another popular travel narrative that included the Dominican Republic and Haiti. Verrill was the son of a well-known Yale zoologist, Addison E. Verrill. The elder Verrill was principally responsible for the overhaul and expansion of Yale's zoological collection, bringing to the university specimens from all over the Americas. He was accompanied on his collecting trips to South America and the Caribbean by his son Adolpheus. Perhaps it is not surprising, then, that the junior Verrill would become an eminent archeologist, explorer, and collector of prehistoric artifacts from Latin America, which he donated to museums throughout the United States and Europe.[90]

With a biography that exemplified the linkages between United States' museums and its travelers, Verrill was also the renowned author of over one hundred books and short stories of science fiction, explorers' guides, children's fiction, and travel narratives. A dozen of these were related to the Caribbean island nations, primarily Cuba, Puerto Rico, the Dominican Republic, and Haiti. Several of these travel accounts were so popular that they had multiple reprintings, including his *Porto Rico Past and Present and San Domingo of Today*. This popular travel narrative was originally released in 1914, before the U.S. occupation of Haiti and the Dominican Republic, and was re-released in 1926 after U.S. withdrawal from the Dominican Republic but during the continued occupation of Haiti. Like his predecessors and followers, Verrill portrayed the two nations as fundamentally antithetical to one another and "as distinct as though situated on different continents."[91] If they had anything in common, it was their history of civil unrest and need for white tutelage, the "guiding hand of the Caucasian . . . to rule and protect them."[92]

Nonetheless, despite this common need for U.S. administration, there was little else in common between the two nations. Indeed, to Verrill they were mirror opposites demographically, socially, and racially. He wrote:

> Whereas the population of Haiti is nine-tenths black and the country is backward and retrogressive, the people of the Dominican Republic are progressive and keenly alive to the importance of sanitation, improvements, and development, and less than one-third of the population are negroes. . . . While the Dominican Republic cannot by any stretch of the imagination be called a "black republic," yet it is distinctly a coloured one. . . . In most places, however, the coloured races outnumber the whites, but the colour is far lighter than in most of the West Indies and to a superficial observer, a large portion of them would pass for white.[93]

While blacks predominated in the Black Republic, in the "coloured" republic, near-white mulattos and whites outnumbered blacks. Elsewhere in the text, Verrill noted that Dominicans retained many Spanish customs and manners in addition to their language. He recounted his visits to several of the Dominican Republic's "white" towns—Santiago de los Caballeros, Moca, San Francisco de Macoris—where the descendants of the Spanish colonizers managed either to retain their racial purity or to mix away most of the residents' blackness.

Verrill's portrayal of the Dominican Republic contrasted sharply with his portrayal of Haiti. Up to the chapter on Haiti, the narrative was a fairly accurate recounting of the island's history, institutions, and landscape. When it came to Haiti, however, his tone shifted from measured delight in the distinctively Spanish flavor of the Dominican Republic to disgust and reprobation:

The term "Black Republic," by which it is commonly know, is far from *a propos*, for while it certainly *is* black in morals, instincts, conditions, and the colour of its people, yet it cannot with truth be considered a "republic" save in theory. . . . Even in the largest towns there is scarcely a sign of modern progress and development, sanitation is conspicuous by its absence, filth and dirt are on every hand, there are comparatively few decent buildings, and ragged blacks swarm everywhere. In the country, conditions are even worse, for the people, unrestrained by a stable government, reared as it were on bloodshed massacre, and warfare, have reverted to almost pristine African savagery in many places.[94]

As this selection reveals, Verrill relied on common Negrophobic tropes in his characterization of Haitians—they were evil, savage, animal-like, bloodthirsty, and incapable of self-governance, all of which was "a shame and a disgrace," given Haiti's "vast resources."[95] Angry at the Haitian constitution's bar on foreign property ownership, Verrill decried the provision as a sign of the country's primitiveness. Although Verrill did recognize the military and political accomplishments of key figures such as Toussaint Louverture, and he acknowledged that "many of the Haitiens [*sic*],—even among the pure blacks,—are intelligent, progressive and broad-minded,"[96] overall the situation in Haiti was one of savagery and backwardness. As if presaging the U.S. intervention in Haiti, Verrill claimed that if white foreign capital were allowed entry, and if "a stable and proper administration" by whites were in place, Haiti's conditions would be improved. Of course, at the time of the second printing of his text, Haiti was indeed under U.S. occupation; its constitution had been forcibly amended by the U.S. military government to lift the ban on foreign investment; and white property ownership rights were firmly established.

"A Contrast to Poor Haiti": Hispanicity and Progress during U.S. Occupation

With the U.S. occupation of Haiti (1915–34) in full effect, and the U.S. Marines still in the Dominican Republic at the halfway point of what would be an eight-year occupation there (1916–24), the renowned travel writer Harry A. Franck published his account of Santo Domingo and Haiti in *Roaming through the West Indies* (1920).[97] Franck was a prolific travel writer whose first book, *A Vagabond Journey around the World*

(1910), established him as the "Prince of the Vagabonds"; altogether, he was the author of twenty-three travel narratives of countries throughout the Americas, Europe, and Asia.[98] This, together with the fact that Franck was a World War One veteran and that his is one of only a few travel narratives that depict the island during the time the United States was occupying both nations, renders his account especially interesting.

Franck began his trip in 1918 from his home state of Pennsylvania and journeyed southward by rail all the way to southern Florida. His description of the passage from the United States' predominantly white North to the Jim Crow South peopled largely by African Americans read very similarly to his account of the West Indies. He described the landscape, the architecture, and the locals, comparing several Southern cities to South American countries he had visited, such as Peru and Brazil. He conveyed to the reader the sense that southern Florida was but a gateway to the Hispanic West Indies, for Spanish was as likely to be heard there as English, and "the Cuban tinge" of the whites-only railcar became the harbinger of Cuba itself.[99]

Franck entered the West Indies on his arrival in Cuba, which itself was little more than a decade past U.S. occupation. From Cuba, he traveled to Haiti on a former New York Yacht Club schooner turned Haitian Navy ship. Like the country itself, he wrote, the ship was under the command of three officers "as Caucasian as a New England village." Contrasted with this racialized metaphor of idyllic order was "the untamable race that peoples [Haiti's] mountainous shores."[100] The reader's first encounter with Haiti in Franck's account was through the "muffled beating of tom-toms" and "a carefree burst of laughter, that could come only from negro throats" as the schooner entered the bay at Port au Prince.[101] Haitians were referred to as "the children of Ham," "negroes," "Africans," and "slaves and savages." Although Franck noted the "easy-going, yet graceful, carriage" of Haitian market women, he portrayed them as shabbily clad, "dirty beyond description," and "primitive" yet "frankly happy with life."[102]

Franck conveyed the sense that this happiness was due not only to the "childlike" nature of Haitians, but also to the beneficent effect of U.S. occupation, which supplanted the incompetent native ruling class. Franck recounted:

The Americans have acquired one by one, as some yellow politician has lost his grasp on the national treasury, the grove-hidden houses in the upper town, some of them little short of palatial. There they live like the potentates of the tropical isles of romance. The blacks are respectful, childlike in their manner, and have of the docility of the negroes of our South before the Civil War. . . . They are usually stupid beyond words, with the mentality of an intelligent child of six, but they are sometimes capable of great devotion, with a dog-like quality of faithfulness; and between them all they swathe the existence of their masters in the comfort of an old-time Southern plantation.[103]

Franck was referring here to the displacement of "yellow" politicians by the Americans' assumption of power that was formerly in the hands of the elite mulatto classes. Drawing on the stereotype of the "happy darkie" and contented slave who needed the paternal domination of white masters, rather than the inept rule of mulattos, Franck failed to acknowledge the role of white violence and repression in creating the fiction of Haitian docility. If Franck had any critique of the occupation, it was of the excesses of those Southerners who made up the great majority of the occupation forces and who had failed to lift up Haiti's "niggers," which he claimed was "the task we have taken upon ourselves in Haiti." Nonetheless, whatever good might be said of Haiti, he claimed, was "thanks to a few hundred of our marines and certain representatives of our navy."[104]

True to his military background and pro-occupation stance, Franck devoted an entire chapter to the military prowess of the occupation forces. He introduced the reader to the *cacos*, Haitian rebel bands who engaged in successful guerrilla warfare against the Americans for nearly a decade. From Franck's vantage point, the cacos were little more than "semi-savage insurrectionists." He appeared oblivious to the fact that, at the time of his travels in Haiti, the occupation forces' commanders were engaged in hearings before the Senate Commission on Haiti and Santo Domingo charged with investigating the illegal origins and violent excesses of the occupation.[105] He recounted with particular admiration, therefore, the exploits of young Marine Captain Herman H. Hanneken, who successfully plotted to kill Charlemagne Masena Péralte, a successful and elusive caco leader. Franck told Hanneken's story, which became part of Marine lore, complete with a citation from Hanneken's military diary. He offered the reader a sense of reassurance that, although cacoism had been "by no means wiped out" by 1920, "the Marine Corps, may be trusted to bring their troublesome careers to a close all in good season."[106] Of course, Franck left out of his narrative not only the fact that Péralte had been assassinated by Hanneken and his comrade William R. Button, but also that they had stripped his corpse nearly naked, bound it prone to a wooden support draped with a caco flag, photographed their display, and circulated the image to demoralize the caco opposition.[107] These actions neatly encapsulate the synecdochical relationships between the political, physical, and symbolic violence of the occupation and its narratives.

If to Franck Haiti was the land of cacoism, the Dominican Republic was "the Land of Bullet-Holes." Like his predecessors, Franck claimed that "the change from civilization—or should I call them two attempts toward civilization?—was as sudden, as astonishingly abrupt, as the dash through the apparently unfordable stream" that separated the two nations, the Massacre River.[108] Franck faced the difficult narrative task of, on the one hand, conveying the justifiability and efficacy of U.S. occupation of both Haiti and the United States, and, on the other hand, distinguishing between the savage Black Republic and the semi-savage "colored republic." This distinction was important insofar as Franck's narrative of the U.S. occupation of Santo Domingo was framed as part of a larger, Dominican project of Haitian containment. Thus, he wrote:

> The Dominican is not unjustified in wishing to keep his land free from the semi-savage hordes beyond the Massacre. . . . Pure white inhabitants were frequent in the larger pueblos; full-blooded African types extremely rare. Santo Domingo has been called a mulatto country; we found it more nearly a land of quadroons. . . . Santo Domingo could be a success so long as some overwhelming power holds it steady by appointing the better class of officials and keeping an exacting eye constantly upon them.[109]

U.S. occupation, in other words, was a racial project that serviced Dominicans who could not themselves contain the Haitian menace. They required the help of "some overwhelming power" to tutor them, and doing so was part and parcel of "the white man's burden."[110]

Franck framed his narrative on the Dominican Republic as part of his larger travels throughout the world and, in particular, throughout the U.S.-dominated world of Latin America. In Santiago, Franck reconnected with George Long, a Marine lieutenant who had worked with Franck on the Panama Canal Zone police force, which was itself the subject of one of Franck's more famous books, *Zone Policemen 88*. "Big George's" career was built largely as part of U.S. imperialist forces in the Panama Canal Zone, Puerto Rico, and, finally, the Dominican Republic. Franck portrayed him as a likeable, all-American character struggling to bring progress, order, and justice to the Dominican people, much like his counterpart Hanneken in Haiti. Unlike Hanneken, however, who had to strategize militarily to overcome Haitian cacos' fierce resistance to occupation, Big George tamed Dominicans through technology and training. Franck wrote that Dominican men "are intelligent youths, on the whole, compared with their Haitian neighbors, with a quick wit to catch a political argument or the mysteries of a mechanical contrivance, though they have the tendency of all their mixed race to slow down in their mental processes soon after reaching what with us would be early manhood."[111] So while having white ancestry endowed Dominicans with greater cognitive skills, being racially impure also impeded their full development into manhood.

Interestingly, Franck gave short shrift to the activities of the *gavilleros*, the bands of guerrilla rebels who offered sustained resistance to U.S. occupation of Santo Domingo until they were effectively routed and disarmed by the occupation forces. Perhaps it was because to pay attention to the gavilleros would be to belie the myth of Dominicans welcoming U.S. tutelage. Franck called the gavilleros bandits and outlaws who were "fighting for good, rather than for either political or patriotic reasons."[112] Although Franck admitted to detecting "a surly attitude toward Americans, a sullen, passive resentment" and noted that "the attitude of silent protest was everywhere in the air" in gavillero-controlled regions, he claimed that for the most part Dominicans benefited from the occupation.[113]

Likewise, although Franck acknowledged that the Marines acted with impunity in Santo Domingo, routinely torturing and murdering Dominicans for sport, he attributed this to the youthful inexperience, Southern ancestry, and effects of popular-media portrayals of the American gangster on a select few. "The great majority . . . were well meaning young fellows," he said.[114] If Haitian and Dominican political and military practices were racially and culturally determined and collectively shown, American actions were circumstantial and idiosyncratic. There was neither collective source nor responsibility for the actions of American interventionists.

Samuel Guy Inman, an instructor of international relations at Columbia University, secretary to the Committee on Cooperation in Latin America, and a Protestant minister, may have crossed paths with Franck, for both visited and were guests of the Marines in Haiti and the Dominican Republic in 1918. Like Franck, Inman published his account, *Through Santo Domingo and Haiti: A Cruise with the Marines*, in 1920.

Although Inman, unlike Franck, was generally critical of U.S. military interventionism and favored missionaries over soldiers as agents of civilization, he shared Franck's racial juxtaposition of Dominicans to Haitians, typically to the disadvantage of the latter. Inman was explicitly sympathetic to the Marines whom he visited throughout the country. In part, that sympathy was due to a sense that they were charged with a task "unaware of the nature of the business they had been caught in."[115] It appears also to have been due to a racial sensibility shared with the Marines in that he framed Haitians as degraded and "unmoral" who behaved in ways "characteristic of animals."[116]

Between Occupation and Dictatorship

Harry L. Foster published his travel account *Combing the Caribbees* in 1929, offering the public a travelogue of the period between U.S. occupation and dictatorship in the Dominican Republic. At the time of Foster's travels, the U.S. occupation had ended in the Dominican Republic but was still in full force in Haiti, where it would last until 1934. Foster, whose Negrophobic rhetoric was far more explicit than Boyce's, Verrill's, or Franck's, traveled throughout the Caribbean. He casually called West Indians "darkies" and, like Boyce, depicted them alternatively as childlike innocents astride donkeys and violent savages engaged in voodoo rituals. Also like Boyce, he depicted Haiti as overpopulated, exceedingly black, and underdeveloped, if adequately orderly under U.S. military rule.

The post-occupation Dominican Republic, by contrast, was more civilized, whiter, and more developed. The difference was so stark as to be immediately discernible upon crossing the border between the two nations.

> The two little nations which share this island have very little in common.
>
> As one crossed the line, one noted the decrease in the density of the population. This Santo Domingo, although it covered two-thirds of the island, had only one-third as many citizens as the contiguous Black Republic. And although complexions were occasionally rather dark, the majority of those one met were predominantly Castilian. On the Dominican side, one found an "Aduana" instead of a "Duane"; the officer who put me through a polite third degree was unmistakably white; and the language was now Spanish, with no French understood. . . . This was a very prosperous land — a contrast to poor Haiti.[117]

The Hispanicity of the Dominican Republic was emphasized throughout the text. Foster perceived Hispanic legacies in the historic architecture, in the people's faces, and in their social customs and culture.

Even the seclusion of women from the overtly public sphere was noted appreciatively as a sign of higher civilization. Dominican women, unlike their Haitian counterparts who roamed the streets and hills of Haiti freely, were more civilized and beautiful precisely to the degree that they were properly constrained by patriarchy.

> Along toward evening, however, the womenfolk would begin to emerge. Windows, shuttered against the tropic sun, opened now to disclose the *señoritas* refreshed from the siesta, and powdered for the evening promenade. . . . In some cases, they were a trifle dark and their hair curled betrayingly, but they scorned the turbans so typical of Haiti. Instead they wore Parisian chapeaux, or more frequently went bareheaded, carrying dainty parasols.[118]

As with other Dominicans observed by travel writers, the hair "betrayed" Dominican women's black ancestry, but their Eurocentric tastes and scorn for Haitian styles distanced them from blackness. Foster summed up the historic, racial, social, and political-economic differences between the Dominican Republic and Haiti this way: "In Haiti one found today a modern capital, with wide rectangularly-arranged streets, but a people completely unchanged since the days of Dessalines. In Santo Domingo one found an old, old city, yet one with a very up-to-the-minute population, addicted to pep and progress."[119] In this interesting set of contrasts, Foster established that Santo Domingo's antiquity linked it to the (white) European metropolis and that its people shared Anglo sensibilities of "pep and progress."

In *Trailing the Conquistadors*, which was originally published in 1930 and later translated and published by the Dominican Society of Bibliophiles, Samuel Guy Inman likewise expressed both his political sympathies for Haiti's violated sovereignty and his at times subtle presumptions of black inferiority through his negative references to Haitians' behavior, sexual practices, relationship to organized religion, and casual nudity. He also cast Haitians as one of the major "influences retarding the Dominican Republic," as when he wrote: "In the early nineteenth century the invasion of Negro despots from Haiti, with the consequent fleeing of the best of the white elements, once again set the country back."[120] This account related his experiences during his second visit to the country in

1929, five years after the U.S. occupation ended. Though he was critical of the intervention as such, he offered example after example of positive outcomes wrought by the Americans in Santo Domingo, from new and improved roads to free public hospitals, from the increasing number of women in the formal labor force to the expansion of literacy and culture, and from the rationalization of the state's finances and administration to the normalization of politics. As he put it, the occupation meant "much for comfort, for education, for commerce, for progress."[121] If there was one drawback to the occupation's legacy, it was that the expansion of foreign (that is, U.S.) capital included the importation of "cheap labor from Haiti, the Negroes bringing with them their strange dialects, their voodoo drums, their magic."[122] This was an assessment shared by Dominican nationalists, who would begin to steadily work toward the removal of the Haitians they viewed as the legacy of U.S. occupation and a long history of Haitian invasions alike.

"As Mimicry Became Mastery": Trujilloist Propaganda and the Institutionalization of Anti-Haitianist Nationalism

During their occupation and military dictatorship of 1916–24, the U.S. Marines had trained the country's infamous dictator, Rafael Leonidas Trujillo. He came away from the experience with a clear understanding of U.S. racial ideology. According to Eric Roorda,

> Trujillo's efforts to create and publicly depict a new Dominican nation are inseparable from his re-interpretation of all references to the colonial past.... In the cultural forms through which foreign relations between the United States and the Dominican Republic were acted out, what began as mimicry became mastery in the process of consolidation of Trujillo's dictatorship and the Dominican state.[123]

Dressed nearly at all times in imposing military uniforms, rife with self-bestowed medals, his shoulders broadened with epaulets, his boots fitted with lifts, and his face lightened with whitening makeup, Trujillo thus offered an embodied display of the new Dominican citizen: virile, powerful, and white.

Frequently violating the proviso of the U.S. Foreign Agents Registrations Act requiring that foreign propaganda be labeled as such, Trujillo planted unattributed stories in the U.S. media written by public-relations professionals that cast his regime in favorable terms. "In addition, the Dominican Republic became a major foreign-government employer of lawyers, lobbyists, and public relations experts, hired to influence the Dominican sugar quota and promote a favorable image of the Trujillo regime."[124] Travel narratives, both officially independent and state-sponsored, played an important role in that project.

In 1932, Arthur J. Burks published *Land of Checkerboard Families*, a memoir of his time in the Dominican Republic as a lieutenant in the occupying Marine force. The memoir bridged the period during which travel accounts of the Dominican Republic began to be replaced by the public-relations propaganda of the Trujillo regime.[125] Burks's account was also interesting in that he was a narrator of lower-middle-class origin directly attached to the U.S. military, unlike his travel-account predecessors who were all observers of the Marines' occupation. Burks's liberal use of the epithet "nigger" in reference to Dominicans indicated the racist dynamics that conditioned everyday interactions between Marines and Dominicans during the occupation.

Burks served in the Marines from 1917 to 1927 in both Haiti and the Dominican Republic, as well as in Brazil, Cuba, Bermuda, Canada, Hawaii, the Philippines, China, Manchuria, and Japan. Immediately upon leaving the Marines, he became a best-selling pulp-fiction author of exotic tales. By 1933, he had founded and acted as the national president of the American Fiction Guild.[126] All together, he published more than 30 million words, including forty-two books and over 1,200 stories, both under his name and under several pseudonyms, earning him the monikers "Dean of American Fiction" and "speed merchant of the pulps."[127]

According to Mary Renda's cultural history analysis of the U.S. occupation of Haiti, Burks's accounts of Haiti formed part of a larger set of paternalist discourses that acted as "one of the primary cultural mechanisms by which the occupation conscripted men into the project of carrying out U.S. rule."[128] Embedded within those paternalist discourses were ideologies of race, class, gender, sexuality, and nation. "The terms with which Burkes and his American heroes described Haitians uniformly conveyed the most pointed hatred and derision, straight from the lexicon of homegrown racism; they were 'dull and stupid' beings, 'beasts of prey,' vengeful 'master-rogues,' great black brutes, aged idiots, and loathsome women."[129] While Burks's account of the Dominican Republic is also denigrating, he nonetheless depicts Dominicans as racially superior to Haitians because of their racially mixed heritages. Perhaps it is not surprising, then, that Burks's account was translated into Spanish by Gustavo Amigó, edited by Diógenes Céspedes, and published in 1990 by the Dominican Society of Bibliophiles.[130]

Burks opened his narrative with the claim that it was the very complexity of race in the Dominican context that led him to write about the place. And while he stated emphatically early on that "there is no Dominican 'type,'" Burks nonetheless endeavored to provide the reader with an "ethnographic" sense of Dominican's racial status.[131] Thus, in his description of Dominicans, Burks engaged earlier descriptions offered by travel narratives, such as his travel-writing predecessor in the Marines Harry Franck, but ultimately drew on his contemporary racial frame of reference:

> Someone has called the Dominican Republic the land of quadroons, which comes as close as any description, perhaps. There can be found blacks, browns, yellows, whites and piebalds. Porto Ricans occasionally, Haitians in plenty, English speaking blacks from Saint Croix and Saint Kitts, and Dominicans. The Dominican, if there may be said to be a true Dominican, looks like a motion picture "type" of Mexican, and even that scarcely describes him. Checkerboard families are not especially rare. A black boy may have a white, brown or yellowish sister and vice versa. Or there may be four children in the same family, presumably the same father and mother, of four different colors.
>
> The basic mixture, however, consists of Spanish and Negro, with a dash of Carib aborigine. The language is Spanish, the religion Creole.[132]

Echoing Franck's depiction of the Dominican Republic as "the land of quadroons," Burks perceived most Dominicans as racially mixed to varying degrees, although not entirely removed from whiteness, as the references to "white" siblings and the Spanish origins and language of the people indicate.

Nonetheless, chapter after chapter is devoted to describing the rampant misery, dirtiness, and leprosy of "the natives," whom Burks was not above calling "chattering apes." The overwhelming image was one of horrible ugliness and decay. Dominican beauty in Burks's account was limited to the lush, natural surroundings and to young women. A recurring theme in Burks's narrative was the desire of "the native" women for his seed. Indeed, his first encounter with a Dominican woman was framed by her explicit desire to have him sire a "white baby" for her. At several other points in his story, Dominican women openly offered themselves to him, usually aggressively. Toward the end of his account, he assisted a Dominican woman in labor and was made her infant son's namesake. The anecdote emphasized his husband-like relationship to her: "At that moment she became as precious to me as though she had been my own wife or sister." He described the fruit of their interaction, his surrogate son, as having all the bearings of a military man, even just a few hours after birth. Like any proud father, he noted that the child was a "husky little blighter" who was "eight years old this spring."[133]

Like narrators before him, and in keeping with his own earlier narratives of Haiti, Burks depicted Haitians as dirty, disorderly, and dumb. He wrote: "The Haitian is capable of going from cradle to the grave unbathed. . . . The Haitians looked as much alike as so many peas in a pod. . . . [T]here isn't anything so dumb!"[134] They were also, of course, "voodoo practitioners." Burks related "one more touch of horror—which is set down here to show something of the difference between Haitians and Dominicans." The horror was Haitian cannibalism. Lest the reader not be convinced that cannibalism existed in Haiti, Burks's account verified that Haitian cannibalism was quite rampant and not contained by Haitian borders. Dominicans, however, punished it harshly, an indication of their elevated degree of civilization and near-whiteness.

Burks devoted an entire chapter, entitled "Tom Tom," to his capture by Haitian caco rebels who planned to torture and kill him. Alluding to popular depictions of cannibals preparing their human catch, he wrote of being encircled by his captors, who beat drums and planned his demise:

> The negroes surrounded us and sat down in the form of a nice black circle. . . . A few rods away a Haitian stood beside the gasoline drum and hammered out the Haitian jungle song—the rhythmic beating of a tom-tom. . . . The tom-tom can easily drive a white man mad. They also drive the blacks mad, for they can work themselves into a frenzy to the tune of the tom-toms.
>
> Another black man built a bonfire near the gasoline drum, so that when darkness fell the whole scene became one from darkest Africa. . . . But this was Santo Domingo, the land of quadroons! That didn't help, though, for the only brown-skinned people present were Garcia and Nicolai. . . . The rest were negroes . . . and negroes had skinned the men I recalled.[135]

In this scene, rather than viewing his capture as the outcome of a military contest between himself as Marine invader and the Haitian forces resisting that invasion, Burks scripts it as emblematic of black nature. Interestingly, although Burks contrasted the "brown-skinned" Dominican from the Haitian "negroes," he also noted elsewhere in the text that there were Dominicans among his captors. But they, evidently, were black Dominicans, for "the only brown-skinned people present were García and Nicolai," his guides. In the tradition of courageous white men throughout the imperial world, Burks managed to escape with the help of his faithful "brown" sidekick, García. After all, according to him, most Dominicans were "utterly different" from Haitians in race, language, and economic condition. The only similarity Burks discerned between Dominicans and Haitians was that both were eloquent, if gesticulating, "born gossips."

In sum, for Burks, Dominicans were "far less primitive" than Haitians; the evidence for this was their lighter skin color. "The people were usually old bronze of color, free of disease, and easy laughers, happy children. . . . The Haitian invasion had trod but lightly here and the 'tar brush' had stroked softly."[136] That is, Dominicans were more like noble savages than like savage Haitians. If they were not yet civilized, the Marine occupation certainly inched them along. Dominicans, then, whom European and U.S. observers would have considered black were it not for growing antipathy toward Haiti and, later, toward Haitians, were affirmed in their Indo-Hispanicity even by their Yankee invaders. Perhaps Burks, in keeping with the times, was simply being a "good neighbor."

Hendrik de Leeuw's *Crossroads of the Caribbean Sea* was certainly written in that spirit.[137] The book was published by an imprint of Doubleday in 1938, but it had been copyrighted in 1935 by Julian Messner, a left-liberal publishing house that promoted racial tolerance in the Americas through its publications. Perhaps that partially accounts for the fact that de Leeuw's is the only travel narrative of the era to present a positive picture of Haiti and Haitians. Renda has pointed out that by the 1930s, U.S. media had begun to portray Haiti as an exotically alluring yet tranquil vacation spot for American travelers, thanks, of course, to the success of the U.S. occupation's program of pacification.[138] I surmise that the text was also self-consciously buttressing the era's Good Neighbor policy of non-interventionism and installation of dictatorial regimes. As Melville Herskovits put it, de Leeuw presented "a picture that should be bright and full of good-will" toward Haiti,[139] which at the time of his visit had transitioned from U.S. occupation to the U.S.-installed dictatorship of Stenio Vincent.

In stark contrast to every other narrator, de Leeuw eschewed the seemingly reflexive tendency to link Haiti to Africa and instead likened Port au Prince to the French Riviera. Likewise, he emphasized the cleanliness and order of the place and its people:

> Perhaps the most novel impression of all is that of an invariable cleanliness. In fact, no where at these bayshore markets did I find any of the squalid filth that one may often see in the crowded districts of northern towns. It seemed that cleanliness was a habit here and a dirty Haitian could not be found anywhere around. He was simply an exception. Even the men on the wharves were clean, even those in rags, and there were many, to be sure, but they had been patched and mended, and gave evidence of much native washing. A most delightful trait.[140]

Rather than being lazy and legion, Haitians were "industrious and ever toiling," "graceful," and "beautifully poised." As for the reputed blood-thirstiness of voodoo-crazed Haitians, de Leeuw insisted that these were "old, cruelly exaggerated, horrific tales, brainstorms of fictitious prattle"[141] which should no longer concern white men. This new Haiti, de Leeuw informed his readers, was attributable to both the benefits of the prior occupation and "the successful administration of Steno Vincent," who ushered in "a period of quiet and order."[142] Indeed, he portrayed Vincent as an erudite and cosmopolitan man who was an "ardent admirer of President Roosevelt." Of course, this admiration might well have been due to the fact that Vincent had been put in power by the Marines before they left Haiti.

The Dominican Republic and Trujillo were likewise presented as good neighbors to the United States, and de Leeuw adopted the language of the regime in his casual reference to Trujillo as "the country's benefactor."[143] If de Leeuw's representation of Haiti's population was radically different from those of the past, he was much more conventional in his depiction of Dominicans:

> The inhabitants of the Dominican Republic have a mixed ancestry. The earliest European settlers, as we know, were Spaniards. Their descendants were deeply influenced by the invasions of the English and the French and later by the Negro occupation under Toussaint L'Ouverture. Today the Creole or mestizo prevails to quite a degree. Yet notwithstanding the modification of the earlier Spanish type, the customs, language and traditions of their proud Castilian ancestors have been loyally preserved.[144]

Of mixed racial heritage, Dominicans were nonetheless predominantly culturally Hispanic. Moreover, the country moved steadily toward modernity and progress under the beneficent tutelage of Trujillo, whose projects and personal virtues de Leeuw extolled in astonishingly syco- phantic language. Indeed, the book closed (and it would appear that the journey ended) with this glowing assessment:

> So I believe that I am not exaggerating when I say that the Dominican Re- public today, under President Trujillo's beneficial reign, is vibrant with progress and with new life, while its Government is as stable as any on earth. The President has exerted his utmost endeavor to establish firmly and securely a national-credit standing and he has devoted himself whole- heartedly to the promotion of his people's prosperity. Under the impetus of his administration the Republic marches toward a brilliant future.[145]

One can easily imagine the regime's propagandists reading this pane- gyric and appreciating fully its usefulness as an endorsement of the dic- tator's power. Perhaps it inspired imitation.

Stanley Walker's account of Dominican history, *Journey toward the Sun- light,* may be just such an example. Published by the Caribbean Library in 1947, *Journey toward the Sunlight* was written under the auspices of the National News-Feature Syndicate, Inc., the publicists for the Dominican Information Center. It is not surprising, therefore, that the entire text is a panegyric to Trujillo and his view of his nation. Nor is it surprising that a recurrent theme throughout the text is Trujillo's anticommunism and evocation of the Good Neighbor policy. In his epilogue, "Notes of a Well Meaning Visitor," Walker indicated his connection to the Trujillo propa- ganda machine by making a passing reference to Morris Ernst. Ernst, whom Walker described simply as "the New York lawyer," was in fact under retainer with the Dominican government and less than a decade later was called on to vindicate Trujillo in the Galíndez affair.[146] While Walker weakly assured his readers that his text was "by no means a po- litical treatise," *Journey* was a propagandistic tract that was all the more insidious for being written in the format and tone of travel writing.

Like his precursors, Walker affirmed the inherent Indo-Hispanic ethno-racial identity of Dominicans. He wrote:

> One must understand that the Spanish influence, which came to this strange and tragic land with Columbus, is still predominant. It is predomi- nant to a degree beyond that which obtains in most, perhaps all, of the Latin-American countries. . . . Spain, in the biological sense, is regarded as the great Mother whose indomitable qualities manifest themselves in the blood stream of generation after generation.

To some observers all this may seem odd, particularly when they reflect that, according to the best statistics available, only about 13 per cent of the Dominican population may be termed pure "white." Nineteen per cent is classified as Negro, and the remainder, the great overwhelming majority is a mixture containing varying percentages of black blood. Such individuals vary considerably in appearance—mulattos who are very dark and whose features would cause them to be classified in the United States without hesitation as Negro; people the color of coffee or chocolate, with more or less aquiline features, in whose veins flows some Negro blood; and a great many others, of different hues and cast of countenance, who defy casual classification. Some are called "Creoles," which is an historically and ethnologically inexact term. Others have been described as "mestizo," which has more justification. An occasional glint of reddish hair, or a luminous golden complexion, may indicate a strong trace of Celtic blood. The "Indian" influence, both in blood and culture, is so nearly non-existent as to be negligible—which is one of the great differences between Dominicans and, let us say, the people of Mexico. . . . They are first of all Dominicans, and even those with a strong admixture of Negro blood have a pride in their Spanish language, the Spanish culture of the country, which is similar to that of any caballero who can trace his descent all the way back to the Conquistadors.[147]

Walker managed to both recognize and diminish the African ancestry and black appearance of Dominicans by emphasizing the predominance of a Spanish cultural heritage that was so strong that it was carried in the blood "generation after generation." Regardless of their appearance, Dominicans identified not with their black ancestors, but with their Spanish Conquistador grandfathers. Indeed, he wrote, Dominicans' Hispanicity was "predominant to a degree beyond" the rest of Spanish America. As Walker's tone indicated, this affinity was not only understandable, but justified.

Walker's description of the Haitian Revolution and of its leaders, by contrast, was rife with racist caricatures. He detailed the savagery of the black insurrectionists in the typical manner. "Vast waves of black men overran the whole western end of the island. It was their custom to kill the white men first. Then came the women and children, who were tortured and at length put to death in all manner of strange and revolting forms."[148] Employing what Toni Morrison has called "the economy of stereotype," which "allows the writer a quick and easy image without the responsibility of specificity, accuracy, or even narratively useful description," Walker drew on existing racist characterization of African American men as alternatively idiotic buffoons, dandies, and savage rapists. Toussaint Louverture was described as "a Negro with an ape-like jaw" and was lampooned as a dandy, an image familiar to North Americans of the 1940s. Walker mocked Louverture's military attire ("powdered and bewigged") and symbolic presumptuousness ("He rode a fine horse"). At the same time, the dandified Louverture was also a potential rapist: "This playful barbarian seemed to find considerable pleasure in poking at the more comely white Spanish women with his cane, laughing as he did so."[149]

Similarly, Dessalines, Toussaint's successor, was cast not as the successful leader of a victorious army of revolutionaries, but as a barbarian: "He loved to kill whites; he took a great satisfaction in dispatching members of his own race; when human victims were not readily at hand, he would torture animals. He tried to surpass even Toussaint L'Ouverture in fancy dress. He was a baboon who sought to be a French fop."[150] The historical and political context in which Dessalines's military policy and governance occurred was completely disregarded and discounted in favor of stereotypes that ridiculed his attempts at masculine authority. He was "a baboon," not a man, and worse still, the man he attempted to emulate was an effeminate "French fop."

Likewise, Walker termed the Haitian Unification period under Boyer "the era of the Great Darkness" characterized by "Haitian savagery," which he claimed was exemplified by the disempowerment of the Catholic church, the closure of the university, the draft into the Haitian Army, the concerted blackening of the nation, and the "rotting away" of Dominican manhood. Salvation arrived, Walker informed readers, in the person of Juan Pablo Duarte, whom, in sharp contrast to Boyer, he described as "a young man, a fine-looking fellow with broad forehead and deep-set eyes." As with the earlier travel narratives, these propaganda pieces established Dominican ethno-racial superiority over Haitians. As their literary predecessors had, they did so by narrating blackness out of the Dominican Republic's history. Rather than depicting masses of native blacks—who would be too akin to the Haitians—iconographic indigenous Hispanic heroes were institutionalized, commodified, and circulated as representatives of Dominican identity.

This culminated in the 1954 English translation and U.S. publication of Galván's *Enriquillo* as *The Cross and the Sword*, translated by Robert Graves and "published in accordance with an agreement between UNESCO (United Nations Education, Scientific and Cultural Organization) and the government of the Dominican Republic, with the cooperation of the Organization of American States." It was the first text published in a series of Latin American classics deemed representative of the "cultural history of mankind."[151] That the Dominican Republic had played an active role in the founding of UNESCO and in this initiative to publish Latin America's great works may have played as great a role in the selection of *Enriquillo* as its literary and historic value.

Enriquillo's devout Catholicism segued nicely with the nation's official Catholicism as personified by Trujillo's anticommunist rhetoric. That Trujillo enthusiastically supported *The Cross and the Sword* project, therefore, should come as no surprise. In many ways, Galván's fictional Enriquillo represented official Dominican identity discourses more subtly and more effectively than Trujillo's vast public-relations campaign. *Enriquillo*, by textually reclassifying Dominicans as Indo-Hispanics, extended the country's foundational fiction beyond its borders and sent it traveling into the broader American reading public.

Triangulating Texts

I am not arguing that these many travel narratives were extensively influential in any given way. Rather, I am arguing that they offer insights into how competing and shifting understandings of whether or not Dominicans were black were developed simultaneously and dynamically in contrastive relation to Haiti and the United States. Those understandings were not simply imperial impositions; they were also reflective of Dominican identity formations. Indeed, one of the country's most erudite scholarly bodies, the Dominican Society of Bibliophiles, has published nearly a dozen of these narratives in translation, including the works of Moureau de Saint-Méry, Fabens, Porter, Keim, Hazard, Ober, Inman, and Burks. Given that the society was founded in 1974 to "promote books and reading through the publication and distribution of single edition works related to Dominican culture originally published abroad and previously untranslated," its translations mark these texts as valuable contributions to the national bibliography.[152]

Anti-Haitian ideologies and discourses have been of central importance in the development of Dominican ethno-racial identity on the island. I view anti-Haitian narratives as "situated and ideological texts" that began as "imperial texts of information" but were utilized subsequently by Dominican intellectual and political elites in their own fashioning of national identity discourses.[153] Many of these texts—which were subsequently used by the Museo del Hombre Dominicano—were written by what Mary Campbell Blaine has aptly called "gentlemen imperialists," travelers who were wedded to the United States' expansionist and imperialist enterprises of the nineteenth century.[154] They also formed part of a larger "capitalist vanguard" whose narrations of Spanish America projected the United States "into the futures of those they sought to exploit, as a kind of moral and historical inevitability."[155] The travel narratives help to illustrate the dynamic interaction between representation of the Dominican Republic and its people to others and the self-representation or identity displays of Dominicans themselves to themselves.

Building on the imperial projections of travel writing of the nineteenth century and early twentieth century, World's Fairs and museums served as principal media in disseminating information about colonized peoples to the colonial center. "Carefully designed exhibits left little doubt that the same set of ideas that had been used to justify the political and economic repression of Native Americans, Afro-Americans, and Asian-Americans were being used to validate American imperial policy overseas."[156] Unlike travel writing and World's Fairs, however, museums proved permanent, widely accessible, and thus more influential nationally than their precursors, as we shall see in the next chapter.

CHAPTER 2.

"The Africans Have No [Public] History"

THE MUSEO DEL HOMBRE DOMINICANO

AND INDIGENOUS DISPLAYS

OF DOMINICAN IDENTITY

> The mission of the Museo is to contribute to the creation of a clear consciousness of the national identity.
> —Dato Pagán Perdomo[1]

> We can expect the negrophobia and Eurocentric notions of Dominicanness to live on for as long as those who are in power remain there, controlling the official tools of cultural definition and the institutions that shape public perceptions.
> —Silvio Torres-Saillant[2]

In this chapter, I argue that the travel narratives discussed in chapter 1 came to be utilized both as primary texts and as ideological discourses that supported the Dominican intelligentsia's meta-narrative of *Dominicanidad* as fundamentally and historically non-black and Indo-Hispanic. I argue also that that meta-narrative has been embedded in the national identity historiography and the displays of leading cultural institutions such as the Museo del Hombre Dominicano. The core of this chapter, therefore, is a close examination of how and why the Museo's permanent exhibit contributes to an indigenist national imaginary at the expense of a more historically complete account of the nation's heritage.

I offer an analysis of how the Museo del Hombre Dominicano narrates Dominicanidad as if it were part of a natural order of things rather than a contestable narration, one that is politically generated and ideologically coded. In undertaking this analysis, I have found Dorothy Smith's work on the conceptual practices of power helpful, particularly her theorization of relations of ruling as "the complex of objectified social relations that organize and regulate our lives in contemporary society."[3] By objectified social relations, Smith means the material conditions under which human lives are ordered and enacted. At the same time, however, these social relations are conceptualized and experienced through discourses. We make and are made by the "actual" world in everyday and every night activities, but these activities are undertaken and organized through "concepts, beliefs, ideas, knowledge, and so on."[4]

In addition, continuing with Smith, ruling relations are expressed through "'ideological codes' that order and organize texts across discursive sites."[5] Because of these ideological codes, we take for granted rather than investigate the conceptual presuppositions of structured social relations, such as "family." These conceptual presuppositions are intrinsically a part of the make-up, or "coding," of the social relations in question. Thus, by "code" Smith does not mean a symbolic system but something more like an organizing structure, as in genetic code. The ideological code ordering and organizing Dominicanidad as text in the Museo del Hombre Dominicano is its conceptual presupposition of "*el Dominicano* [the Dominican]" as a racially typifiable and racially progressive man. Ideologically, the typicality of Dominicanidad elides or naturalizes the normative conceptual schema on which that typicality relies: pigmentocracy, Negrophobia, indigenism, Hispanophilia, and androcentricism. That conceptual schema is organized through the Museo's exhibitionary technologies, which encourage visitors to internalize that normative conceptual schema.

As the museum historian Tony Bennett has noted, museums generally have organized exhibit space so that the physical interaction with and movement through the space itself organizes visitors' perceptions and trains visitors to accept viewing conduct (how to dress, walk, look at, talk about the exhibit). Thus, "mind–body dualities" are overcome simultaneously with the assimilation of the museum's message. Bringing Smith and Bennett together, one could say that the Museo del Hombre Dominicano fosters the internalization of its ideological code through "behavior-management" technology, one that I will argue in subsequent chapters becomes manifest in individual embodiments and displays of

Dominican identity.[6] As Bennett puts it, "The museum provide[s] its visitors with a set of resources through which they might actively insert themselves within a particular vision of history by fashioning themselves to contribute to its development."[7]

Moreover, through its exhibitionary technologies—its architecture, display strategies, and "narrative machinery"—the Museo del Hombre Dominicano not only links past to present in a seamlessly progressive continuum from pre-Columbian to Dominican, but also promotes a "simultaneously bodily and mental" subjectivity that conceptualizes Dominican identity as naturally indigenous and historically Hispanic. Thus, the Museo del Hombre Dominicano acts as a particular discursive site within a larger web of ruling relations. Perhaps it is not surprising, then, that when asked what she had learned about Africans in Dominican history, one of my New York respondents laughingly declared that "the Africans have no history." And indeed, she is correct. In the Dominican Republic, Africans are conceptually disappeared through "text-mediated modes" of action such as the Museo del Hombre Dominicano's display.

I begin the chapter with an overview of the historical precursors to the Museo, followed by an examination of the political and ideological context of the Museo's birth. I argue that the Museo del Hombre Dominicano formed part of a decades-long series of attempts to recognize and protect the national patrimony from U.S. imperial agendas beginning at the end of the nineteenth century. U.S. archeologists and ethnologists were always present when the U.S. government intervened in the Dominican Republic, beginning with the Customs Receivership, which began in 1905, and through the occupation of 1916–24. At the same time, U.S. intervention not only threatened national sovereignty in relation to Dominican–U.S. relations; it also brought with it increased Haitian presence in the country and tapped into longstanding anti-Haitianist politics and ideologies. A key aspect of interventionist policies was the expansion and foreign capitalization of Dominican sugar economies, which relied increasingly on the importation of labor from Haiti and the Windward Islands. To Dominican nationalists, particularly those of the landed oligarchy who found their interests undermined by this turn of events in the national economy, the marked increase in the Dominican Republic's Haitian population was tantamount to a "silent invasion."[8]

Attempts to protect the national patrimony were principally legislative and often held little more than symbolic importance before the 1916 occupation, as the various Dominican presidential administrations did little to enforce this legislation. During the occupation, the country was subjected to U.S. military governance that not only disregarded Dominican legislation in this area, but provided support for U.S. naturalists,' archeologists,' ethnologists,' and travel writers' plundering of indigenous artifacts. The U.S. occupation government helped its countrymen researchers in their excavation and extraction endeavors, from informing them of important archeological sites to accompanying and providing security for them and transporting artifacts within and outside of the country.

These white men were the product of an era in which Native American nations in the United States were being systematically disappeared through legislative, political, and military action into either reservations or death, both symbolic and real. Framed in the United States as a dying and vanquished race through various exhibitionary techniques—the exhibition of living beings as "the last of their race"; via visual media such as photography, caricature, paintings, and the plastic arts; or through their material cultural objects and artifacts—contemporary Native Americans in the United States were routinely displayed at World's Fairs and museums as part of the vanquished past.[9] Native Americans were scripted by founders of the national literature such as James Fenimore Cooper as belonging to the United States' prehistory and as remnants of a past from which the new nation had risen and evolved.[10] They were represented in popular culture as the natural and the primitive antithesis to the rational and modern citizens of the United States. As the anthropologist John Borneman put it, "The formidable cognitive and emotional task for white Americans was to (re)create oneself as and to occupy the category 'American,' though fully 'foreign' oneself, through the expropriation of native lands and the liquidation of those natives."[11] Thus, as Philip Deloria has pointed out, by "playing Indian"—through literary and physical masquerade—Anglo Americans authenticated their claims to power over the lands and resources they had violently appropriated first from native peoples, and then from the British.[12]

Shepard Krech and Barbara Hail argue further that if playing Indian was central to American nationalism in the nineteenth century, "collecting native America" was an expression of American imperialism, one in which museums played an important role from the 1870s to the 1950s.[13] Thus, major ethnological museums such as the Smithsonian Institution and the Museum of the American Indian–Heye Foundation built their Native American collections with artifacts from throughout the Americas, which came to be seen as legitimately within the purview of the United States. Whether publicly or privately funded and operated, these institutions routinely relied on and contracted the collecting services of both amateur and professional ethnologists, anthropologists, archeologists, naturalists, and, yes, private travelers whose writings would memorialize their collecting adventures, such as A. Hyatt Verrill, whose account of the Dominican Republic was discussed in chapter 1.[14] Indeed, private collectors and museum founders such as George Gustav Heye often funded the educational and professional development of these collecting agents, who in turn secured artifacts for his collection and published their findings in his museum's research notes.[15] Likewise, those in the employ of or who were recipients of research grants from the Smithsonian Institution's Bureau of Ethnology, Natural History Museum, or Anthropology Department secured artifacts along with new knowledge for the institution.

In both cases, these collectors exploited the political and military activities of the U.S. government, which created access to sites that were previously inaccessible, both on the North American continent and beyond. There was, as C. Richard King succinctly puts it, an inextricable link between "empire and exhibition" so that "the collection and exhibition of Native American artifacts depended on and energized American empire, transforming disparate objects from diverse contexts into monuments" celebrating expansionism.[16] This was the context in which the Dominican government's attempts to define, protect, and, later, display the national patrimony developed.

In addition, the Dominican state was a weak one throughout the nineteenth century and into the first decades of the twentieth century. Thus, until the consolidation of the state under the Trujillo dictatorship, the best defenders of the Dominican national patrimony—at least, in terms of keeping native artifacts in the country—were personal collectors, principally men who belonged to the country's small intelligentsia and social elite. The first government-sponsored archeological dig was undertaken by Louis Alphonse Pinart in 1881 in the caves of the Samaná Bay. In his subsequent report to the Ministry of Justice, Public Works, and Public Education, Pinart also documented that the country's leading nineteenth-century historian, José Gabriel García, the nationalist General Francisco G. Billini, and the oligarch Luis Cambiaso each had sizable artifact collections. Likewise, Jesse Walter Fewkes's pioneering 1902–4 study of Caribbean archaeology documented the private collections of the former president and renowned nationalists Archbishop Fernando Arturo de Meriño, A. Llenas, and Ramon Imbert.[17] Finally, the unparalleled personal collection of indigenous artifacts of Narciso Alberti Bosch, a La Vega pharmacist and lay ethnologist, formed the basis of the founding collection of the Dominican Republic's first National Museum.

The founding director of the National Museum, Abigaíl Mejía, had noted as early as 1926 that "only the State is capable, if not the wealthiest then certainly not the poorest entity, the most powerful entity with the executive capabilities to mandate and establish a [National Museum]."[18] By March 1930 that Trujillo, who had been elected to office just the month before, funded and opened the museum, laying claim to being the first regime in the republic to do so.[19] This was the first in a series of state efforts to display the country's Indo-Hispanic identity to the world at large. The rise of the Good Neighbor era and the concomitant withdrawal of the United States from the internal affairs of the Dominican Republic after having set the stage for the Trujillo regime allowed for a proliferation of legislation protecting, restoring, and preserving the national patrimony.

Inspired by his 1939 trip to the impressive New York City World's Fair, Trujillo set out to create a positive image for his regime in the eyes of the international community through his own public-history projects. He regularly displayed Columbus's remains at the National Cathedral to visiting dignitaries and military men.[20] He also reactivated dormant plans to build a Columbian Lighthouse to commemorate the Columbian expeditions. With the support of the Pan American Union, through which the project had been initiated at the 1923 Pan-American Conference in Chile, two international lighthouse-design contests were held in 1929 and 1931.[21] The winner of the second contest, J. L. Gleave of Nottingham, England, had a model of his design displayed at the Dominican Pavilion of the 1939 New York World's Fair.[22]

But perhaps the grandest of Trujillo's international public-relations schemes was the Feria de la Paz y la Confraternidad del Mundo Libre (Fair of Peace and Brotherhood in the Free World).[23] The fair was mounted to improve Trujillo's international image, which had been particularly damaged after the kidnap and murder of the Basque exile Jesús Galíndez in 1954, and commemorated the twenty-fifth anniversary of the "Era of Trujillo." With seventy-one permanent buildings and a $25 million budget, the fair was a spectacular extravaganza that displayed the progress the country had made under the dictator's rule.[24] Among other publicity strategies deployed for the fair, Trujillo contracted Xavier Cugat's slick New York City Latin band to record an album of merengues arranged for cosmopolitan tastes and distributed throughout the United States and

Latin America. The spoken introduction to the song "¡Ay, que merengue!" from the album exhorts:

¡De todos los continentes,	From all of the continents, let's go to the
a la Feria en Santo Domingo!	Fair in Santo Domingo!
¡Bravo!	Bravo!
¡Allá los esperamos a todos!	We are waiting for you there![25]

Unfortunately, the fair generated neither international attendance and the revenue nor the public-relations payoffs Trujillo had hoped for. Despite a huge international propaganda machine, the fair failed to overshadow the excesses of the Trujillo regime at home and abroad.

Following the fall of the Trujillo regime with his assassination in May 1961, the 1960s were a time of enormous upheaval and struggle over national representation, both political and cultural. Many of those struggles were contests over: (1) who was entitled to represent the nation; (2) how the nation was being represented; and (3) what was represented. At the center of these contests was Joaquín Balaguer, whose rise to power would portend the institutionalization of his conservative visions of Dominicanidad through repressive techniques of power. Among the challengers he faced were progressives who styled themselves as a "New Wave" of committed political and cultural activists pressing for full political participation and representation across class, race, and gender lines. Despite their ongoing efforts, they have had limited success in decentering indigenism and hispanophila.

Representational Struggles: Whose Story Is Told?

In 1989, the Permanent Dominican Commission for the Celebration of the Fifth Centennial of the Discovery and Evangelization of America organized *Primacías de América en La Española (1492–1542)*, a poster exhibition that presented twenty-nine social, political, economic, demographic, architectural, and cartographic "firsts" achieved during the first fifty years of the Spanish colonial project in the Americas. The exhibition traveled from the Dominican Republic to the United States, and several hundred exhibition catalogues were ultimately distributed throughout the world, though primarily in the United States.[26]

In the presentation statement of the exhibition's inauguration, Archbishop Nicolás de Jesús López Rodríguez noted that the commission "want[ed] all Dominicans to be more aware of this historical truth, especially the younger generation, often so distanced from their past and therefore ignorant of the roots of their own culture."[27] The exhibition celebrated the fact that the island was the first home of the key Spanish colonial-era events: the development of governing apparatuses, maps, settlements; conversion to and institutionalization of Catholicism among indigenes; effective resource extraction and land tillage; money and market development; and slave rebellion. Interestingly, although slave rebellion is claimed, the fact that Hispaniola was also the first place to import enslaved Africans, thus becoming what Torres-Saillant has called the "cradle of blackness in the Americas," is unclaimed among the exhibition's celebration of "firsts."[28]

It is not coincidental that the state's desire to spread the "truth" of Dominican Hispanicity, particularly among the young, should bear fruit during Balaguer's Hispanophile regime's second period (1986–94), co-incident to the international debates around the Quincentennial. Balaguer himself insisted that the poster exhibition was part of a worldwide celebration of the island's "outstanding role as the catalyst that integrated the American Continent into European Civilization and the Christian Faith."[29] Indeed, in its entirety, the project was one of Hispanophile erasure of the violently genocidal aspects of Spanish colonialism on Hispaniola, as well as a diversion from the anti-Haitianist tenor of contemporary Dominicanidad in the Dominican Republic.[30]

Balaguer's celebration of the Columbian quincentennial formed part of a seventy-year career built on extolling the Hispanicity, Catholicism, and whiteness of the Dominican people. Balaguer had begun his professional life as a schoolteacher in Santiago de los Caballeros, the country's second-largest city. A scholar of Spanish and Spanish-American literature who was critical of the first U.S. occupation, he formed part of a patriotic nucleus that included the likes of the famous nationalist feminist schoolteacher Ercilia Pepín. Following the end of the occupation and Trujillo's rise to power, Balaguer became the dictator's leading ideologue as well as his secretary of state. He was rewarded for his sycophancy and loyalty when Trujillo had him appointed to the vice-presidency and later to the presidency of the republic, the post he held when Trujillo was assassinated.

Following Trujillo's assassination and his own exile to New York City, where he founded the Partido Reformista Social Cristiano (PRSC), Balaguer astutely negotiated the Trujillo family, the Trujillistas, the church, the military's various factions, and the administration of U.S. President Lyndon Johnson to get himself "elected" to the presidency again in 1966. The contest was between the ultraconservative and Trujillista factions, who organized themselves into a triumvirate lead by Colonel Elías Wessin y Wessin, who sought to nullify the secular and progressive 1963 constitution, and the Constitutionalistas, led by Colonel Francisco A. Caamaño Deñó, who sought to reinstate the 1963 constitution. The constitution had been developed and instated under the short-lived presidency of Juan Bosch. It reflected the social-democratic ideals of the Partido Revolucionario Dominicano (PRD), which Bosch founded, and was thought to threaten the interests of the military, the elite, and the Catholic church. Bosch's presidency lasted a mere seven months before the conservative sectors joined forces to oust the country's first freely elected president.

Following the coup, Bosch was deported to Puerto Rico, and a civil war that came to be known as the *Guerra de Abril* broke out during the month of April 1965.[31] The Constitutionalistas were gaining ground in the reinstatement of constitutional rule, and by all accounts they were about to take control of the government when the U.S. Marines invaded. The invading forces eventually consisted of a force more than 30,000 strong—as many U.S. troops as were concurrently stationed in South Vietnam.[32] For the second time in less than fifty years, a U.S. occupation order was established in the Dominican Republic, ostensibly to protect U.S. lives. The U.S. government's explicit justification for the occupation was that, given Bosch's socialist-democratic politics, the Dominican Republic would follow Cuba, an untenable prospect in the context of the Cold War. Although it framed itself as a peacekeeping and democratic stabilization force, the U.S. occupation force effectively collaborated with local conservative political factions of the military and civil society.[33] The final outcome of the collaboration was Balaguer's 1968 "election" to the presidency. Balaguer remained in power for three terms all together (1966–78), a repressive period now known as "the twelve years."[34]

Coincidental to and surviving beyond the Balaguer regime's first period was the rise of *La nueva ola* (the New Wave) movement, a reclamation of African heritage and cultural legacies in the Dominican Republic that was inspired at least in part by anticolonial struggles, revolutionary movements, and negritude movements being organized throughout the Americas of the 1960s. The U.S. intervention and occupation during the Guerra de Abril had a radicalizing effect on the racial ideologies and politics of the progressive sectors of Dominican society. That effect was born out of the ironic coupling of anti-U.S. imperial politics and the initiation of an informal policy of using massive emigration to the United States to quell dissent in the Dominican Republic.[35] The irony lay in that it was precisely those who were most threatening to the United States' interests in the Dominican Republic who were either exiled or forced to emigrate to the United States. Following three decades of the Trujillo regime's carefully engineered isolation and insularism, these Dominicans came into personal contact with the United States at precisely the moment when black liberation movements, anti-Vietnam War protests, and Marxist-inspired responses to injustice and inequality were rife. These charged national and international political contexts formed the background against which the New Wave movement would rise.

"*Exigencias de un cimarrón*": Blackness Represented

The New Wave movement was composed of leftist scholars, academics, cultural workers, students, artists, peasants, and wage laborers who attempted to vindicate the country's political and economic sovereignty. Many who participated in *La nueva ola* were members of the PRD or of the Partido Comunista Dominicano (PCD). In part, their political project turned on challenging the ideological legacies of the Trujilloist state through revisionist historiography and cultural concientization about racial oppression. Thus, New Wave publications began to appear in 1969; the First Colloquium on the African Presence in the Antilles was held in 1973 at the Universidad Autónoma de Santo Domingo; the first research monograph on the African diaspora and slavery in the Dominican Republic was published by Carlos Larrazábal Blanco in 1967; the first negritude-inspired folk festival was organized at Atabales in 1975; and the Casa Identidad Mujer Negra was founded in the early 1980s by self-identified black feminists.[36]

According to Moya Pons, from 1966 onward, New Wave-inspired actors began to draw attention to what they called "the racial and cultural alienation of the Dominican people."[37] Blas Jiménez, for example, in the title poem of the collection *Exigencias de un cimarrón*, decries the over-representation of Iberian and indigenous people in the public sphere, whose histories are literally embedded in the country's landscape, where "many streets bear [their] names" and "lots of marble bears [their] likeness." By contrast, Jiménez observes, there is "not a single street, not a bit of marble, not a memory" for the descendants of Africans who "sculptured your rocks, worked your lands, washed your minerals, built your temples and cut your cane."[38] Deploying the figure of the *cimarrón*, the runaway slave who established communities independent of the colonial regime, Jiménez as cimarrón demands recognition and remembrance.

These thinkers and cultural workers challenged a long tradition of Hispanophile and white-supremacist Dominican thought that ranged from the work of nineteenth-century *pesimista* (Pessimist) intellectuals to Trujillo's three-decade-long project of institutionalizing of Indo-Hispanic Dominicanidad. The *pesimistas* were convinced that Dominicans were racially doomed because they had inherited the worst traits of each of "the three races" that made up "the national character": the Spaniard's laziness, the Indian's primitivism, and the African's lechery. Trujillo, in turn, assured Dominicans that they could exterminate the African presence (the Haitian Massacre), reinterpret the Indian's savagery as a noble resistance (Enriquillo), and extol the Spaniard's "Europeanizing" influence (through the arts and protection of the national patrimony).[39]

In the aftermath of the Trujillato, and confronted once again with U.S. imperialism, the extrication of political nationalism from the cultural nationalism that was the ideological legacy of Trujillo's repressive politics and the anti-Haitianist ideologies that had most effectively fostered and institutionalized Dominican identity became increasingly thorny for New Wave activists and thinkers. Those grouped together under the banner of Dominican nationalism were anti-imperialists as well as anti-Haitianists, Marxists as well as liberal capitalists, and Hispanophile as well as pro-negritude cultural workers. Although New Wave intellectuals and cultural workers managed to establish themselves as legitimate interlocutors and actors in the interpretation of Dominican nationalism and, later, in the display of Dominican identity, they did not manage to institutionalize their vision in any extensive way.

Thus, Dominican scholars who challenged anti-Haitianist and white-supremacist ideologies were lauded for "having distanced themselves . . . from the traditional reactionary currents" that reject negritude.[40] This Negrophobic tradition is so dominant that the use of the word "black" in reference to the Dominican population has to be qualified and justified, even in the context of one of the few works on African slavery in the Dominican Republic, Carlos Esteban Deive's *La esclavitud del negro en Santo Domingo, 1492–1844*, published in 1980 by the Museo del Hombre Dominicano. Deive wrote in his introduction that

it is worth underlining the fact that the use of the word "black" has no pejorative connotation. It refers, instead, to a semantic practice justified by historical and practical reasons evidenced in an abundant bibliography. The phenotypical markers of black Africans are not manifestations of their racial or intellectual inferiority relative to whites, as has been scientifically demonstrated.[41]

That Deive evidently felt behooved to remind a presumably literate and educated reading audience that "black" was not an implicitly pejorative term, and that black Africans were not inferior to whites, offers evidence of the everydayness of Negrophobia. Embedded in Negrophobia's racial project is a foreclosing of critical political action because Negrophobia is naturalized and normative.

"¿Y tu abuela, ¿donde está?": Blackness and Anti-Haitianism

Deive has written that when someone "pretending" to be white "crows in the yard about his pure whiteness and upper class status, there is without exception always some caustically forward soul who will immediately ask: 'And where is your grandmother?' an inquiry which is intended to 'lower the "cupcakes" from their heights.'"[42] The rhetorical question, "Where is your grandmother?" is usually asked of one who is perceived to be putting on airs or claiming the sort of social status accorded only to the legitimately privileged: the white upper class.

Illegitimate claims to privileged status breach the ascribed distinctions between *gente* (persons) and *individuos* (people). As Roberto Da Matta has suggested with regard to Brazilian society, persons "are those who have the power and status to make themselves known to others through affirming their social relations and position in society. . . . Individuals, on the other hand, have no such social connections and relations, and are thus part of the anonymous masses."[43] In the Dominican context, those of "the anonymous crowd" are the poor, the black, and the otherwise socially marginalized.[44]

In *Tres leyendas de colores*, the New Wave poet and essayist Pedro Mir reconceptualized the notion of the faceless (black) masses as nameless and inverted the relationship between mass anonymity and social status:

> History could not get his name. The black had no time to pose for the lens of history, which is a dialectical form of photography. . . . He is, thus, anonymous. To be anonymous is to be unanimous. Not to have a name is to contain all names. . . . Anonymity is a kind of sum total, collectivity, unanimity. To be no one is, at the same time, to be everyone. Anonymity is plural.[45]

Here Mir inverts the notion that *individuos* are anonymous nobodies. He argues that it is precisely that overwhelming, majority presence that makes "the black" *the* "collectivity," "the Dominican." Mir, in other words, is arguing against the power of the elite, those who are *gente*, to imagine and represent Dominicanness as the exclusive terrain of persons. Dominicanness is everyone's, it is "unanimous" peoplehood. In his three legends, Mir writes of the history of Africans and their descendants in the formation of the Dominican Republic, reclaiming and legitimizing work that has been repudiated, diminished, and, perhaps worse, ignored by the Dominican elite and authors of state-sanctioned histories.

Scholarly narrators of the nation's history from the late nineteenth century onward have linked blackness with foreignness and Dominicanness with Indo-Hispanicity. Perhaps it is not surprising, then, that little historiography and anthropological or sociological research has been done in the Dominican Republic on blackness. Much of the work has focused on slavery, on communities explicitly acknowledged to be slave-descended, or on communities descended from the British West Indian or African American diaspora. The major works on slavery to date have been written by Celsa Albert Batista and Alejandra Liriano, both of whom have written short monographs on women in slavery, and by Deive, Carlos Larrazábal Blanco, and Ruben Silié, who have written fairly extensive research monographs on the political-economic history of slavery on Hispaniola.[46] Franklin Franco Pichardo has likewise written about slavery as a key component of Dominican culture, politics, and ideology,[47] while the folklorist Dagoberta Tejada Ortíz, the poet Blas Jiménez, the singer Xiomara Fortuna, and the black feminist social critic Ochy Curiel have established a corpus of negritude-inspired literature and cultural works.[48]

The Dominican diaspora scholar Silvio Torres-Saillant likewise has called for the universal recognition of African ancestry, exclaiming that Dominicans "are all ex-slaves!"[49] As Torres-Saillant explains, his intent is to ask "Dominican historians, in effect, to embrace a narrative that privileges the many rather than the few."[50] Torres-Saillant argues that Dominican scholars traditionally have internalized, and continue to propagate, a white-supremacist and Eurocentric model of Dominican history. Thus, they "have learned to see slave-masters and planters" rather than the slaves, freed people, and maroons who predominated demographically and culturally as their ancestors. It is that identification with the (white) slave masters and their descendants that informs "the State-funded distortion of Dominican ethnicity and culture."[51] Today, only a handful of scholars, many of them now elder leaders of the New Wave vanguard, continue to research, write, and lecture on blackness in the Dominican Republic. Their intent is to challenge white supremacy, undo Negrophobia, and celebrate black history and culture through a recovery and recognition of African ancestries and cultural heritage.

"¡Carajo Quisqueya! No recuerdas a Toussaint": Travel Narratives as Primary Texts

Despite the efforts of pro-negritude cultural workers and scholars, for the most part blackness and Haitianness continue to be consistently vilified in Dominican texts. In her book *Mujer y esclavitud en Santo Domingo*, for example, Celsa Albert Batista points to the simultaneously visual and historiographic misrepresentation of blackness in educational materials:

> The majority of textbooks' illustrations of people have white phenotypes and when a black person is illustrated, it is in a position of inferiority. There is rarely a black female figure in these educational materials, but when illustrations of blacks and mulattos from our history appear they are caricatured in troubling ways inconsistent with their actual phenotypes, in which manner our historical reality is deformed.[52]

Similarly, the historians María Filomena González Canalda and Rubén Silié undertook a systematic analysis of the national history curriculum's textbooks for grades three to five approved by the government's Primary Education Secretariat and used throughout the country's primary-school classrooms. They found a consistent pattern of historical inaccuracies geared toward the mythification and glorification of the country's colonial and indigenous past, along with a nearly total exclusion and routine denigration of the country's African heritage and history. In addition, these texts present the island's current division into Haiti and the Dominican Republic as arising from the very landscape of the island, so that even the island's indigenous population of the pre-Columbian era is presented as inhabiting "Haiti" in the west and "Quisqueya" in the east. Moreover, the two country's populations are represented as being both culturally and racially distinct—to Haiti's disadvantage, of course.[53]

The works of the anti-Haitianist historians José Gabriel García, Bernardo Pichardo, Pedro Henríquez Ureña, Emilio Rodríguez Demorizi, Ramón Marrero Aristy, Joaquín Balaguer, and Jacinto Gimbernard were institutionalized in the curriculum, and in their mutual referentiality their flawed claims about Haitians and Haiti were perpetuated through the generations.[54] For example, Gimbernard's *Historia de Santo Domingo*, used by Dominican schoolchildren for generations, borrowed liberally throughout its text from his anti-Haitianist predecessors and peers. An illustrative example is the following quote from Balaguer's *El centinela de la frontera*, with which Gimbernard closed his brief chapter on "Toussaint's Death, Independence from Haiti, Dessalines' Invasion":

> The year 1806 was flowing. The late echo of the French Revolution, swollen with human grievances, still reverberated in the western part of the island of Saint-Domingue, which at the time served as the seat of the most prosperous colonial organizations in the world.
>
> A native African lion, Toussaint Louverture, had launched the battle cry that penetrated the soul of more than six hundred thousand slaves of the African race. From the start, the uprising took on the cast of a battle to the death inspired by the desire for liberty, but nourished above all by profound racial antagonisms. Jean Jacob Dessalines, Toussaint's successor in that epic battle, launched his famous "Decree of Death to Whites" and a legion of tribal chiefs, convened by the noise of the drum in impressive ceremonies improvised in the midst of the jungles, responded, sinisterly, to that macabre order. The European-descent colonists were run through with knives or burned alive in their own bedrooms.[55]

Although this passage hardly requires interpretation, I think it is useful to point out how similar Gimbenard's depiction is to those of nineteenth-century travel narratives discussed in chapter 1. Louverture is equated with an animal native to Africa. The references to echoing and reverberating battle cries, tribal chiefs, and jungle drums impute primeval savagery to "the African race." The Haitian revolutionary leader's "profound racial antagonisms" seem to spring from mere blood lust rather than being a political response to colonialism, enslavement, barbarous treatment, and genocide. The Europeans and their descendants are the victims, rather than the victimizers, of blacks. Highly organized and successful military men are cast as nothing more than "a legion of tribal chiefs." Finally, the account subsumes Dominicans under those of "European-descent."

Gimbernard's presentation of African slavery in the Spanish part of Santo Domingo was sketched in the briefest of terms, while several chapters were devoted to the Taíno and Spanish colonial legacy, including a chapter each for Enriquillo and Bartolomeo de las Casas. Later in his text, Gimbernard affirmed the seemingly essential differences between nascent "Dominicans" of the early and mid-eighteenth century, when there was no Dominican Republic, and "the Haitian invaders." He wrote:

> The new Haitian occupation increased the out migration of the most distinguished families, a process that had been developing, in its latest stage, since the 1795 signing of the Treaty of Basel.
>
> The abandonment by the people most capable of opposing the invader based on a solid culture and tradition of sustaining a Hispanic society that would be a bastion against the efforts to Haitianize the Dominican population, did not manage to quash the conviction among the inhabitants of the ancient Spanish part of the island that unity with Haiti was impossible.
>
> The permanent resistance of Spanish Dominicans to assimilation with Haiti remained firm throughout the twenty-two years the occupation lasted.
>
> Boyer's government was particularly characterized by its determination to blacken the Dominican population and to destroy the culture it had enjoyed.[56]

Once again, the narrative frames Africanness and blackness as foreign impositions on an essentially white and Hispanic Dominican population. Although the Spaniards themselves abandoned the colony, "the Dominican population" in the "ancient Spanish part of the island" retained their Hispanicity to such a degree that they could resist efforts to Haitianize them. Even Boyer's "determination to blacken the Dominican population" signals the population's non-blackness. Gimbernard formed part of an intellectual elite reliant on primary texts such as foreign travel narratives that confirmed their ideological presumptions. As Torres-Saillant notes, "When they imagine Dominican history and the Dominican people only the experience of their ancestors come to mind, the experiences of others, meaning the majority of the population, receiving only tangential, if any, treatment."[57]

However, as the economist and historian Raymundo González argued more than a decade ago,[58] and the historian Richard Turits has more fully elaborated, this project of rejecting blackness is not simply one of symbolic domination or ideological hegemony of the elite. It also has roots in the social worlds of the peasant masses that formed the majority of Dominican society well into the last quarter of the twentieth century. "The spectacular failure of Santo Domingo's sixteenth-century plantation society, the long history of Spanish neglect, the dearth of commercial agriculture, the irrelevance of legal property forms, and the transformations provoked by the Haitian Revolution and the Haitian occupation all provided the conditions under which successive generations of Dominicans were able to liberate themselves from slavery and constitute a vital, independent peasantry."[59] By the late eighteenth century, when the slaves of French San Domingüe were revolting, three-quarters of the population of the Spanish part of Santo Domingo was composed of free people of color who sustained themselves independently of the master class through subsistence agriculture. The major social classes, according to them, were the enslaved and the free. That peasantry operated relatively independently of state control throughout the nineteenth century, and it was not until the early twentieth century that the white elite were able to consolidate control of the state.[60]

As a result, even as the Spanish and Creole elite perpetuated white-supremacist and patriarchal ruling relations, the peasant masses of color were able to fashion themselves as Creole and native rather than black and enslaved. These are the social roots of Indo-Hispanicity. Thus it was that these peasants could consider themselves "the whites of the land" or "negroes with a white heart," as foreign observers had noted in astonishment in their travel narratives.[61] Throughout the nineteenth century and into the twentieth century, as foreign narrators were producing texts that represented Dominicans as somewhere between Haitians and Americans in the hemisphere's racial hierarchy, Dominican social realities likewise affirmed relational and hierarchical understandings of Dominican whiteness and Haitian blackness.

As my examination of travel narratives and Turits's historicization of Negrophobia both illustrate, that ideology cut across class lines and had its antecedents in a triangulated dynamic of geopolitically framed ideological relationships between the Dominican Republic, Haiti, and the United States. Throughout historically shifting and contested political contexts, a constant was the symbolic position of the Dominican Republic as being between Haiti's Black Republic and Ben Franklin's "lovely White Republic." Dominicans were symbolically positioned, in other words, as non-white in relation to the United States, but as non-black relative to Haiti. And always, they were indigenous.

A Single Archeological Field? Dominican Artifacts and Symbolic Nation Building

The Caribbean islands were valuable to Europe and the United States not only in terms of economic and geopolitical assets, as has been amply documented elsewhere,[62] but in terms of cultural resources, as well. Indeed, much as Latin American resources helped fuel U.S. political, economic, and military projects in the nineteenth century and twentieth century, Latin American material culture and archeological artifacts proved important to the country's racial projects. The Monroe Doctrine of 1823 and Manifest Destiny ideologies had already laid solid political and ideological foundations for continental expansion, but it was not until the post-Civil War years that expansion beyond continental boundaries began to be contemplated seriously and undertaken. Although Cuba and the Dominican Republic both had been viewed by certain political, economic, and social sectors of the United States as potential territories, those desires were not realized until the Cuban–Spanish–American War of 1898. Establishing the United States as an imperial power with colonial possessions and as the hemisphere's hegemon, the War of 1898 also created the conditions for enriching not only U.S. capitalists, but also U.S. cultural institutions, particularly those dealing with ethnology, anthropology, and archeology.

Although the existence and availability of indigenous artifacts on Hispaniola was documented by Europeans as early as 1760, when Thomas Jefferys's *Natural and Civil History of the French Dominions in North and South America* was published, and later the British diplomat and naturalist Sir Robert Schomburgk undertook extensive archeological, ethnological, and natural explorations of the Dominican Republic immediately after its separation from Haiti,[63] earnest archeological explorations of the country began in the last quarter of the nineteenth century. That period saw the proliferation of U.S. interests in the indigenous legacy of the Caribbean islands being considered for annexation or colonization, principally Cuba, Puerto Rico, and the Dominican Republic. Sacking of material culture operated hand in glove with the extraction of natural resources, colonization of lands, and military intervention.

As discussed in the introduction, like their contemporary sociocultural institutions—the World's Fairs, department stores, and beauty shops—museums were part of the democratization and diffusion of scientific knowledge in Europe and the United States. Ideologically, they incorporated massive numbers of immigrants, women, and even newly emancipated African Americans in the project of "building the continental empire,"[64] even as they simultaneously hardened national racial, gender, and class hierarchies and institutionalized a representative, rather than a participatory, democratic system. Those who were marginalized or excluded from representative democracy were offered superficial social democratization through access to these new public spheres, even as the creation of those spheres became increasingly professionalized and regulated from above, and spectators were trained into passively consuming the displays organized for them by the ruling elites. In other words, at these new exhibitionary sites people came *to see themselves and their Others represented*, rather than to represent themselves. That is, even as it *appeared* that the public sphere was more democratic because it was made concretely visible and available for mass consumption, it was actually less democratic because it was reliant on a passive consumer class rather than on direct creation of and engagement with public goods.

Thus, from the late nineteenth century onward, hundreds of thousands of U.S. residents attended World's Fairs and their more permanent counterparts, museums. Indeed, the country's preeminent museum, the Smithsonian Institution, funded in 1829 by James Smithson and opened in 1846, participated actively in the organization, staffing, and exhibiting of World's Fairs throughout the nineteenth century and twentieth century. Moreover, as the historian Robert Rydell has argued, the World's Fairs "muted class divisions among whites, providing them with a sense of shared national purpose," even as the fairs themselves were the outcome of "the intermeshing of upper-class purpose and federal power."[65] The manifest mandate of the Smithsonian has long been "the increase and diffusion of knowledge." Its latent mandate was the creation and display of a symbolic universe that generalized the authority of the ruling classes to rule both at home and abroad.

U.S. archeologists and anthropologists were active participants in the mythicization project both in the United States and abroad. Peter Hulme explains:

> In a country conscious of its own Manifest Destiny, it was inevitable that interest in the history of the coveted islands would arise. Descriptions of the islands were undertaken, as well as of the anatomy of their political systems, their natural resources were enumerated and there were interminable discussions of the strategic positions they occupied. Thus, their indigenous

and colonial histories were reconstructed until they were endowed with an adequate image.[66]

That "adequate image" was that of the Noble Savage, who symbolically embodied both the noble pursuit of liberty in the face of foreign rule and oppression at the hands of the British, and the savagery of the "naturals" who would now be replaced by the new "native" Americans, those of European heritage.[67]

At the same time, U.S. expansionism confronted the colonial power of Spain, France, and England on the North American continent. Distinctive strategies were utilized to ideologically and politically de-legitimize each. In the case of Spain, the Black Legend offered an economical and useful rhetorical device that both deflected attention away from governmental and private atrocities committed against the native peoples of the United States and undermined Spanish dominion over territories the United States wanted to claim.[68] From the Louisiana Purchase to the Seminole War to the War of 1848, the Black Legend surfaced in justifications of U.S. expansion onto Spanish territory. Finally, the War of 1898 tolled the death knell for Spanish colonialism in the Americas and ushered in U.S. imperialism in the Caribbean.[69]

Just as Native North Americans had been converted to useful, if fraught, symbols of an authentically American identity for the descendants of European colonists and immigrants in North America, similar indigenist ideologies were encouraged in the Caribbean. For the United States, Caribbean indigenism offered both a nationalist identity resistant to Spanish colonialism and a way of positioning Caribbean islanders as indigenes who could be handled as North America's native peoples had been, though supposedly with more felicitous outcomes for the Caribbean "natives." Of course, this was belied by the fact that in establishing itself as an imperial power in the Caribbean, the U.S. government drew directly on the legal, political, and social precedents it had developed in subjugating Native Americans in the North.[70] As John Borneman argues, anthropology and U.S. foreign policy shared "the conceptual apparatus created in Indian policy as part of a global strategy in dealing with foreignness outside the territorial boundaries of the United States."[71]

If in the United States the concern of anthropology and archeology was with preserving the supposedly "rapidly disappearing" languages and material culture of native peoples who would be cast as patriotic symbols even as the material conditions and political demands of contemporary Native Americans themselves were ignored, in the Dominican

Republic there was no similar tension between indigenist myth-making and social and historical facts of native peoples' experiences because no native communities remained. Thus, Dominican indigenists could extol and manipulate the extinct "prehistoric" or pre-Columbian period without disputation by native peoples themselves. However, as "Caribbean natives," Dominicans did have to deal with the United States' interests in the island's indigeneity.

Government moves to protect the Dominican national patrimony had begun during the Báez era on February 3, 1870, with Decree No. 1164, which declared Diego Columbus's fortress a national monument. That this was also the period during which U.S. annexation of the Dominican Republic was being hotly debated and contested, and just before the U.S. Senate's investigative commission left for Santo Domingo, is probably not coincidental. Indeed, the monument was one of the commission's stops on its tour of the country. As discussed in chapter 1, Dominican annexationists and independence leaders alike worked to represent the Dominican Republic as an Hispanic nation. The 1893 World Columbian Exposition offered an excellent opportunity to display that vision abroad.

Frederick Albion Ober, ornithologist, Caribbean traveler, novelist, and the Smithsonian Institution's special commissioner for the World Columbian Exposition of 1893, was charged with obtaining Columbus's remains from the Dominican Republic for the exposition. Although Consul to the Dominican Republic Reverend Henry C. C. Astwood was removed by President Grover Cleveland for his "indecent proposal" to travel the United States displaying Columbus's remains at circuses and expositions,[72] Ulises (Lilís) Heureaux, then dictator of the Dominican Republic, was willing to send the remains to the exposition for a $100,000 loan, as Ober documented with derision.

It was not until more than a decade after Ober's unsuccessful attempt to secure Columbus's remains for the Chicago World's Fair that Decree No. 4347 of October 15, 1903, declared existing archeological objects the property of the state and proposed the creation of a National Museum in the Dominican Republic. An indication of the perceived importance of the matter to the ruling classes is that this decree was issued during the exceedingly short-lived, three-month presidency of Alejandro Woss y Gil, in an era of considerable political upheaval.[73] Later, in 1913, the Dominican government, under the leadership of Archbishop Alejandro Nouel, decreed the establishment of a National Museum to be housed in Diego Columbus's fortress (figure 3). It was not until 1927, during the

3. Alcazar de Diego Colón (Diego Columbus's fortress)
4. and 5. Exhibit halls, National Museum of the Dominican
Republic

brief Horacio Vásquez presidency, however, that funds were appropriated for the creation and operation of the National Museum. The new National Museum was to house the items previously held by the Municipal Museum, opened in Santiago by Amado Franco Bidó in 1907.[74]

The principal mandate of the Municipal Museum of Santiago and the National Museum was the collection, preservation, display, and diffusion of knowledge about the country's pre-Columbian artifacts and legacy (figures 4–5). The importance of this mandate to the nation's symbolic capital is underscored by the fact that, even during the most politically unstable times, the Dominican government acted to protect the archeological evidence of the country's Hispanic and indigenous heritages, as the colonial-era buildings became national monuments and pre-Columbian artifacts and remains became archeological treasures. By contrast, there was no language in any of the legislation relating to the research, preservation, display, and diffusion of knowledge about the country's African heritages and artifacts.[75]

It is noteworthy that this was not long after the 1924 end of U.S. military's 1924 occupation of the Dominican Republic and on the cusp of the Trujillo era. Coincidentally, 1924 was also the year in which the founder of the Smithsonian Institution's Anthropology Department, Dr. Herbert Krieger (1889–1970), a specialist in pre-Columbian archeology, joined the Smithsonian. Although Krieger was not the first Smithsonian official to excavate and collect in the Dominican Republic, he was the most prolific.[76] As Krieger himself documents, William M. Gabb (who had accompanied President Grant's Commission of Inquiry in 1871) had collected pottery and bones from Samaná Bay between 1869 and 1871, which were exhibited at the U.S. National Museum in 1872. Dr. William Abbot, also of the National Museum, began his Dominican expeditions in 1883, making "repeated visits" from that date to the first decades of the twentieth century. However, unlike these predecessors, Krieger lived and worked in the Dominican Republic, from 1929 to 1953, and would build his career on Dominican artifacts.

Krieger's work was indebted to the model of excavation and collection in Puerto Rico established by the eminent archeologist Jesse Walter Fewkes, who was employed by the Bureau of American Ethnology at the Smithsonian. Fewkes's classic work, "Prehistoric Puerto Rico" (1902), was written to bring newly colonized Puerto Rico and Cuba to the attention of U.S. archeologists.[77] Fewkes also traveled to the Dominican Republic, as noted earlier, and was sponsored by the Museum of the American Indian–Heye Foundation. A major result of his expedition was his acquisition of more than 1,200 artifacts from the Dominican Republic and Puerto Rico, which "equaled in number the West Indian objects previously existing in the Smithsonian collection, which was already one of the largest in the world."[78] It is telling, therefore, that Krieger cast his work with Dominican artifacts as following Fewkes's model.

Krieger corresponded regularly with leading Dominican nationalist intellectuals, including Emile de Boyrie Moya, an engineer and the subsequent founder of the Anthropological Research Institute of the University of Santo Domingo; Abigaíl Mejía, the feminist writer and director of the National Museum; Frederico Henríquez y Carvajal, poet and educator; the feminist schoolteacher Ercilia Pepín; and the historian E. Rodríguez Demorizi.[79] And he evidently found a colleague in Narciso Alberti Bosch, whom many considered "the most important pioneer of archaeology in Santo Domingo" and whose "untiring labors" between 1908 and 1932 yielded one book and fifteen articles on archeology in the Dominican Republic.[80] Yet despite these ties, what Dato Pagán Perdomo, director of the Museo del Hombre Dominicano from 1996 to 2002, generously called Krieger's "questionable professional ethics" were evident in Krieger's unapologetic sacking and robbing of pre-Columbian archeological artifacts and graves in the Dominican Republic for over three decades.[81] This was in direct violation of the Dominican government's 1903 Decree 4347, which "declared existing archeological objects property of the Dominican State and territory." The decree was issued by Provisional President Carlos F. Morales Languazco specifically "to prevent the removal and exportation of the country's indigenous archeological pieces."[82] Decree 4347 was irrelevant under U.S. occupation, however.

This is perhaps best illustrated by Krieger's employment of Harry E. Hurst, a former U.S. occupation officer, to travel through the Dominican Republic collecting artifacts on his behalf as the occupation came to an end. Hurst, who supplied both Krieger and Mark Harrington, an anthropologist in the employ of the Museum of the American Indian–Heye Foundation, was quite successful in his incursions.[83] Just from March 5 to June 6, 1924, Hurst made six shipments of archeological objects to Harrington in New York City, evidently in anticipation of the withdrawal of U.S. troops in July.[84] The Museum of the American Indian–Heye Foundation had begun collecting in the Dominican Republic in 1913 when it commissioned the archeologist Theodoor De Booy's expedition to the caves of Saona Island, off the coast of San Pedro de Macoris.[85] De Booy returned during the summer of 1916, again under the auspices of the Museum of the American Indian–Heye Foundation, but this time excavating a kitchen middens and burial mound on the Cristóbal Colón sugar plantation in San Pedro de Macoris itself. As De Booy reports in the museum's research monograph, the plantation's owners and administrators gave him "a large number of specimens" for the museum.[86] Krieger likewise openly reported not only his archeological findings but also his acquisitions through private purchases, even of artifacts taken from public lands. As Pagán Perdomo noted:

> The purchases were an important and permanent means of acquiring indigenous objects and [Krieger] shamelessly admitted to his friends that he had purchased in Santo Domingo all sorts of artifacts that interested him for the Smithsonian Institution, exulting over the fact that his best collector in Constanza was the police commissioner. In 1930 he removed from the country hundreds of ceramic pieces and various crania obtained from La Caleta.[87]

Between purchases and his own excavations, Krieger acquired pre-Columbian artifacts from Monte Cristi, Samaná, Dajabon, la Bahia de Andres, La Caleta, Azua, La Vega, Constanza, Los Picos Culo de Maco, Rucilla, Pico del Yaque, Monte Cucucho, and Chinguela for the Smithsonian Institution.

The occupation era had created a degree of political stasis through disarmament and repression of the population, and it had "accelerated the growth of a plantation economy highly dependent on the world sugar market over which the country had little control."[88] These political-economic changes influenced Dominican identity formations. Moya Pons informs us that

> the U.S. occupation also left a marked taste for the consumption of U.S. goods. In the following years, Dominicans resumed their use of European products, but more than half of the country's imports continued to come from the United States. A marked Americanization of the language also took place during these years with the dissemination of U.S. trade marks on almost all the products consumed in the country. U.S. games and toys became popular, and baseball eventually replaced cockfighting as the national sport. Among the urban elite U.S. music became a sign of good taste, although the inverse phenomenon took place among the mass of the population, which espoused the merengue as a sign of protest against foreign domination.[89]

In such a context, the role of a National Museum in the development and display of an "authentic" Dominican identity was all the more ideologically pressing for the nationalist sectors of Dominican society. To this end, the ethnically Hispanicist and racially indigenist projections of the increasingly nationalist post-occupation and emergent Trujillo-ist Dominican state were institutionalized permanently through venues exhibiting the national patrimony, ranging from the architectural to the artifactual.

Thus, in 1926, the renowned Hispanophile feminist Abigaíl Mejía began an "unceasing lobbying" campaign in the nation's leading news-papers and magazines on behalf of the development of a National Mu-seum. Mejía demonstrated the kind of nationalism that articulated well first with President Horacio Vasquez's post-occupation regime and later with the Trujillato's agenda. Mejía, a normal-school teacher, poet, and essayist from one of the country's "leading families," had been in Spain during the U.S. occupation and for much of her adolescence taking her teaching degree. She returned to Santo Domingo in 1925 and immedi-ately began to lecture and publish on feminism, arts and culture, and protecting the national patrimony.

In article after article, she made the case for the establishment of a National Museum. She acerbically noted in 1926 that the "ill-fated era of Yankee intervention" witnessed the "avid exploration of every corner that secreted something worthy of admiration and worth taking casu-ally as booty to their country of merchants."[90] Now, she exhorted, "the State had to prove its patriotism" and pay its "patriotic debt" by founding a National Museum to safeguard the country's treasures.[91] She pointed out that if the "Old World" capitals had their colonial treasures, artistic masters, and histories arrayed for proud exhibition in monumental mu-seums, the Dominican Republic had its archeological treasures, national artists, and rich cultural heritage meritorious of proud display. And she laid out a plan for the National Museum that would include indigenous artifacts, colonial- and national-history exhibits, national paintings and sculpture, natural-history exhibits, and a library collection of works writ-ten by Dominicans.[92] All that was needed, she claimed, was a small ap-propriation, a small house, and the patriotic will to make it happen.[93] She presented her fully elaborated plan and budget to the Vasquez ad-ministration's secretary of state and public education in November 1926, and in 1927 the Vasquez government agreed to set aside appropriations for the museum.[94] However, the museum was not actually funded or opened until Trujillo won the 1930 election, as the country's leading newspaper, Listín Diario, reported in March of that year.[95] Soon after, Trujillo named Mejía the National Museum's first director, a post she held for eight years.[96] In that capacity, she continued to publish articles in the national press educating the public about the didactic role of the National Museum and offering instructions on how to comport oneself in the museum and how best to view the exhibits.[97]

A decade later, the National Museum became part of the Dominican Institute for Anthropological Research of the University of Santo Domingo. The institute was a state office created in 1947 by Emile de Boyrie Moya to centralize archeological and ethnological research activities, itself part of a larger mandate to consolidate and rationalize the state bureaucracy during the Trujillato. In addition, the institute's establishment was Trujillo's response to the recommendations made by the Inter-American Union of the Caribbean and the Caribbean Archaeology Conference, which had been celebrated the year before in Honduras. As part of its cultural research and diffusion mission, therefore, the institute presented its "First Exhibit of Autochthonous Indigenous Art" at the university in 1948.[98] It is important to note that this state-sanctioned professionalization of efforts to protect the national patrimony responded not only to nationalist interests in promoting indigenist ideologies, but also to regional cultural currents, and international relations and developments.

Ethnological museums had originated as institutions intended to bring knowledge about colonial and native others to Europe and the United States. "As such," as Faith Ruffins of the American History Museum of the Smithsonian puts it, "these museums became the primary scholarly means by which the public came into contact with the 'primitive'—that is, people of color."[99] But ethnological museums and their exhibitionary techniques were also adopted and adapted by the natives for their own ideological and political purposes. The Dominican archeologist Manuel García Arévalo has argued that the habitualized turn to the indigenous past, is an expression of nationalist ideologies. Identifying with the "autochthonous past" allows for an expression of Dominican identity as distinct from two of the historic foreign threats to Dominican sovereignty: the Spanish and the Haitian.[100] Indigenism also allowed for ideological and ethnic unity because of its "telluric solidarity."[101] In other words, nineteenth-century indigenism elided the emergent fact of social stratification and political contestation within the Dominican Republic by creating an identity that emerged from the very land on which the nation was built. In the face of multiple internal and external claims upon that land, indigenism worked to counter the legitimacy of those claimants.

In 1945, the United Nations was founded by twenty-six Axis nations, including nine Latin American states, of which the Dominican Republic was one. By 1946, the United Nations Organization had founded UNESCO. Part of UNESCO's mission was the preservation of cultural heritages, and an aspect of that project was support for the development and institutionalization of museums and museology. The historian Frederick Elwyn Kidder has argued that the founding of UNESCO owed a great deal to the work of Latin American countries that had joined the United Nations when it was founded in 1945, for many of those countries had long participated in international intellectual co-operation efforts.[102] The Dominican Republic was one of the eleven Latin American countries that signed the Acte Internationale of the League of Nations' Institute of International Intellectual Co-operation (which had been founded in 1926 in Paris) to establish the Intellectual Cooperation Organization (ICO) in 1938. The Republic also established a National Committee of Intellectual Co-Operation as part of its membership in the ICO.

As a UNESCO member nation, the Dominican Republic simultaneously could access resources for preserving what it deemed its autochthonous cultural heritage and traditions and signify its status as a thoroughly modern state because of that international affiliation. Thus, by 1948, when the Anthropological Institute was founded, the Dominican Republic was an active participant in the yearly UNESCO conference and presented the international body with a six point set of suggestions: "special issues of postage stamps to raise money for an International Fund; UNESCO-prepared textbooks on history; better pay for teachers; free postage for school to encourage correspondence between students of different countries; exchange of students and teachers; and Spanish as a UNESCO working language." A key outcome of the Dominican Republic's participation in UNESCO during this period was that Manuel de Jesús Galván's *Enriquillo* was the first book to be selected by the organization as part of its project of translating and publishing "a selection of classical and contemporary works from the literature of Latin America."[103] *Enriquillo* was published as *The Cross and the Sword* in 1954.

Although few Dominicans were allowed to leave the Dominican Republic during the Trujillato, *The Cross and the Sword/Enriquillo* traveled as an exemplar of the state and the nation it represented. Dominicans were represented via Enriquillo's story, and in the absence of a large body of actual Dominican travelers or community, foreign readers could imagine Dominicans as Enriquilloesque—that is, as modern-day Indians. Better still, foreigners could visit the country, tour the national monument, and attend Trujillo's showcase Fair of Peace and Brotherhood at which only those Dominicans thought to embody Indo-Hispanic Dominicanidad were employed and admitted.[104]

These disparate efforts at protecting and showcasing the national patrimony coalesced in 1969, when Balaguer decreed the formation of the Office of the National Patrimony (ONP), which would oversee national monuments, arts, archives, and folklore.[105] The ONP reported directly to the president from 1971 onward; that year, the Dominican Commission to UNESCO was reorganized, as well. Finally, in 1972, Law No. 318 decreed the establishment of the Museo del Hombre Dominicano, which would become the new home of the National Museum's holdings and would be situated in the Plaza de la Cultura. The Plaza de la Cultura includes the National Library, the Museo del Hombre Dominicano, the Museo de Historia y Geografía, the Museo de Historia Natural, and the Museo de Arte Moderno. The plaza was built in an effort to centralize the collection and display of materials related to the national patrimony for the benefit of educating the national public and of serving the burgeoning tourist industry.[106]

The Museo del Hombre Dominicano

The relationship between the Museo and the Dominican state has been somewhat embattled when its vision and the current presidential administrations clash. Both Vega and Pagán Perdomo have alluded to the direct and indirect government constraints on the Museo's exhibition policy and research, programming, and education efforts, particularly during the Balaguer years. In 1978, Balaguer lost internationally monitored elections to Antonio Guzmán of the PRD. Guzmán was much more supportive of—or, at least, did not impede—research into the African roots of the nation. It was during Guzmán's tenure as president of the republic and Vega's tenure as director of the Museo that anthropological and ethnographic research on and exhibits of African heritage were undertaken, and several research monographs on the country's black heritage were published. As Pagán Perdomo emphasized subsequently, "It was the era in which the most serious research projects were undertaken."[107] Upon Balaguer's return to power in 1986, however, research into the country's black heritage was again stymied. What had been accomplished, however, was not undone. Vega put it simply: "It wasn't expanded, but it wasn't reversed."[108]

Currently, indirect impediments to expanding the Museo's African heritage and history research agenda generally consist of poor and insufficient funding for salaries, research, and publications by the legislature in its general national budget appropriations to the Museo. Harold Olsen Bogaert, Fanny García, and Mayra de Jesús have argued that "whether or not the approved budget is executed depends on various factors: the Government's availability of funds at any given moment, the redirection of those resources to other areas, political or personal motivations to approve, withhold or reject a given request based on the Approved Budget, etc."[109] In recent years, as much as 56.5 percent of the Museo's approved budget has not been rendered to it.[110] Thus, even when there has been an institutional interest in or willingness to expand the standing exhibit, the funds for doing so have not materialized.

The Museo del Hombre Dominicano is an archeological and ethnological museum located in the Plaza de la Cultura in the capital city of the Dominican Republic, Santo Domingo. Inaugurated on October 12, 1973, the anniversary of the "discovery of America,"[111] and opened in 1974, the Museo was mandated to collect and exhibit Taíno artifacts. The Museo del Hombre Dominicano's permanent exhibit was developed over a decade of negotiations and transitions from Balaguer-era administrators, PRD-era administrators, and New Wave scholars. In 1984, the Museo expanded its mandate to include more expansive anthropological projects. According to Bernardo Vega, the Museo's director during the early 1980s, "Its basic function is actually the study of the Dominican man, past and present, from an anthropological perspective. With that study, which considers both sexes, the Museo del Hombre Dominicano has been converted into the Museum of Dominicanness. What is sought is an exhaustive understanding of the Dominican people's culture and its museographic representation."[112]

The Museo del Hombre's *Catálogo General* states unequivocally, "Spanish influences predominate in Dominican culture."[113] At the same time, the Museo is dedicated almost entirely to the collection, preservation, and display of pre-Columbian artifacts. Currently, it houses the largest collection of pre-Columbian artifacts in the world and receives over 30,000 visitors per year.[114] It is by far the most visited of the country's museums, and among tourist sites it is surpassed only by Diego Columbus's fortress (the Alcazar de Colón) in Santo Domingo, the cathedral, and the infamous Columbian Lighthouse.[115] Catering primarily to students and the Dominican general public, who make up 94 percent of its visitors, the Museo receives twice as many visitors as the National

6. Entrance, Museo del Hombre Dominicano

History Museum and one-third more visitors than the Museum of History and Geography, which is located right next door.[116] In short, it is a prominent Dominican cultural institution.

At the entrance of the Museo stand three imposing, larger-than-life-size statues of Fray Bartolomeo de las Casas, Enriquillo, and Lemba (figure 6). When the Museo first opened, the Enriquillo statue was situated inside the main lobby and was said to symbolize the fact that the Dominican people had a long history of constant struggle and rebellion against oppression.[117] Later, the other two statues were added. Together, these three figures are said to represent the ethno-racial trilogy that forms Dominican identity. They were chosen as archetypal of the three ethnic antecedents of Dominicanness because they each lived during the first sixty years of the colonial system and played important roles therein. According to the Museo's administration, their commonality lies also in their

> search for a common goal: the liberty of man, the right of every human being — notwithstanding his social status or the color of his skin — to be free and to express his ideas freely. The three battled, pacifically or violently, against the oppression that subjects man. Taíno, Spanish and African in origin, each one of them appear historically committed to one goal: the de-

fense of human dignity, in his reason and his free conduct, in short, they fought for what we know today as human rights.[118]

Las Casas, also known as "The Protector of the Indians," was a Spanish friar based in Spanish Santo Domingo during the early colonial period. He launched the now famous debates over the enslavement of indigenous peoples in the Americas from Santo Domingo, a battle that he ultimately won, if only morally. His early concern was not with slavery as such— indeed, Las Casas owned indigenous slaves himself until 1544[119]—but with the enslavement of American natives, whom he came to perceive as endowed with souls and therefore as humans who should not be enslaved. As an alternative to natives, he suggested the importation of enslaved Africans into Santo Domingo and other Spanish colonies, a suggestion he subsequently regretted and recanted. By then, of course, the trans-Atlantic slave trade had already been set in motion.[120]

As was noted in chapter 1, Enriquillo was a Taíno *cacique*, or chief, and convert to Christianity in the early sixteenth century. He collaborated with *encomenderos* (or beneficiaries of land grants and slaves titles from the crown) and slaveholders in tracking and returning *cimarrones*, both Taíno and African. When in 1619 his wife Mencia was assaulted by a Spanish colonist who was not duly punished by local colonial authorities, however, Enriquillo became disillusioned with Spanish authority and began to wage war on his former patrons together with the same cimarrones he had formerly hunted. Although he waged war on the Spanish for over a decade, ultimately Enriquillo made peace, though he refused to live among them and lived the remainder of his days in the Baoruco mountain region as the leader of a free indigenous community.[121]

Sebastián Lemba was a sixteenth-century maroon of Cameroonian origins who waged continuous war for nearly two decades on Spanish encomenderos. He commanded a standing army of four hundred rebels at any given time. He was, according to Jane Landers, "one of the most feared of the maroon leaders of the 1540s."[122] The details of Lemba's demise are uncertain—either he died in the *palenque* (cimarrón settlement) named for him and his head was hung in the capital, or he was taken prisoner and executed there. In any event, Governor López Serrata recorded his death with great relief in 1547. Unlike Enriquillo's, Lemba's story has been neither mythologized nor nationalized in any extensive manner. Indeed, his statue was not added to the Museo's frontispiece until 1980, nearly a decade after the Museo opened, and then only because the political climate—a brief, post-Balaguer economic and political

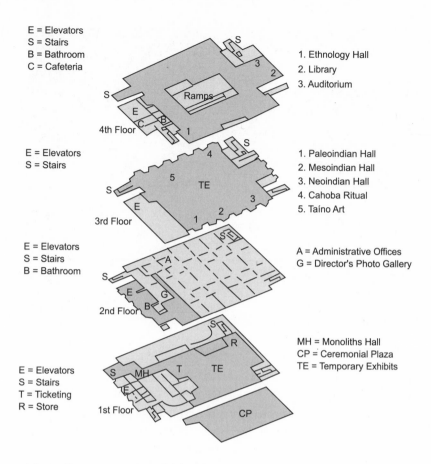

E = Elevators
S = Stairs
B = Bathroom
C = Cafeteria

1. Ethnology Hall
2. Library
3. Auditorium

S
3
2
Ramps
E
C B
4th Floor 1

E = Elevators
S = Stairs

1. Paleoindian Hall
2. Mesoindian Hall
3. Neoindian Hall
4. Cahoba Ritual
5. Taíno Art

S
4
5
TE
E
3
3rd Floor 1 2

E = Elevators
S = Stairs
B = Bathroom

A = Administrative Offices
G = Director's Photo Gallery

S
A
S
E G
B
2nd Floor

E = Elevators
S = Stairs
T = Ticketing
R = Store

MH = Monoliths Hall
CP = Ceremonial Plaza
TE = Temporary Exhibits

S
R
S MH T TE
E
1st Floor
CP

7. Floor plan, Museo del Hombre Dominicano

restructuring moment that coincided with the New Wave's increasingly visible activism—allowed for a revisiting of official Dominican historiography.

Naturally Male and Indo-Hispanic: Displaying Dominicanidad through Pre-Columbian Artifacts

The Museo has four levels—a ground-floor lobby level plus three exhibition levels—that are connected by an elevator, a stairwell (generally used by employees), and a series of ramps (figure 7). The visitor is expected to take the elevator from the ground-floor entrance level to the first ex-

8. Central hall, second-floor ramp to exhibition floor

hibit level and then proceed upward via the ramps. Each exhibit level is arranged so that visitors must enter the exhibit and proceed in a counterclockwise direction through the exhibit area until once again at a foyer and at the base of the ramp up to the next level (figure 8). The physical space and the bodily negotiation of that space both imply an upward spiraling, a progression of sorts through the story of Dominican archeological and ethnological history. Because of the content and space allocation, the upward spiral is experienced as progressive and evolutionary.

The entire first exhibition level and large parts of the second exhibition level are dedicated to Taíno archeology, culture, dioramas, and contributions to contemporary Dominican culture. Taíno artifacts are disproportionately present through space and motion, spatially reinforcing the notion that the indigenous heritage makes up the original racial base of the national trilogy. The exhibits are arranged chronologically in a series of exhibition halls, beginning with the Monolithic Room. According to the Museo's *Catálogo*, displayed there are artifacts "whose common denominator is their sculptural engravings. These confer a symbolical, religious, and magical context to the introductory physical space of the Museo." Named for and dedicated to the pioneering archeologist

Dr. Narciso Alberti Bosch (1860–1932), the room and its contexts act as "evidence of the aboriginal culture" of the country.[123] The artifacts, consisting primarily of ceremonial, masculine anthropomorphic figures, are displayed singly and collectively in glass cases.

The second exhibition level, located on the third floor, has four exhibition halls.[124] The first two halls present the predecessors of the Taínos encountered by the Spanish colonizers in 1492. Taínos appear, in both text and artifacts, in Hall Three. Distinguished from both their contemporaries and their predecessors by their "important artistic abilities," Taínos are presented as conquering, absorbing, and improving on the Mesoindians who lived on the island on their arrival. Their rituals are more elaborate, their material culture is more artistic, and their economies and political systems are more developed. They are, in other words, emblematic of progress. They become historical rather than natural actors. With natural and human-made artifacts as a background, we are introduced to Taínos in the Taíno Peoples Hall.

A curious combination of archaeological artifacts, dioramas, and photography makes up the representation of Taíno life and culture on "Quisqueya."[125] The artifacts predominate, both in quantity and spatially. However, the use of dioramas and photography in the Taíno Hall is fairly extensive. According to the catalogue, the dioramas depict "scenes from the daily life of Antillean aborigines of the neo-Indian or agricultural period." These scenes were developed using descriptions provided by Spanish chroniclers along with data collected by contemporary ethnologists. As the Museo's inaugural exhibit catalogue puts it, "They are a cultural synthesis of more than five hundred years of study."[126] As a companion to the dioramas, nearby cases display Taíno artifacts of daily life depicted in the dioramas alongside items currently utilized by Amazonian and Orinoco River Indians in contemporary Venezuela. This placement connects a Taíno Dominican past with an indigenous South American present. Of additional note is the use of unlabeled photographs of contemporary indigenous people from South America to represent "Quisqueyan" Taínos who have long been gone from the island.

According to the Museo's inaugural exhibit catalogue, these photographs are "dramatic and authentic representations of the daily lives" of "members of the Arawak people who populated the Antilles" (figure 9). Use of the photographs is explained in the catalogue as illustrative of the continuity between the Spanish chroniclers' descriptions of Taíno communities and peoples in the Antilles and current Arawak peoples in "the jungle zones of Venezuela, Brazil, and Colombia."[127] No similar ex-

9. "Indigenous Peoples of Orinoco River region of Venezuela," Museo del Hombre Dominicano

planation is offered in the exhibit itself. The photographs are unlabeled. Given that the catalogue is not available for purchase, and exhibit-goers are routinely left to their own interpretive devices, the contemporaneous nature of photographic technology buttresses the contention that contemporary Dominicans are the descendants of and kin to the people depicted in those images.

In other Latin American nations, indigenous communities exist in the here and now, and American Indians are physically present, confronting and challenging indigenist myths.[128] In the Dominican Republic, the "Indians" exist only in one-dimensional photographs and three-dimensional glass-cased dioramas and cannot challenge the indigenist identity myth making of Dominicans. Also, the photographs solve a practical museological problem: how to display a heterogeneous and nearly extinct people as a homogenous and living community. The Museo del Hombre Dominicano thus reifies the mythical Dominican *Indio* through its exhibitionary techniques.

Archeology, the Museo's principal methodology, could just as easily be used to unearth materials and data concerning African life on Hispaniola. For example, in her study of La Isabela, the first Spanish colonial settlement in the Americas located in the Dominican Republic's north coast, the U.S. archeologist Kathleen Deagan has documented the existence of artifacts from the daily life on colonial Hispaniola. Deagan worked the La Isabela site with the Venezuelan archeologist José Cruxent in collaboration with the Museo del Hombre Dominicano and the Dominican government. They spent three years at La Isabela, securing the site, documenting it, and collecting and preserving artifacts.[129] Employing a gendered analysis, Deagan has focused her research on the tools of domestic life. Insights into the daily lives of and relations between Spanish, indigenous, and African peoples, for example, come "from one of the most humble categories of material culture, the cooking pots and food in colonial kitchens."[130]

Deagan elaborates:

> In general, both traditionally "male" categories and socially visible categories of the material world remained Spanish or European in form from the fifteenth through the eighteenth centuries. This situation is especially evident in the areas of spatial patterning, architecture, and the built environment. . . . One of the most profound of the post-Isabela changes in the Spanish Caribbean colonies, however, was also one of the least visible historically. This was the adoption and incorporation of American [Indian] traits and technologies in domestic spheres of activity. . . . [B]y the sixteenth century, archeological evidence has demonstrated both the regular and systematic incorporation of African and Indian elements in Spanish colonial domestic life and a clear divergence from household material patterns of Spain.[131]

Looking at cookware and foodstuffs, in other words, provides clues about how the division of labor was both gendered and racialized. More important, it indicates three-way cultural contact, influence, and adaptation in a realm that is often symbolic of cultural group identity—foodways. Spanish women were enlisted by the Spanish crown to help domesticate, as it were, the new colonies. Part of that domestication involved the importation of foodstuffs unavailable in the "new world," even if at great physical and monetary cost.[132] That Eurocentric domestication, however, could not be sustained. Instead, the foodways and domestic practices of Taínas and the various African ethnic groups present on the island eventually held sway.[133]

Yet indigenous and African women's central role in those processes of adaptation and survival are not evident in the Museo's display. The first introduction to women is in diorama exhibits of Taíno life. These dioramas create a visual economy of gendered indigenism. Taíno men are depicted as hunters, often standing and wielding bows and arrows, while the Taínas are shown squatting below and behind the men, cooking and serving. Each fulfills a traditionally gendered role. Taína bodies are always presented nude or semi-nude, and their positioning emphasizes their reproductive functions.[134]

The use of dioramas alongside artifacts is exemplary of what Barbara Kirshenblatt-Gimblett has termed in situ display. "In-situ approaches to installation enlarge the ethnographic object by expanding its boundaries to include more of what was left behind, even if only in replica, after the object was excised from its physical, social, and cultural settings." The Museo's displays of Taíno artifacts are in situ because they are arranged in period rooms, re-create dioramic villages, depict Taíno rituals, and utilize photo murals.[135] Considered in the context of larger Dominican political, sociological, and economic history, each of these displays reinforces indigenist identity imaginaries.

At the Museo, interestingly, the Spanish heritage is less dominant in terms of space allocation, taking up only one-third of the fourth-floor space, with an emphasis on "the discovery," conquest, and the colonial period. At the entrance to the exhibit, a life-size bronze sculpture by Aberlardo Rodríguez Urdañeta of the cacique Caonabo in shackles foregrounds a panel depicting the arrival of the Spanish. The *Catálogo General* informs readers that "the word GENOCIDE has been greatly utilized in reference to the conquest of our island," but argues what while it is "undeniable that there were excesses on the part of the conquistadors," a great deal has been "exaggerated." Maps of the Caribbean are displayed alongside demographic information on the indigenous population. Their conquest, we are informed, was motivated by the desire to "convert the Indians to Catholicism, to take gold and plants to Spain, and to control the new territories politically." These agendas are symbolized by the display of swords, epaulets and spurs, church bells, and a cross. Government institutions, the encomienda socioeconomic model, religion, and language are presented as the major cultural legacies of conquest and colonization.

Large, colorful panels arranged in a series of aisles contain text historicizing the conquest, the Devastations, the arrival of buccaneers, the French colonization, and subsequent political intrigues between the French and Spanish colonial powers. We are reminded here that the contact between the Spanish and the Taínos affected the culture and lifeways of each, albeit with devastating results for the Taínos. Yet the message is that, although Taíno people may have disappeared, their cultural forms live on in contemporary Dominican culture.

10. "Punishments," Museo del Hombre Dominicano

The "third" heritage, the African, is relegated to the remaining space, also about one-third of the second level.[136] This section was added to the Museo in the early 1980s, after the publication of *Ensayos sobre la cultura dominicana*.[137] This edited volume served as the research basis for both the African-heritage display and the ethnographic displays of contemporary Dominican culture and people on the fourth floor.[138] The focus is a limited account of slavery and, more marginally, African antecedents of contemporary Dominican culture.

The section on slavery covers the "capture" of Africans, their "transportation" to the Americas, and the conditions of slavery in Santo Domingo. This history is presented primarily through ink depictions on large panels. In this panel, the methods used to control and punish enslaved Africans are depicted (figure 10). The accompanying label begins by documenting the use of punishment and torture. In this way, the display attempts to counter the myth of "benevolent" slavery in Santo Domingo. However, it ends by emphasizing the lessened social distance between master and slave early in the colonial period.

For example, several of the images—"A Negro Hung Alive by the Ribs to a Gallows" and "Flagellation of a Female Samboe Slave," among others—used in the section on African slavery in Santo Domingo are drawn from the collection produced by William Blake for John G. Stedman's *Narrative of a Five-Year Expedition, against the Revolted Negroes of Surinam, in Guiana, on the Wild Coast of South America, from the Year 1772 to 1777*, which was published in London in 1796 (figure 12). These

11. Slave shackles,
Museo del Hombre
Dominicano

12. "A Negro Hung
Alive by the Ribs at the
Gallows," Blake

drawings formed part of at least sixteen engraved plates, each of which depicted some scene described in Stedman's travel narrative. The narrative, together with Blake's sympathetic visual renderings, was published in the aftermath of the Haitian Revolution and at the height of the British abolitionist movement; together, narrative and images offered ambivalent but starkly compelling evidence "that the Europeans were 'the greater barbarians.'"[139] According to Mary Louise Pratt, read "in the context of the Santo Domingo slave revolt," Stedman's narrative was part of a larger late-eighteenth-century crisis of colonial legitimization spurred by Latin American and Caribbean independence movements and abolitionism.[140] Their use in the Museo del Hombre Dominicano's display similarly conveys the barbarity of slavery and the "dignity" of the subjugated. In this way, they act as visual metaphors for nationalist imaginaries. This is classic auto-ethnography: It appropriates the language of the center for its own hegemonic purposes.

However, because the Museo's display of slavery is primarily narrative and visually represented through pen-and-ink drawings drawn from nineteenth-century travel narratives, it is not shocking and is, indeed, much less visceral than the Taíno displays. The only artifacts of slavery are a pair of manacles displayed in a glass case (figure 11) and an actual *trapiche*, or sugar press used on cane plantations. This display makes it easy to imagine that slavery in colonial Santo Domingo was not quite the foundational and brutal institution it was.

Similarly, while marooning—or the rebellion and independent community formation of previously enslaved Africans from both the French and the Spanish colonies—is depicted in several pen-and-ink drawings, the full depth and breadth of this phenomenon are underexplored. Maroon communities, archeological and historical researchers have found, developed richly diverse material cultures, and they were able to organize militarily in self-defense across ethnic and linguistic differences. "By 1545 it was estimated that some seven thousand runaway slaves were living in such communities."[141] Landers informs us that

surface collection and shallow excavations of an early eighteenth-century maroon settlement in eastern Hispaniola, the Maniel José Leta, confirm some of Archbishop Cueva Maldonado's observations in the Bahoruco mountain settlements. The José Leta site yielded seventeen copper bracelets, metal arrow tips, and a variety of iron objects, including tongs and a lance point. Iron slag deposits are evidence that the runaway [black] smiths were manufacturing the objects on site. The simple bracelets of coiled metal may have only been body decoration but perhaps, as in Kongo, they also implied status or leadership functions for those who wore them. In nearby caves explorers have also found metal daggers, clay water jugs, and triton shell trumpets which they identify as the work of African runaways. . . . The Dominican archeologist Manuel García Arévalo has assembled an important collection of pots made by African runaways and retrieved from water-filled caves near the Santo Domingo airport.[142]

García Arévalo is one of the few Dominican archeologists who has worked on the island's African heritage. He notes in his report on his archeological findings on the Maniel José Leta that, although the location of cimarrón communites (palenques and maniels) necessarily are difficult to access even today, the principal barrier to their exploration has been lack of interest.[143] Given this seeming wealth of archeological materials related to the country's African heritage and history, it is all the more surprising that the Museo currently only has four artifacts related to slavery.[144] Why, one wonders, are those types of artifacts not pursued and displayed? When asked this question, the former Museo director Pagán Perdomo referred several times to the lack of sufficient resources for a proper and full-scale research project and to the reliance on foreign and private funds for such research. Yet funds are available for indigenous archeology and research.[145]

Likewise, the cultural and biological mixture that occurred between the Spanish, the indigenous peoples, and Africans is emphasized in several panels and labels throughout this area. I do not wish to argue that cultural and physical contact and mixture should be excluded from the exhibit. However, in the larger ideological context that minimizes or denies black heritage, repeatedly emphasizing cultural mixture reinscribes the racial-democracy thesis and the Tannenbaum thesis—which held that slavery was more a benevolent institution in Spanish America than in North America[146]—implicitly, if not explicitly, in the public display of Dominican identity.

When asked for his impression of the Tannenbaum thesis's validity, Pagán Perdomo similarly engaged in both refutation and affirmation:

That's a thesis that has argued that slavery here was softer. That means less torture, fewer punishments because the system, the slave system, is one of humanity's undeniable disgraces, in the history of humanity there isn't any other period as repugnant as slavery. I'll confess that there are books on slavery which are jewels such as Moreno Fraginals's on Cuba, which my students at the university, when I asked them to summarize some of them, used to confess that they couldn't complete the assignment because they would be disgusted by what they read about slavery in Cuba, Puerto Rico, Jamaica, in all the Lesser Antilles, and the things that were done to slaves and their children—horrors that made their hair stand on end and are disgusting and give umbrage. Especially in those places where they don't have the black in the skin; they have it behind the ears, as we say.[147]

Although slavery as an institution is "repugnant" and disgraceful in general, it is slavery in Cuba, Puerto Rico, and Jamaica that makes Dominican students' "hair stand on end" rather than slavery in their own country's history. This sense of "umbrage" is especially strong in the Dominican Republic precisely because blackness resides "behind the ears." Thus, the history of slavery is all the more shocking, all the more disruptive. Slavery and blackness, in other words, are not part of the Dominican student's historic past; they are only a part of others' pasts.

In the absence of factual narratives of racialized systems of marginalization, it becomes easy once again to overlook the continued disadvantages faced by the Domincan Republic's darkest citizens. As the archeologist Jalil Sued-Badillo has observed, much Caribbean archeology focused on the "pre-history" of the region, defined as the pre-Columbian era to the disadvantage of the colonial and national periods. As a result, Caribbean archeology remains, "by and large, a distant hacienda, monotonously repeating itself. There are obvious reasons for this, because in that pre-colonial past the Caribbean people expect to encounter the confirmations of their social worth and the confidence to persevere as nations in the future."[148]

Likewise, though excluded or marginalized elsewhere in the Museo's displays, women's bodies are in the narrative and portrayal of Dominican *mestizaje* and social reproduction. Cultural maintenance, transformation, and transmission are encoded visually as women's work. All of the images emphasizing the survival of African cultural forms and practices—be it hair care, basket weaving, modes of carrying babies or bundles, worship, music, and dance—are depicted as women's practices. The reproduction of the Creole, likewise, is an implicitly feminine function. An ink drawing of a slave cabin and its primarily female inhabitants is made symbolic of the process of "transculturation" by the accompanying label and by the copious presence of infants. Again, although the ostensible emphasis is on "hybridity" and retention of Africanisms, the final word is had by the "dominant group"—that is, the Hispanics. In

13. Pen-and-ink drawings from Hazard used in Museo del Hombre Dominicano exhibit panels

fact, the Spanish were militarily and politically dominant. However, read against the context of the Hispanophilia that defines the Dominican educational system and official identity narratives, dominance comes to be understood as superiority.

A final interesting note about this part of the exhibit is the use of pen-and-ink drawings from some of the very same U.S. travel writings discussed earlier. In particular, Hazard's *Santo Domingo, Past and Present* is heavily used as a primary visual source. Several of the ink drawings—"Dominican American," "Old Negro," "Uncles and Mammies," "Water-carrier," "A 'Guajiro,'" and "Market Square"—are reproduced in the panels (figure 13). They illustrate nineteenth-century life and modes of dress, but their provenance is left unmentioned. Interestingly, the Dominican translations of Hazard's text altered some of the U.S.-derived racial language used in the original, so that, for example, "Uncles and Mammies" become "Ancianos," or "the elderly."

The final area of the exhibit contains a typical Dominican wood cabin, complete with rough-hewn furnishings and a set of light-skinned and straight-haired mannequins representing a peasant family. The kitchen and the family altar are highlighted in the display, and visitors are informed that this continues to be a typical Dominican home. However, this area also displays the carnival masks made and worn during the Easter season. Like carnival masks elsewhere in the Caribbean, they signify the black heritage of their makers and wearers. The final note of the exhibit, in other words, resonates with ambiguity.

Conclusion

As the integration of travel narratives and their images into Dominican elite discourses and state-sanctioned identity displays illustrates, Dominican identity formations have developed historically against the backdrop of Spanish and French colonialism, Haitian Unification, and U.S. imperialism. Rather than simply being impositions of foreign racial ideologies, those accounts supported the emerging state's and the elite's project of separating from Haiti and establishing clear national boundaries between it and the Dominican Republic. A key aspect of that distancing and boundary-maintenance project has been the development and institutionalization of indigenist ideologies and discourses.

Ironically, indigenist ideologies served both Dominican nationalist and U.S. imperialist interests simultaneously. Indigenist identity claims legitimized Dominican independence from Haiti and Spain alike, because both were framed as inherently foreign to the Dominican Republic and its people. At the same time, indigenist ideologies played a role in U.S. imperialism in the Caribbean, whether political, military, or cultural. Framing themselves as legitimate inheritors of the North American continent from both their British forefathers and the Native Americans, the Americans supported Latin American indigenist nationalisms that helped to expel Spain from the hemisphere and to open those new territories to the United States. Thus, the discursive work of U.S. travel writers, naturalists, archeologists, anthropologists, and ethnologists worked toward cultural conscription of Dominicans to U.S. political projects in the region and vice versa. And, of course, the United States' political projects in turn opened the region to U.S. cultural workers. Moreover, for those with annexationist and imperialist interests, Caribbean indigenism in particular allowed for both the rejection of Spanish authority and the elision of the region's predominant African heritage, which was considered by many in the North to be a major obstacle to annexation or incorporation of those territories.

Attempts at the historicization and display of the history and heritage of the country's African diaspora have been made, mostly beginning in the 1960s, as part of the New Wave movement. The New Wave is largely responsible for the slowly institutionalized challenges to indigenism, such as the introduction of the *Presencia Africana en Santo Domingo* (The African Presence in Santo Domingo) into the Museo del Hombre Dominicano's permanent exhibit in 1980. Most recently, the Museo's current director, the anthropologist Carlos Hernández Soto, has also brought several major exhibits and programs on Haiti, Dominican Vodun, and Africa to the Museo. Hernández Soto, who has published extensively on the country's African heritage and diasporic cultures, deliberately had the summer 2007 exhibit of West African fertility statues, *Mama Africa*, installed prominently in the third-floor central exhibit hall (figure 8) in order to signal the Museo's emerging commitment to exploring and exhibiting the country's black heritage.[149] However, the exhibit's symbolic meta-narrative continues to insist that the country has "three roots," of which the indigenous is artifactually dominant, the Hispanic is symbolically foundational, and "the African" is folklorized and symbolically equated with rurality and backwardness.

Thus, the exhibit forms part of a larger discursively mediated racial project that elides blackness into indigeneity and subsumes women to "Man" even as it rhetorically affirms a cultural nationalism that supposedly incorporates all Dominicans. In the exhibit's ideological code, the subordination of women, blacks, and Haitians appears as a natural feature of the republic's evolution from pre-Columbian society to modern society. A Dominican who claims, rejects, or is ambiguous about a black identity, then, references and contends with multiple histories, codes, and states. The next chapter considers what happens when Dominicans are re-socialized in the ideological codes of a predominantly black-identified community in another capital city, Washington, D.C., and how they are represented by its leading museum, the Anacostia Museum of the Smithsonian Institution.

CHAPTER 3.

"I Could Go the African American Route"

DOMINICANS IN THE BLACK MOSAIC
OF WASHINGTON, D.C.

> The fear is that anyone who voluntarily agrees to be black is in some sense not really black, because our culture has defined blackness as something that you can never escape.
> —Gerald Torres[1]

> To claim to be a Hispanic is to make some claim about the ways in which one's specific Latin American ethnic heritage is made concrete within the general culture of the United States. . . . The fact that Hispanics can be of any "race" suggests that what you think and even who you think you are is determined by more than who you look like.—Gerald Torres[2]

I have argued thus far that Dominican identity formation in the Dominican Republic must be situated within the historical triangulation of relations between Haiti, the Dominican Republic, and the United States. As my examination of travel narratives illustrates, those triangulated relations generated a set of national discourses and ideological codes that were institutionalized through the national historiography and public-culture venues such as the Museo del Hombre Dominicano. Both vehicles encouraged the internalization of anti-Haitianist and Indo-Hispanic identity discourses through their narrative and exhibitionary echniques. In this chapter, I argue that, despite the hegemony of Indo-Hispanic ideology in the Dominican Republic, the experience of Dominican immigrants in Washington, D.C., belies the notion of a universally internalized Negrophobic and indigenist Dominican identity. The evidence lies in the life histories of black-identified Dominican immigrants to Washington, D.C., and their representation in an African American public-history museum.

I will explain why, instead of conforming to national identity discourses, Dominican immigrants to Washington, D.C., are more likely to identify as black than Dominicans anywhere else in the United States. I argue that this is so for a variety of reasons, including their regional origins in the Dominican Republic; the epoch of their migration; their age and generation; their residential and occupational patterns in Washington; and the nature of their social contact with other Latin Americans and with African Americans. They exemplify, therefore, the fact that identity is *social* rather than essential and dynamic rather than reified. Thus, in the context of a stratified, predominantly black-identified community in Washington, D.C., where black self-identification has been imposed by the local racial order, on the one hand, and has become a means of access to economic, social, cultural, and political capital, on the other hand, Dominicans have multiple incentives to identify racially as black.

Nonetheless, they continue also to identify ethnically as Dominican and as "Latin." Although they are demographically a national-origin minority among the new Latino immigrant community, which is now predominantly of Central American origins, they were also among the founding members—or, as they put it, the "old guard"—of the capital's early Latin American community. Because of this, they share similarities and differences in identity with other Latinos and African Americans alike. At the same time, African Americans in Washington, D.C., grapple with Dominicans' ethno-racial distinctiveness. This becomes evident when one examines Dominicans' participation in *Black Mosaic: Community, Race, and Ethnicity among Black Immigrants in Washington, D.C.*, an African American public-history project undertaken by the Anacostia Museum of the Smithsonian Institution.

"How Do You Connect Different Notions of Race?" The Anacostia Museum's Challenge

The Anacostia Neighborhood Museum opened in 1967, five years before the Museo del Hombre Dominicano and at the height of the Civil Rights Movement and the Black Power Movement. Washington, D.C., was a central axis of the Civil Rights Movement's agenda and actions. Faith Davis Ruffins, an African American curator at the Smithsonian Institution's National Museum of American History, describes the historic moment this way:

> Between 1963 and 1972 hundreds of thousands of Americans came to Washington to protest government policies or to lobby for various political goals, including civil rights and an end to the Vietnam War. In 1968, the Poor People's Campaign brought many tens of thousands of black and activist people to the Mall. Erecting masses of tents—nicknamed Resurrection City—between the Capital and the White House, in the shadow of five governmental museums, these people almost certainly included many who had never visited the Smithsonian. But the simple presence of masses of black people created pressure on the institution.[3]

The struggle for African American self-representation in public-history and public-culture venues dated back to at least the Philadelphia Centennial Exhibition of 1876. Most World's Fairs in the United States excluded African Americans from development, planning, construction, and curation and included them only as objects of spectacle and as consumers on special "Negro days." It was not until the Atlanta Cotton States and International Exposition of 1895 that "Negro" sections and buildings were allowed.[4]

Tellingly, it was at that exposition that the prominent African American educator and principal of the Tuskegee Institute, Booker T. Washington, made his infamous "Atlanta Compromise" speech. Washington reassured whites that African Americans would accept segregation as long as they were supported in their pursuit of the "education of head, hand, and heart." As he put it in one of the speech's most quoted lines, "In all things that are purely social we can be as separate as the fingers, yet one as the hand in all things essential to mutual progress."[5] Washington's speech and the social vision it proffered may have been reassuring to segregationist whites of the Jim Crow era, but it engendered a maelstrom of debate within the African American community. Among the key issues was whether segregation or integration would best serve African Americans' social, political, and economic interests, given that segregation was a system that relied on both physical and symbolic violence against African Americans.

David Roediger, David Nasaw, and Eric Lott have each argued convincingly that throughout the nineteenth century, U.S. public culture had long cast African Americans as the racialized foil against which the ideology of white supremacy was formed and white privilege was institutionalized.[6] As they had done in other segregated social and economic arenas, African Americans developed their own cultural institutions to service their community's needs and to counter the ideology of white supremacy and "Negro" inferiority. Thus, the expansion and institutionalization of black churches; schools; media, including film and radio; black letters; black theater; black visual arts; even black beauty culture in the first quarter of the twentieth century was an unintended consequence of Jim Crow segregation.[7] Likewise, black museums began to be founded in the United States in the nineteenth century.[8]

But it was the last three decades of the twentieth century that witnessed the proliferation of museums dedicated to presenting African American experiences from the community's vantage point. "The courses, classes, lectures, exhibitions, concerts, archives, and libraries of these 'democratized' cultural institutions provided neighborhoods and families with opportunities for achievement and accomplishment."[9] The Anacostia Neighborhood Museum's founder, John Kinard, a former minister and Washington native, actively integrated local residents into the museum's workforce, volunteer staff, and Neighborhood Advisory Committee. In turn, those residents became the Anacostia's leading constituents. For Anacostia staff, the museum "became a way of doing things, an approach to the work of the museum and a key to its self-perceived identity as a community-based institution."[10]

Like the Museo del Hombre Dominicano, the Anacostia Museum of the Smithsonian Institution is a state-funded institution. However, unlike the Museo, it is a community-based museum with a founding mandate to serve and reflect the community in which it is located. Originally intended by the Smithsonian's Chairman S. Dillon Ripley as a vehicle for bringing the Smithsonian to the people, the Anacostia community transformed the museum quickly into a way of putting themselves into the Smithsonian.[11] Anacostia is a poor and working-class African American neighborhood located across the Potomac River and about fifteen minutes' driving distance from the Smithsonian Institution's mall in downtown Washington, D.C.; thus, the Anacostia Museum is a far-flung Smithsonian outpost.[12]

The Anacostia Museum was founded and operated in the spirit of community self-representation for nearly two decades. The increasing professionalization of the Anacostia over the 1970s, however, eventually created barriers to the kind of daily and full community participation that had characterized its first five years. "By the mid-1980s, museum–community interaction was largely confined to the education department's programs and the director's individual activities."[13] According to Portia James, the exhibition's originator and curator, *Black Mosaic* represented a modified return to the Anacostia's original methodology and orientation because of its extensive community involvement. However, that return was conditioned by new internal and external political circumstances.

The most salient internal change was the death of the Anacostia's founding director, Kinard.[14] In his absence, Anacostia staff was forced to reconsider its mandate and constituency. "From the museum's inception, there had been questions about which groups were being included in the museum's community. *Black Mosaic* further underscored such questions. Although encountered every day, black immigrants form an invisible community existing within the very core of Washington's African American community life and social history and yet still exist on the margins of the city's public history."[15]

Internal discussions about how to integrate that "invisible community" into Anacostia exhibits began in 1990 in the context of larger Smithsonian plans to mark the Columbian Quincentennial. In 1991, the Mount Pleasant riots highlighted festering tensions between the African American and Latino communities. In May 1994, three months before the opening of *Black Mosaic*, the Smithsonian Institution Task Force on Latino Issues published *Willful Neglect: The Smithsonian Institution and U.S. Latinos*, an indictment of the nearly total exclusion of Latinos from Smithsonian staff, curators, exhibits, and collections. The task force wrote:

> The findings of the Task Force are extremely clear: The Smithsonian Institution almost entirely excludes and ignores the Latino population of the United States. This lack of inclusion is glaringly obvious in the lack of a single museum facility focusing on Latino or Latin American art, culture, or history; the near-absence of permanent Latino exhibitions or programming; the very small number of Latino staff, and the minimal number in curatorial or managerial positions; and the almost total lack of Latino rep-

resentation in the governance structure. It is difficult for the Task Force to understand how such a consistent pattern of Latino exclusion from the work of the Smithsonian could have occurred without willful neglect.[16]

Willful Neglect argued that exclusion was unconscionable because Latinos, with "their indigenous roots and their Spanish heritage," predated British colonization in the Americas. This formulation, while partially accurate, perpetuated a mestizo notion of Hispanicity—one that glaringly excluded the fact of African heritage both within Spanish heritage and within Latin American heritages. Both Africans and Asians are mentioned later in the report as part of the mestizo "roots of the Americas" when the methodological and empirical lessons of the Quincentenary Commemoration for Latino initiatives are presented.

The Quincentenary Commemoration itself offered two critical lessons for future Latino initiatives: the model it generated of a true consultative process, and the message it communicated of mestizaje and multiculturalism. In preparing Quincentenary programs, the secretary demonstrated a model of internal and external cooperation and consultation by opening up the institution to outside experts and community scholars in an unprecedented way. Several key Latinos within the Smithsonian served as catalysts for the Quincentenary programs. This model could become the foundation for a broad-based and inclusive Latino initiative. The Quincentenary programs were also unique in being truly multicultural. Their message of mestizaje reflected the Spanish, African, Asian, and indigenous roots of the Americas.[17]

A second report published by the Latino Oversight Committee in 1997, "Towards a Shared Vision: U.S. Latinos and the Smithsonian Institution," attempted to be more historically accurate. "Because of both their indigenous roots and their Spanish and African heritage," notes the report early on, "Latinos predate the British in the Americas."[18] Taken together with the repeated use of the word "mosaic" in this report, one could easily conclude from this revised definition that the Anacostia and *Black Mosaic* had been influential in the Smithsonian's approach to Latino histories. At the same time, the Anacostia was still the only Smithsonian museum with a Latino board member.[19]

In addition, Anacostia curatorial staff was influenced by the national discussions about immigration and the "changing face" of U.S. society, as echoed in a review of *Black Mosaic* by *The Torch, A Monthly Newspaper for the Smithsonian Institution*.[20] According to Steve Newsome, director of the Anacostia, *Black Mosaic* was intended to serve as a connection between the African American community and the Latino community in Washington, D.C.[21] Indeed, Newsome received special acknowledgment from the Latino Task Force, which noted that the Anacostia was "among the museums making a positive effort" to represent Latinos at the Smithsonian.[22] *Black Mosaic* was mentioned several times in *Willful Neglect*, both for its utilization of community scholars and its documentation of "the fact that many African Americans are also Hispanic."[23] Speaking to a *Torch* reporter, Newsome expressed the hope that "the exhibition [would] give us inroads to communities that were totally disenfranchised from the Smithsonian as a whole and from the Anacostia Museum in particular. There was no consistent relationship between the Afro-Latino community and [the Smithsonian Institution]."[24] Nor would there be after *Black Mosaic* came down, for reasons I think are illustrative of the difficulties of attempting to display Dominican identities within the constraints of hegemonic U.S. notions of blackness.

After more than a century of regional and local variability in the application of the one-drop-of-blood rule, by the twentieth century it was accepted that as little as one ancestor out of sixty-four was enough to classify an individual as black in the United States.[25] The Anacostia has helped local educators train African American children to understand and accept the one-drop-of-blood rule. For example, in *How and Why African People Came to North America*, an educational kit developed by the Anacostia's Department of Education in 1979—which is still used, including in the context of tours of *Black Mosaic* for student groups[26]—educators are told:

In working with groups of Black children, we usually begin by asking whether there are any Black people in the room with us. If children recognize themselves as being Black, we go on to talk about a place—as yet unidentified—that is the home of all Black people. If children are confused as to who they are, we point to ourselves and say, "I am Black," and to others, and say, "He is Black, and she is Black." We speak of the commonality of Blackness in terms of our ancestors who came from that special land where most of the Black people in the world lived then and still live now. And we say that because our ancestors—our great-great-great-grandmothers and - grandfathers—were Black, and came from that land of Black people, we, too, are Black, even though some of us may be lighter or darker than others.[27]

As is evident from these instructions, African American children can be "confused as to who they are" because they may not appear black to themselves or to others. Their physiognomy may not match their genealogical status as black in the United States. Thus, when the Anacostia staff undertook to display Afro-Latino history and life in D.C., they were understandably perplexed and in some cases downright annoyed by the seeming unwillingness of Dominicans, Puerto Ricans, Cubans, Costa Ricans, Brazilians, and Haitians of African descent to identify simply or primarily as "black." Internal memos and research notes for the exhibit document the ongoing dialogue among Anacostia staff, and between the staff and participants, over issues of ethno-racial and national identity.[28] Anacostia staff accustomed to the primacy of hypo-descent-based blackness in the United States asked themselves and one another how it could be that nationality could be as salient an identity referent as race. Ruffins likewise has pointed out that "the use of the term *diaspora* to describe the experience of black people in the Americas" by scholars of African American history and culture began in earnest in the early 1970s.[29] The African diaspora in the Americas was first made "manifest" at the Smithsonian at the 1976 Festival of American Folklife's African Diaspora Festival, organized by Bernice Johnson Reagon. "Perhaps for the first time ever in American public history, a black American mythos—the notion of the unity of African peoples across time and space—was presented by a preeminent cultural institution."[30] By the time the Anacostia began its discussions about *Black Mosaic*, in other words, the Smithsonian had had some experience presenting the African diaspora in the Americas.

However, despite the Anacostia staff's attempts to understand and present the complexity of racial identity, the ethno-racial identity of Dominicans in D.C. was flattened by the structure of *Black Mosaic* because of its insistence on blackness as a universal experience that predominates over ethnic or national differences. Anacostia staff struggled with this throughout the development of the script, the recruitment of participants and community scholars, the collection of artifacts, and the preparation of the exhibit itself. In her notes on race for an early script, for example, Sharon Reinckens, project director for *Black Mosaic*, wrote:

> Race is a concept, not a biological given. Changes through time and space.
> . . . Race different in countries of origin; racial terms from different communities. History of nationalities in Cuba, Brazil, Haiti. . . . Race is dynamic elsewhere. Here it is cut and dry. How do you connect [different] notions of race?[31]

This was a key area of difficulty for *Black Mosaic* and, ultimately, its greatest conceptual weakness. In part that paradigmatic difficulty is itself a legacy of the history of the socio-racial terrain of Washington, D.C.

The U.S. capital is simultaneously a provincial Southern city and a cosmopolitan international city, and various ethno-racial systems are mapped on it. These mappings overlay one another at key historic and institutional points and diverge at others. In domestic terms, black–white relations have been the defining paradigm of community formations in the United States. In international terms, U.S.–foreign relations have mapped the borders of communities in Washington, D.C. Dominicans in D.C., therefore, have had to be "world travelers" in the sense developed by María Lugones, who writes: "Those of us who are 'world'-travelers have the distinct experience of being different in different 'worlds' and ourselves in them. . . . The shift from being one person to being a different person is what I call 'travel.'" Those shifts, Lugones notes, may or may not be conscious or willful. And "even though the shift can be done willfully, it is not a matter of acting 'world.'"[32] Rather, in phenomenological terms, it is a matter of "being in the world."[33]

The "World" of Washington, D.C.

Washington, D.C., is a city with a complex racial history. It was founded in 1791, less than a year after the Naturalization Act of 1790 restricted citizenship to white, landowning males. By 1800, enslaved African Americans made up one-quarter of the population. In the pre-Civil War era, the District of Columbia suffered a severe labor shortage and became increasingly attractive to free African Americans seeking employment. By 1860, 84 percent of the nearly 11,000 African Americans in D.C. were freedmen and, "together with their slave brethren, accounted for 17.9 percent of the total D.C. population."[34]

European immigration to D.C. was not substantial during the nineteenth century. "In 1900, a year in which 37 percent of the population of New York (and 35 percent of Boston's population) was foreign-born, the District of Columbia counted only 7 percent of its residents as foreign-born."[35] Consequently, African Americans were able to gain an impressive foothold in skilled fields:

Unlike most urban centers along the Eastern Seaboard, the District of Columbia did not develop an industrial economy. Instead, the aftermath of the Civil War witnessed the rapid expansion of the civilian government work force. . . . The growing demand for blue-collar tradesmen and urban services led to impressive levels of entrepreneurship and relatively high socio-economic status among African Americans in the late nineteenth century.[36]

These accomplishments were offset by the post–Reconstruction-era institutionalization of Jim Crow. Jim Crow policies and practices restricted African Americans' work opportunities to unskilled occupations, forced them out of self-employment, denied them government employment, concentrated them in the inner-city residential districts, limited their access to public services and spaces, and severely restricted their personal and social mobility. "This deteriorating occupational status of African Americans, which pervaded both private and public sectors, became official U.S. government policy following the election of Woodrow Wilson in 1912; it not only reserved most federal jobs for whites but it offered only the most menial jobs to blacks."[37]

The 1920s extended the Wilsonian legacy to a "new nadir" in African American life in D.C. At the 1922 dedication of the Lincoln Memorial, for example, seating was segregated. Consequently, African American dignitaries—including the keynote speaker, Robert R. Morton, principal of the Tuskegee Institute—sat below the speakers' platform, while white dignitaries sat on top. Three years later, some 50,000 Ku Klux Klan members paraded down Pennsylvania Avenue to the Washington Monument in an apparent effort to show their strength in Washington, D.C.[38] Although the federal government's demand for labor expanded exponentially, African Americans were excluded from that job market.

By the 1930s, however, African Americans in D.C. were organized politically to combat Jim Crow and racism generally. The New Negro Alliance, for example, boycotted businesses that would not hire African Americans and protested segregation in public places.[39] "In 1939, the famous black singer Marian Anderson was refused permission by the Daughters of the American Revolution to sing in Constitution Hall."[40] The sponsors of the concert, the Howard University School of Music, arranged to have Anderson perform on the steps of the Lincoln Memorial, which had been offered by Secretary of the Interior Harold Ickes. This shift in the location of African Americans at the memorial from a Jim Crow seating area to the platform mirrored the evolving position of African Americans in D.C.

The exigencies of World War Two created new employment and political opportunities for African Americans in the U.S. government bureaucracy. Segregation in the public school system was declared unconstitutional in 1954, and integration was mandated. However, white families preferred leaving the city to having their children attend integrated schools. "The exodus of whites to the suburbs and continued influx of southern African Americans to Washington, D.C. led to a dramatic shift in the racial composition during the 1950s; by 1960, over one half (53.9 percent) of the District of Columbia is comprised of African Americans."[41] Although they made up a numerical majority in the district's central city, and were becoming increasingly present in the suburbs, black D.C. was heavily segregated and disadvantaged through the 1960s.

The Civil Rights Movement and the Black Power Movement changed that. Although nationally the most remembered event was the 1963 March on Washington for Jobs and Freedom, in which Martin Luther King Jr. delivered his famous "I Have a Dream" speech, a great deal of local, grassroots activism had been taking place in education, health, housing, and public accommodations, as well. Following King's assassination on April 4, 1968, the capital burst into riots, as did many other U.S. cities. Howard University was shut down by teach-ins. Local African American leaders and residents alike banded together and, once again, brought local and national attention to the plight of African Americans in D.C. The election of Walter E. Washington to the mayoral seat in 1967 was the outcome of African American civil- and economic-rights politics in the district.

Latin Americans Meet Jim Crow in the Capital

Although Latin American commercial agents, consuls, foreign ministers, and other government representatives had been present in Washington, D.C., from the birth of their republics in the early nineteenth century, it was not until the turn of the twentieth century that those countries began to establish fully fledged legations and embassies. Thus, Jim Crow was in the flower of its youth, the last of the Indian Wars were being fought,[42] and U.S. interventionism in Latin America was beginning in earnest when the Latin American diplomatic community began to establish itself in Washington, D.C.[43] The Pan American Union, officially established in 1910 and headquartered in Washington, D.C., was the first organized venue of the Latin American diplomatic community as a whole.[44] That community provided the small but evidently sufficient demographic basis for the emergence of a self-aware Latino immigrant community, initially drawn from those who accompanied diplomatic missions as staff, as well as from Puerto Ricans who came to work with the federal government.

In the case of the Dominican Republic, once the U.S. occupation and military government ended in 1924, newly elected President Horacio Vasquez reestablished the Dominican diplomatic corps, which had been defunct since the assassination of President Ramón Cáceres in 1911.[45] It was not until Trujillo's election in 1930, however, that Dominican diplomatic relations expanded and became fully institutionalized.[46] In terms of Dominican–U.S. relations, this meant a substantial growth in the diplomatic corps, concentrated primarily in New York and Washington, D.C.[47] This coincided with the growth of the Latin American diplomatic corps in general, whose numbers had expanded during the Hoover administration and were solidified by Franklin Roosevelt's Good Neighbor policy. By 1940, there were at least 720 "white [individuals] of Spanish mother tongue" residing in Washington, D.C.[48] Since the Latin American diplomatic community relied primarily on the domestic labor of black and indigenous women and men from their countries, we can surmise that there were more than 720 Latin Americans in the capital in 1940. In the 1940s and 1950s, these Latin American service workers lived alongside African Americans south of Columbia Road, the racial dividing line of the Adams Morgan neighborhood, where much of the international community had settled due to its proximity to the embassies being established.[49]

During the Trujillo era, migration out of the Dominican Republic was severely limited and controlled. Other scholars have noted that Trujillo-era migrants were primarily of three types: those who Trujillo felt furthered the interests of the regime, those Trujillo felt would not undermine him, and those who were exiled.[50] Members of these groups were primarily from elite white-identified families in Santo Domingo. Dominican migration scholars have overlooked a small but interesting fourth class of migrants who arrived in the United States during this time: the domestic servants of the first two. Mirroring socio-racial and political conditions in the Dominican Republic at the time, these domestic-labor migrants were women who typically hailed from the traditionally English-speaking African American-descended and West Indian-heritage communities in the Dominican Republic.[51]

Ironically, it was precisely because they were poor, female, and black that members of this group were able to leave Santo Domingo and stay in the United States, even after their employers left the country, as was often the case. Their working-class and peasant cousins, by contrast, had few opportunities to migrate and were subjected to the full force and effect of the Trujillato's ideological and repressive apparatus. Although their diplomatic-corps employers often engaged in a variety of repressive measures to retain control over their staff, including keeping their passports, many managed to remain in the United States nonetheless.

Simultaneously, large Hispanic communities were beginning to form on the U.S. East Coast. In New York City, Philadelphia, and other urban manufacturing centers, poor and working-class Puerto Rican migrants pushed out of Puerto Rico by Operation Bootstrap were arriving and settling in unprecedented numbers, while middle-class Puerto Ricans began entering the U.S. government bureaucracy in Washington, D.C. Elite Cubans continued to travel and study across the country, as they had throughout the nineteenth century.[52] At the same time, carefully controlled images of "Latin Americans," both abroad and in the United States, began to proliferate in film and television, offering viewers in the era of Roosevelt's Good Neighbor policy a companion script with which to understand Latin America and the Latin Americans increasingly present on this side of the border.[53]

By the time *Black Mosaic* was being developed, some 1,779 Dominicans lived in Center City, Washington, D.C.[54] By 2000, the number had increased to 2,904.[55] Center City includes the area of Washington, D.C., where Dominicans tended to settle on their arrival in the capital, particularly the Adams Morgan and Adams Pleasant neighborhoods. Latinos generally made up small percentages of the Center City population, although their presence nearly doubled from 6.82 percent in 1990 to 10.04 percent of the 2000 population. Dominicans composed a small percentage both of Hispanics (5 percent in 1990 and 2000) and a negligible percentage of the city overall (2.1 percent in 1990 and 3.5 percent in 2000).[56] In other words, they are a small group in both absolute and relative terms.

At the same time, Dominicans were more likely than any other Latino group to live among African Americans and other blacks and the group least likely to live among non-Hispanic whites. In 2000, 45.2 percent of the city's population was black and 39.3 percent was white. Although the dissimilarity index between Dominicans and blacks was very high, Dominicans tied with Puerto Ricans for the lowest index of dissimilarity between Latinos and blacks and with Central Americans for the highest index of dissimilarity between Latinos and whites. In other words, Dominicans and Puerto Ricans were the Latinos likeliest to live among blacks, and Dominicans and Central Americans were the Latinos least likely to live among whites. In addition, Dominicans had the highest residential exposure levels to blacks, average exposure levels to other Latinos, and lowest residential exposure levels to whites of any Latino subgroup. In 2000, Dominicans in D.C. tended to live in neighborhoods that were 51 percent black, 20 percent Hispanic, and 24 percent white.[57]

By comparison, Dominicans in New York City were less likely to live near blacks than Puerto Ricans, although they were more likely to live near blacks and Latinos and were the least likely to live near whites than other Latino subgroups. Specifically, Dominicans in New York City live in neighborhoods that are 22 percent black, 12 percent white, and 58 percent Hispanic.[58] Moreover, in New York City, Latinos make up 27 percent of the overall population, while blacks make up 25 percent and whites make up 35 percent.[59] Thus, where D.C. is predominantly divided between blacks and whites, New York City is far more "Latinized," as a recent anthology has put it.[60]

For Dominicans in particular, New York is certainly a much more Dominican city than Washington, D.C. Approximately 20 percent of Dominicans' neighbors in New York City will be other Dominicans, indicating a much more ethnically concentrated settlement pattern than for any other group besides Puerto Ricans, who are only slightly more likely to have co-national neighbors.[61] Indeed, a common refrain among Dominicans is that New York is the Dominican Republic's second-largest city, as it is home to more Dominicans than Santiago de los Caballeros, officially the second city of the country. Washington, D.C., conversely, is popularly known as "Chocolate City" because of its black majority population.

Black Mosaic

> Every museum exhibition, whatever its overt subject, inevitably draws on the cultural assumptions and resources of the people who make it. Decisions are made to emphasize one element and to downplay others, to assert some truths and to ignore others.
> —Steven D. Lavine and Ivan Karp[62]

Black Mosaic was organized in five major thematic areas: Identity, Memories of Home, Migration, Race and Ethnicity in D.C., and Community Life (figure 14). The Anacostia staff used its signature innovative research methods in the development of *Black Mosaic*. Through a

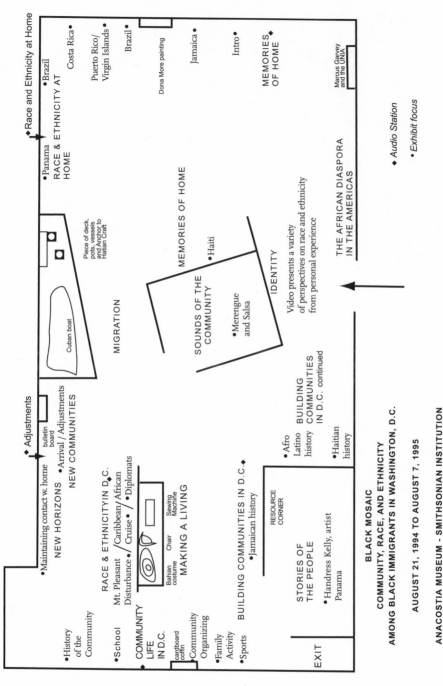

14. Floor plan, *Black Mosaic* exhibition

Race and Ethnicity at Home

RACE & ETHNICITY AT HOME
• Panama
• Brazil
• Costa Rica
Puerto Rico/
Virgin Islands
• Brazil
Dona More painting
• Jamaica
• Intro

MEMORIES OF HOME

Marcus Garvey and the UNIA

◆ Audio Station
• Exhibit focus

MIGRATION

Cuban boat

Piece of deck, pots, vessels and Anchor to Hatian Craft

MEMORIES OF HOME
• Haiti

SOUNDS OF THE COMMUNITY
• Merengue and Salsa

IDENTITY
Video presents a variety of perspectives on race and ethnicity from personal experience

THE AFRICAN DIASPORA IN THE AMERICAS

◆ Adjustments
bulletin board
• Maintaining contact w. home
NEW HORIZONS • Arrival / Adjustments
NEW COMMUNITIES

• History of the Community

RACE & ETHNICITY IN D.C.
Mt. Pleasant • /Caribbean/African
• School   Disturbance • / Cruise • / • Diplomats

Bahian costume   Chair   Sewing Machine

COMMUNITY LIFE IN D.C.   MAKING A LIVING
cardboard coffin
• Community Organizing
• Family Activity
• Sports   BUILDING COMMUNITIES IN D.C.
• Jamaican history

BUILDING COMMUNITIES IN D.C. continued
• Afro Latino history
• Haitian history

RESOURCE CORNER

STORIES OF THE PEOPLE
• Handress Kelly, artist Panama

EXIT

BLACK MOSAIC
COMMUNITY, RACE, AND ETHNICITY
AMONG BLACK IMMIGRANTS IN WASHINGTON, D.C.

AUGUST 21, 1994 TO AUGUST 7, 1995

ANACOSTIA MUSEUM - SMITHSONIAN INSTITUTION

15. *Black Mosaic* visitors viewing Cuban refugee raft, Anacostia Museum

series of meetings held in each of the communities represented, oral-history interviews, use of community scholars, a fifteen-member Community Advisory Committee, and traditional bibliographic research, the exhibit's researchers and staff gained increasing insight into Afro-Latin American community, race, and ethnicity in Washington, D.C. It used videotaped interview displays, audio-taped interview listening stations, music, participant artifacts (family photographs, documents, clothing, and furnishings), documentary photographs, and artifacts collected for the exhibit—most notably, a Cuban raft recovered off Florida's coast (figure 15).[63] By all accounts, it was a rich and textured display that appealed to audiences in both audio and visual terms.[64] This was *Black Mosaic*'s greatest success.

Anacostia-trained community scholars interviewed nineteen Afro-Latinos.[65] Of those Afro-Latinos, nine were Dominican, two were Cuban, three were Puerto Rican, four were Panamanian, and one was Costa Rican. In other words, Dominicans made up nearly half of the Afro-Latino respondents and twice the number of the next largest national-origin group, Panamanians. Of the nine Dominicans, seven were women and two were men: Francia Almarante, Daniel Bueno, Juana Campos, Luís E. Druyard, Julia Lara, Juanita Laureano, Casilda Luna, Maricela Medina, and Esperanza Ozuma. In addition, Juana Campos's children, Ramberto Toruella and Carmen Quander, provided artifacts and oral histories of the Latino/a community. Dominican participants, particularly Juana Campos and Sofía Mora, were featured prominently in promotional literature and local media coverage of the exhibit. Finally, *Black Mosaic*'s lead community scholar was Héctor Corporán, a Dominican forty-year resident of D.C.

The issue of black immigrants' racial identity was taken up immediately in the exhibit. Visitors were informed that

> this exhibit looks at the immigration of people of African descent from Central and South America and the Caribbean to the Washington metropolitan area. It examines how the perceptions and the realities of race, color, and ethnicity have shaped people's identity. It also illustrates their impact on the community life of these groups of Black people in their homelands and in the Washington metropolitan area.[66]

A video of various *Black Mosaic* participants speaking about their identities played on a television screen just inside the exhibit space. In it, the featured participants discussed their understanding of nationality and race and of their pre- and post-immigration experiences of these. Lara, for example, recalled growing up in the Dominican Republic essentially unaware of race, despite her poor economic circumstances. She explained:

> Well, although I was the darkest child in my family at the time, color was not an issue in any way that influenced my relationship with my parents, my aunt, my uncles, my cousins. It just was not an issue. I was never made to feel that I was less than a full human being. It wasn't an issue for me growing up in the Dominican Republic. It just wasn't. And so feelings of difference in ways that one feels here in the States when one is growing up was not something that I experienced until I came to the States.[67]

Many visitors noted that this video was especially compelling and useful in advancing their understanding of the communities represented.[68]

The first historically substantive section, "The African Diaspora in the Americas," followed. A brief definition and history of the African diaspora, a map of the diaspora from the sixteenth century to the nineteenth century and a chart titled, "Blacks and Mulattoes in Latin American Countries," were displayed. The accompanying label read:

> It is difficult to determine the exact numbers of people of African descent in Central and South America and the Caribbean. Different regions and countries have different definitions of who is Black. In addition, African an-

cestry is often overlooked or ignored in official censuses, particularly where people of African descent exist in small numbers or where intermarriage with other groups has been common.[69]

The next panel displayed black Ecuadorians as a case study of the African experience in Latin America. The story of the sixteenth-century Maroon leaders Francisco and Juan Mangache of Esmeraldas was presented alongside current literature produced by the Centro Cultural AfroEcuatoriano and photographs of the Esmeraldas.

Next, "The Diaspora as Pan-African Community" panel made the connection between this history of Africanity in Latin America and the Caribbean, and blackness as understood in the United States. The work and experiences of Marcus Garvey and his Universal Negro Improvement Association (UNIA) were explored in a large label, together with the work of "the activities of Black writers and intellectuals of the Harlem Renaissance and the Negritude cultural movements in the 1920s and 1930s." Photos and memorabilia of the UNIA and such pan-Africanist luminaries as Jean Price-Mars, Aimé Césaire, Langston Hughes, Leon Damas, Claude McKay, Leopold Senghor, Frantz Fanon, and W. E. B. Du-Bois were displayed alongside the label. The connection between their work and Afro-Latin America was not made until the display of the artifacts of the Congress of Black Culture in the Americas meetings of the 1970s and 1980s.

This section glossed over the eighteenth century and nineteenth century, periods of anticolonial revolutionary foment and Latin American nation building. Most striking was the lack of reference to the Haitian Revolution, particularly given the inclusion of the Haitian community in *Black Mosaic*. The Haitian Revolution was undeniably a pivotal event in the development of blackness and institutionalizations of nationhood throughout the Americas, including the United States. The only reference to that history in this section is elliptical and gives short shrift to the distinctive ways in which race was used in Latin American and U.S. nation-building projects. "Although individuals may have thought of themselves as, say, Haitians or Cubans," visitors were told, "some Black religious and political leaders argued that people of African descent should look to Africa as their ancestral home and echoed slave folk beliefs of an eventual return to Africa."[70] That many blacks in Latin America often did not agree that they should "look to Africa," preferring instead to focus on their countries of birth, is left unexamined.

Following a list of common race terms from the region, however, a later section on "Race and Ethnicity in Latin America and the Caribbean" explained that

> the racial and ethnic environments of the English- and French-speaking West Indies where there are large Black majorities, are significantly different from those in Central and South America and the United States. In the final years of the colonial era, the emergence of Black political leadership, economic and social institutions have encouraged the expansion of the Black middle class. Recent economic difficulties and political crises, however, have prompted significant immigration from these islands.[71]

Accompanying objects included photographs, newspaper articles, dolls of several skin tones in traditional folk dress, Colombia's antidiscrimination law, a Dominican passport, a *Dictionary of Latin American Racial Terms*, and a copy of Moreau de Saint-Méry's famous *Descripción de la Partie Francaise de Saint Domingüe*. Together, these objects conveyed—at least, in part—the importance of colonialism and imperialism in the development of Latin American racial identities. Case studies of black-consciousness movements in Brazil and Panama were presented and situated in their respective political-economic contexts. The focus was on the relationship between U.S. imperial interests in Panama, the racist work and living structures experienced by British West Indian laborers in the U.S.-controlled Canal Zone, and the formation of an Afro-Panamanian identity.

In a following section, "Migration," an analogy was drawn between the history of British West Indians in Panama and African Americans in D.C. Visitors were reminded that the African American community was established in D.C. following the great labor migration of African Americans from the U.S. South during the 1930s and 1940s. "But," the opening panel in the section explained, "international migration has also made its mark. The vast majority of Black immigrants to this country come from Central and South America and the Caribbean." The Great Migration north coincided in Washington, D.C., with the arrival of a Latin American diplomatic community. That community relied primarily on the domestic labor of its respective countries' Afro-Latino migrants. Mirroring socio-racial and political conditions in the Dominican Republic at the time, for example, Dominican domestic labor migrants typically hailed from the traditionally African American and West Indian communities in the Dominican Republic.[72]

Black Mosaic situated the experience of Dominicans in the context of African American history in the United States. Because of this, it missed the opportunity to note that the hemisphere's African American history began in Santo Domingo. For example, the first enslaved Africans arrived in Santo Domingo, and the first African revolutions occurred there, as well.[73] The absence of that historic connection was glaring even to visitors:

> Throughout the *Black Mosaic* exhibit, two concerns clearly emerged from the expressions of support and feedback from visitors: Visitors communicated that the concept of the African Diaspora as presented by the exhibit was not sufficiently explored. They were intrigued by the concept and wanted a more concrete, historical discussion. Also, many in our traditional (African-American) community miss seeing themselves. They want an examination of how the histories of the African-American and immigrant communities were linked.[74]

It would have been possible, for example, to explore those centuries overlooked by *Black Mosaic* during which the African presence in the Americas was principally located in the Spanish, French, Dutch, and Portuguese colonies. At the same time, the migration of African Americans from the United States and establishment of colonies in places like Samaná during the early nineteenth century would have added an often overlooked dimension to African American history.

Similarly, there was no discussion of how the diverse slave economies affected subsequent racialized nation-building projects. While the Museo's exhibit may have overstated the case for racial democracy, reliance on a cattle-ranching-based slave economy in the context of an impoverished and abandoned Spanish colonial outpost certainly must in fact have had an impact on the social, political, cultural, and economic distance between the "white" Creole elite and the African and Afro-Hispanic masses in Santo Domingo until the mid-nineteenth century.[75] That legacy in turn has had an impact on subsequent Dominican ethnoracial identity formations and representations, at home and abroad.

Every Mosaic Has Its Fissures

> In this sense, all history is an interpretation of the past.
> —Faith Davis Ruffins[76]

The first job of the public-history museum in the Americas has been to document, preserve, and interpret the past in ways that are innovative yet familiar. The display of Africa, Africans, and the African diaspora in museums has long been conditioned by that fact:

> Museum exhibitions draw on the resources of public culture and public imagery to produce their effects. They are as much an arena of discourse about the "other" as editorial cartoons or travel books. They also use the organizing principles of difference and similarity to produce the imagery of the "other." Which principle predominates in the account or image of a cultural "other" often determines the strategy for how the "other" is portrayed. Usually we think of the "other" as represented primarily as different. Quite the opposite can occur, however. Similarity can be used to assert that the people of other cultures are no different in principle than the producer of the image, or that the differences that appear so great are only surface manifestations of underlying similarities.[77]

Ivan Karp calls this strategy "assimilating." Such displays "appeal to the audience's sense of the familiar and natural. They don't stop exhibition-goers in their tracks and produce a 'what in the world is that?' response."[78] This was the strategy of *Black Mosaic*.

Dominicans were assimilated into the organizing principle of the exhibit—"black" immigrants to D.C. In this regard, *Black Mosaic* was a conservative presentation. It erased ambiguous Dominican identify formations, both on the island and in the diaspora, simply by not exploring it. Dominicans in D.C. were conditioned by historical socioeconomic and political circumstance to identify as black; likewise, those Dominicans who reject a black identity are operating in context. If the Museo del Hombre Dominicano's displays are classically in situ, then the Anacostia's *Black Mosaic* is classically "in context." As Barbara Kirshenblatt-Gimblett explains:

> Objects are set in context by means of long labels, charts, and diagrams, commentary delivered via earphones, explanatory audiovisual programs, docents conducting tours, booklets and catalogues, educational programs and lectures and performances. . . . In-context approaches to installation establish a theoretical frame of reference for the viewer, offer explanations, provide historical background, make comparisons, pose questions, and sometimes even extend to the circumstances of excavation, collection, and conservation of the objects on display. . . . In-context approaches exert strong cognitive control over the objects, asserting the power of classification and arrangement to order large numbers of artifacts from diverse cultural and historical settings and to position them in relation to one another.[79]

Yet on another level, the overrepresentation of Dominicans in *Black Mosaic* represents a shift in Dominican identity displays. As argued in the previous chapter, most elite and official representations of Dominican identity in the Dominican Republic have emphasized Indo-Hispanic origins and have silenced or denigrated African heritages. However, because they were working from within a U.S. African American frame of reference, the Anacostia's curators and researchers placed Dominicans inside that context rather than interrogating the connection between contexts. Although as cited above in this chapter Reinckens had posed the question early on in the exhibit-development process, it appears that it was never completely answered. Nonetheless, the Anacostia staff worked hard to display Dominicans in what it considered respectful terms. After *Black Mosaic* came down in November 1995, there were continued attempts by Anacostia researchers and staff to institutionalize a relationship with the Latino community. Several programs geared toward Caribbean and Afro-Latino communities were organized after *Black Mosaic*, primarily around music. These had petered out, however, by mid-1996.[80] Corporán was charged with researching possible sites for a Latino Community Museum initially sponsored by the Anacostia but located in Adams Morgan, a predominantly Latino neighborhood in Washington, D.C., as a community-based museum. Although internal discussions, research, and community outreach progressed to the point where two sites were being actively considered, the project was ultimately dropped, and Corporán subsequently did not have his contract renewed at the Anacostia.[81]

Despite the Anacostia's failure to institutionalize the incorporation of Afro-Latinos into its curatorial and didactic agendas, it did create an important fund of knowledge about that community through its collection of oral histories. As Olivia Cadaval, a researcher with the Smithsonian's Center for Folklife Programs and Cultural Studies, has noted: "There is little scholarship on or documentation of Washington's Latino community. Its evolution has been recorded and critiqued primarily by its members through anecdotes, oral histories, interviews and newspaper editorials."[82] Were it not for those sources that the Anacostia helped to collect and archive, we would know little about the experiences and memories of Dominicans in Washington, D.C., to which I turn next.

If the world of Washington, D.C., was a racially complex one, then being in that world was equally complex, especially for those new to it. Returning to Lugones's notion of "'world'-travelers," we learn from the oral-history accounts of their experiences of their identities in Washington, D.C., that Dominican participants in *Black Mosaic* certainly experienced themselves as different in each of the worlds they traveled. They were both Dominicans who identified or were identified as black and blacks who identified as Dominican. *Black Mosaic* attempted to convey this through Dominicans' life stories, most prominently through that of Juana Campos, one of the community's venerated elders.

Juana Campos arrived in Washington, D.C., in 1940 after having docked in New York City and spent several weeks with a cousin who resided there. She had been contracted to work as a seamstress for a Dominican diplomatic family in Washington, D.C. When the family left the capital, she stayed and continued to work independently. She met and married Ramberto Toruella Sr., a Puerto Rican migrant who had arrived in the capital in 1941 to attend American University, where he earned a bachelor of arts degree in electrical engineering. They had two children, Ramberto and Carmen Toruella (subsequently, Carmen Quander). Juana Campos divorced her husband following his marital infidelity and raised her children as a single mother. She is considered a "godmother" of the Dominican community due to her long history in D.C. and her service to the community. She was instrumental in the provision of Spanish-language masses in the local Catholic diocese. In 1954, she organized an annual celebration for the Dominican Republic's patron saint, La Virgen de la Altagracia, which continues to be observed. And together with her then adult children, she was an early participant in the annual Latin American Festival.

Similarly, Casilda Luna arrived in Washington, D.C., as a domestic with a Dominican diplomatic family in 1961. Like Campos, she chose to remain in the city when the family returned to Santo Domingo. An outgoing person, Luna organized weekly social gatherings in her apartment. Those gatherings became community discussion sessions during which social problems would be presented and collectively considered. It was in those sessions that Luna "cut her teeth" in community organizing. She subsequently became involved with the Latin American Festival organizing committee and, most recently, with the Latino Affairs Office of the District of Columbia.

Daniel Bueno was a sixteen-year-old teenager when he arrived in Washington, D.C., from Santo Domingo. The son of *Ingleses* (British West Indian immigrants to the Dominican Republic and their descendants) and a politically progressive youth, he left the country during the post-Trujillo political turmoil. His father had migrated ahead and was a self-employed mechanic. Bueno worked for his father, obtained a General Educational Development (GED) high-school equivalency diploma, and became a well-established East Coast record-industry entrepreneur. He married a Salvadoran woman, Coco, who is also his business partner.

Following a three-year separation, Maricela Medina was reunited at age twelve with her mother in Chevy Chase, Maryland, where her mother was employed as a domestic for a white family. Medina quickly learned English and graduated at the top of her class from the local Catholic high school in which her mother had enrolled her. She was awarded a full scholarship to Howard University, where she majored in Latin American history. Again a top student, she received a fellowship to study in the Ph.D. program in history at the University of Michigan. She completed her doctorate in 1986 and joined the faculty at Howard in a tenure-track appointment. Although she became tenured, Medina became disillusioned with academic life and went on to open her own insurance-services firm.

Francia Almarante arrived in Washington, D.C., in 1974 to live with her mother, a domestic at the Moroccan Embassy (figure 16). They lived at the embassy for several years, during which time Almarante attended the Americanization School, learned English, obtained a GED, and went on to become a licensed cosmetologist and hairdresser. After apprenticing at a Georgetown beauty shop that primarily served white customers and, later, at an African American shop in the district, Almarante opened her own shop in the Adams Morgan neighborhood. Juanita Laureano, who arrived in 1977, and Esperanza Ozuma, who followed in 1983, are also licensed cosmetologists. They work together as hairdressers in a beauty shop. Laureano also attended the Americanization School, now known as the Carlos Rosario Center, where she obtained a GED. Ozuma likewise obtained a GED, although through the program run by Lincoln Junior High School.

Finally, Julia Lara arrived in Washington, D.C., in the late 1980s as an adult professional relocating from New York City. She had arrived in

16. Francia Almarante newly
arrived in Washington, D.C.

New York City as a twelve-year-old child. She attended primary and high
school in the New York City Catholic school system, entered the College
of Staten Island, and subsequently received a full scholarship to Middlebury College in Vermont. At Middlebury she completed a bachelor of
arts in political science. Following several years working in New York
City, she moved to Washington to join her husband, an African American professional. Once settled in Washington, she entered the graduate
program in education at George Mason University, where she completed
her Ed.D. in 1998.

The Dominicans who participated in *Black Mosaic*—and who I subsequently re-interviewed for this project—are exceptionally well educated
as a group, and they have the highest rates of higher education and occupational rankings of Dominican communities in the United States. In
2000, only 10.6 percent of all Dominicans in the United States had a
college degree or more.[83] Although high-school-completion rates among
Dominican immigrants and U.S.-born Dominicans are not significantly
different, at 20.5 percent and 21 percent, respectively, they do have significantly different college-graduation rates. While only 9.5 percent of
Dominican immigrants have a college degree or more, 21.9 percent of
U.S.-born Dominicans have completed college or more.[84] Still, as table 3
illustrates, the Dominican participants in *Black Mosaic* all had at least a
high-school degree, one had a bachelor's, another had a master's, and

Table 3 Dominican Participants in *Black Mosaic*

Name	Sex	Year Arrived in Washington, D.C.	Highest Grade Completed	Where Educated	Occupation
Juana Campos	F	1940	*Bachillerato*[a]	Dominican Republic	Seamstress
Ramberto Toruella	M	Native-born	B.A.	Ohio	D.C. government
Carmen Quander	F	Native-born	M.A.	New York	Artist
Casilda Luna	F	1961	*Licenciatura*[b]	Dominican Republic	Social worker
Daniel Bueno	M	1963	7th grade; GED	Dominican Republic; Carlos Rosario Center Cardosa	Entrepreneur/ record shop
Maricela Medina	F	1964	B.A.; Ph.D.	Howard University; University of Michigan	Historian, Howard University; entrepreneur/ insurance agency
Francia Almarante	F	1974	Nearly *Bachillerato*[a]; GED; cosmetology license	Dominican Republic; Carlos Rosario Center; D.C. Beauty Academy	Beautician Entrepreneur/ beauty shop
Juanita Laureano	F	1977	GED	Carlos Rosario Center	Beautician
Esperanza Ozuma	F	1983	GED	Lincoln Junior High; NCIT	Beautician
Julia Lara	F	1984	Ph.D.	George Mason University	Educator/ researcher

[a]Dominican degree equivalent to a high-school diploma.
[b]Dominican university degree.

two had Ph.D.s. Most obtained some, if not all, of their education in Washington, D.C., which may account in part for their high educational levels.

By their own accounts, all were exposed to the race problem in the United States in both academic and daily life. The participants in *Black Mosaic* simultaneously identified with African Americans and understood themselves to be Dominicans. In Washington, D.C., they shared a sense of being racialized "black" while being culturally distinctive as Dominican. According to the participants, their identities, high educational-attainment levels, and middle class socioeconomic standing were dynamically interrelated. In some cases, identifying as Dominican enabled them to circumvent educational and residential segregation during the 1950s. In the wake of desegregation and the successes of the Civil Rights Movement, however, identifying as black allowed them greater access to the gains of the Civil Rights Movement and Black Power Movement. In each of their life stories, access to education was mediated by how they identified and were identified racially. What these experiences taught them is that there were situational advantages and disadvantages to each of their ethno-racial affiliations, but that, in general, identifying as "black" would offer them opportunities for upward mobility. Through them we gain key insights into how Dominican identity formations are responsive to local conditions and institutions.

Coming of Age in Washington, D.C.

Corina Sallaint arrived in Washington, D.C., in 1921 from Monte Cristi, in the northwestern part of the Dominican Republic. She came employed as a domestic for a U.S. family who had met her while in the Dominican Republic during the U.S. occupation period. Local Dominican lore has it that she was among the first Dominican domestics to settle in Washington. Mamá Corina, as she came to be known, married an African American man, Nelson Washington, had seven children, and made her home in Maryland a social haven for Latin American immigrants and their children.[85] Carmen Quander recalled in a 1998 interview: "Mamá Corina and her house were like an international house. And we would all go out to her on Sunday, and every nationality. . . . This is why in Washington we didn't have the racism between Latin Americans that you do in New York: because all Latin Americans could go to Mamá Corina's house." Dominican domestics organized their social lives with one another because they were primarily a Spanish-monolingual, female group. Maricela Medina, whose mother worked as a domestic for a family in Chevy Chase, Maryland, recalled:

> There were a number of men who were brought and who worked at the embassy, but for the most part, it was a female staff. You always had a few to do the driving and do the gardening and stuff like that, but the bulk of the staff was female. And the stories about people who mistreated them, who overworked them and didn't want to pay them and would keep their passports. And remember, many of these women were working for people out in the suburbs, and I'm talking about when the suburbs—when you saw cows over there by the Naval Hospital, ok? So this was the country.[86]

At the same time, however, because of their status as Spanish-speaking immigrants and their work connections to Latin American legations and embassies, Dominicans worked and socialized primarily with other Latin American immigrants. "On Thursdays, which was the maid's day off," Medina recalled, "all of them would come together, and there were only a few that had a partner. So you met at someone's apartment, and they would socialize, and you would go shopping and buy clothes or this and the other." As independent mothers, these women combined their parenting responsibilities—providing food, clothing, and household goods—with their social needs for contact with other women similarly situated. At the same time, they trained their daughters in the ways of Dominican culture.

Daniel Bueno, now the owner of Zodiac Records and a prominent East Coast Latin music distributor, explained the role of music and parties in Dominican community building:

> We grew up in house parties. We would ask, "Where's the party?" every Saturday. There were very few clubs and we would visit the parties and our friends. And that was our life. We grew up in house parties, which doesn't exist anymore. People would share, and we would get to know each other. People used to spend time together, and we would get to know one another. Parents were there with their children; they would take their children. The house parties we would go to, almost everyone was older.[87]

Dominican immigrants in Washington, D.C., in other words, replicated patterns of socializing typical in the Dominican Republic. Young and old alike dance to the same music, using the same—or, at least, similar—dance steps, inside the same spaces, often relatives' and friends' homes.

There was no "generation gap" in terms of Dominican cultural practices in the United States.

While regular daily or weekly socializing was organized along class lines, because the Latino community was so limited, service staff also had fairly regular social contact with elite embassy and legation families during the 1940s and 1950s. Ramberto Toruella, Juana Campos's son, who was born and raised in D.C. during the 1950s and 1960s, recalled:

> The only Latinos in this town were embassy personnel, the support staff of the embassy. So we grew up with all the embassies. If the embassy of Venezuela would have a celebration to celebrate their Independence Day, all the Latinos were invited. And we'd go to the Venezuelan Embassy, eat Venezuelan food, and dance Venezuelan dances. And the same with the Mexican Embassy, the Dominican Embassy. There was a handful; within a fifty-mile radius, there must have been one hundred Latinos. We knew every Latino in D.C. Every Latino in D.C. knew each other.[88]

This working and social relationship with Latin Americans of all classes and with white Washington, D.C., shielded early Dominicans somewhat from the sort of Jim Crow policies and practices their contemporary African American neighbors and co-workers were experiencing. It also enabled the retention of a Latin American identity for the first generation and the formation of a generalized Latino identity for the second generation, expressed particularly through foodways, music and dance, religion, and the retention and use of Spanish.

The vast distance between African Americans and whites in the United States had perplexed Juana Campos when she arrived in 1940. An astute reader of the social landscape, Doña Juana recalled more than fifty years later that "people here were separated like tuberculosis patients, black and white apart."[89] Neither in New York City, where her boat from the Dominican Republic had docked, nor in her hometown of Pelmar had she experienced the kind of visibly entrenched Jim Crow segregation that characterized the U.S. capital. Indeed, it was a new Puerto Rican friend who "instructed" the recently arrived Campos on the rules of Jim Crow. A brown-skinned woman to U.S. observers, Juana Campos was clearly of African descent to some degree or another and, her friend warned, likely to experience discrimination. From the first, Juana Campos was determined that neither she nor her children who were born in Washington, Ramberto and Carmen, would be constrained by Jim Crow (figures 17 and 18).

17. Juana Campos,
Washington, D.C.,
1998
(below) 18. Ramberto
and Carmen Toruella,
Washington, D.C.,
1950s

Ramberto Toruella described the socio-racial geography:

In those days, we were the first Latino family in the black section. North of Columbia Road was all white. South of Columbia Road was all black. The north side was very wealthy. The south side was the poor people. And the south side, that's where all your black chauffeurs and nannies and cooks and housekeepers lived. So we were always on the fringe of the good area. The wealthy area. And my mom was a seamstress, and she sewed for all the rich white folks on the north side. We were raised by my mom being a seamstress sewing for the rich white folks.[90]

For second-generation Dominicans coming of age in the 1950s and 1960s, Spanish-language use became a means of affirming a Latino identity, and for Afro-Latinos it became a shield against anti-black racism. As *Black Mosaic* pointed out, a series of widely publicized racist incidents leading to diplomatic debacles occurred in 1961. International attention was focused on the United States, and on Washington, D.C., in particular, when several dignitaries from newly independent African nations were refused service at Maryland and D.C. establishments on repeated occasions.[91] As a result, President John F. Kennedy sent identical letters to the governors of Connecticut, New York, New Jersey, Pennsylvania, Delaware, Maryland, and Virginia—states through which diplomats frequently traveled. These letters asked the governors for their cooperation in assuring "friendly and dignified receptions for diplomatic representatives of foreign countries who may be working, living, and traveling in your State during their Assignment in the United States."[92]

Thus, local businesses, government officials, and residents were encouraged to distinguish between U.S.-born blacks and foreign blacks who, unbeknownst to the local white racist, might be a foreign dignitary or official. Since appearance was not necessarily enough of a distinctive marker of foreignness for individuals who appeared black to local segregationists, the use of languages other than English or speaking English with a foreign accent served as a salient marker of not being African American. Here Ramberto's recollections of what that diplomatic exigency meant for him and his Dominican family are instructive:

All we spoke at home was Spanish, so we didn't know any English. All our friends were Spanish-speaking. And when we started learning English, my mom would always say, "Never speak English in public. Always speak Spanish." At the People's Drug Store, blacks couldn't eat. "No coloreds." Coloreds could not sit at the counters, and my mom would take us there, and the waitresses would look at her and look at us. We were actually speaking Spanish, because then they'd say, "Oh, they're not colored; they're foreigners. You can feed them." We grew up like that. We grew up going everywhere because my mom knew how to play the game. So we grew up knowing it was important that we were *Dominicano*, Latino, *Dominicano*.[93]

Doña Juana clearly understood that she and her children could be taken for African American. She was also, it seems, aware of the foreigners' exemption.[94] Through her use of Spanish she actively resisted the social and spatial segregation that African American identification implied, and she taught her children to do the same. As her daughter Carmen explained, "I grew up as white, and I fit into the white community, and it's the black community that I've had a problem with because I don't have the baggage." The "baggage" Carmen referred to is the experience of residential and public segregation and racial violence. Growing up "as white" meant making full use of the public resources Washington, D.C., offered to whites.

Doña Juana's refusal to be perceived as African American can be understood as a negation and a refusal of a black identity. And, indeed, Doña Juana does not identify as black; instead, she understands herself to be *India*, just as she did nearly sixty years ago when she left the Dominican Republic.[95] However, soon after her arrival in D.C., Doña Juana understood that her racial self-perception differed radically from the perception of both whites and African Americans. To them, she was "black," and that meant subordination. She understood quickly that Spanish-language use and retention would mediate anti-black racism.

The issue for Doña Juana was not one of allegiance to one group or the other, however. Rather, it was a refusal to be relegated to second-class citizenship by either community. Doña Juana was a labor migrant who left the Dominican Republic in 1940, during the Trujillo era and shortly before the end of the decades-old U.S. Customs Receivership.[96] Her premigration experience of the United States, in other words, was in the context of a country deeply affected by U.S. economic, political, and military intervention.[97] It is understandable, then, that Doña Juana did not feel herself to be caught in the horns of the United States' "American dilemma."[98] The issue for Doña Juana, instead, was her family's ability to negotiate both "the [U.S.] racial state," as Michael Omi and Howard Winant put it, and the socio-racial geography of D.C. on pragmatic terms.[99]

Ironically, Doña Juana's story was at the center of *Black Mosaic*. The pedal-footed sewing machine with which she made her living in Washington was prominently displayed in *Black Mosaic*, and a picture of her alongside it at the exhibition's opening day was widely circulated in promotional materials. She derived great pleasure from her participation in *Black Mosaic* not because she understood herself to be a black immigrant, but because she understood the exhibition to be a celebration of Latin American immigrants' survival in Washington, D.C.[100] For Doña Juana, *Black Mosaic* was a more permanent version of the yearly Latin American Festival she had helped establish in Washington twenty or so years earlier.[101] Why, then, did Doña Juana participate in *Black Mosaic*? Simply stated, as she had done throughout her experience in Washington she ignored the racial context of the event and focused on the ethnic part of the exhibition that served her purposes. For her, *Black Mosaic* was an affirmation of her success as an immigrant and as the "godmother" of the Dominican community in Washington.

By contrast, for Doña Juana's children and those of their generation who came of age in Washington during the 1960s and 1970s, *Black Mosaic* was successful in affirming their membership in several communities: Dominican, black, Latino, Afro-Latino. As it was noted in *Black Mosaic*'s section on race and ethnicity in D.C., "Afro-Latinos had to adjust to an unaccustomed social distance between the races and to U.S. classifications that sought to divide their ethnic community into two racial groups: 'blacks' and 'Hispanics.'"[102] However, the underlying sociological and historical reasons for those affiliations were not sufficiently explored by *Black Mosaic*. Although it recognized and presented race and ethnicity in Latin America as distinctive from that in the United States, *Black Mosaic* never questioned, and therefore never explained, why this particular group of Latin American immigrants identified as black.

A Legacy of Migration

The Dominicans who participated in *Black Mosaic* came from very particular ethno-racial backgrounds in the Dominican Republic. They were nearly all either from communities that had historically received large contingents of West Indian labor migrants ("*cocolos*" and *Ingleses*[103]) in the late nineteenth century and early twentieth century or were themselves the descendants of those migrants. For example, Maricela Medina was born in San Juan de Maguana, which is in the southwestern part of the island in the vicinity of the border with Haiti and a traditional locus of the sugar industry. British West Indian migrants from the Lesser Antilles were brought to the Dominican Republic to work in the newly industrialized sugar plantations owned by Cubans, Puerto Ricans, and North Americans, while others came from the Dutch Antilles. Like the African American colony in Samaná (the "*Americanos*"), these migrants sustained a unique ethnic identity—typically through English-language use and membership in the African Methodist Episcopal Protestant church—even as they became integrated into Dominican society.[104]

As in other Latin American regions where they migrated, Dominicans of West Indian descent perceived themselves as superior to the Dominican natives, due in large measure to their ability to speak English with North American owners and managers, who put them in skilled and supervisory positions:[105]

> In spite of the slur campaigns in the press, the *cocolos* progressively achieved acceptance in the communities where they lived. The white elite and mulatto masses of the nation began to view the *cocolos* in a positive manner. Their superior formal education, strict child rearing practices, discipline in the capitalist system, the ability of most to speak to the North American plantation owners and managers in English, and the specialized skills of many, converted the image of these black immigrants in the Dominican society to that of the "*negro blancos*" (white blacks).[106]

Unlike in the Haitian experience, *cocolos* and *Ingleses* in the Dominican Republic have been able to sustain a unique ethno-racial identity that is positively perceived. They do not, therefore, necessarily understand black self-identification as negative. They are "white blacks" because, although they are racially identified as "black," they are socially and economically positioned as "whites" because of their Anglo ethnicities.

Julia Lara, a Dominican policy analyst and daughter of immigrants from St. Kitts who had grown up in the Dominican Republic and had lived in Saint Thomas before migrating to the United States, arrived in Washington from New York in the early 1980s and was profiled in *Black Mosaic* (figure 19). In her interview with Corporán, she explained:

> I was very well aware in the Dominican Republic and in St. Thomas, that I was black. But it wasn't institutionalized and what that means, the meaning of that was not the same in the U.S. as it was in the Dominican Republic and in St. Thomas, because while there was somewhat of a negative attribute attached to it, it wasn't a source of high status in the Dominican Republic or in St. Thomas. It was certainly not a negative characteristic, personal

19. Julia Lara and her childhood best friend, Ofelia,
Dominican Republic, circa 1960

characteristic, as it is in the United States and was at that point in time. So
I guess what I'm trying to do is establish gradations of differences. I think
there is a difference in terms of how people are perceived as you go from
the Caribbean and you come to the U.S. primarily because in the Caribbean
and in the Dominican Republic you had for many, many, many years people
of color, specifically people of African descent, living with others who are
lighter skinned. Beyond that, the reality is that it is a very small population
in the Dominican Republic who could be considered in American terms
white. Very small. So Dominicans are people of color, and while there is a
lack of consciousness, historical consciousness and knowledge about where

we came from, because there was never institutionalized racism, the impact is different.[107]

That Lara does identify as black is due in large measure to her experiences within the U.S. educational system and her subsequent political consciousness of the salience of race as an organizing principle here. That she also continues to identify as Dominican and more generally as Latina, however, points to the multiple ethno-racial negotiations Dominicans undertake.

Finally, nearly all of the Dominican participants in *Black Mosaic* worked either for or with African Americans at some point in their lives. Often they had African American bosses and mentors who modeled appropriate professional behavior and black upward social mobility for them. Today, Washington's black population is the most highly educated in the nation. More than half of the black population has attended college, and 80 percent of adults over twenty-five have completed at least high school.[108] Ironically, the class stratification of the African American community in Washington, D.C., actually served as an incentive to Dominican assimilation into a black racial identity. As Carmen Quander explained:

> So that the Dominican blacks that come here or the mixed blacks, like myself, that come here, we get involved in the African American community, and we see that there is a very, very deep class consciousness and that there is a place for us. A positive place. But, for example, in New York City, although there are affluent African Americans, they are not in a mass concentration the way you have in D.C.[109]

Conversely, the relative political and economic disempowerment of African Americans in New York, particularly those next to whom Dominicans live, work, and go to school, reinforces the prevailing Dominican association of blackness with low socioeconomic standing.

In Washington, D.C., there was and continues to be a structural incentive to black self-identification. There, African Americans are a numerical majority, wield increasing political power, hold the vast majority of government posts and jobs, and occupy a diversity of socioeconomic statuses. (For example, just outside D.C., Maryland's Prince Georges County has the highest percentage of affluent blacks in the country[110]). In 1991, the D.C. Latino Civil Rights Task Force found that, "even though Latin American residents represented between 10 and 15 percent of Washington's population, African Americans monopolized the city government as well as city services and outreach programs. None of the city council or school board members was Spanish-speaking, and Latin Americans constituted only 1 percent of the bulging D.C. municipal workforce of forty-eight thousand."[111]

While the Dominican women arriving in D.C. during the 1960s and 1970s may have come from positions of disadvantage and arrived in much more segregated communities than their New York counterparts, over the long term they have been able to experience greater upward mobility because they have been able to benefit from the political activities of African Americans. The U.S. Civil Rights Act of 1960, for example, opened up clerical jobs to African Americans, prompting a shift out of domestic service and into pink-collar and white-collar labor. Terry Repak informs us that

> the percentage of African American women who were private-household workers in 1960 (37.5 percent nationwide) plummeted by the end of the 1980s, when only 3.5 percent of employed African American women still worked in domestic service. The move out of service and into clerical occupations enabled African American women to improve their occupational distribution to such an extent that their median income increased from 51 percent of white women's income in 1955 to 98 percent in 1975.[112]

It was a shift that Dominican women who arrived as adults or came of age alongside African American women in D.C. experienced with them.

A case in point is that of Casilda Luna, who emigrated from Santo Domingo in 1961 to work as a domestic for a Dominican Army general and his family in Washington and went on to become a professional community organizer employed by the Office on Latino Affairs.[113] Carmen Quander explained:

> You have to understand that Dominicans that constitute the District of Columbia came originally . . . in a servant capacity, and so they came here as maids and chauffeurs and stuff like that. So the class that came to New York is working-class poor. They're still not servants. So the servant class that came here are in fact the black people. The difference here also and then in New York, the servant class here has managed to still serve, but their children go on to college, whereas in New York they don't.[114]

For example, black Dominicans have been able to make use of affirmative action in higher education at Howard University, a local, historically black university. As Maricela Medina, a Howard University alumna and former professor, put it:

Well, in my case, I didn't have to go the Dominican route. I could go the African American route. And that was another thing that I found out, as opposed to people who think there are only disadvantages to being African American. There were a lot of advantages when I went to school, because this was the time of the Civil Rights Movement. The Black Power Movement. The militancy on campus. A lot of things were changing, and there were a lot of opportunities offered to African Americans. Puerto Ricans were always included and Mexican Americans, but if you were Hispanic of any other origin, unless you qualified as African American, you weren't able to participate.[115]

Participation for Dominican immigrants, who had made so many sacrifices to get to Washington, was, of course, of the utmost importance. As Medina further explained:

That's why you came to the United States. You came to the United States for opportunities. Your parents made this big trip. See, this was always very clear to me that my parents . . . my mother, because at that time it was just my mother . . . my mother came here, and she sacrificed. I could not let my mother down by getting poor grades. I could not let my mother down by failing. So this was not even an issue.[116]

In short, the combined demonstration effects of African American political activism and upward social mobility and high immigrant expectations for the second generation's success supported black identity in the Washington, D.C., context.

Choosing Ambiguity

Both whites and African Americans expected Dominicans to declare their racial identities and, presumably, their attendant loyalties. For whites, the issue was whether one was willing to establish belongingness in the United States by rejecting blackness and African Americans, as immigrants have been required to do historically. Maricela Medina explained it this way:

Americans, period, required that you make choices. Because even whites, even though you were black, whites would make that kind of . . . [T]hey put you in a separate category because you were Spanish. But they always wanted you to choose. It seemed like society was always asking you to choose between being black and being Hispanic.[117]

African Americans, historically and contemporarily, insisted that Dominicans (and African diaspora communities generally) identify as black. Other Latinos, conversely, insisted that ethnicity supersedes race in the structuring of Latino identity. *Black Mosaic* explained, "Unlike other immigrants, black immigrants must also adjust to and successfully situate themselves within two distinct environments—society at large and the African American community. Thus they must often negotiate a conflicting set of expectations."[118] Afro-Latinos negotiated yet another "set of expectations": those imposed by the Latino community at large.

Julia Lara's college experience is illustrative:

> Well, it was an experience because it was for the first time when I was caught between an African American population, a Latino population, who were not of African descent. . . . The Latino students who were not from the Caribbean did not view me as legitimately Latina because I was of African descent. These are people who, for the most part, came from South America, some from Mexico. But they were not Latinos of African descent. They were Latinos who might have been Spanish or Indian and did not recognize or value their heritage as Indian people. So being Latina and being of African descent was strange for them. And for the African American population, being of African descent yet speaking another language and having some sense of pride in where I came from and not in any way denying where I came from was interesting to them.[119]

Lara distinguished between Latinos from the Caribbean, who presumably are either themselves Afro-Latino or familiar with Latinos of African descent, and those from South America and Mexico, who presumably are not. This group, Lara explained, did not perceive her "as legitimately Latina" because they were either unfamiliar with Afro-Latinos or "did not recognize or value their [own] heritage as Indian people."[120] That tension over her recognition and legitimization as a Latina by other Latinos is one that has gained increasing salience for Dominicans in Washington, D.C., due to the influx and numerical predominance of Central Americans.

Until the late 1970s, the Latin American community in D.C. was small and highly heterogeneous. The largest subgroups were Cubans, Dominicans, and Puerto Ricans. Although South Americans and Central Americans were present, as well, the series of civil wars in Central America created a large Central American community of over 200,000 as of the 1990 census. "Within a single generation, Washington could claim the second largest settlement (after Los Angeles) of citizens from

El Salvador to the United States and the third largest community of Central Americans overall."[121] According to the Dominicans interviewed for this project, this sea change in the ethno-racial composition and size of the Latino community affected African American–Latino race relations. Maricela Medina explained:

> The composition of the community now is completely different. You have mostly Central Americans . . . of Amerindian background who don't necessarily mix well with blacks, whether Hispanic or African American. Many of them are openly antagonistic to blacks. They harbor many of the prejudices that whites harbor against blacks . . . and one of the things that bothers me is that when they talk to you—or not necessarily to me, but to a person— and they are relating something that happened to them, they will always say, "*El policia negro* [The black police officer]." My thing is: Why do you have to specify that he was black? Because when they are talking about a policeman who is white, they don't say, "*policia blanco* [white police officer]." They only make the reference to race when it's a black policeman. "*El Negro* [The black guy]." And I never thought I would learn to dislike a word like that, because I never had any problems accepting . . . I shouldn't say "never had any problems," but I don't have a problem accepting who I am or what I am. But the way that word is used carries a similar connotation to the word "nigger." I don't mean any disrespect by that, but the way it is said, it always had that kind of meaning, the expression in which they express that word. . . . And, of course, I am speaking heresy when I say this because, you know, Hispanics are not supposed to . . . [W]e're not prejudiced, you know. It doesn't matter to us whether you're black or white, right?[122]

As an Afro-Latina, Medina signified her membership in the larger "Hispanic" community, which Central Americans belong to, through her use of "we" and "us." At the same time, she signaled that blacks can be both African American and Hispanic. She took offense, therefore, at the pejorative way in which the Central Americans she had encountered use the term "black." This anti-black prejudice marked the tenuous nature of Dominican inclusion in the categories "Hispanic" and "black" in Washington, D.C.

The lack of familiarity with African American history in the United States also marked Central American–African American relations in D.C. Several respondents indicated that African Americans deserved to be respected both in terms of their ancestors' status in Africa and in terms of their own survival and accomplishments in the United States. As Casilda Luna put it, "They were kings and queens in Africa, and now you want to treat them badly?"[123] Carmen Quander expressed similar sentiments:

> Something happens to the Latin American who comes here . . . to the Washington area, because everything is so divided between black and white. And all of a sudden, all of these other people become white, whereas their own . . . They don't have blacks in their country? . . . Come on, get out of here! And you have to remind these people, and this is why the blacks have so much resentment towards the foreign—because they come in and they have to step on somebody. The white men have to step on somebody. So they come in and step on a black person as lower than they are. But this is the black man's country. They built it. They made it. They've been here much longer than the whites. How dare you come in and condemn them in their own country?[124]

These Dominican respondents, while sustaining a separate ethnic identity from U.S. African Americans, expressed their rejection of the Negrophobia expressed by their Latin American peers, an ideology of which they are aware because they speak and understand Spanish, because they are familiar with Latin American race ideologies, and because it is part of Dominican culture, as well.[125] While their kin and countrymen in the Dominican Republic were being encouraged to internalize an Indo-Hispanic identity based on anti-Haitianist nationalism, coming of age in the United States they witnessed and were forced to negotiate Jim Crow segregation, the Civil Rights Movement, the Black Power Movement, and Afrocentricism. Accordingly, they felt that their own histories were tied to African American history.

At the same time, as Latinos they helped organize the first Spanish masses, the first community dances, the first Spanish-language films at the Colony Theater, the first Latin American Festival, the first bilingual education programs, and the Office on Latino Affairs.[126] They were, in other words, invested in several communities and their histories. And they had had to fight and push each to acknowledge their perspective. The hair stylist Esperanza Ozuma explained:

> I consider myself black, and I have considered myself black since I was in my country. The difference is that when they call you black here, it's because of problems African Americans have had with white Americans, with the differences, with that blacks can't be and whites can. So that exists also in that sometimes there are Latinos and they don't know where you are from and they are talking about you and they don't know if you speak Span-

ish, and then after they know that you are Dominican they don't know how they're going to apologize, due to the same difference they mistake people a lot. I don't agree with that racism where you're black and I'm lighter.[127]

When African Americans ask her what she considers herself, she said, she responds "black," in part because she identifies as such, but also as a gesture of solidarity. Similarly, Maricela Medina noted that

the black Hispanics would be caught in the middle because the African Americans wanted to kick the Hispanics' butt because they were white— or, as the African Americans say, "They think they're white." And then the black Hispanics would say, "Hey man, you can't beat up my friends. How can you be a friend with that whitey?"[128]

Likewise, Carmen Quander, who married into a prominent African American family in D.C., recalled ongoing negotiations with Washington's African American elite:

Why do you want to take my heart and soul just because you see the color of my skin? Toruella is my last name. That's from the south of Spain. I said, "I'm Dominican. I am a person of color. I am of the African diaspora, but you know what you talk to me about other stuff, too, OK? We came here knowingly. I know my roots. I took my family to the grave of all of my ancestors." I am a person of color and very proud of it, but you cannot stay in that box.[129]

The "box" Quander refers to is the one that gives racial identity primacy over national or ethnic identity. It is the one based on hypo-descent that would have identified her solely as black because she has African ancestors. As she reminded her questioner, however, she felt as connected to her European ancestors (who are from the south of Spain) as to her African ones. What is more, she felt herself to be more than the sum total of the "parts" that constitute her background. She refused to be boxed into a strictly racial identity at the exclusion of her ethnic one.

Speaking of her interactions with her co-workers at the African American beauty shop, Francia Almarante expressed a similar sentiment in a 1998 interview:

I have arrived in places where I've noticed the looks, but as soon as I speak Spanish, everything changes. Their faces change. I notice the difference immediately, from both whites and blacks, because blacks here are a little discriminatory, too. They also discriminate a little bit. As soon as I speak Spanish, things change because now they know I'm not black American.

And everything changes. I did notice a bit of difference between the other Latinas who had white skin and me. They treated me better than them, friendlier. I don't know why. They identified with me more than with the other girls because I am black.[130]

Almarante identified both with Latinas, of whatever color, and with African American women. She was, in other words, both at once. Sofía Mora explained:

[If I am] asked where I came from, I will say I'm Dominican. But that's a nationality. It's not a race. If they want to know where I'm coming from in terms of race, then I am of African descent—recognizing that in many Latin American countries, being of African descent really means being that and some other things. But certainly I am an Afro-Latina. I am an Afro-Latina who was born in the Dominican Republic.[131]

Maricela Medina was even more emphatic: "I'm still Dominican, but there is no question in my mind that I am African. Of African descent. I describe myself as a black Hispanic woman."[132] Almarante put it succinctly: "I am black, but that's not all I am."[133] For these Dominican women, physical appearance and the reception it inspired in both white and black Washington is only part of their being in the world of Washington, D.C. The other part is formed by their social networks, which continue to consist primarily of Latinos.

Medina, for example, attended Howard University and went on to become a member of its history faculty. She was a member of Howard, and the African American community it encompasses, for three decades. Nonetheless, as she explained, "Howard changed my life, my outlook. But my social outlet was in the Hispanic community."[134] When she left the Howard faculty to establish an insurance agency, it was Latinos who came to be heavily represented among her clientele.

Similarly, Almarante found herself working alongside African Americans and servicing many African American clients, but she continued to organize her social life primarily in the Latino community. She lived in Mount Pleasant, attended Spanish mass, and attended Latin dances. Nonetheless, after several years of working with African Americans, and especially as her English language proficiency increased, she began increasingly to socialize in that community, as well:

Despite the fact that I worked there, I just worked. I didn't have any other contact, nothing. As I went entering a little bit, conversing and leaving behind the friends I had years earlier, that's when I began to familiarize myself with Americans. I began to make friends with the girls. I used to go to birth-day parties; they'd invite me to their Thanksgiving. . . . I'm very grateful to them, They showed me a lot of things I didn't know.[135]

Her African American co-workers shared their professional knowledge and skills, their foodways, and their English-language skills, each of which facilitated Almarante's entrepreneurial success as a hairdresser in D.C. While her clients include many Latinas, African American women predominate. Ultimately, however, Almarante opened her beauty shops in Mount Pleasant, where she lived, with Latina partners and em-ployees.

Similarly, Ramberto Toruella, who now works in the District of Colum-bia Office of Human Resources, said in 1998 that he felt connected to D.C.'s larger "Latin" community, despite the cultural and ethno-racial shifts in that community:

> It's different now in that with the influx of Salvadorans and Central Ameri-cans from the wars down there, from Nicaragua and so forth, and the Lati-nos that are coming in, this is different. I know I'm part of the Old Guard by being on the Latino Civil Rights Center and the Wilson Center and staying in Adams Morgan instead of moving out of the city into the suburbs, where they've started to actually lose their Latino roots. But I'm staying in. I want to bridge that gap. . . . And I'm learning a lot about Salvadorans that I just didn't know. I'm working with them and around them all the time, and I know there are a lot of derogatory remarks made about Salvadorans, but just like anybody else, there's good and bad.[136]

The Latino "Old Guard" has been an established presence in Latino so-cial and political institutions since the early 1970s. Many of those folks, as Toruella alludes, had attained a degree of economic success and had moved out of the Adams Morgan neighborhood and into the suburbs of Maryland and Virginia. The new Latino community is as foreign to the Old Guard as it was to African Americans. Yet while many of my respon-dents noted the racial tensions that exist between African Americans, Afro-Latinos, and Central Americans, they also spoke of professional, social, and kinship ties with the Central American community.

Daniel Bueno had been married for more than three decades to a Sal-vadoran woman, Coco, to whom he gave credit for his professional suc-cess. Maricela Medina had a *comadrazgo* relationship with a Salvadoran couple and counted many Salvadorans among her clients. Francia Alma-rante's beauty-shop partner was Central American, as were many of her clients. A question for future research will be whether the presence of, and increasing social and political relations with, other Latino communities will influence Dominican identity in Washington, D.C.

For Dominicans who came of age in D.C. during the 1950s and 1960s, black racial identity was a gendered public identity, while their ethnic identities as Latinos—and, specifically, as Dominicans—centered on and developed through the home, family life, and social gatherings with other Latinos. Dominican women were shielded from anti-black racism both through their use of the Spanish language and because of their position in the labor force and in their communities. As domestic laborers, they were confined to private households for the majority of the workday. Although as immigrant women of color engaged in menial domestic labor they were structurally subjected to gendered, racialized, classed, and sexualized inequities, they were nonetheless comparatively shielded from overt institutional assertions of racism.[137]

As Dominican immigrant women, they socialized in each other's homes and continued to socialize their daughters into the traditional division between "house" and "street." As in many Latin American communities, Dominican culture holds that "good" girls and women should organize their lives in and around their homes.[138] Men and boys, by contrast, are defined as *"de la calle,"* or "of the street." While the exigencies of economic need may have forced women out of their homes to work, it was often in the homes of others that work was found, and all other activities were centered there. Moreover, their constant contact and dialogue with older Dominican women in home settings facilitated their assimilation of Spanish and Dominican foodways, music, domestic arts, and religious practices. Thus, Carmen Quander, for example, remained in her home cooking, cleaning, sewing, and so forth with her mother and her mother's friends. Maricela Medina lived at home while she was a student at Howard and went to campus only for classes. Francia Almarante left the Moroccan Embassy, where her mother was a domestic, only to attend classes at the Americanization School and, later, the D.C. Beauty Academy. Small Dominican boys, such as Ramberto Toruella, who traveled in their mothers' social and work circles were likewise shielded.

Dominican adolescent males and men who organized their social and work lives outside the home were far more exposed to anti-black racism. Daniel Bueno, for example, arrived in the United States in 1964 at sixteen. He went to work immediately. Many of his co-workers were African American men who socialized Bueno into the rule of race in Washington. He explained:

I was an Afro-Latino teenager. The word "Afro" wasn't used. We were still divided into two races, black and white. When we spoke Spanish in the 1960s, people would be surprised that we could speak Spanish, and we were surprised that there were so many people of color in this country, because we were under the impression that they didn't exist, that here everyone was white. I experienced racism—minor, of course. I went to a restaurant in Alexandria where they didn't let me sit down in 1964. I worked for [a company that] painted cars, and they sent me to Alexandria to drop off some cars, and when it was lunchtime, you had to eat across the street. I didn't know English. I was in a group of blacks, and when we went to the restaurant, I went in, sat down, and asked for my food. The owner came and told me that I couldn't eat there. And the guy who was with me told me, "No, ours has to be carry-out." So, in Alexandria, in the 1960s, in the early '60s and maybe in the late '60s, you still couldn't eat in certain restaurants. You know, this is a country of racists, where thirty years ago blacks couldn't walk the streets, and if we were on buses, we had to sit in the back. I didn't come to that. Papá had problems with that. Racism, even if you don't want to believe it exists, it lives in the United States, because it hasn't been that long since it was outlawed. Sometimes you get a complex over it because you don't know if you're black—you know, you speak Spanish, that you don't know English. . . . It was very confusing. It took me time to adjust.[139]

Although Bueno arrived when the Civil Rights Movement was in full swing and was not subjected to segregated public accommodations, transportation (as his father had been), and education, he did experience U.S. anti-black racism firsthand. The son of *Ingleses*, Bueno had never experienced what he considered racism in the Dominican Republic; it was in the United States that he "sometimes [got] a complex" over his racial status. Bueno sustained an intact Dominican ethnic identity as he came of age, due in large measure to his continuing involvement in Dominican politics. He also understood himself to be a "black" man in terms of his physical appearance but considered that more a descriptive than a salient identity.

Ramberto Toruella, by contrast, went through what he called his "black phase" once he became an adolescent and went "out into the streets":

I just went black. I went and started living in the streets. I was partying. I was playing basketball. I became streetwise. I was working at a shoeshine shop. I had a steady job. I was a short-order cook. I started working when I was fourteen years old, and I stayed on the streets. And then I went to the service at nineteen, as soon as I graduated from high school. I joined the military. Two weeks after I graduated I joined the service. . . . I graduated in June '63 from high school. Street black. I was black. And when I was in the service, it became worse, because they sent me down South. Mind you, all I ever knew was D.C., and a couple of times my mom took us up to New York. We went to New York three or four times. So all I ever knew was D.C. I knew nothing else. Born and raised in the city, and I didn't know anything else. Then at nineteen I joined the military to get away and see the world. They sent me to San Antonio, Texas. They sent me to Montgomery, Alabama, and they sent to me to Greenville, Mississippi. This was all in 1963, before the Civil Rights Act. In Greenville, Mississippi, I got put in jail. I got into a bar fight. I went into a bar and asked for a beer, and the bartender said, "No colored here." And I said, "I'm Dominican," and they said, "You're a fucking nigger" (*laughter*).[140]

Again, both his work and his social life exposed him to the sort of racist violence his sister Carmen was shielded from. Whether playing basketball or partying, cooking, shining shoes, or training for the Vietnam War, Toruella was reminded forcefully time and again that he was "a fucking nigger," Dominican or otherwise.[141] It is not surprising, then, that Toruella "went black" for nearly two decades. He adopted an African American identity, attended a historically black university, and refused to speak Spanish. It was not until 1988, when he visited the Dominican Republic for the first time and "saw all these people who looked like" him, that he reclaimed a Dominican identity. Now, as he put it, "I'm all about Latin again."

Conclusion

It is precisely because the Dominican community in D.C. is a small community with origins in West Indian and African American communities in the Dominican Republic, that came of age in a segregated Southern city and in the midst of a large, economically and politically diverse African American community, that these Dominicans identify as black nearly twice as often as Dominicans in New York City. As Corporán put it, "I didn't have a choice." The lack of a large Dominican community, Hector explained, "creates a discontinuity of all the racial classifications that we use in Santo Domingo, which has been transplanted in New York City, but here that disappears."[142] It is noteworthy that D.C.'s Dominicans have continued to sustain an identity as Dominicans—or, more universally, as Latinos. In that regard, the story told by *Black Mosaic*'s Dominican participants should be considered an important chapter in Dominican history.

As I indicated earlier, Dominicans who participated in *Black Mosaic* in Washington, D.C., were world travelers in sociological and phenomenological terms. They repeatedly crossed national, racial, cultural, geographic, ideological, and social borders. The complexity of their identity narratives and displays highlights the routes they have traveled across and within those borders. If for some observers Dominican ambiguity is difficult to grasp and equivocal, for the Dominicans I interviewed in Washington, it is consistent with their travel routes and destinations. *Black Mosaic* Dominicans experienced themselves as black in Washington, D.C., in ways that simultaneously linked them to and distinguished them from their African American neighbors. They could, as Maricela Medina put it, "go the African American route," but they would continue to carry their Dominican identities with them. I will turn next to Dominicans in New York City for a contrasting case.

CHAPTER 4.

"They Are Taken into Account for Their Opinions"

MAKING COMMUNITY AND DISPLAYING IDENTITY AT A
DOMINICAN BEAUTY SHOP IN NEW YORK CITY

Use to be
Ya could learn a whole lot of stuff
Sitting in them
Beauty shop chairs
Use to be
Ya could meet
a whole lot of other women
Sitting there
along with hair frying
spit flying
and babies crying
Use to be
you could learn a whole lot about
How to catch up
with yourself
and some other folks
in your household.
Lots more got taken care of
than hair.
—Willi M. Coleman[1]

The national museum and the beauty shop are physical, social, and cultural spaces that simultaneously display, mediate, and construct social identities. That both of these sites historically developed as institutions contemporary with department stores, which also arose in the nineteenth century as explicitly, gendered, and classed cultural displays, is important to this project. Museums borrowed heavily from department-store display and architectural models; beauty shops originated from the department stores' "ladies' parlor," which had been used by women to try on dresses and to rest.[2] On the similarities between museums and department stores, Tony Bennett writes, "Both were formally open spaces allowing entry to the general public, and both were intended to function as spaces of emulation, places for mimetic practices whereby improving tastes, values and norms of conduct were to be more broadly diffused through society."[3] What has not been noted elsewhere is the connection between the beauty shop and the museum as locations with civilizing agendas predicated on gendered bodily displays and the internalization of techniques of the body.

As I discussed in chapter 2, the national museum is endowed with a mandate to protect the national cultural patrimony and thus is an official institutionalization of identity ideologies par excellence. On the one hand, museums draw their collections and exhibit themes from the communities they represent, and ostensibly they reflect a reality. On the other hand, those collections are scripted in particular ways and act to inform the community of its contours and contents. The act of educating the public about itself discursively *creates* the public as much as it reflects it. The national museum, then, acts as a vehicle for the collection, dissemination, and institutionalization of national identity discourses. What is more: Access to the museum and control over exhibits is an implicitly gendered, racialized, and class-bound phenomenon.

Like the museum, the beauty shop is an institution that provides access to culturally particular aesthetic norms as it creates and disseminates discourses that culturally conscript women to those norms. For example, while beauty shops respond to industry standards and fashions, they also innovate and market their own products and services. One goes to one's hairdresser for aesthetic guidance as much as to attain a previously determined "look." Aesthetic norms are loaded with racial, gender, class, and sexual meanings. As an openly and avowedly gendered space, the beauty shop is explicitly dedicated to producing certain kinds of female beauty while at the same time implicitly providing a space where *certain kinds* of women come together regularly.

Moreover, beauty shops operate within specific ethno-racial contexts and communities. Indeed, they are one of the last public–private spaces in the U.S. where social segregation is generally accepted without challenge. Several African American men and women have successfully brought lawsuits against white beauty shops that have refused them service, but beauty shops' racially and ethnically exclusionary practices have not been subjected to broad legal review.[4] Accordingly, they are often ethnically and racially segregated social spaces. Beauty shops also openly cater to particular economic classes. Given this confluence of race, gender, class, and sexuality practices and ideologies, the beauty shop is an excellent source of information on how identities are scripted and displayed in everyday life. As Coleman offers in her poem, "Ya could learn a whole lot of stuff / Sitting in them / Beauty shop chairs."

Both the museum and the beauty shop operate on the premise of display. "Individual and state formation take place, in part in the visual sphere through a complicated play of looks: looking, being looked at, identification, recognition, mimicry."[5] The issue of looks, both in terms of appearances and in terms of the act of perceiving, must be understood as dialectical and structured by power relations. If Dominicans are said "contrary to appearances" to promote themselves "as a white Hispanic society,"[6] the issue is as much who is doing the looking as it is who is being looked at. Looks operate within the context of a "political economy of bodies" in that the "materiality of the body" is central to "the production of gender, sexuality, and other cultural values"[7]—cultural values that dialectically buttress and create national identity narratives and paradigms and that are performed on and via the body.[8] Frida Kerner Furman notes that the "beauty salon is one place, among others, that assists women in attending to their appearance: by setting its standards, by maintaining it at an acceptable level, and just as critically, by improving it. In these ways the beauty salon serves as an important tool in the creation and maintenance of femininity."[9] In this chapter, I argue that it also functions in the creation and maintenance of group identities and authentication by training Dominican women in the techniques of the body that will enable them to embody and display Dominican identity in keeping with the hegemonic ideological codes of Dominican ruling relations.

I begin this chapter by introducing a Dominican salon in New York City in which I undertook extensive ethnographic research and interviewing about salon clients' racial perceptions and identity-display strategies. In the course of that work, I came to understand that the

Dominican salon offered insights into how racial perception is trained and how identity-display strategies are learned. As an institution, the salon works toward what Mary Renda has called "cultural conscription" of Dominican women into racialized, gendered, and classed norms of Dominican identity. Although Renda limits cultural conscription to "the process by which discourses shape human actors,"[10] if we return to Dorothy Smith's theory of relations of ruling discussed in chapter 2 with regard to the Museo del Hombre Dominicano, we are reminded that cultural conscription through beauty-shop use could be understood as a conceptual practice of power. "Conceptual practice of power" refers to the ways in which habits of the mind and body are organized through both material and discursive practices in "everyday/every night" life.[11] Thus, the Dominican salon is a discursive site ordered by Dominican ideological codes (pigmentocracy, Negrophobia, indigenism, Hispanophilia, and androcentricism) that operate across a transnational social field with its particular relations of power. Just as the Museo del Hombre Dominicano's exhibitionary technologies encourage visitors to internalize the naturalness of Dominican Indo-Hispanicity, so, too, does the salon offer Dominican women the techniques of the body they need to externalize that ideological code. Further, though the details of this case are specific to Dominicans, I would argue that U.S. beauty shops in general are discursive sites in Smith's sense.

For example, although small, locally owned and operated beauty shops generally create what Julie Willett has called a women's culture of intimacy, there are distinct differences between the function and meaning of beauty shops owned and operated for and by white women and beauty shops owned and operated by women of color. Willett argues that one of the boundaries is gender, because beauty shops arose in response to the exclusion—or, at best, tolerance—of women seeking hair care in barber shops. Another boundary was the professionalization of the industry on an androcentric and classist model that sought to divest hair care of its earlier connections to domesticity and servitude, particularly given that prior to the twentieth century, much hair-care work was done by enslaved blacks and later by black and European immigrant women. Finally, another boundary is that of race, for as Willett lays out in careful detail, the beauty-culture industry was racially hierarchical and segregated from its origins in the late nineteenth century.[12]

Many white women in the United States simply do not know what "black hair" feels like, how it is maintained, what products are used, and what beauty technologies are employed. Nor are white women who work in the beauty industry generally any more familiar with black hair. "White stylists and clients embraced and helped create a racially exclusive beauty shop that played an important role in the development of a larger culture of whiteness around which men and women fashioned their identity."[13] For example, in his account of a white beauty shop in Chicago, David Schroder relates the story of the disruptive effect of a new hire's "ethnic clientele" in the implicitly (if not explicitly) white racialized "atmosphere existing in the salon."[14] African Americans and whites alike hesitate to frequent each other's shops, although from the mid-1980s a series of individual and legal challenges to those social norms have been made.[15] As a result, white women, who because of persistent patterns of residential segregation rarely have the opportunity to interact with African American women as they are coming of age, particularly around beauty regimes, do not experience firsthand the variety of hair textures in the African diaspora in terms of touching, washing, or styling "black hair" or seeing local media depictions of black hair care. African American women, conversely, are constantly exposed to white women's hair-care routines and hair textures through a variety of media: dolls, television, cinematic and print media representations, and firsthand observation of white women's hair ministrations throughout the day.[16]

It is not until they reach college, the armed services, or other situations with dormitory housing that many white women are exposed to black women in close quarters. An experience commonly narrated in African American women's stories is that of the white undergraduate who asks to touch her black classmate's hair, thus exposing her segregated upbringing, the novelty of African diaspora hair textures, the racial distinctiveness of black women, and, ultimately, her own racialized aesthetic privilege. Black women often recount the impact and significance of these encounters, while white women seem surprised at the hostility with which their seemingly innocent desire to touch another woman's hair is met.[17]

Dominican women, conversely, do not experience this particular type of racially segregated upbringing. Simply stated, people with a variety of hair textures, facial features, and skin tones make up Dominican families. Consequently, girls and young women are allowed "hands-on" exposure to a range of hair textures throughout their lives. Yet while this might appear to be an expression of Dominican "racial democracy," it could also be read as an expression of Negrophobia, pigmentocracy, and indigenism, for often hands are being laid on black hair to change it from its natural form to a style that marks the body as "Indian" rather than black. As the Dominican anthropologist Casandra Badillo has put it, "The problem is not changing the hair per se, but rather the power relations it expresses and in the attitudes of domination it reflects."[18]

Central to Dominican hair culture have been the twin notions of *pelo malo* (bad hair) and *pelo bueno* (good hair). *Pelo malo* is hair that is perceived to be tightly curled, coarse, and kinky. *Pelo bueno* is hair that is soft and silky, straight, wavy, or loosely curled. There are clearly racial connotations to each category: the notion of *pelo malo* implies an outright denigration of African-origin hair textures, while *pelo bueno* exalts European, Asian, and indigenous-origin hair textures. Moreover, those with *pelo bueno* by definition are "not black," skin color notwithstanding. What is instructive about the Dominican case is the seeming possibility of racial transformation through hair care. As one respondent noted, "For Dominican women, it's not just straightening but transforming it into white hair" and, by extension, themselves into "whiter," but not white, women. The goal is an approximation of idealized "Dominican" looks as those are popularly understood: straight haired, tan skinned, "fine" featured.

At the same time, there is a fair amount of ambivalence toward *pelo bueno*. For example, while *pelo bueno* is usually defined in positive terms, it is also called *pelo muerto* (dead hair) and *pelo lambío* (limp hair). Hair can be (as each of the hairdressers I interviewed mentioned) "too good." Similarly, while light skin is generally valorized, white skin in and of itself is insufficient, and skin that is too white is considered unsightly. In other words, it is the "*India*," the embodiment of the "not-black" icon, that is displayed at the museum, in the history books, in the media, and in the beauty pageant that is desired, literally and figuratively, politically and culturally. That desire has been historically narrated and displayed in venues such as the national museum. But it has been enacted through spaces such as the beauty shop, which offer training in the "techniques of the body" required for the proper display of Dominicanness.

The Dominican beauty shop thus is the discursive site that provides the technology to sustain and create "good hair" and to militate against the effects of having "bad hair." Dominican women with a broad range of hair textures employ more hair-straightening techniques, such as through chemical hair relaxers, roller sets, *toobies*, and blow drying, than non-Dominicans might imagine.[19] For example, Dominican women with curly hair that is neither coarse nor kinky often employ chemically assisted straightening techniques, while other women with similar hair textures do not necessarily feel compelled to straighten their hair. Furthermore, while in African American communities — and lately among white youth, as well—Afrocentric hair-styling techniques and styles such as braiding, corn rowing, and dreadlocking, have a committed following, such a following does not currently exist in Dominican communities.[20] This is so, even though many Dominicans have hair textures that would be amenable to those styles and practices. Indeed, it is to hair culture that Dominican women often point when asked what distinguishes Dominicans from Haitians and African Americans. In addition, the daily practices and technologies of Dominican beauty culture in New York City speak to the role Dominican women's bodies play in displaying Dominicanness and in differentiating Dominicans from other immigrant and racialized communities.

"Compared with Other Women in the Rest of the World, Dominican Women Visit Beauty Parlors More Often": The Dominican Beauty Shop in New York City

When large numbers of Dominican women began to arrive in New York City in the 1960s and 1970s, they generally frequented shops owned by other Latina/os, especially Cubans and Puerto Ricans who were already established in upper Manhattan.[21] Over time, they began to establish themselves as employees in these shops, later as "booth renters," and eventually in their own shops.[22] The increased flow of Dominican women into beauty-shop occupations, whether as owners, hairdressers, manicurists, shampoo girls, estheticians, or masseurs, reflects changes in the New York economy from manufacturing to service industries, changes in the demographics of New York City's Washington Heights neighborhood, and changes in beauty culture in the Dominican Republic.[23]

Historically, female Dominican immigrants to New York City were over-represented in the manufacturing and service industries, particularly during the 1970s and 1980s. However, in the 1990s the manufacturing industry in New York began to collapse, leaving "tens of thousands of Dominican workers temporarily unemployed" and creating "economic distress in the City, particularly among Dominican women."[24] At the same time, Dominicans' participation in the manufacturing sector declined from a high point in 1980, when that sector employed 48.6 percent of Dominican workers, to 2000, when only 12.4 percent of Dominican workers worked in manufacturing.[25] Thus, while Dominican women continued to be over-represented in the non-durable-goods manufacturing sector, particularly in the apparel industry, the volatility of that sector, together with the regimentation, occupational hazards, low pay, and low status, made beauty-shop work and ownership appealing.

The large number of Dominican women in this sector also reflects both the importance of the shifting opportunities available to Dominican women in the New York beauty-culture economy and the growth of the beauty industry in the Dominican Republic, where many developed the appropriate beauty-culture work skills prior to immigrating. In the Dominican Republic, commercial beauty shops have been a salient feature of urban life since the 1950s, but it was the outstanding economic growth of the Dominican Republic in the 1990s that spurred a dramatic increase in the number of shops and a drive toward professionalization of the occupation.[26] Through the last decades of the twentieth century, beauty shops in the Dominican Republic were usually frequented on special occasions—"weddings, baptisms, graduations, and birthdays"— with most women caring for their hair at home. As one Dominican journalist put it, "Large curlers, some bobby pins, a hairnet, and an old hair dryer were enough."[27] Shops were usually sole proprietorships operated by women out of their front parlors or converted garages. They provided a basic menu of services, typically consisting of shampoos, curler sets, bonnet drying, hair relaxing—most often using home-made products— and manicures and pedicures. Clients typically spent two hours in the shop, and the busiest times were Friday afternoons and Saturdays.

In the 1990s, however, the industry underwent a sea change in the Dominican Republic. "Hair stylists of the '90s are guided by a different concept, from simple family businesses they have developed into enterprises."[28] In 1998, there were more than 15,000 beauty-shop workers and 4,000 shops in Santo Domingo alone, according to the Dominican Association of Beauty Specialists. That is, there was on average one shop for every seventy-five women residing in the capital. Start-up costs ranged from $400 to $3,200. In a country where the average weekly income was $125, hairstylists in the late 1990s could earn $133–$400, plus tips, for a six-day, seventy-two-hour workweek. Today's shops offer not only the basic services of the past but also new tints, cellophanes, and hair "re-texturizing" services. Foreign products and hair dryers are more often used, and visits have become one-hour affairs. At the same time, shops are now busy all week, the slowest days being Wednesday and Sunday.

According to a 1998 article published in *Listín Diario*, "Compared with other women in the rest of the world, Dominican women visit beauty parlors more often, spending as much as 30 percent of their salaries on these services."[29] The cost and quality of services purchased depends on a combination of class and status factors: location, physical plant, shop decor, stylist's reputation, and products used. "A wash and dry costs from [$2.67] to [$8.33], a [$5.66] difference that reflects the service and the air conditioning, since a change in the products used (shampoo, rinse, and conditioner) are reflected in the total bill."[30]

Meanwhile, in New York City, the beauty industry was experiencing growth of its own, due at least in part to the transnational entrepreneurship of Dominican women. In New York, the Dominican beauty shop—while not entirely providing autonomous or especially well-paid work—offers greater flexibility, earnings, and community status than the leading employment alternatives in the low-wage service industries available to Dominican immigrant women.[31] In addition, the Dominican beauty shop represents a female-dominated entrepreneurial sector somewhat parallel to the male-dominated Dominican bodega.[32] In his study of Dominican entrepreneurs in New York City, the sociologist Luís Guarnizo found that entrepreneurial Dominican women chose beauty shops as their niche:

> One out of every five respondents is a woman. Unlike male owners, however, women are clustered in a single sector: 60% of women own service firms (especially beauty salons and other personal service establishments) while only 25 and 15% of them own commercial or manufacturing firms, respectively.[33]

The appeal of the beauty industry for Dominican women is manifold. Barriers to entry are fewer both in terms of fixed capital and human capital.[34] Beauty-shop start-up costs are substantially lower than those for commercial or manufacturing firms, and the industry is therefore more accessible to low-earning, poorly capitalized, or less-educated women. As Guarnizo found, Dominican women "are more likely to own smaller and less profitable firms than their male counterparts."[35]

Guarnizo has also argued that Dominican entrepreneurship in general has both relied on and created new forms of social capital as a result of the transnationalization of the community. It has also created new forms of cultural capital specific to the transnational experience. He writes:

> The ethnic-oriented production and distribution of goods and services—that is, not only *what* is produced and sold, but *how* it is done—recreates culture and by so doing facilitates the life of immigrants upon arrival, making

it easier for them to adapt to their new world. Of course this does not mean adaptation, let alone assimilation into the dominant culture. It relates to the culture the immigrant situation creates, which never duplicates fully that of the immigrants' native land, but is close enough to prevent a potential culture shock to both new and old immigrants.[36]

Luís Guarnizo also found that Dominican businesses tend to cater primarily to other Dominicans and Latinos.[37] Dominicans in New York City are more residentially and occupationally segregated than their Washington, D.C., counterparts. They live, work, and socialize primarily with other Latinas/os, usually Dominicans.

At the same time, Anneris Goris-Rosario found that Dominicans who work outside their community are no more integrated into the larger New York City community than those who work among Dominicans. Dominicans working outside their ethnic enclaves, although more likely to have non-Latino employers and supervisors and to speak English in their workplaces, work primarily alongside other Latina/os with whom they speak Spanish and sustain ethno-racial norms. Goris-Rosario suggested further that Dominicans reproduce the characteristics of Dominican businesses in Washington Heights and Inwood in their workplaces outside those communities.[38] Thus, they are able to sustain and reproduce pre-immigration ethno-racial identities that are somewhat more independent of local African American communities than their D.C. counterparts.

In terms of Dominican ideal culture norms, beauty-shop work is considered women's purview, while commercial or manufacturing ventures are generally considered male domains.[39] *Bodegueras* (female bodega owners) for example, while not uncommon, often have male kin "*representándolas* [representing them]" at the store counter. Likewise, while Dominican men do own beauty shops, they are less likely to be owner-operators, preferring instead to hire women as managers. Guarnizo notes that in a classic case of entrepreneurial succession, Dominican *bodegueros* have stepped into an entrepreneurial niche abandoned by Puerto Rican men.[40] Dominican women have followed a similar pathway into the beauty-shop niche in that they have stepped into chairs and shops previously owned and operated by Cuban and Puerto Rican women in Manhattan. Commercial Dominican shops range in size from small, three-chair operations to large, more expensive salons with eight to ten chairs. At the same time, many women continue to work out of their kitchens, operating on the basis of word of mouth, without licensing and unlisted in the telephone directory. A typical Dominican salon in Washington Heights has four styling chairs and two hair-washing sinks, includes a manicurist, and occasionally employs an esthetician who provides waxing, facials, and massages. Currently there is a thriving Dominican beauty-culture industry in New York City, supported primarily by Dominican women (table 4). In Washington Heights and Inwood alone—that is, in northwestern Manhattan, from 155th Street to the 190s and from the Harlem River on the east to the Hudson River on the west, where 40 percent of the Dominican population in New York resides—there are 146 salons (figure 20). On average, these salons are less than a quarter-mile (or one-and-one-half blocks) apart from one another. There is, in other words, a salon on nearly every block in Washington Heights.

By comparison, there are only 103 (or 40 percent fewer) beauty shops on Manhattan's far wealthier Upper East Side, which is the area from East 61st Street to East 94th Street and from Fifth Avenue to the East River. The salons are just over three-quarters of a mile apart, on average. In Harlem, where average per capita income is nearly identical to that in Washington Heights and Inwood, there are 112 shops. Shops in Harlem, which ranges from 114th Street to 138th Street and from the Fifth Avenue to the Hudson River, are just under half a mile apart, on average.[41] Washington Heights and Inwood are only somewhat more densely populated than Harlem. That there are 30 percent more shops in Washington Heights than in Harlem, therefore, indicates that the provision of beauty-shop services is even more visible and pronounced among Dominicans than among African Americans.

Interestingly, the community district with the largest number of shops was Hamilton Heights, a border district between Harlem and Washington Heights. In the 1990s, 45 percent of its residents were African American, and 33 percent were Dominican. While many shops in this area do advertise a mélange of African American and Dominican services, most cater specifically to either one community or the other. Increasingly, however, African American women are turning to Dominican hairdressers, especially in areas like Hamilton Heights, where they are residing alongside one another.[42] Perhaps this is why there is one shop for every 877 residents, making Hamilton Heights the most beauty-shop-dense district in Manhattan.

These upper Manhattan neighborhoods have received large contingents of Latin American and Caribbean immigrants (often dispropor-

Table 4 Beauty Shops and Beauty-Supply Centers in Residential Upper Manhattan

Community Districts and Zip Codes	Total Number of Shops	Shops with Employers	Percentage of Total	Beauty-Supply Centers
Upper East Side				
10128	18	22	100	0
10021	61	104	100	0
10028	24	32	100	0
Total	103[a]	158[a]	100[a]	0
Average number of residents per shop	1,958	1,277	N/A	0
Upper West Side and Cathedral				
10024	16	16	100	0
10025	11	18	100	0
Total	27[a]	34[a]	100[a]	0
Average number of residents per shop	6,877	4,854	N/A	0
El Barrio				
10029	23	5	22	0
10035	18	1	6	2
Total	41	6	15	2
Average number of residents per shop	2,511	17,158	N/A	51,471
Harlem				
10026	13	0	0	0
10027	58	5	9	4
10030	21	0	0	1
10037	2	2	100	1
10039	18	1	6	1
Total	112	8	7	7
Average number of residents per shop	1,288	18,033	N/A	20,610

Table 4 *Continued*

Community Districts and Zip Codes	Total Number of Shops	Shops with Employers	Percentage of Total	Beauty-Supply Centers
Hamilton Heights				
10031	64	9	14%	4
Total	64	9	14%	4
Average number of residents per shop	877	6,245	N/A	14,043
Washington Heights and Inwood				
10032	42	7	17	0
10033	51	9	18	3
10034	23	5	22	3
10040	30	7	23	0
Total	156	28	18	6
Average number of residents per shop	1,286	7,168	N/A	33,450

Sources: 1990 U.S. Census, database c90STFSB, Zip code summary level; 1992 Economic Census, Service Industries, Firms Subject to Federal Income Tax, Zip code statistics; New York City Department of City Planning, *The Newest New Yorkers, 1990–1994;* "Beauty Salons," *Manhattan Yellow Pages,* April 1999–April 2000, 159–68.

[a]Reflects a discrepancy between census figures and personal count based on *Manhattan Yellow Pages* and telephone census conducted June 1999.

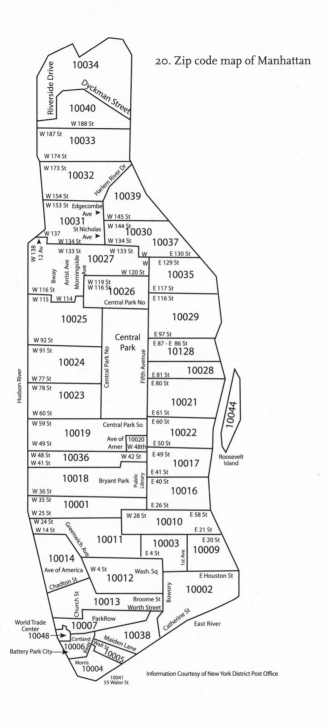

20. Zip code map of Manhattan

Information Courtesy of New York District Post Office

tionately female) in the past three decades. The immigrant women bring with them not only a demand for culturally specific hair-care practices and services, but also culturally specific hair-care skills and beauty-culture practices. Thus, the rise in owner-operated shops in Manhattan and Brooklyn, for example, parallels the growth and establishment of large, predominantly female Caribbean communities in those boroughs.[43] According to the U.S. Bureau of Labor Statistics, by 1998 6,140 Latinas were employed as hairdressers and cosmetologists in New York State; of those, 915, or 15 percent, were self-employed. This number does not include women who operate in the informal sector, selling their hair-care services either through their home or at the homes of their clients, a fairly common practice in the Dominican community. It is also likely that undocumented workers would be excluded, as well as those working in unlicensed facilities. Even so, the 5,225 Latinas employed as wage and salary workers in beauty shops represented roughly 25 percent of the sector's 1998 workforce, although they are only 7 percent of the population overall.[44] In other words, Latinas are over-represented in the industry.

Salon Lamadas: A Dominican Beauty Shop in New York City

> Cause in our mutual obvious dislike
>
> for nappiness
>
> we came together
>
> under the hot comb
>
> to share
>
> and share
>
> and share.

—Willi Coleman[45]

Salon Lamadas, where I did my fieldwork, was in many ways a typical Dominican salon (figure 21).[46] It was located in the heart of Washington Heights, on St. Nicholas Avenue, several blocks south of the 181st Street shopping district. The streets were very busy there. There was a constant parade of people. Women with strollers predominated during the week, followed by young women alone or in pairs, single men, and occasionally couples. The bodega next door sold fruit and vegetables; out front, a lady

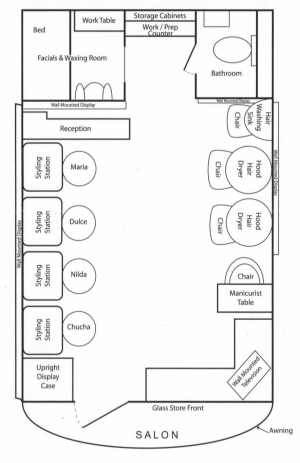

21. Salon Lamadas on a typical day

22. Floor plan, Salon Lamadas

sold contraband makeup and nail polish from a makeshift stand in the shade of a small tree in front of the bodega, and the "*jodedores* ("fuckers," troublemakers, or drug dealers) stood around chatting behind her. They were mostly older men in their forties, flashily dressed but discreet about their business. They kept their drugs stashed in a nearby apartment and used one or two of the neighborhood *tigüeritos* (punks) who also stood there to distribute the goods. On the other side of the salon were a telephone station, a pharmacy, a Pronto Envío remittance agency, and a family restaurant.

Founded in 1992 by an owner-operator, Salon Lamadas was an average-size shop with four stylists, including the owner, a shampooer, a manicurist, and a facialist/masseuse. Music was always playing at the salon, sometimes quite loudly. It was generally merengue and salsa, although one or two *boleros* were occasionally heard. Often the television was turned on, as well, and it was usually tuned to *Cristina*, a popular Miami-based, Spanish-language talk show. In addition to the music and the television, the blow dryers were constantly going. Despite all this noise, the women heard each other quite well and carried on conversations across the room.

Salon Lamadas was open seven days a week. Although many salons close on Mondays, Dominican salons do not, for several reasons. First, Dominican women use salons for regular, weekly hair care, not for intermittent haircuts and hair treatments. Therefore, there was demand for services throughout the week rather than only toward the weekend, when more formal social gatherings occur, although Fridays and Saturdays are still the busiest days. Second, the staff needed to work six days a week to earn enough money to survive in the city and, for many, to send home to the Dominican Republic. Third, because Dominican women are heavily represented in blue-collar and pink-collar work, the salon accommodated their varied and long working hours.[47]

Every possible inch of floor and wall space was fully utilized in Salon Lamadas. As the shop's layout indicates (figure 22), income was generated both through the provision of services and through product sales. Salon Lamadas's shop space was rectangular, about fifteen feet wide and thirty-five feet long. The entire storefront was glass, and the walls facing and behind the styling chairs were mirrored, giving an illusion of light and space where both were limited. A small waiting area was located to the right of the entrance, consisting of a low, L-shaped, built-in storage area that was carpeted for comfortable seating space. The L was four feet long at its long end—long enough to seat about three average-size women—and three feet long at the base, where another two people could sit. A manicurist's table was positioned at the long end of the L, facing the door. Customers who were having their nails done sat facing the manicurist and at a right angle to others sitting behind her. Behind the manicurist were two more chairs for waiting customers. Behind those chairs were four bonnet hair dryers, followed by a hair-washing sink. Along the wall above the sinks and the hair dryers were display cases that extended to the ceiling. The cases were jammed with hair products, primarily Sebastian, Joico, Razac, Paul Mitchell, and Salerno.

Behind the hair-washing station and at the end of the shop was a tiny bathroom, where housekeeping supplies, peroxides, and other chemicals were stored. Along the far wall of the shop's rear, between the bathroom and the facials room, was a waist-level counter, with cupboards above and below. Hair dyes were stored and prepared there; Dominican coffee was percolated on a hot plate; and occasionally someone ate lunch standing at the counter. Across from the bathroom and next to the counter was the facials room. The space was about six feet wide by ten feet long. Because both it and the hallway were so narrow, a pocket door was used rather than a conventional swinging door. A black-vinyl-padded massage and facials table that was pushed up against the far wall dominated the room. At the end of the room and at the head of the table were steam machines and magnifying mirrors, as well as shelving that contained skin-care products, again primarily Sebastian. A small, dorm-size refrigerator sat in a corner, on top of which was the hot wax pot.

Across from the hair-washing station was a tall and narrow pink Formica counter. The shop's only telephone, a pay phone, sat there. Behind the counter were stored the hairstyle books, the cash box, and ledger. Along the wall above, behind, and beside the counter were more Plexiglas display cases reaching to the ceiling and filled with hair-care products. The largest case in the store was alongside the shop counter, facing the hair dryers, where women often sat for at least an hour. In front of this case were two more bonnet dryers. Next to the case and along the remaining fifteen feet of wall space were the shop's four hairstyling stations.

Each station had a narrow, pink Formica hairdressing counter with a drawer and equipment slot protruding from the mirrored wall. The styling chairs were padded in pink vinyl and covered in plastic. Each stylist had one or two personal effects at her station, but otherwise the stations were identical. Next to the first station closest to the front door and behind the front door was another floor-to-ceiling display case. As the floor plan reveals, hairstyling, relaxing, and coloring were central public activities, while skin care was an intermittent private task. Food consumption had a place, but one that was limited and, when possible, hidden. The expectation that clients would be waiting for a while was evident in the maximization of seating areas.

The prevailing colors were light pink, gray, black, and white. The floor of the work area was covered in light-gray linoleum tile, and the waiting area was covered in dark-gray industrial carpeting. The walls and drop ceiling in the general shop and facials room were painted white, while the bathroom was pink. The manicurist's table was white Formica, as were the many display cases. The two rolling curlers and pins carts stored behind the manicurist were white plastic. The furnishings were light pink with either black or chrome accents and trim. The large storefront awning was a deeper "shocking pink." The shop's name was written in large black cursive script on both sides and on the front of the awning. The pink motif was carried through to the shop's business cards, which were pink and lavender.

The colors employed in Salon Lamadas's decor are symbolic. Salons have historically used white as a base color in their decor to connote hygiene and health care, themes that are historically related to beauty culture. The grays, blacks, and chromes connote modernity and technological advancement.[48] Finally, pink is traditionally a feminine color. However, in the context of Salon Lamadas, pink had a deeper meaning, as did the salon's name.

Salon "Lamadas," while superficially a nonsensical nomenclature, was a coded declaration of the shop's "open secret": Salon Lamadas's owner-operators, Leticia and Chucha, were lesbian partners. "Salon Lamadas" was actually code for "salon *de las dos amadas* [the two beloved women's salon]."[49] Further, pink is now the color of gay and lesbian liberation and pride in the United States. In this way, Leticia and Chucha were "secretly declaring" in bold black letters covering the bright-pink front awning that they were the besotted lesbian owners of this enterprise.

Leticia and Chucha openly lived together, traveled together, ran the shop together, and bickered and joked with the intimacy of life partners. At the same time, their sexuality was unnamed and explicitly unacknowledged by them and by staff and clients. No one called them a couple, much less a lesbian couple, or even "partners." Thus, their relationship was an "open secret." When asked to characterize their relationship, customers giggled, shifted about uncomfortably, whispered that while others had passed on rumors that Leticia and Chucha were gay, they personally had never seen anything to verify that. The "anything" missing for those observers was public physical contact and affection. And, in fact, Leticia and Chucha studiously avoided touching, hugging, or kissing, even when posing together for pictures during their celebration of the salon's anniversary.

The "open secret" displayed by Chucha's and Leticia's partnership was the defining theme of Salon Lamadas, and, I would argue, it offered an apt metaphor for the role of hair culture in the management of blackness and Dominican identity displays. On the surface, the work of the shop operators and the meaning of hair care seem fairly straightforward. Beauty-shop work can be poorly paid and tiring, and it requires limited amounts of education and training. Similarly, the common Dominican practices of chemically relaxing and blow drying hair into straightness seem supportive of Eurocentric aesthetics. Below the surface — or perhaps one should say, "behind the ears" — however, lie other meanings. Dominican women's hair culture practices are intended to create "authentic-looking" Dominican women who, as I will elaborate in the next chapter, embody an Indo-Hispanic appearance. The open secret was the artifice required to keep the "black behind the ears," a task that Salon Lamadas workers and clients undertook with the same mixture of recognition and disavowal with which they approached the fact of Chucha's and Leticia's "queerness." Whether they were getting their hair done or dissimulating their recognition of the lesbian partnership, Dominican women at Salon Lamadas were collaborating in the cultural work of "saving face" while being true to themselves.

The Culture Workers

The owner, Chucha, was an attractive and stylish forty-something-year-old woman from the capital of the Dominican Republic (figure 23).[50] Her partner, Leticia, was a forty-something-year-old woman from Santiago de los Caballeros, the Dominican Republic's second-largest city. Although Chucha was the legal owner of the shop, she and Leticia were partners in its day-to-day operation. Chucha had a loyal following and worked behind the chair every day except Tuesday. Standing behind the first chair, Chucha was clearly in charge of the shop's personnel and services, and she actively set the tenor and tone of the shop's routine. She had been in New York City since the mid-1980s, working in beauty shops nearly from the moment of her arrival. Leticia was in charge of promotions,

23. Chucha blow drying a client's hair

product sales, inventory, cash receipts, and the shop's ledgers. She also maintained the shop's physical plant, doing small repairs, purchasing furnishings, and overseeing the cleaning of display cases and the storefront. As I noted in my field notes, Leticia was "the front person, the public person. She did the client reconnaissance for the salon, she knew other salon owners in the area, she worked the street, she spoke for the salon." Prior to migrating "permanently," she had traveled frequently to New York. Finally, in her mid-thirties, she moved to New York City permanently.

Behind the chair next to Chucha was Nilda, who was from Dajabon, a small town on the Dominican–Haitian border. Nilda arrived in New York when her daughter was three, following her divorce. Next to Nilda was Alma. She was in her late thirties, a more jovial person than the others, frequently telling funny stories and jokes and spontaneously breaking into song when a favorite tune played on the shop's radio. A native of

La Vega, she moved to Santo Domingo when she married, and raised her children there. When her youngest daughter was of school age, she divorced and migrated to New York City.

Then there was María. She and Alma were sisters-in-law and were similar in temperament. However, María was the quietest member of the shop. Short and plump, she was seven months pregnant with her second child when I first arrived at Salon Lamadas. Born, raised, and married in Santiago, María had migrated to New York with her husband after the birth of her first child. The facialist, Nené, was also in her third trimester of pregnancy when I first entered the shop. Nené was the "third in command" of the shop in Chucha's and Leticia's absence. She migrated to New York in her late twenties.

When I first arrived at Salon Lamadas, Leonora was the manicurist. Born, raised, and married in San José de las Matas, a rural area of the Dominican Republic, she migrated to New York in her thirties. Three months into my fieldwork, however, Leonora gave up her table and went to work from home. She was replaced by Fannie, who had previously helped around the shop on weekends and during staff vacations. At twenty-four, Fannie was the youngest member of the shop. A native of Barahona, she migrated to New York City while still in high school with hopes of attending college here. Like Alma, she was prone to singing out loud to her favorite songs. After Leonora left the shop, Fannie took over the manicure table full time. Finally, Flor, a Santiago native, was the shop's shampooer, receptionist, janitor, and all-around assistant. A former nurse, she had migrated to New York just two years earlier and almost immediately began working at the shop. Although pleasant and warm, she was as quiet as María.

There was a clear social and professional hierarchy at Salon Lamadas. Who was asked to run errands, answer the phone, and assist Chucha indicated who had more or less status. As in U.S. salons generally, staff were organized along a professional, personal, class, and race continuum. Chucha was the most privileged member of the shop, primarily because she was its owner. However, status also accrued to her by virtue of her class background and color privilege. The daughter of upper-middle-class professionals in the Dominican Republic's capital, Chucha attended the Universidad Autónoma de Santo Domingo. She grew up in Gazcue, an upper-middle-class neighborhood,[51] and traveled frequently to Puerto Rico while coming of age. In addition, Chucha was universally considered "una mujer fina [a fine woman]." "Fina [fine]" is a socio-racial descriptor that encompasses both physical features and deportment. To be *fina* is to be light-skinned or white with thin nose and lips, to be tall, and to be tasteful. Since she was thought to have all of these qualities, she was considered *legitimately* in charge by the staff for socio-racial reasons as well as obvious economic ones.

Alongside, but slightly below, Chucha on the status chain was Leticia. As Chucha's partner, Leticia was endowed with relational status and authority. Further, as the shop's financial manager, she wielded a degree of power. However, her physical appearance only partially legitimated her status because she was perceived to embody a contradictory mixture of socio-racial signs. She was light-skinned and had "*pelo bueno* [good hair]." Yet she was also was described as short and "*media ordinaria* [somewhat ordinary]," where "ordinary" meant that she had a broad nose, full lips, and a broad mouth, all considered to be signs of African ancestry. To be "somewhat ordinary," in other words, meant to be somewhat black. Thus, Leticia was powerful and "white," but not as powerful and "white" as Chucha.

The third on the status chain was Nené. Like Leticia, she was described by the others as embodying a mixture of socio-racial signs. She was considered light-skinned and of medium height, bodily features they considered white. At the same time, she had relaxed "*pelo malo* [bad hair]" and was characterized by her co-workers as "*ordinaria* [ordinary]" and "*áspera* [rough]," in terms of her facial features and her personality. Accordingly, her authority in the shop was tenuous, relational, and situational. She had a close and trusting relationship with Chucha, and secondarily with Leticia. In their absence, she handled the cash flow, sold the products, and generally managed the shop. Nonetheless, she was often directly challenged, and occasionally ridiculed and chastised, by the stylists and the manicurist, who considered her stupid.

As a group, the stylists were subordinate to Chucha and Leticia. None of them identified or was identified by the others as white. They were instead classified as *India* or *India clara*, intermediate categories between black and white. However, the degree of subordination varied depending on their compensation structure; their education, experience, and licensing; and their personalities. Of the three, María was the most economically autonomous and thus the least subordinate to Chucha and Leticia. She rented her chair at Salon Lamadas for $300 per week and kept all her earnings. She set her own hours and was the only staff member who took Sundays off, a privilege neither the wage-based nor commission-based staff was allowed. While she was considered to be the darkest skinned of the shop stylists, she had naturally thick and lustrous "*pelo bueno*" and "regular" features; because of this, she was classified as "*India clara*." She was also licensed by New York State, held a cosmetology degree from a Dominican beauty school, had attended university in Santiago, and had owned her own shop in the Dominican Republic prior to migrating. Each of these features positioned her almost at par with Chucha. Because she was quiet and reserved, however, she was perceived as "too sweet" to be in charge. However, María was never asked to serve Chucha. Given that María was the only stylist who had a *silla rentada* (rented chair) and thus was not as profitable for Chucha as the employees were, María was fairly independent of and respected by Chucha.

Next was Nilda, who was never asked to serve Chucha and, indeed, re-fused to answer the phone, but who worked for commissions. A licensed stylist, she had worked in the industry since she was a teenager and had participated actively in the professionalization of the Dominican beauty-shop industry prior to migrating. By contrast, Alma was the only stylist ever asked to run errands, answer the phone, serve *café*, or hand things to Chucha. Alma was not licensed, and she had come to professional hair-dressing late in life, following her divorce. She was the least experienced of the stylists and, as she put it, was "grateful to Chucha" for employ-ing her. Her lack of credentials and Chucha's professional patronage, in other words, lowered Alma's status in the shop.

Flor was expected to assist and serve Chucha and Leticia first, and then all of the others. Flor also responded "*¿Señora?* (Yes, ma'am?)" when Leticia called to her, which is how maids typically respond to their employers in the Dominican Republic.[52] Similarly, although all the staff partook of mutual grooming activities, she was the only staff member who was expected to disrupt her own grooming to tend to clients. For ex-ample, if someone arrived and asked to see or purchase a product while Flor was having her hair dried or set, she was expected to stand and as-sist the client, even if the others were unoccupied. Indeed, Flor worked longer hours and did more physically strenuous work than any of the staff. The salon opened at ten in the morning, but she arrived two hours earlier to clean the salon and set up for the day's work. On Mondays she arrived at seven in the morning and did a full cleaning, including the large glass doors of the display cases. She also washed hair, set rollers, and applied relaxers and hair dyes. She rarely sat and rested, as the others did when there were no clients to attend to.

Leonora, the manicurist, was exempted from this hierarchy in that she did not have to answer to Chucha because she rented her space for $150 per week and because she was not competing with the others for her

24. Salon Lamadas staff. Clockwise from top: María, Chucha, Letitia, Nilda, Nene, Fannie, Alma, and Leonora

customers. Conversely, when Fannie replaced Leonora, she was working on a commission basis utilizing Chucha's products and equipment. Thus, she was subordinate to Chucha. As this analysis illustrates, a complex web of interactions between class background, phenotype, and employment status within Salon Lamadas operated to organize hierarchical relationships between owners and staff. At the same time, however, in contrast to the dynamic in white salons, Salon Lamadas's beauty culturalists were positioned at par, and at times above, their clients in terms of status and prestige (figure 24).

In "Pamela's Place: Power and Negotiation in the Hair Salon," Debra Gimlin finds that white beauty operators engage in particular strategies to diminish the class distance between themselves as personal-service providers and the clients who purchase those services. White operators emphasize their overall fashion expertise, their superior technical skills, and their greater knowledge of the client's beauty needs. In this way, they position themselves less as personal-service providers than as professionals and artisans.[53] Schroder likewise points out that while some white hairstylists have developed a degree of fame and elite status, white clients see hairdressers "as rather *déclassé*, perhaps reflecting the fact that beauticians deliver a rather intimate service."[54] Similarly, in an article for

Ms. magazine, Louise Kapp Howe emphasized the drudgery and exploitative nature of beauty-shop work, which she considers to be "pink-collar" work and by definition less prestigious than professional or "white-collar" work.[55] It would seem from these assessments that the only white beauty shops where operators and clients share status levels and develop relationships across class lines are those depicted in film and television where "the beauty salon seems a much more benign place than it often is in life," as the *New York Times* writer Caryn James put it.[56]

By contrast, Dominicans, like African Americans have historically endowed beauty-culture workers with social status and professional standing incommensurate with their educational attainment or class backgrounds. This is likely due to the fact that beauty shops have provided women of color with entrepreneurial employment and social opportunities that are not otherwise offered by dominant white society. In traditionally African American neighborhoods such as Harlem, owner-operated shops have predominated since the 1920s. Studies of African American shops were conducted during the Great Migration of the 1930s in Philadelphia, New Orleans, St. Louis, and Columbus, Ohio. "Of the 75 Negro shops included in this study over four-fifths (62) were independently owned; approximately two-fifths of these were small commercial concerns, while more than one-half were connected with the owner's living quarters."[57] Conditions in African American shops were similar across the nation, as a New York State report on the beauty shop industry noted in 1931:

> Unlike white operators, the majority of Negro women engaged in beauty culture in Harlem work independently, either in their own shops in which they generally do all the work or in booths which they rent in a larger shop. The few women found who did not own their shops or rent their booths, and who might be regarded in some respects as employees rather than independent proprietors, generally work exclusively on a commission basis rather than on a wage basis. In some cases they set their own hours, working when they please and dividing their earnings with the shop owner.[58]

In addition, African American shops tended to stay open later to accommodate the work schedules of their patrons, many of who were themselves service workers with long workdays. Similar patterns are evident today among Dominicans in Washington Heights and Inwood and, to a lesser degree, among Puerto Ricans in the El Barrio neighborhood of East Harlem.

Moreover, beauty shops in minority communities have relayed socially, politically, economically, and culturally valuable information to their clients. For example, Diedra Forte has noted the success of African American beauty shops used as agents in community-based breast-cancer intervention programs directed toward older African American women.[59] Similarly, in his study of Latina beauty shops in Lawrence, Massachusetts, Melvin Delgado pointed to the multiple roles played by the shops in the community: "The Latina owners expressed willingness to involve themselves in leadership roles on social agency boards, advisory committees, task forces, and so forth. . . . The women, with few exceptions, recognized the impact of social problems on the customers and their families."[60] Certainly, that was the case at Salon Lamadas.

"A este salon hay que respetarlo":[61]
Conflicting Agendas in the Shop

At Salon Lamadas, Dominican immigrant women simultaneously reproduced their Dominican beauty-culture norms and learned about consumer culture and taste in the United States. As Nurka, a regular client, explained to me, the salon owners and stylists arbitrated taste:

> I think that they are taken into account for their opinions. Once I was there and a lady called on the telephone, she called the owner, regarding a brand of clothing or something. And Chucha says, "Yes, that is a good brand." For a reference! On clothes and such. It's as if they consider them to know it all. Everything about everything, fashion, beauty. About everything in terms of personal beauty.

As gatekeepers to both Dominican and U.S. cultural norms, salon staff negotiated conflicting gender, race, and class codes and symbols. Their right to do so was based on their status as technicians of the body. After all, they had been professionally trained into the Dominican beauty-shop industry, both on the island and in New York.

Professionalism and its maintenance were a guiding and oft-repeated theme at Salon Lamadas. Central to that project were the licensing of its staff, their level of personal grooming, and the exclusion of children and food from the shop. Chucha and her staff took great pride in the fact that most of them were fully licensed by the state. Their status as professionals, in other words, was verified by their ability to negotiate the industry in this country as well as in the Dominican Republic.

Chucha, for example, often emphasized the difference between "*mujeres que saben hacer rolos* [women who know how to do curler sets]" and "*estilistas* [stylists]." The first she described variously as "*mujer de barrio* [ghetto woman]" and "*una qualquiera* [an any nobody]" who is willing to operate as if on a "factory assembly line," producing routinized and un-imaginative "heads." Thus, as Leticia pointed out, the streets of Washington Heights were covered with Dominican factory workers sporting nearly identical shades of "*pelo colora'o* [red hair]." Stylists, by contrast, were trained professionals who approached their work with "artistic" vision and dedication. In sum, as Chucha put it, "Anyone can wash and set hair. Few can create style." Yet most of her, and the others,' days were spent setting, drying, and blow drying set hair. What is more, Chucha was well aware of the profitability of clients' willingness to imitate other women.

Following a training seminar in new color products, Chucha insisted on dying Flor's hair, in her own words, "*Para vender, para vender. Porque a la gente lo que le gusta es lo que ven* [To sell, to sell. Because people like what they see]." This tension between ideal professional status as artists and everyday business practices reflects the lot of stylists more generally. The stylist is the taste and fashion expert. Yet she is also constrained by the personal-service and non-essential nature of her industry and must ultimately concede to her client's desires or risk losing her following and her income.

For example, one Wednesday, a Dominican woman in her forties came in. She had very short, coarse, reddish hair with patches missing by her ears, at the back of the head, and at the crown. She explained to Chucha that she had had a bad *derrizado* (chemical relaxer) at another salon and that she wanted to have her hair fixed for an important family event that was taking place the following Sunday. Chucha told her that her hair was too damaged for further processing and that she should wait for more growth before relaxing or coloring the hair again. The woman insisted that she could not stand to see herself looking so unkempt. Chucha re-fused to take her as a client that day.

That Friday, however, the woman returned and insisted on being ser-viced. Chucha conceded and spent several hours working to treat and style the woman's hair. After the customer left, I approached Chucha and asked her whether that was the same woman from Wednesday.

GINETTA: Chucha, wasn't that the same woman from the other day that you couldn't tend to?

CHUCHA: Girl, don't say anything. That nut has me ill! I told her that she wasn't in any condition to do anything in those kinks. You know what that is? She comes here with that head so ugly so I can fix what can't be fixed.

GINETTA: And did it turn out well?

CHUCHA: For what she had of hair, yes.

GINETTA: I noticed that she is kind of missing some hair.

CHUCHA: Some? She's missing chunks.

GINETTA: What happened to her?

CHUCHA: She says that someone did a bad relaxer on her. I think she did it herself, fucking around at home with stuff you can't play with. Look, I'm so pissed. No, no, no, it's just that I can't. I told her that she had to cut off all that rotten hair and let it grow again. I'd even buzz her.

GINETTA: And she didn't want to?

CHUCHA: No. Supposedly she couldn't go around like that, without hair, through the streets. She prefers going around with those kinks, with that rotten head. You know what that is?

LEONORA: If it were me, I'd shave my head in order to not go around like that. That old lady is crazy; she looks like a clown.

Chucha's anger stemmed from the sense that her profession and her professionalism had been doubly undermined. First, the client's attempt to relax her own hair flew in the face of the skills and experience a "delicate" process requires; only a professional has both in sufficient quantities. Second, the client's insistence and Chucha's ultimate concession to have her errors corrected heightened the service nature of the profession. Having in effect to clean up another person's mess highlighted the servile nature of hairdressing precisely at the same time that its artistry and professionalism were being dismissed. It also tested the limits of what was possible in terms of "fixing" so-called bad hair and creating an appropriately Dominican look. The client's botched beauty efforts made the artificiality of an "authentic Dominican look" more obvious. By going around "with those kinks," the client was "looking like a clown," a spectacle.

The fulfillment of her Dominican clients' needs was often in direct contradiction to Chucha's perception of appropriate professional norms and shop culture. For example, she believed that the presence of children and food created an informal atmosphere based on familiarity and community care. Central to the professionalization project was the exclusion of children and food from the shop. There were as many as nine neon-colored paper signs taped up throughout the store that prohibited eating and drinking in the shop and exhorted patrons to leave their children at home, particularly on Fridays and Saturdays. People brought their children to the shop with them and let them run around, Chucha explained, but the space was far too tight to accommodate them. It was clearly one of her pet peeves, together with people eating "full meals" at the salon, as it undermined her efforts toward professionalism.

Yet on most days, the ambulatory vendor who sold *empanadas de queso y de pollo* (meat and cheese patties) and tamarind, carrot, and passion fruit juices came by, and nearly everyone in the salon purchased food from her, despite the signs prohibiting eating in the shop. Also, clients continued to bring their children, including infants. While in the shop, children were treated as if they were kin to all, even when they were strangers to the shop. A selection from my field notes illustrates:

> One of the clients brought her twenty-three month old with her while she had her hair washed, set, and dried, all of which took about two hours. All the women there treated him as if he were a nephew. Nené fed him empanadas, Leticia roughhoused with him, Alma caressed him, etc. When he left with his mother, Chucha said that having him there all that time was "*un abuso* [abusive]" and that she didn't understand how women can do that.

Chucha herself was childless and often made disapproving comments about children and about the mothers for bringing them to the shop. While the child was in the shop, however, Chucha cooed over him and stroked his head several times. The misbehavior of clients' children and the inappropriateness of their presence in the shop was a frequent topic of conversation.

Indeed, all three of the stylists said that Chucha's prohibitions against children had diminished their client base. María explained:

> And like that, a lot of people have left. I had a lot of clients who are moms, too, who have left me. I have worked in a lot of places, and nothing had ever been said, but now, now, you see that they go, when they go, when their children go and start in, they insult them. "Boy! Be careful! This is a salon!" And the moms, you see, they feel bad. A lot of people have told me that they've stopped going because of that. Because sometime you don't have anyone to leave them with, and twenty dollars for washing your hair and then having to pay for a babysitter, it's a lot. A lot of people have stopped going now. [Chucha tells them,] "No, this is not a day care!" And you see, when you're with someone who has children, who has children? It's stressful for them not to move. And you see that people don't like it very much. A lot of people tell me. I have a good client, she's not coming back ever again. She bought a meat patty and a drink, she came in to eat it, and Chucha threw her out. She

told her that eating isn't allowed in a shop. In other words, it was in order to make her feel bad. And like that, many have left.

That is, what Chucha *says* indicates that she is hostile to children and food; but what she *does* indicates her acceptance of their presence. Paulina, a longstanding and loyal client, explained: "Yes, sometimes Chucha is a little hard on the children, but not with my daughters so far. No, she's treated them well. If not, I don't think I'd go back." There was a degree of tension, in other words, between her clients' and her staff's personal and material needs and her attempts to assert the professionalism from which she drew her class and cultural authority.

The eating of meals at the salon was another area of tense negotiation. Staff members were required to eat the lunch a neighborhood woman named Nana delivered for them in the privacy of the facials room. Previously, they had had to go to Nana's apartment across the street to eat. After Chucha began to eat in the shop, the stylists soon followed her example. Nana brought lunch by around noon, although it often was not eaten until two or three in the afternoon. Everyone except Flor and Alma ate Nana's food. They each paid $6 per meal each day. Since a similar meal could be had across the street at a small restaurant for $3.50, I asked Leonora why they used Nana's costlier services. She explained that Nana cooked especially for them. She prepared low-fat, low-salt, diet-conscious meals, and she delivered. She began by cooking occasionally for Chucha and the others when they worked together at another salon. When Nana was laid off from her job, Chucha and the staff contracted her for full-time provision of home-made, delivered meals.

Having food delivered to the salon was a status-marking activity that referred back to the upper-middle-class Dominican custom of having household maids deliver afternoon meals to their employers' offices or workplaces. Having Nana deliver to Salon Lamadas affirmed Chucha's and the others' professional and class status. To be able to spend $36 per week on lunch, the thinking went, one must be earning well. Thus, Flor and Alma, the two workers with the least status and lowest earnings, did not eat Nana's delivered food. They either skipped the noon meal or brought food from home. The rest of the staff ate in the facials room, usually two at a time, except for Chucha, who preferred to eat alone and who was not to be disturbed while she ate. All used the padded massage table as a dining table, to which they pulled up chairs. They ate and chatted but were generally done eating in twenty minutes or so. It was not an especially comfortable place to eat, and it was against local health codes to eat where massages, waxing, and facials are performed. But it was the only private space in the salon, and Chucha insisted on removing food from the salon's public workspace as much as possible.

"Ni a los salones ni a los medicos se va huyendo": Dominican Hair Culture Takes Time

Dominican beauty culture, with its requisite time investment, also provided regular and extended opportunities for developing intimacy and sharing information. The salon acted as a "third place"—a "generic designation for a great variety of public places that host the regular, voluntary, informal, and happily anticipated gatherings of individuals beyond the realm of home and work."[62] Salon Lamadas was an intimate social space beyond the home and the workplace where women could congregate and talk about topics that ranged from their assessment of local, national, and international politics and happenings to the provision of information about how to negotiate local institutions and bureaucracies and the emotionally and psychologically taxing terrains of romantic relationships, health issues, and workplace experiences. As Antonia put it:

> I go to the salon to clear my mind, to rest. For me, it's like therapy. I don't have to do or think about anything if I don't want to. I spend a few hours taking care of myself. I partake of the jokes they make, I laugh a little bit, I listen to their stories—although I don't tell my stuff—and so on, you see?

As Antonia indicates, at the salon women can reaffirm their personal worth beyond their roles as mothers, wives and lovers, and workers. Like her, they can participate in a culture of lighthearted exchange to which they set limits of their own choosing. Thus, Antonia connected with other women by listening rather than by sharing her own affairs. In so doing, she met her needs for companionship and sociality, together with the needs of her countrywomen who wanted to be heard. However, because of the porous boundaries of that sociality, Antonia guarded herself from the possibility that her affairs could become part of the "gossip."

When asked what they liked best about Salon Lamadas, many other respondents also mentioned the talk and laughter that occurred there. Aleida, for example, noted:

> It's funny to me just to see how all these women talk, and they are so expressive when they're talking. They use their hands. They act it out. And you

pick up on so much gossip that you haven't heard elsewhere. You pick it up there *(laughter)*. It's fun. That's what I like. It's just women who dominate the work area. What you hear in conversation, is "my husband" or "We're going to a party" or "Let's plan for this." They're always, "On Friday, we have a party, don't forget." Things like that. They are very close. They were talking about Nené. The fact that she was so worried about her family in [the Dominican Republic after Hurricane Georges] that she kept walking up and down the salon saying, "Oh my God, you know what happened? I have to go call." And then she started laughing and crying at the same time. While she was laughing, her tears were coming down. So they were making fun of her. She was loud!

Aleida viewed the salon as a "loud" and "fun" place where women "dominate the work area." The level of expressiveness and interaction struck her as both informative—"you pick up so much gossip that you haven't heard elsewhere"—and intimate. Social activities, both spontaneous and planned, were inclusive of clients and staff and occurred regularly. Special events in the women's lives were celebrated in unison, while trying moments, such as 1998's Hurricane Georges, were coped with together. But as in all groups, togetherness required the exclusion of those marked as outsiders.

Salon Lamadas had no regular African American or white clients. Indeed, the absence of African American and white clients marked the salon as an almost exclusively Dominican and, secondarily, Latina space. This became especially apparent one afternoon when a young African American woman came into the shop. She wore a baseball cap with all her hair tucked inside, a T-shirt, a denim jacket, jeans, and sneakers. When she arrived, she spoke in English to Alma, saying, "I want to get a perm. I just took braids out my hair." Confused, Alma and María conferred in Spanish for a few minutes on what she meant by "perm."

MARÍA: What's she having done?
ALMA: She's getting relaxed. I think. She said "permanent."
MARÍA: That's how they say it.
ALMA: Just out of braids and getting relaxed. That's dangerous. Her hair will break. Have Stefani translate then.
MARÍA: We have to see the hair—they could be small braids.

They then turned to Stefani, María's eight-year-old daughter, and asked her to confirm their translation, which she did. First Alma and then

María walked over to the woman and examined her hair. The client's hair was tightly curled, blonde, and shoulder length. I asked Alma and María why having had braids was a problem. María explained: "They lock; their hair rots. Relaxed hair, bad hair. Not with good hair." After they discussed whether they should do the *derrizado* (relaxer) for her, which they agreed could only be on the roots because the shaft and tips were too "mistreated" by the braids, they asked Stefani to explain to her.

After Stefani's explanation, the client agreed and sat down to wait. Unlike other clients who were actively engaged by the staff, this client was allowed to sit without interaction. Neither Alma nor María seemed anxious to relax her hair. They began to take care of other customers who came in after her while she was still waiting. Alma, for example, did a roller set, while María began another *derrizado*. Their response, in words and actions, indicated their hesitation to engage her and her hair, although it was not different from the other hair types they worked on. The silence was both verbal and gestured, as not a single smile, wink, nod, or other sign of friendly communication commonly used to integrate clients into the shop was directed her way. Ultimately, after waiting about thirty minutes or so, this young woman made a call on the salon phone and left.

The mood of the shop had changed with the presence of a "stranger," a non-Latina. The prospective African American client and the two Dominican hairdressers were "foreigners" to one another. The client, in the context of Salon Lamadas, was "foreign" to Alma and María because of the language barrier, because of the unfamiliar hair-culture practices and technologies, and because of the strangeness of her presence. At the same time, Alma and María's own foreignness were highlighted by the client's presence. In that context, because of her English monolingualism, her attire, and her use of certain terms, the client represented U.S. society at large. In the absence of non-Latinos, the shop was *normal*; in their presence, it was *ethnic* and *foreign*. The shop, in other words, acted as a boundary-marking and maintaining institution. As this interaction illustrates, Salon Lamadas affirmed for its staff and clients that they are not like African Americans and that African Americans are not like them, either.

At the same time, while Salon Lamadas was generally welcoming to Latina clients, admittance into the salon's inner circle of clients even for Dominican women was contingent on socioeconomic status outside the shop, as well as on personal patronage within the shop. A core group of about ten clients socialized with Chucha and Leticia in and outside of the shop. They were all Dominican women who visited the salon weekly and who were willing to spend freely in purchasing gifts, salon services, and the accoutrements of middle-class status. They participated in all staff birthdays, baptisms, and other ritual celebrations, including the yearly *Angelito* (Secret Santa). And they invited Chucha and Leticia to their own celebrations and rituals.

In addition to this core group, there was a larger, looser configuration of regular clients who participated occasionally in salon social activities and who had more personal relationships with the other stylists. They were mostly Dominican women but included Cuban, Puerto Rican, and Colombian women, as well. On the whole, they were aware of the "inner circle" and evidently chose not to participate in it. Nonetheless, there was clear evidence of co-centric groupings, radiating outward from Chucha and Leticia.

"*Es que aquí nos ayudamos mutuamente*": Fictive Kinship and Community

Where the journalist Mimi Valdés saw only female rivalry over men and economic and racial posturing in her snapshot of the Dominican salon, I would argue that, although they are certainly present, they are only part of what happens in the salon.[63] Many social and cultural rituals were performed in the salon itself and outside the salon for and by the staff and clients that created fictive kinship links, support networks, and social capital. Several of the staff and many of the clients were lone female migrants who had left their children in Santo Domingo until they could secure visas for them. Consequently, they were childless mothers who found and offered kinship to other women through their work in the salon.[64]

For example, in the six months I was at Salon Lamadas, three baby showers were held in the salon itself or in the women's homes—two of them for staff members (María and Nené) and one for a staff member's sister.[65] Perhaps the most representative case, however, was Nené's shower. Again I refer to my field notes:

This afternoon, Leticia and Nené arrived at the salon excited and jubilant. Leticia was especially well dressed (she called her attire "*vestuario dominguero* [Sunday best]"): linen, cream-and-tan plaid blouse, tan leather belt, tan linen slacks. Nené wore a blue denim maternity top with black collar and cuffs and with her hair done (*derrizado* [relaxed and pulled up]). Leticia was jubilant. She and Nené had gone to the medical center where Nené has been receiving prenatal care (apparently insufficiently and intermittently). Leticia went to represent Nené and confront the doctor regarding Nené's condition.

Nené has had a difficult pregnancy and, it seems, has not been able to advocate for herself with the doctors at the medical center because they don't speak Spanish well enough and because of her self-declared ignorance of her rights and needs. Leticia went to advocate for her. She recounted how she had forced the doctor to test Nené for possible complications during delivery such as those she suffered with her first child, Daniel. Daniel was born at [nine and a half pounds] and was delivered with forceps. The doctor agreed to conduct an amniocentesis to test for fetal age and development, particularly lung maturity. If the baby is developed enough, they will induce labor on Tuesday or Thursday so that the baby doesn't get too large.

To emphasize how well she had represented Nené, Leticia repeated several times that the nurse and doctor had insisted that Nené take several of the sample diapers they distributed, while other patients had only been given two samples each. Because Leticia told this story about five times, I understood that she took it as an indication of her success in advocating for Nené.

What also struck me was how important the interaction among Nené, Leticia, the doctor, the nurses, and the social worker seemed to be. This could have been a routine prenatal exam; instead, it was an event, a confrontation with the foreign and a victory over somewhat adversarial forces. Leticia had acted as Nené's cousin throughout the remainder of their interactions with the hospital and its staff. She and Chucha attended the birth and left their names and numbers as emergency contacts. Although Nené was married, she received federal welfare benefits. Thus, her husband, Alex, was not allowed to attend the birth for fear of disclosure of their violation of benefit-eligibility regulations. However, it was clear that his exclusion was not merely a response to the disruptive exigencies of welfare regulations.[66] Subsequent interactions around Nené's labor, delivery, and post-partum care, and around the newly born Nenita, indicated that Alex was in fact marginal to the experience. It was Chucha and Leticia as a unit who were full co-parents to Nenita.

Both Chucha and Leticia attended Nené's labor and delivery. After sixteen hours of labor, Chucha left the hospital at 4:30 A.M. Leticia stayed through 6 A.M., when Nené finally gave birth. Back at the shop, Chucha kept saying *"estoy pari'a* [I'm birthed]"—that is, that she had just given birth—to all who entered. She also agreed to wash and deliver the baby clothes that Nené's *compadre* (the child's godfather) had dropped by the store. Having had no prior experience with baby clothes, Chucha asked María later in the day what detergent products to use and accepted María's advice. Rather than go home upon her discharge from the hospital, Nené took Nenita straight to the shop. Leticia guarded the baby and monitored access to her. Indeed, Chucha took pictures not only of Nené with the baby, but also of Leticia with the baby. Leticia repeated several times that someone at the hospital had asked her if the baby was hers— *"Creian que es hija mia!* [They thought she was my daughter!]," she exclaimed—to which she had replied that she was the baby's godmother.

Throughout Nené's pregnancy, labor, delivery, and post-partum period, Chucha was simultaneously critical and protective of Nené, as was the entire staff. For example, they threw a surprise baby shower for Nené at the salon to supply her with a layette and furnishings, none of which she had. In attendance were the whole salon staff, as well as about ten or fifteen clients and neighborhood folks. All together, there must have been about thirty people in the small space. The salon was decorated with pink and blue balloons, streamers, baby shower signs, and a large "Surprise" sign on the window. There was also a baby shower chair and a gift table and miniature gift well, both of which were filled to capacity. The hairstyling stations were converted into a buffet area. Leonora, María, Alma, and several clients prepared the food. The fare consisted of large aluminum trays of typical Dominican dishes such as *arroz con güandules, lechón, carne guisada, ensalada,* and *ensalada de coditos.*

At the same time, the staff commented often on Nené's failure to prepare properly for the baby, on her overall stupidity, and on how she was wearing on their collective patience. Nonetheless, they advocated for her, helped her care for her children, attended her labor, and prepared for her baby. Nenita was subsequently also baptized by Chucha, who hosted a large sit-down dinner at an expensive local restaurant (figure 25). The kinship circle extended beyond Chucha and Leticia to include other staff and intimates. For example, in keeping with a Dominican folk belief, it was said that Nenita's mouth resembled Nilda's because she and Nené argued often during Nené's pregnancy.

Moreover, birthdays were regularly celebrated for staff and for regular clients. During my fieldwork, three staff birthdays occurred. Each was recognized with a bouquet of flowers, a cake, and small presents.

25. Nenita's baptism

During the Christmas season, the staff and clients orchestrate an *Angelito*, a Secret Santa-like gift exchange with a $50 minimum. The financial and social investments each of these events entail indicated a real commitment to the salon as a quasi-kinship-providing space. In sum, these women thought of themselves as family—they advocated for one another, socialized together, depended on one another, and criticized one another mercilessly and with deadly precision. And like family, they acted as an institution that socialized its members into normative identities, including ethno-racial ones.

Baby Hairs: Racialized Reproduction

The presence of babies—the staff's and mine—inspired discussions of hair texture and color. After Nenita's birth, Leticia said several times that she was concerned about the baby's gender and size, not about her hair texture or color: "That she be a girl, beautiful and fat, nothing else matters to me. She can have a head worse than the devil's." The disavowal itself, of course, reiterated the importance of hair, as did the equation of "bad hair," blackness, and the devil. In addition, strangers and friends alike often commented directly on the quality of Nenita's hair texture and the tone of her skin. Nené's landlady, Miguelina, for example, was present when Nenita was brought home from the hospital. On seeing the baby, Miguelina turned to Alma, who had accompanied them home, and cooed, baby-like, "Alma, you're going to have to relax my hair, Alma." Alma cooed back "No ma'am, it'll be a curly perm that I'll be getting. I have good hair."

Later that day, a spontaneous discussion occurred regarding whether Alex, the baby's father, had *pelo malo* or not. Ultimately, no consensus was reached on what kind of hair Alex had, due in large measure to the fact that he wore it closely cropped. Chucha seemed to have the last word on the matter. "Alex has good hair that's wavy. Bad hair is hair that breaks. There's good hair and bad hair, there's limp hair—like you, Leticia and María—curly hair, kinky hair, curly hair. People are mistaken. Bad hair is simply hair that breaks." Here Chucha was defining hair in terms of relative ease of care and health, and was rejecting as mistaken the racialized categorization of hair. Nonetheless, the use of the negative term "bad" rather than, say, delicate (which conveys the meaning Chucha insisted on) implied that it was not simply the manageability of the hair that was being assessed. It was also its nearness to blackness.

Good vs. Bad Hair

Jackie, a young client, made explicit the relationship between reproduction, race, and aesthetics. Sitting next to my infant son, Christian, and me, she asked if I was Dominican. I replied that I was.

JACKIE: You don't look Dominican.
GINETTA: Why not?
JACKIE: Because of your hair.
GINETTA: How so?
JACKIE: Because it's so soft, so fine, so good.
GINETTA: And we Dominicans aren't like that?
JACKIE: No. We have bad hair, hard hair.
GINETTA: What makes *pelo bueno*?
JACKIE: That it's easy to take care of. That you don't have to work so hard. That it's pretty. I'm very racist. I don't want to know about blacks.
GINETTA: Which blacks?
JACKIE: None. Because I don't like hard hair. I want to have a baby like yours, blond and white. Although I shouldn't be like that since I have

Haitian race myself, but anyway. . . . I've been mistaken for Indian, Arab, Moroccan.

As this exchange indicates, there was an enormous amount of ambiguity about race and reproduction. First, because of the connection between fine hair and whiteness, the assertion that Dominicans do not have fine hair means that they are not white. Second, Jackie's insistence that Dominicans have "bad hair, hard hair," together with her later equation of bad hair with blackness, indicated that Dominicans must be black. Yet Dominicans could reproduce blackness away. While Jackie described herself as not quite white—indicated by her sense that she "shouldn't be racist" because she had "Haitian race" herself—she claimed a degree of distance from blackness because she had been "confused for Indian, Arab, Moroccan" in the past.

Further, she desired whiteness for her children—defined not by virtue of their ancestry, which would unalterably include her Haitian ancestors, but by virtue of their white skin and blond hair, which are within reach. Thus, she did not "want to know about blacks." After all, she asked rhetorically at the end of our conversation, "Who wants to be struggling with kinks?"

Similarly, when María's baby was born, the conversation once again turned to race:

GINETTA: How did it go for María?

CHUCHA: Fine.

GINETTA: What did she have?

CHUCHA: An eight-and-a-half-pound girl. She already knew that it was going to be a girl.

ALMA: She's a pink white girl.

NENÉ: María's girl is white, white.

ALMA: That baby girl made María really black.

LEONORA: She's getting better. She's getting white already; her feet went down. She's OK. . . . That girl looks like Frank [her husband]. She's going to be fine.

ALMA: Poor Stefani.

NANA: That girl is rough. Who'd she come out so rough like?

ALMA: I don't know. The poor thing. She's got such a wide face.

NENÉ: But the baby is going to be pretty. She's going to be the pretty girl.

In this exchange, the baby's color was volunteered freely and casually. Nené, whose own baby was described as olive-skinned with softly curled hair, noted that María's baby was "really" white. Alma reminded those present that María, too, was "really" white and that her previously dark skin was related to her pregnancy. Leonora responded consolingly that María was "getting better" because her skin was becoming white again, as if dark skin were an illness. She then offered that the baby looked like her father, Frank, who was "fine featured." Alma then pitied her niece, Stefani, who now looked blacker compared with the baby. The "poor thing" had a wide face and "coarse" features. The baby, conversely, would "be the darling girl" of the family because she was "pretty" and white.

"The First Shop I Used Myself": Learning to Look Like a Dominican Woman

The Dominican salon acts as a socializing agent. Salon use is a rite of passage into Dominican women's community. It is at the salon that girls learn to transform their bodies—through hair care, waxing, manicuring, pedicuring, facials, and so on—into socially valued and culturally scripted displays of Dominican femininity. Many of Salon Lamadas's clients recalled visiting beauty shops as children with their mothers. Charity, for example, recounted:

> I used to go always with my mother to this shop in Flushing, where I grew up. She would go all the time, and I'd go with her. I must have been real little because I remember being, like, "Wow" and "Ooh" about everything. They all looked glamorous to me *(laughter)*. She still goes there, and it was the first shop I used myself. I still go there sometimes just to catch up on the neighborhood gossip.

As in Charity's case, it is often at the mother's shop that young women first experience beauty-shop culture. Generally, however, they do not become beauty-shop clients until they are about fifteen, the age at which Latin American girls of means are introduced into society and Latin American girls across class are physically considered "women."[67] Kathy recalled her first salon visit when she turned fifteen:

> The first time I went to a shop I was already, like, fifteen years old. And it was to have my hair trimmed a little. But I wanted to get out of the ponytails

and buns already. And so I went to a neighbor who had a shop in her house, and I had my hair washed, trimmed, and set. Oh, I looked so pretty.

Others recalled first visiting a beauty shop in preparation for their migration to the United States, a moment that also marked the transition from girlhood to adolescence for some of them.

Nurka, for example, recalled that before she migrated when she was fourteen, her mother took her and her sisters to a beauty shop in town:

Look, it was to come here. Exactly. Yes. (Chuckles) I had never gone to a salon. I always . . . had two ponytails, like this, and that was it. But I went. When we were coming here, mommy went to pick us up. And she took the three of us to the salon. I think my brother also had a haircut. And it was, we were in the country, and mommy took us to the east, to Bayaguana, the place was called. She took us there to have us all have our hair cut. They trimmed our hair, they washed our hair, and it was, "Oh!" Everyone, "Oh! What pretty hair! Oh, how pretty!" (Laughs) And that was true—yes, of course. I remember it as if it were today, yes.

For Nurka, the transition from childhood to adulthood was marked as much by the change from pigtails to hair done at the shop as by the move to New York. Her transformation into young womanhood was socially recognized by people who acclaimed her "pretty hair," now loose and womanish. The repeated refrain of how pretty they looked after their first beauty-shop visit also marked the transition from innocent childhood to sexualized young womanhood. All of the respondents raised in the Dominican Republic, and several who were raised here, recalled that the loosening of their hair from ponytails and *moños* (buns) marked the transition from childhood to young womanhood.

Like Nurka, Charity remembered her grandmother styling her hair into pigtails and, later, *moños* for neatness and ease of care. As long as mothers and grandmothers were responsible for their children's hair, these were the preferred styles. As Nana explained:

Look, I hated those buns. It was three buns—one here, one here, and one here. My grandmother used to make them with a piece of string. And the other children used to make fun of them, saying, like, *"Tin marín de dos pingó, cucara macara titire fué"* [a nonsensical children's rhyme]. I used to tear them [the buns] apart when I was walking to school. So then, when I became a little bigger, my grandmother told me that I was already old enough to take care of my hair myself. And that was such a joy for me! Oh! I started wearing curlers and styling my hair well.

26. Fannie and her cousins

The transition of hair care from one's caretaker's hands into one's own hands thus paralleled the increasing responsibility for one's own body and self.

For example, Fannie, the manicurist at Salon Lamadas, used one hair-care regime at home suited to her mother's and her own fine, lank hair, and another when ministering to her cousins' hair-care needs. As Fannie came of age and began to socialize with her cousins, whose hair-care regimes included roller sets, relaxers, and *toobies,* she became versed in those methods, as well (figure 26). As she recalled:

> We would all go to the beach together, in Barahona, there are a lot of beaches. And when we would come back from the beach, I would return with my hair dry and straight, you know? And then they would come with their hair, you know, curly. You know, bad hair that is relaxed? That when it comes into contact with seawater, it comes, you know, Dominican hair, black women's hair? And they would say to me, "Oh! You're all set to go dancing, but not me. Come on, then, and get to work fixing my hair, too." And so I, in order to hurry up and for us to all get ready at the same time, I wanted to help. And that's how I started practicing. "Let me set your hair." "Here, fix my hair." You know? Between ourselves, girls to the end, getting together. The family is very large.

Responding to the question about how she had come to work in a beauty shop, Fannie explained that her first experiences with Dominican beauty culture occurred in the context of her family, which was "very large" and very diverse. It was while participating in her cousins' hair-care regimes that she began to practice setting hair. Further, her cousins marshaled her assistance in caring for their hair, evidently undaunted by the fact that her own hair was different from theirs. In helping to care for each other's hair, a spirit of feminine intimacy—"between [themselves], girls to the end"—was developed and sustained. Finally, although Fannie was Dominican and was described as having fine, lank hair, light eyes, and freckled white skin, she equated "Dominican hair" with "black women's hair" and "bad hair that is relaxed." It was her cousins, in other words, who "typified" Dominican women's hair culture.

Dominican mothers and daughters also often have dissimilar hair textures, and mothers have to care for and style their daughters' hair. Doris, for example, never used curlers but had to set her daughter's hair:

> I myself haven't used them yet. It was out of necessity . . . that I learned. I'd put them and they'd come out more or less, with lots of pins and things like that. . . . I saw at the salon how they did it, and I more or less, in my mind, I had an idea of how they were done, and I did them, and they didn't come out too badly. Because, you know, it's very difficult to get them to come out as nice as they do.

Again, although Doris did not, and still does not, use curlers because she has what she considers thin, lank hair, her daughters had thick, curly hair that "needed" to be set. Since Doris's sisters and mother also had hair they did not set in rollers, Doris had to learn how to do roller sets at the salon. What this indicates is that the salons she frequented, both in the Dominican Republic and in New York City, catered not only to clients with hair like hers, but also to clients who used roller sets. In other words, unlike most U.S. shops, Dominican beauty shops cater to Dominican women with various hair textures within the same shop. Further, the work done in the shops, as Doris points out, is "very difficult" and requires a high degree of skill. Finally, as with Fannie and her cousins at home, the beauty shop helped to socialize Doris and, later, her children into Dominican beauty culture.

Cause with a natural
there is no natural place
for us to congregate
to mull over
our mutual discontent
Beauty shops
Could have been
A hell-of-a-place
To ferment
a. . . . . . . .revolution

—Willi M. Coleman[68]

As Willi Coleman so evocatively depicts in this poem, for African American women the beauty shop historically has been a paradoxical site of sociality for African American women. On the one hand, it existed because of a "mutual obvious dislike for nappiness" that brought women together to work on "fixing" that hair. On the other hand, at the beauty shop "you could learn a whole lot about / How to catch up / with yourself / and some other folks / in your household." Thus, for example, black beauty shops were used as organizing networks and meeting sites during civil-rights actions such as the Montgomery bus boycotts. Because they serviced other blacks exclusively, they operated autonomously of local white economies and therefore could not be subjected to economic retribution for political organizing, as were most black women workers, the vast majority of whom were dependent on white employers.[69]

The black beauty shop has also acted as a source of social and economic support in the present, as when they are used to promote public-health initiatives such as HIV/AIDS prevention and early breast cancer screenings.[70] In addition, in a historically racially segregated and still discriminatory labor market, black beauty shops offer the possibility of self-employment and professionalization for beauty operators.[71] At the same time, shop clients have often engaged in an informal shop economy in which they exchange food, housing, transportation, child care, money, and other material resources as a survival strategy. Finally, of course, are the psychological and emotional supports black beauty shops offer their clients, along with regular access to women's culture and sociality, as Kimberly Battle-Walters lays out in her description of Sheila's Shop, a small, African American neighborhood shop in northern Florida.[72]

The Dominican beauty shop likewise offers Dominican women workers and clients access to social, cultural, and economic capital, operating in ways similar to the African American beauty shop. It could also be an informal locus through which Dominican women organize politically, socially, and economically to confront transnational Dominican concerns, including poverty, residential concentration, poor schooling, lack of adequate health care, police brutality, and more mundane expressions of sexism and racism. With shops proliferating in neighborhoods with large concentrations of Dominicans throughout New York City, New Jersey, Boston, Rhode Island, and Florida, the potential for creating a network out of those atomized shops is clear. At the moment, however, instead of being "A hell-of-a-place / To ferment / a . . . revolution,"[73] or even a place to consolidate Dominican women's economic power, it acts as a gendered site of community development and racial boundary maintenance.

The socioeconomic positioning of the salon within the Dominican transnational community, the culture of its daily operations, and the sociality of its members are manifest expressions of Dominican cultural norms and ideological codes. Through extensive and intensive interactions between and among the owners, staff, and clients, the normative ethno-racial Indo-Hispanicity of Dominicanidad is ideologically coded, and Dominican women are culturally conscripted into the relations of ruling. Thus, shops such as Salon Lamadas tend to reproduce the socioracial dynamics of Dominican identity. However, the *meaning* of those dynamics is altered somewhat in their New York City context, as I argue in the next chapter.

CHAPTER 5.

"Black Women Are Confusing,

but the Hair Lets You Know"

PERCEIVING THE BOUNDARIES

OF DOMINICANIDAD

> As organic matter produced by physiological processes, human
> hair seems to be a natural aspect of the body. Yet hair is never
> a straightforward biological fact, because it is almost always
> groomed, prepared, cut, concealed and generally worked upon
> by human hands. Such practices socialize hair, making it the
> medium of significant statements about self and society and the
> codes of value that bind them, or do not.—Kobena Mercer[1]

> One of the great paradoxes of Dominican national formation is
> that while the Hispanic population became increasingly blacker,
> the Dominican mentality became whiter.—Frank Moya Pons[2]

The transformation of Dominican women's hair into racially acceptable signs hinges their sense of being Dominican on certain norms and
models. For Dominicans, hair is the principle bodily signifier of race,
followed by facial features, skin color and, last, ancestry. Harry Hoetink
discerned the connection between identity and race in his coining of the
term "somatic norm image" to improve on "race" as an explanatory concept in the Caribbean. He defined somatic norm image as "the complex
of physical (somatic) characteristics that are accepted by a group as its
norm and ideal. Norm, because it is used to measure aesthetic appreciation; ideal, because usually no individual ever in fact embodies the so-

matic norm image of his group."[3] Hoetink convincingly argued that the somatic norm image of whiteness in the Hispanic Caribbean is distinctive from the somatic norm image of whiteness in the United States.

Specifically, the "Iberian variant" of whiteness that defines the region's somatic norm image is darker featured than the more Nordic somatic norm image of the United States. Hoetink attributed this darker whiteness to both precolonial contact and mixture in Spain and Portugal among native Europeans, conquering Moors, immigrant Jews, and imported North African slaves, and later to colonial contact among Iberians, or *Peninsulares*, and indigenous and African women. Further, the expansion of social and legal whiteness to include racially intermediate individuals (mestizos and mulattos), also called *morenos* and *trigueños* in the Hispanic Caribbean, who phenotypically approximate the somatic norm image is distinctive from the closed nature of hypo-descent-based whiteness in the United States. Thus, in the Hispanic Caribbean, if one *looks* white—and the variety of phenotypes contained within the Hispanic somatic norm image of whiteness is fairly extensive—then one *is* white, for all intents and purposes. "So much so," Hoetink argues, "that certain somatic categories of the coloured group may be regarded by the Latin American (Iberian) whites as white and as being 'within the fold'; though they would not be accepted as white by those dominated by the North-West European somatic norm image."[4]

Hoetink goes on to argue that, although throughout the Americas features identified with black somatic norms are universally construed as ugly and undesirable, and features identified with white somatic norms are considered beautiful and desirable, "the somatic norm image of Latin American whites is 'darker' than that of the North-West European American."[5] Because of this, the "somatic distance" between Latin American whites and mulattos/mestizos is much shorter than it is between North American whites and blacks (who because of the U.S. hypo-descent rule include those who would be considered mulattos in Latin America). Moreover, because of the darker somatic norm image in Latin America, some who are genealogically mulatto/mestizo are classified as white "by the criterion of the dominant somatic norm image."[6] Thus, the willingness to accept mulattos and mestizos as whites—or, in other words, the incorporative rather than the exclusionary nature of whiteness—in and of itself indicates a darker somatic norm image of whiteness. Hispanic looks, in other words, are those that are light without being so white as to be beyond normative somatic images.

Normative *"white"* Hispanic looks, therefore, are those that show some mixture of European, indigenous, or African ancestors but are somatically distant from the indigenous or African somatic norms. Thus, as the anthropologist Nancie L. González remarked some three decades ago, although "the basic white Dominican . . . is not without admixture . . . , a black Dominican sees no contradiction in cursing the Haitian for his negritude."[7] However, migrant Dominican self-perceptions and somatic norm images clash with those of their host societies (such as the United States or Puerto Rico), which classify and label them as black.[8] Thus, lineage, appearance, and perception must coincide in the United States for inclusion in whiteness. As José Itzigsohn and Carlos Dore-Cabral have argued, "For some Dominicans, embracing the Hispano or Latino label is a way of rejecting being labeled as black and choosing what is perceived as an intermediate label. In the field of symbolic racial classifications, the *Hispano/a* label parallels the *Indio/a* label in Santo Domingo."[9]

Given that Dominicans are endowed with many of the physical signs to which they attribute blackness, and that they draw a distinction between blackness and Hispanicity, how do they discern who is "Hispanic" and who is not?[10] Hairstyle books offer an invaluable window into how Dominicans read bodies ethno-racially. I employed the books both in formal and informal settings. Formal responses were elicited during interviews with clients of Salon Lamadas in New York City. In addition, on several occasions, when the shop was quiet and there were no clients present, I opened the books and asked the staff, individually and collectively, for their opinions of the hairstyles and models depicted.

In her study of older women and beauty shop culture, *Facing the Mirror*, Frida Furman employed photo elicitation as a method of discovering how her informants evaluated themselves—physically, socially, and so on—across time. Accordingly, she asked each informant to gather together photographs from various stages and ages of her life and to describe herself to her in each photograph. She then took a Polaroid picture of the informant and asked her to describe herself in the present moment. She found that this methodology provided an excellent window into informants' self-perceptions and self-representations, as well as into the larger social contexts within which they developed.

Employing photo elicitation in my study was meant to draw out self-evaluation not only across time but also across place for those who immigrated to the United States. The background assumption here is that both national and individual identities are temporally and spatially fluid yet constrained by social structures. Moreover, photo elicitation is a subtle way to explore cultural narratives of race and racial self-conceptions, allowing them to emerge from the informants' evaluations rather than being guided by the researcher. Thus, participants were asked to collect pictures of themselves across their lifetimes, as well as of their families. They were asked to describe each person in terms of perceived physical appearance and personality traits. Usually, these photos were informal shots taken at social gatherings and family events, in places key to their life stories or while performing activities that reflected their sense of self.

In addition, each of the respondents was shown a series of head shots selected from the hairstyle books kept at the salon. Those particular books were utilized because they reflect the salon owner's and staff's tastes, and they are the hair-culture texts to which the Salon Lamadas clientele had access while there. Moreover, these books depict "real people," not professional models or celebrities whose countenances are widely familiar and whose ethnicities are public knowledge. Of the thirteen books available to customers at Salon Lamadas, three featured African American hairstyles modeled by presumably African American women. The others featured hairstyles and models that were meant to represent white women. There were no Asian or Asian American hairstyle books in the shop or any models who were perceived to be Asian in the available books. Color photocopies of the photos were made to remove them from the context of the books, which were explicitly directed at either white or black audiences, so that the respondents could evaluate the photos independent of their bindings. Many of the models from the books directed at African Americans were utilized. A selection from each of the white books was employed. I felt that it was important to use a sample drawn from as many of the white books as possible, given that I had no predetermined assumptions about which was particularly popular or influential.

Respondents were shown pictures of women with short, medium, and long hair; of men; and of female children. Each of the groupings contained an equal number of photos from the African American and white books. The photographs of women were divided by hair length to control somewhat for the relationship between hair length and perceptions of race. From each of those groupings respondents were asked to select the prettiest and least pretty;[11] those most and least qualified for political office; those best and least suited for business endeavors; and those who appeared to be Latina based on appearance alone. Among the photographs of the men, respondents were asked to select the most and least handsome; those most and least qualified for political office; those best and least suited for business endeavors; and those who appeared to be Latino based on appearance alone. Respondents were also asked to select the girls they considered to be the prettiest, the smartest, the most likely to succeed, and who looked Latina to them.

The core research questions guiding the elicitation were: Who do Dominican women consider beautiful? Is the somatic norm closer to or further from whiteness or blackness? How are "Hispanic looks" conceptualized? What is the relationship between aesthetic preferences and social status? While a sample of eighteen respondents is not a statistically valid one, the results resonate with larger, historical indications of Dominican race ideologies, as well as with my ethnographic findings in the beauty shop. Furthermore, my interviews provide substantial support for Hoetink's hypothesis of an "Iberian somatic norm image" among Dominican immigrants.

Of the thirteen hairstyle books referred to by customers at Salon Lamadas when selecting a hairstyle, ten were labeled as displaying white models and hairstyles. Three of the books feature black or dark-skinned women. All of the books available at the salon had been purchased by Chucha. One afternoon I approached her with one of the three books of African American hairstyles and asked her about the styles it contained.

CHUCHA: I just bought that book. I bought it because my clients have to locate themselves in the hair they have.

GINETTA: How so?

CHUCHA: Why, Dominican women don't want to see that book. They ask for the white women's book; they want their manes long and soft like yours.

GINETTA: Why?

CHUCHA: It's because of racism. It's just that we don't even know what race we are. That if we're white, that if we're black, *Indio*, or what. . . . I don't want to know about blacks so I don't have to be fucking around with kinks. Look, I came out like one of my aunts and that was suffering in my house in order to lower my kinks. The Dominican woman wants her soft mane, long hair. I bought that book now so they can start to locate themselves well. They don't want to see that book. They ask for the white women's book, the one for good hair like yours. Look, I have a client who brings me a three-year-old girl so I can blow dry her hair. You know what that is? Three years old. And in the end, when she gets home and starts playing, her hair stands on end again. (*Laughs*) The latest was that she wanted her to have her hair set. That little girl sat under the dryer better than some grownups, reading her magazine. Do you think that's right? That's suffering. It's not fair. I tell her, "Leave her with her curly hair. Put a ribbon in it and leave it!" But no, they want their soft manes.

That Chucha's purchase was recent and geared toward pointing her clients out to themselves, and given that the book featured women of the African diaspora, the selves Chucha was pointing Dominican women to were black. But it was an image rejected by her clients, who "don't want to see that book." Instead, she said, they "ask for the white women's book." Attributing the desire for long and soft hair to racism and to racial confusion, Chucha reiterated the equation of blackness with kinky, difficult hair that results from failed *blanqueamiento*. As she indicated by tracing her own "*greñas* [kinks]" to her aunt, blackness is errant and betrays girls and women. It leads to "suffering."

Interestingly, Chucha depersonalized her own suffering and hairstyle, referring instead to "Dominican women," to her clients' and to her family's suffering. The ambiguity Chucha expressed as a woman whose own hair was treated as a cause of sorrow in her childhood and as a stylist who actively participated in the very system she condemned typifies the paradox of Dominican beauty culture. She was critical of her clients' choosing the white book, subjecting their three year olds to "suffering" under the dryer, and preferring "long manes." She relished the resiliency and unruliness of a child's kinky hair that refuses to relax. Yet she was an active agent of the very system she criticized. Further, she was subjected to it herself, even as an adult.

The texture of Chucha's hair was variously described as "*pelo macho* [macho hair]," "*pelo durito* [slightly hard hair]," and "*pelo fuerte* [strong hair]" by her staff and as "*greñas* [kinks]" and "*pasas que hay que bajarlas* [kinks that have to be tamed]" by herself. Much like the customers who pretend not to notice the waiter's gaffe in order to support his role, Salon Lamadas's staff politely overlooked and worked to fit Chucha's hair texture to her high status, both through their grooming of her hair and through their softened descriptions of it. Chucha herself was open about her hair's secret, as the following selection from my field notes indicates:

Chucha and Leticia attended a Sebastian hair-product seminar in New Jersey today. The topic was how to use a new color product. Chucha sat down and recounted the details of her experience to María: "They don't work on bad heads there. It's all for good hair, like hers [pointing to me] and yours [María]." I asked why not and whether they had ever asked for a different kind of hair on the dummies. Again Chucha responded: "There it is! Our job is to adapt straight hair, good hair products, to ours. I was dying laughing, thinking about the surprise they'd experience if my hair got wet!" she laughed. "If my hair got wet!"

The "they" Chucha referred to were the white producers, marketers, and beauty culturalists at Sebastian. Chucha's laughter and pleasure in relating the story indicated to me awareness on her part of her corporate host's ignorance. Water would return her hair to its natural, tightly curled state. Her looks, she recognized with relish, were deceiving; she too, was a "bad head." So it seemed that Chucha was well aware that she was transforming herself racially when she did her hair. The question is: What is she transforming into? I argue that it was not a desire for whiteness that guided Dominican women like Chucha. Instead, it was an ideal notion of what it means to "look Hispanic," an intermediate between white and black "types" grounded in the Iberian somatic norm image.

When asked for their opinions of the appearance of women depicted in an African American braiding book, Salon Lamadas's staff members were vehemently derogatory in their commentary. At one point, a debate ensued over whether the woman depicted in one of the hairstyle books, and who Chucha had previously described as having "*una cara de arroz con habichuelas* [a rice-and-beans face]," was Latina or African American. Nilda, María, and Flor felt that she was Hispanic; Nené, Alma, and Leonora disagreed—particularly Nené, who felt that she was definitively black.

NENÉ: Her features are rough, ordinary black muzzle, big mouth, fat nose.

NILDA: Blacks are dirty and they smell. Hispanics are easy to spot! [Turning to me:] You have something Hispanic.

GINETTA: What?

NILDA: Your nose. Fannie is white with good hair, but her features are rough black ones.

LEONORA: It's just that black shows.

NILDA: Black is not the color of the skin. Really pretty, really fine. The person has black behind the ears.

In this exchange, several things become apparent. First, those who "look" Hispanic could easily be African American, and vice versa. Second, "blackness" is discerned through a sometimes contradictory, but cohesive, system of bodily signs: hair, skin, nose, and mouth. When these features were "black," they were perceived to be animalistic and crude, as the terms "rough" and "muzzle" and the attribution of filth and odor indicate. Yet they were also common, if denigrated, among Dominicans, as the term "ordinary" implies. At the same time, an intermediate category—"Hispanic"—was deployed to contain the fluid middle between black and white. Ancestry, even if not discernible through skin color and facial features, is immutable. Thus, my nose indicated my African ancestry to them. But as the repeated references to my "good" hair as a signifier of whiteness indicated, ancestry does not determine current identity. Finally, the use of the one-hundred-year-old term "black behind the ears" is striking.

In keeping with their rhetorical denigration of blackness, these Dominican women considered women they perceived to be "Hispanic," and specifically "Dominican," as most beautiful.[12] Both "Hispanic" and "Dominican" were taken by the women at Salon Lamadas to mean "a middle term" or "a mixture of black and white," an intermediate racial category. "Hispanic" looks are accordingly those that contain elements from each constitutive "race." For them, therefore, "Dominican" was often synonymous with "Hispanic." And evidently they were not alone, for subsequent to my work at Salon Lamadas, Census 2000 data indicated that of all Latino groups, Dominicans were the "most identified with general Hispanic responses" when asked to write in a racial identity.[13]

Looking Hispanic, Being Latina

To investigate these racialized ideological codes, I color-copied a total of thirty images of women from the four most popular of the white hairstyle books at Salon Lamadas and from the African American hairstyle books.[14] I divided the images into three groupings by hair length—short, medium, and long—with half of each group being drawn from either the white or the African American books. I showed my respondents one hair-length grouping at a time and asked the following questions for each grouping:

1 Which of these women do you consider prettiest?

2 What makes her pretty?

3 Which of these women do you consider least pretty?

4 What makes her the least pretty?

5 Do any of these women look Latina to you?

6 (If yes) Which ones?

7 What makes these women look Latina?

8 Which of these women looks like she'd make the best business partner?

9 What makes her look like she'd make a good business partner?

10 Which of these women looks like she'd make the worst business partner?

11 What makes her look like she'd make a bad business partner?

12 Which of these women would you be most likely to vote for?

13 What makes her look like she'd make a good candidate?

14 Which of these women would you be least likely to vote for?

15 What makes her look like she'd make a bad candidate?

I weighed all the responses equally. Nine of thirty women depicted were selected as prettiest three times or more. The nine prettiest were ranked according to how frequently they were selected (figure 27). Three of the depicted women were each considered prettiest by nearly half of my respondents. Similarly, twenty-one of the thirty women were perceived to "look Hispanic" by at least one respondent. The more often a given woman was perceived to "look Hispanic," the more often she was thought to be Latina. Of the twenty-one women perceived to "look Hispanic," thirteen were selected three or more times by the respondents.

Thus, the woman selected most often as looking Hispanic was also the one most often selected as prettiest. Indeed, the top three "prettiest" women were all thought to be Latina. The top eight of the nine women selected as prettiest were thought to be Latina by nearly a quarter of the respondents. Only the ninth woman of those selected as prettiest was a blonde-haired, white-skinned woman who was universally declared to "not look Hispanic." Still, it is noteworthy that seven of the nine prettiest women were light skinned and had "good hair." At the same time, there were no "white" women among the women perceived as "least pretty." Instead, as the "looks Hispanic" ratio indicates, the women considered "least pretty" were those African diaspora women who were furthest away from the most "Hispanic"-looking woman (figure 28).

27. "Top nine prettiest" (women). From *Before and After; Family Album III; Family Images*, Vol. 2; *Ultra World of Hair Fashion*

Prettiest

Least Pretty

28. "Prettiest" and "least pretty" (women). From *Before and After; Family Album III; Family Images*, Vol. 2; *Ultra World of Hair Fashion*

TOP FIVE

| 1st choice | 2nd choice | 3rd choice | 4th choice | 5th choice |

SECOND FIVE

| 1st choice | 2nd choice | 3rd choich | 4th choice | 5th choice |

THIRD FIVE

| 1st choice | 2nd choice | 3rd choice | 4th choice | 5th choice |

FOURTH FIVE

| 1st choice | 2nd choice | 3rd choice | 4th choice | 5th choice |

29. "Looks Hispanic" (women). From *Before and After*; *Family Album III*; *Family Images*, Vol. 2; *Ultra World of Hair Fashion*

30. "Does not look Hispanic" (women). From *Before and After*; *Family Album III*; *Family Images*, Vol. 2; *Ultra World of Hair Fashion*

Since the "looks Hispanic" category included women in nearly equal proportion from both the white and black hairstyle books, there did not seem to be a preference for "pure" or "European" whiteness. Rather, as my respondents indicated in their interviews, the women they perceived to be Latina were selected because their faces or hair were perceived to indicate some degree of *both* African and European ancestry (figure 29). Thus, those thought not to show any degree of mixed ancestry were also those thought to "not look Hispanic" (figure 30).

The question remains, however: How do Dominican women and girls look at pictures of African American women who look like them and yet distance themselves from this similarity? What is taking place when women at the salon ask to see the women in the white hairstyle books and adamantly reject looking at the African American hairstyle books? Does this do psychic violence to them? I argue that it does not, to the extent that these Dominicans identified as "Hispanic"; they considered those who showed a degree of mixture to "look Hispanic," and they considered those whom they perceived to "look Hispanic" as most beautiful. Thus, if one were to be guided simply by the fact that Dominican women at Salon Lamadas preferred to look at the white hairstyle book, it could easily be concluded that Dominican women prefer "white" looks.

Table 5, for example, illustrates the preference for images selected from the "white" book and the concomitant rejection of images from the "black" book. Only one-third of the women considered "most attractive" were selected from the images drawn from the African American hairstyle book. Likewise, three-quarters of the women who were considered "least attractive" had been featured in the African American hairstyle book. At first glance, this would appear to reflect white preference and pigmentocracy, which would be very much in keeping with the ideological codes of race hegemonic in the Dominican Republic. Once the

Table 5 Binding of "Prettiest" and "Least Pretty" Images

Image	Percent
Prettiest	
Images selected from "white" hairstyle book	65
Images selected from "black" hairstyle book	35
Least Pretty	
Images selected from "white" hairstyle book	29
Images selected from "black" hairstyle book	71

images are considered outside the context of their bindings, however—as they were by Salon Lamadas's clients during the photo-elicitation interviews—it becomes clear once again that the preference is not for U.S. whiteness but for "Hispanic" or mixed looks. That is, the symbolic and literal binding of the images into one of two choices—black or white—reflects U.S. dichotomization of race. At Salon Lamadas, there are no "Latina" or "Hispanic" hairstyle books. In other words, it is neither the white book nor the black book per se that Salon Lamadas's clients prefer or reject. It is the images contained in each book that they consider to approximate or not a "Hispanic" ideal, an ideal defined as containing elements from both blackness and whiteness, where Dominicans are concerned, and more generally of indicating identifiable outcomes of mestizaje and blanqueamiento: thick but "manageable" dark hair, dark eyes, medium skin tones, medium facial features.

Thus, nearly all of the women selected from the "white" book, and all of the women selected from the "black" book, who were perceived by respondents as attractive were also thought to "look Hispanic" (table 6). And while neither of the two women from the "black" book who were considered to be unequivocally black was considered among the prettiest, only one of the two women considered to be unequivocally non-Hispanic white was perceived as being among the prettiest of the women pictured. None of the top three choices as the prettiest of the women was perceived as white. The woman most often considered attractive was considered to be unequivocally Latina, while the second- and third-most-attractive women were said to be "probably" Latina and "possibly Latina, possibly black," respectively.

Although women perceived to be non-Hispanic white were not considered prettiest, they were also less likely to be categorized as "least pretty." All three of the top choices for "least pretty" were perceived as closer to

Table 6 Perceived Ethnicity/Race and Perceived Prettiness by Hairstyle-Book Bindings

Attributes	Percentage of Perceptions of "White" Book			Percentage of Perceptions of "Black" Book		
	Latina	"White"	"Black"	Latina	"White"	"Black"
Prettiest	92	8	0	100	0	0
Least pretty	71	29	0	83	0	17

31. "Looks Dominican" (women). From *Before and After*; *Family Album III*; *Family Images*, Vol. 2; *Ultra World of Hair Fashion*

blackness and further from Hispanicity. What is more, those perceived to be whiter Latinas were more heavily represented among the top nine prettiest women. Most interesting, however, was the assessment of the appearance of the woman selected both as most Latina-looking and prettiest.

The top choice in both the "looks Hispanic" and "prettiest" categories was perceived to have what several respondents called "prototypical" or stereotypically Hispanic looks. Clara Rodríguez has noted that the media representation of "Latin looks" in the United States consists of skin that is "slightly tan, with dark hair and eyes,"[15] a reasonable description of the top choice in this study. That said, it is important to note that half of the twenty women my respondents perceived to be Latina were drawn from the African American hairstyle book and had features that they considered to connote a degree of ancestral blackness. Further, all of the women my respondents selected as looking "typically" Dominican were drawn from the black hairstyle book (figure 31). "Looking Dominican," as noted earlier, evidently means having more visible African ancestry, while looking Hispanic is more generally about mixedness. Thus, discerning who is simply "black" and who is "Dominican" is aided not only by signs of mixture—lighter skin, looser hair, thinner features—but by reference to hair culture, because, as the Salon Lamadas client Paulina explained, "Black women are confusing, but the hair lets you know." It is the lack of "naturalness" in sculpted and obviously processed hairstyles that Dominican women point to as disconcerting and as distinguishing Dominican hair culture from African American hair culture.

"The Difference Is to Look More Natural": Hair, Membership, and Status

These Dominican women placed great emphasis on hair that appears "healthy, natural, and loose." As Nuris put it:

> The difference between here and there, black women here, they use a lot of grease, their hair . . . doesn't look as loose as Dominican women's. Dominican women don't use it that way, they wear their hair processed, but the hair looks healthy, it stays well, very pretty the hair, the hair always looks healthy. . . . I think the difference is like to look more natural. To look more, like, for the hair to look looser. That's it.

In other words, the extensive body technology, time, and effort employed to make the hair "loose and manageable" must not show. Indeed, it is precisely the emphasis on naturalness that signifies the techniques of the body required by Dominican hair culture and elides the ideological codes of pigmentocracy, indigenist blanqueamiento, and Negrophobia. In this way, Dominican whiteness rejects U.S. Anglocentric white supremacy based on the "one drop of blood rule," where "one drop" of African "blood" makes one black.[16] But Dominican whiteness also rejects the notion of shared blackness and politics of black solidarity that arose as a result of African American responses to the institutionalization of that rule in the United States.[17] As Casandra Badillo put it, for a Dominican woman to refuse to straighten her hair into a "naturally" indigenous look would be "an affirmation, a symbolic act of going over to the other faction—the faction of the maroons."[18]

Not surprisingly, therefore, there is a stated preference for *pelo bueno* and an awareness that having (or making) good hair endows one with certain privileges. As Fannie put it:

[My cousins would tell me] that I always had an advantage. "You always have an advantage. When you arrive from the beach, your hair is all set." They always wanted to have my hair. Always, you know. . . . "Why didn't God give me your hair?" But they know that it's because of the mixture of races that I have also. Perhaps if dad had married a Dominican woman, not so much Dominican, because we are mestizos, but a person with bad hair, I, too, would have had it like that. But they always, about my hair, there wasn't any egoism. Never, never.

As Fannie's narrative indicates, her cousins who had "bad hair" may have been aware that what was at stake was not simply aesthetics but also "advantages" and disadvantages, often quite material ones. Having "good hair" will often mean having increased access to good jobs and "good" families through mate-selection preferences.[19] At the same time, rather than questioning that system of privilege or expressing negative feelings about Fannie because she was advantaged, Fannie's cousins question "God" or nature for putting them at a disadvantage by giving them "bad hair." Fannie likewise attributed her advantage to nature—her biological heritage of a "mixture of races" accounted for her hair—rather than to a system of racial privilege that endowed that physical attribute with positive social value. Finally, Fannie's account highlighted that there is a pervasive discourse emphasizing the racially mixed nature of Dominicanness—"because we are mestizos"—even as it recognized that some mestizos have "bad hair."

There was an aesthetic preference for bodies that are *"termino medio,"* the middle term, particularly as this is symbolized by straight and loose hair. Furthermore, straight hair was worn for formal social events, clean paid labor, and occasions where prettiness was required. Conversely, curly hair was equated with sports and recreation, parks and beaches, and dirty work. Straight hair was equated with upper-class pursuits, while curly hair was connected to middle- and lower-class ones. Indeed, curly hair was seen as *inappropriate* for certain social activities, while straight hair was inappropriate for others.[20] Alma explained:

And so if one is always used to being in salons and having one's hair done, one always likes one's hair straightened, one never likes to go about, because in order to do curly hair, that is for going to sit in a park, for going to the beach, to go to that. But it's not for going to a restaurant, for going to a party where one wants to look pretty. For that you do an updo; you do dead hair.

In other words, curly hair is for sports and recreation, where one can look casual and unkempt. But social spaces that require one to display higher social status, such as restaurants and parties, require one to "look pretty," which means creating "dead hair." Indeed, nightclubs in the Dominican Republic routinely refuse admission to women who do not conform to these expectations and who wear their hair unprocessed or braided.[21] If class mediates race for Dominicans, as has often been argued, then by implication hair that makes blackness excessively visible does not jibe with privileged social and economic status. The goal is not Nordic or Aryan whiteness but mixedness that is more an approximation of Hispanic looks as those are popularly understood: straight haired, tan skinned, aquiline featured.

This is reflected in the ambiguity that exists around *pelo bueno*. For example, while *pelo bueno* was usually defined in positive terms, it was also called *pelo muerto* (dead hair) and *pelo lambío* (limp hair), and hair could be, as each of the hairdressers mentioned, "too good." Be that as it may, however, the ambivalence was more rhetorical than not. For example, although perms for curling *pelo muerto* are taught in Dominican cosmetology programs and are known to exist, they are rarely, if ever, performed. I never once, in the six months I was at the shop, saw a curly perm performed. Indeed, when I inquired into where the perm rollers, lotions, and papers were kept, it took all of the stylists together nearly ten minutes to locate the equipment, as no one could remember where they had been stored.

Similarly, while light skin was generally valorized, white skin in and of itself was insufficient, and skin that was too white was considered unsightly. As Chucha put it: "There are blacks who have pretty faces. And there are whites who have ugly faces." Nonetheless, the fact that each of these possibilities was constructed as an exception to the norm pointed to the standard equation of whiteness with beauty and blackness with ugliness. Consider the following exchange between Doris, a white-skinned, straight-haired Dominican woman married to a brown-skinned, curly-haired Dominican man, and me, a similarly white-skinned, straight-haired Dominican woman. Recall that Doris is the woman who said that she had learned to set her daughter's hair by going to Dominican beauty shops and observing how the stylists did it.

GINETTA: Tell me something: You've just told me that we value hair a lot and color less, in the sense that if hair is "good," you are placed in the white category. What happens in the case of someone who is very light but has "bad hair"?

DOLORES: No, that one is on the black side because it's just that the *jabao* in Santo Domingo is white with bad hair, really tight hair. Well that one is on the black side because I myself say, "If my daughters had turned out *jabá*, it's better that they would have turned out brown, with their hair like that, trigueño." Because I didn't want my daughters to come out white with tight hair. No. For me, better trigueña. They're prettier. I've always said that. All three of my children are trigueños.

GINETTA: Why? What makes them prettier?

DOLORES: Well, their color. Because for me, someone white, an ugly, ordinary white person, looks worse than a brown one, a black one who doesn't, who really is black. If they're white like that, the way there are some white, those white people, white, white, fine, they look exaggeratedly white like that. They don't look good. To me, they're not attractive. I prefer someone of color.

Of color, but not black—in other words, the embodiment of the Indo-Hispanic norm of Dominicanness that is displayed at the Dominican museum, in the Dominican beauty pageant, in the Dominican media, and in Dominican history books. To the extent that the mulata has been semantically erased in favor of the *India* (who is understood to be representative of Dominican "in-betweenness"), the *India* operates as an iconographic stand-in for contemporary Dominican women.

Several of the younger Salon Lamadas clients, members of the one-and-one-half generation, said they had experimented with "Spanish" and "black" identities when they were coming of age as a result of pressure from peers in each group. Tanany, for example, who described herself as brown skinned with hair that she now relaxes and wears short, recounted that in high school she adopted a black identity:

So I was going through my black phase, having to do nothing about Dominicans. I didn't know what to be. So we're like, "Okay, black." So we started dressing—the sneakers. I never wore shoes. I never wore a dress. Everything is sneakers and boots and bigger pants. I mean, I was wearing like a size thirty-three, and I was thinner than what I am now. And now I'm a twenty-seven. So, these pants were huge. And the earrings and the chains.

For Tanany, and for her Puerto Rican best friend who accompanied her in experimenting with a black identity, being black meant wearing certain clothing and accessories. It signified, further, a rejection of Dominican identity defined as "not black." That she ultimately "returned" to a Dominican identity did not for her indicate a rejection of blackness. Rather, it was a translation of blackness into Dominican terms. Nonetheless, she recounted that among Dominicans, she was "*una India oscura* [a dark Indian]," although she could also negotiate non-Dominican codes that defined her as black—or, at least, "not white."

Employed as a flight attendant, Tanany traveled to Europe and the Caribbean regularly, and she continued to live in Washington Heights. Consequently, she frequently interacted with Dominicans, Europeans, African Americans, and Anglo-Americans. These interactions led her to conclude that identity is situational:

> The whites are afraid of us, the Spanish and the blacks. I'm not going to say afraid; I'm just going to say it's different the way you talk, the way you express yourself. It's not the same the way I talk in the salon to the way I talk when I'm around my friends at work. It's not that I have two personalities, but it's just different. Because you have to sometimes come down to people's level. And I do that very well. Or go up to their level. (*Laughs*) That's how I see it . . . Where I work, it's like I'm considered different. . . . They don't know what I am. "Is she black? Is she Spanish?" They don't know. But I see sometimes that they would rather deal with me than with my African American co-workers. . . . But if there's a white girl, the customers feel more comfortable. I don't know what it is, they just feel more comfortable. It's happened to me a lot of times. Blacks just call me light-skinned. That's because I have curly hair and they think that I'm black.

If as an adolescent it was Tanany who did not know "what she was," as an adult it was others who were unsure of her racial status. Fluent in several idioms, both linguistic and cultural, Tanany wryly noted the difficulty both whites and blacks had in translating her identity intelligibly. She understood that relative to whites in the United States, both "the Spanish and the blacks" are not white and thus are considered not only different from, but inferior to, whites. At the same time, she considered herself distinct from African Americans, who just "call her light skinned" and thus erase her Dominican identity. Finally, she also engaged other Dominicans, here referenced in terms of the salon, for which she also had to adopt a particular code or "way of talking."

In terms of the relationship between perceived personality attributes and appearances, these women's most frequent choices for best and worst potential business partners indicated the gap between Negrophobic rhetoric and blanqueamiento-oriented practices, particularly in

Most
Businesslike

Least
Businesslike

32. "Most and least businesslike"
(women). From *Before and After*;
Family Album III; *Family Images*,
Vol. 2; *Ultra World of Hair Fashion*

the areas of marriage, social reproduction, and political representation. Nearly half of the women selected by my respondents as the "most and least businesslike" were from the black hairstyle book (figure 32). The woman most frequently selected by more than half of the respondents as the "best potential partner" was also from the black hairstyle book. When asked why, respondents such as Tania replied, "Because she looks very professional and charming." While the woman selected as the least attractive potential business partner was also from the "black" hairstyle book, she was notably lighter skinned and had looser hair than the others. Again, she was assessed based on her "unprofessional" appearance, due primarily to her hairstyle and her dress, which were "too sexy," as Aleida put it.

Similarly, the women selected by my respondents as the ones they would be most likely to vote for were fairly evenly split between the images from the white and black hairstyle books. Nonetheless, both of the women most frequently selected as best potential candidates were selected from the images from the white hairstyle book. When asked to comment on the attributes that gave them a positive impression, many responded, as Paulina did: "*Porque lucen serias* [Because they look seri-

Most Likely
to Vote For

Least Likely
to Vote For

33. "Best and worst potential candidates" (women). From
Before and After; *Family Album III*; *Family Images*, Vol. 2;
Ultra World of Hair Fashion

ous]." To "be serious" in Dominican cultural terms has both social and
political connotations. Christian Krohn-Hansen explains:

> A basic concept is that of the person as *serio* (or, if used as about women,
> *seria*), that is, serious. To claim that a man isn't serious is to imply that
> he is shameless. Used of men, the label *sinvergüenza*, or shameless, most
> often connotes "wrongdoer" or "thief." Bosch and his followers consistently
> argue that the other political parties—in particular, that of Balaguer—are in
> the hands of men who lack seriousness or are *sinvergüenzas*, or shameless.
> This discourse is a powerful one because it mobilizes key concepts used
> frequently in everyday life in all sectors of society; in saying that the other
> parties' leaders "rob" the state, this discourse (the *Boschista* discourse) at-
> tempts to deprive them of any legitimacy.[22]

While one of the two best candidates was also among the top nine of
those perceived to be Latina, the other was among those least often perceived as to be Latina. Further, both of the two women perceived as the
worst candidates were also perceived to be Latina (figure 33). One (on the
left) was among those selected as "typically" Dominican. The other was
frequently perceived to be "Puerto Rican-looking," as Essie put it. This is

Table 7 Personality Attributes and Appearance by Hairstyle-Book Bindings

Attribute	Percent
Most Businesslike	
Images selected from "white" hairstyle book	56
Images selected from "black" hairstyle book	44
Least Businesslike	
Images selected from "white" hairstyle book	26
Images selected from "black" hairstyle book	74
Best Potential Candidate	
Images selected from "white" hairstyle book	56
Images selected from "black" hairstyle book	44
Worst Potential Candidate	
Images selected from "white" hairstyle book	46
Images selected from "black" hairstyle book	54

significant in light of contentious political relations between Dominicans and Puerto Ricans in New York City, as well as in light of the decidedly masculine nature of Dominican politics in the city and in the Dominican Republic. Perceived class status was also a factor in their assessments. Both of the women selected as best potential candidates were perceived to be "*de categoría*," or "upper class," while the worst potential candidates were perceived to be "*de montón*," or "of the masses," due principally to their hairstyles and attire (table 7).

"Accommodation and Dissimulation": Race and Reproduction

In his article "The Tribulations of Blackness: Stages in Dominican Racial Identity," Silvio Torres-Saillant pointed out that there is a distance between Dominicans' "rhetorical Negrophobia" and racially tolerant action. He cited a 1995 Gallup poll of 1,200 people in the Dominican Republic in which the majority of those polled (56 percent) did not care about the skin color of a relative's potential spouse. At the same time, 51 percent said they would mind a relative marrying a Haitian.[23] Dore-Cabral, who reported the poll's results in *Rumbo* magazine, concluded, "The study indicates that the Dominican population's rejection of its neighbors is more for their condition of being Haitian (generally synonymous with poor and 'backwards') than for being predominantly black."[24] Américo Badillo and Casandra Badillo questioned this finding strongly, doubting that a survey instrument such as the Gallup Poll could accurately reflect the opinions of a population "that prefers to develop discursive strategies of accommodation, dissimulation, that avoids extremes and prefer to situate themselves on neutral, less compromising grounds."[25]

In light of this methodological challenge, photo elicitation undertaken after rapport and trust had been established with the respondents proved especially appropriate and instructive. Respondents were shown images of men selected from Salon Lamadas's hairstyle books and were asked to select the men they found most and least attractive physically, most and least suited to marriage, and most and least attractive as reproductive partners.[26] Because nearly all of the men pictured wore their hair short, the respondents were shown one grouping of twenty. They were asked the same questions about the men as about the women. In addition, they were asked:

1 Which of these men strikes you as most marriageable?
2 What makes him look like a potential husband?
3 Which of these men strikes you as least marriageable?
4 What makes him look like a bad potential husband?
5 Which of these men strikes you as good for having children with?
6 What makes him look good for having children with?
7 Which of these men strikes you as not good for having children with?
8 What makes him look bad for having children with?

Like the images of women, when considered independent of their bindings, the images of men selected by Salon Lamadas's clients as most attractive were also those men perceived to be "Hispanic" (figure 34). Two white men, one considered possibly Hispanic and the other probably white, were selected as the first and second most attractive and as best for having children with. The men considered least attractive included the two men considered to "not look Hispanic" at all, one perceived to be black, the other perceived to be white (figure 35). The most attractive men, in other words, were not necessarily the men perceived to be potentially better husbands (table 8).

These men's potential suitability for marriage was based on their perceived Hispanicity, maturity, and economic well-being. In their marked preference for "Hispanic" men as marriage partners, my respondents'

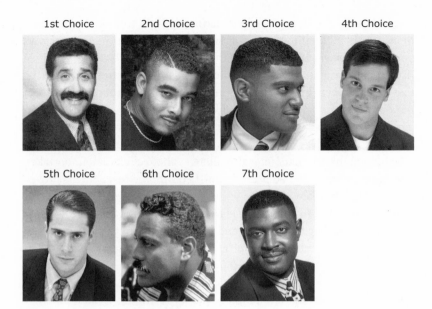

1st Choice   2nd Choice   3rd Choice   4th Choice

5th Choice   6th Choice   7th Choice

34. "Looks Hispanic" (men). From *Before and After*; *Family Album III*; *Family Images*, Vol. 2; *Ultra World of Hair Fashion*

35. "Does not look Hispanic" (men). From *Before and After*; *Family Album III*; *Family Images*, Vol. 2; *Ultra World of Hair Fashion*

choices echoed larger demographic patterns of endogamy among Dominicans in New York City. According to Greta A. Gilbertson, Joseph P. Fitzpatrick, and Lijun Yang, 54.8 percent of first-generation Dominican women's marriages in New York City were to Dominican men in 1991. An additional 39.8 percent married other "Hispanics." In other words, nearly 95 percent of Dominican women's marriages in New York City were to "Hispanics" of some nationality or another. The rates for

Table 8 Physical and Personal Attributes by Perceptions of Ethnicity (Men)

Descriptors/Attributes	Percentage Perceived to be Latino	Percentage Perceived to be "White"	Percentage Perceived to be "Black"
Most attractive	94	6	0
Least attractive	0	50	50
Most marriageable	100	0	0
Least marriageable	40	0	60
Would bear children with	100	0	0
Would not bear children with	67	0	33
Most businesslike	100	0	0
Least businesslike	40	60	0
Most likely to vote for	100	0	0
Least likely to vote for	0	60	40

the second-generation Dominican women's marriages in New York City were surprisingly similar. Forty-eight percent married Dominican men, and an additional 27.7 percent married other "Hispanics." All together, then, nearly 86 percent of second-generation Dominican women's marriages in New York City were to "Hispanics."[27]

Another factor I assessed was how the women at Salon Lamadas perceived and judged the appearance of men's work status based on attire and hairstyle (figure 36). A man with a thick gold chain, for example, was perceived as potentially involved in illicit activities and was therefore deemed an unsuitable husband. By contrast, men wearing suits or neat and casual attire were perceived to be "more serious." Thus, while the least marriageable man was also one who was perceived to look very "Hispanic," it was his youthful appearance rather than his physiognomy that made him an unsuitable candidate.

Salon Lamadas's clients considered a man who was possibly Latino or possibly African American as the most businesslike, followed by one who was possibly Latino or possibly white. This would indicate that in matters of professionalism, dress and perceived demeanor matter most. They selected non-Hispanic white men as less businesslike in their appearance and as less viable political candidates, again because of their dress and demeanor. Neither the long, layered hair worn by the blond man in figure 35 above nor the short twists worn by a man they per-

| Most Attractive and Best for Having Children | Least Attractive and Worst for Having Children | Most Marriageable | Least Marriageable |

36. "Attributes" (men). From *Before and After; Family Album III; Family Images*, Vol. 2; *Ultra World of Hair Fashion*

ceived to be a black man connoted professionalism to these respondents. Antonia's comment with reference to the group's top choice for most businesslike—"There are a lot of men like this in Santo Domingo"—was echoed by several respondents, by which they indicated that dark businessmen are not an anomaly, although economic success and professionalism are most often associated with whiteness. Hispanic looks for men, as for women, were those that indicated a degree of "mixture." Thus, the group's top choice in the "looks Hispanic" category was a man who most approximated the stereotypical notion of what a Latino looks like: medium-tone skin; dark, wavy hair; regular features; and a mustache. The respondents considered the subsequent selections as representative of "*el prototipo dominicano* [the Dominican prototype]" (figure 37). Again, as with the women, these men were all drawn from the black hairstyle book and had more visible African ancestry. Of those, one had been selected as most marriageable and another as businesslike and politically viable. By contrast, none of the women selected as looking "typically" Dominican were among those perceived to be the prettiest, nor were they selected as businesslike or viable candidates for political office.

My respondents clearly preferred lighter-skinned men as reproductive partners, by more than two to one, and 100 percent of the men they perceived to be the least suitable for bearing children with were selected from the black book, of whom 67 percent were also perceived to be Latino. On the other hand, 100 percent of the men from the black hairstyle book who were selected as most marriageable were also perceived to be Hispanic. Of those perceived to be least marriageable, 40

37. "Looks Dominican" (men). From *Before and After*; *Family Album III*; *Family Images*, Vol. 2; *Ultra World of Hair Fashion*

percent were perceived to be Latino, while the remaining 60 percent were perceived to be non-Latino blacks. None of those perceived as least marriageable were white. Similarly, none of those rejected as potential reproductive partners were white. What, then, of the children that might result from these unions?

"She Looks Like My Youngest": Giving Girls a Racial Pass

In the United States, studies have been conducted on the racial identity and psychological health of African American children since the 1950s. The most famous, conducted by Kenneth and Mamie Clark, used dolls to determine whether black children attributed more positive physical and social characteristics to whites than to blacks due to racist conditioning and social settings. The Clarks found a significant preference for white physical attributes among black schoolchildren and interpreted this as indicative of racial self-hatred.[28] Other studies have contradicted the Clarks' findings.[29] For example, William E. Cross Jr. has most thoroughly and convincingly critiqued the doll study and its intellectual progeny on the grounds of methodological and theoretical flaws.[30]

Apparently unaware of this critique, Ashindi Maxton, a master's degree candidate in anthropology at Vassar, undertook a similar study in the Dominican Republic.[31] Maxton spent four months in La Joya, a middle- to lower-class neighborhood of Santiago,[32] and replicated the Clarks' doll test with sixty-two kindergarten and first-grade schoolchildren from that neighborhood. She concluded that "the children were intentionally deluding themselves" in terms of their racial self-perceptions because the majority classified themselves as white in response to her questions. Although Maxton repeatedly stressed the importance of not applying a

U.S. interpretive paradigm to the Dominican context, she nonetheless did so. The dolls she used, although meant to represent three "different races"—white, black, and "*Indio*" or mulatto—were identical in all regards *except skin color*. Thus, the fundamental methodological and theoretical issues aside, the study was flawed in its cultural assumptions. As I argued earlier, skin color is not the primary determinant of racial identification or identity in Dominican settings. Hair is. Since the dolls all had the same hair texture (which Maxton does not describe in her report, so we do not know what it is), the children were being asked to make a primary assessment based on a model that privileged a secondary race marker in the Dominican context. Maxton's interpretation, in other words, is flawed due to lack of sufficient cultural knowledge.

While studies of Dominican children's ethno-racial-identity development are clearly needed, they must be undertaken in a methodologically appropriate and culturally competent manner, such as that used by Claudina Valdez, a Dominican researcher.[33] Valdez used photo elicitation to explore how children racially identified the subjects shown to them and how those perceptions related to their perceptions of the subjects' personal and professional attributes. She interviewed thirty-six children in two primary schools, one serving a predominantly working-class community and the other a predominantly middle-class population, in Santo Domingo. She found that the children considered the women they perceived as white to be most suited to high-status jobs and work and those they perceived as black to be most suited to low-status and menial jobs and work. These children also considered men across race lines to be more suited to high-status jobs and positions than women in general, although black women were deemed particularly incompetent if they did not relax their hair. "A black woman with relaxed hair has more opportunity to be an executive than a woman with kinky hair," the children told her. "That is, the more a person approximates the white, western model of loose hair, the more opportunity she has to do work that requires intellectual dexterity and that is symbolically associated with physical appearance related to the Occidental model (white and with loose hair)."[34]

Valdez argues that these children's responses indicate burgeoning racial ideologies that are Negrophobic and white supremacist. She takes those responses as an indicator of how various socializing agents—the family, school, church, media—contribute to racist ideologies and practices that particularly disadvantage black Dominican women. "The study found that regardless of social class the children have internalized codes of valorization and classification of people according to their pheno-

Table 9 Perceived Attributes of Children by Hairstyle-Book
Bindings

Descriptors/Attributes	Percentage of Perceptions of "White" Book	Percentage of Perceptions of "Black" Book
Looks Latina	27	73
Most attractive	29	71
Least attractive	43	57
Most intelligent	8	92
Least intelligent	43	57

types: 64% of the children classified the black women as janitors, with 41.7% of these assignations attaching to women with kinky hair; that is, the more unaltered black features a woman has, the closer she is to the stereotypes of the black woman."[35] Valdez argues that as black Dominican women come of age, their experiences foment their "endoracism," or internalized racism.[36] Valdez was not able to study how parents perceive the physical and personality traits of their children. Parental perception is sure to have a formidable impact on children's self-perception. In that vein, I asked my respondents to evaluate images of little girls selected from both the white and the black hairstyle books (table 9).

The Salon Lamadas women expressed a marked preference for children they perceived to be Hispanic. In this case, however, the children they chose as most attractive were markedly dark skinned and broader featured, and they wore more typically African-diaspora hairstyles than the adults ranked similarly (figure 38). Children drawn from the white book were only half as likely to be selected as most attractive as those drawn from the black book. Similarly, the "most intelligent" and "most likely to be successful" selections were almost entirely drawn from the black book's images. At the same time, those perceived to be "least intelligent" were as likely to have come from the white book as from the black one.

The child selected as "most attractive" had her hair styled in small buns similar to those worn by children in Santo Domingo. Not surprisingly, she was perceived by all my respondents to "look Dominican." The child selected as most intelligent was perceived as possibly African American, again because of her hairstyle. Nonetheless, as Tanany put it, she had an "intelligent face." Similarly, the little girl selected as most likely

	Attractive	Intelligent	Likely to Succeed
MOST			
LEAST			

38. "Attributes" (girls). From *Before and After*; *Family Album III*; *Family Images*, Vol. 2; *Ultra World of Hair Fashion*

to succeed was perceived to have a combination of good looks and personality. By contrast, the three children selected as least attractive, least intelligent, and least likely to succeed were described as "too bland" and "too advanced" (that is, too sexualized) for their age and elicited negative responses.

How do we account for these results in light of the negative racial assessments of each other's children in Salon Lamadas made by some of these same respondents? Are these results exemplary of the sort of "dissimulating" strategies Dominicans use to avoid exposing themselves to interviewers with unknown agendas that Badillo warns of? After all, would not attributing negative characteristics to the darker girls reveal these women's Negrophobia and pigmentocratic ideologies? Yet like the women Badillo interviewed, some of these women recalled being subjected to denigration and humiliation as children because of their hair textures.[37] It appears unlikely, therefore, that they were actively dissembling to avoid the stigma of being considered racist. To be sure, they had no qualms about expressing very negative opinions of women they perceived to be black. Instead, I would speculate that they responded to the girls as they did because they perceived the girls as similar in appearance to their own children and children in their extended families.

Indeed, several made that perception explicit by saying, as Paulina did, "She looks like my youngest."

Like Torres-Saillant, I would argue that, while Dominican women might discursively engage in Negrophobia and in practice might seek out reproductive partners they perceive will enable them to "improve the race," their responses to the children in their lives are far more ambiguous. If their responses to the children depicted in these images are any indication, I would conclude that, while these Dominican women hold themselves to a standard of attractiveness that valorizes a femininity predicated on Hispanicity, they are tolerant of a greater distance from that norm in men and female children. Men can compensate for their racial status through their access to social, economic, or political capital. Female children, according to my respondents, are not held to those standards, even as they are being socialized into them. Once they approach womanhood, however, they are expected to conform to the prevailing aesthetic norm.

Hair Race-ing Conclusions

The importance of hair as the defining racial marker for Dominicans highlights the social constructedness of race, class, and gender. Hair, after all, is an alterable sign. Hair that is racially compromising can be mitigated with care and styling. Skin color and facial features, conversely, are less pliant or not as easily altered.[38] Confronted with the U.S. model of pure whiteness that valorizes racial "purity" and pale femininity, the Dominican staff and clients at Salon Lamadas continued to prefer a whiteness that indicates Afro-European mixture. That whiteness was considered "Hispanic," and it was preferred to the white and African American somatic norm images of the host society, both of which rely on hypo-descent to categorize anyone with African ancestry as black.

Who is black in the Dominican context of New York City is mediated by the historical relationship between blacks and whites in the United States, the current relationship between Dominicans and African Americans, and the mutual constituitiveness of beauty and race. Racial identity is enacted through racialized reproduction practices and gendered beauty practices. For this reason, the open secret of Dominican hair culture situates Dominican ethno-racial formations at the crossroads of multiple identity discourses and displays.

In stretching the bounds of whiteness in the United States to accommodate and include their definition and understanding of it, Dominican women's hair culture forced a sharp contrast between Dominican and African American hair culture and an alteration of white hair culture. Chucha was pointing to precisely that alternative understanding of both whiteness and blackness when she noted that the job of the Dominican hairstylist is to "adopt white products to our hair." African Americans, by contrast, have developed their own, unique system of hair care and hair-care products—at times in opposition to, at times parallel to, and at times simply oblivious of white aesthetic ideals. For Hoetink, it was "illogical" that African Americans, "despite [their] adoption of the whole [white] preference pattern, nevertheless place [themselves] at the top of the [aesthetic] preferences list," as a study of St. Louis African Americans' aesthetic preferences found.[39]

What Hoetink overlooked, and what therefore makes African Americans' self-valuation "illogical" in the context of white supremacy, was that segregation forced African Americans to create their own social, economic, and symbolic spaces. Thus, straightening their hair, for example, was not necessarily or simply a "white wish" on the part of African Americans. Nor was it merely a reflection of black women's internalization of sexist ideals of feminine beauty. Rather, as Kobena Mercer points out, it is often simply a means to an explicitly "black woman's" hairstyle. For example, certain sculpted hairstyles require processed "black" hair for their construction. The explicit artificiality of hair sculpting stands in sharp contrast to naturalness on the European model, indicated not only by "hair that moves" but by "natural" styles such as Afros and dreadlocks.[40] That is, it is a strategic gendered signification and affirmation of racial-group membership. Further, both natural and processed hairstyles require substantial investments of time, money, and sociality, which, when viewed through the intersecting prisms of race, class, and gender, contest both beauty and anti-beauty ideologies.

Put more directly: If, as some feminist scholars and activists have argued, for white women in the United States the beauty shop and beauty culture have been manifestations of misogyny and vehicles for patriarchal oppression,[41] for Latina and African American women who belong to racially and economically marginalized groups, the ability to invest in self-care and self-beautification is an expression of a sense of entitlement to economic, emotional, and social well-being and an effort at its attainment.[42] Beauty culture creates modes of producing what Lynn Chancer has termed "bodily capital," extending Pierre Bourdieu's insights on the relationship between social and cultural capital and economic capital.[43]

Margaret Hunter concurs, arguing that "beauty is a crucial resource for women" and thus is a form of social capital that Latina and African American women use to improve their life chances.[44] For these women, engaging in beauty culture is therefore one strategy among others for capital accumulation in the face of systematic barriers to their individual and collective access to well-being. Dominican women's hair-culture practices, in other words, are complex and complicated negotiations of self in the face of social inequality, and not a simple internationalization of racist, sexist, or heteronormative ideals imposed by patriarchy, the state, and social institutions.[45]

"Black behind the Ears, and Up Front, Too"

IDEOLOGICAL CODE SWITCHING AND AMBIGUITY IN DOMINICAN IDENTITIES

> If people can be close or remote from one another in many ways, it is the compresence of characteristics of closeness and remoteness along any of those dimensions—the very dissonance embodied in the dualism—that makes the position of strangers socially problematic in all times and places. When those who should be close, in any sense of the term, are actually close, and those who should be distant are distant, everyone is "in his place." When those who should be distant are close, however, the inevitable result is a degree of tension and anxiety which necessitates some special kind of response.—Donald Nathan Levine[1]

> As group markers the difference between citizenship and identity is that, while the former carries legal weight, the latter carries social and cultural weight.—Engin F. Isin and Patricia K. Wood[2]

The sociological aspects unique to Dominican techniques of the body are signaled precisely in the remainder of the Dominican poet Juan Antonio Alix's famous nineteenth-century décima "El negro tras de la oreja," whose opening stanza was quoted in the introduction and from which this book draws its title. Alix began his exegesis by claiming that he "employ[ed] his weak pen . . . to teach a lesson" to more than one "person" overwhelmed by the preoccupation with race. He ended the first stanza with the assertion that "the black behind the ears" is "abundant nowadays." Further on, he crowed that those who are "fine whites" never notice whiteness. Instead, those who notice are those who are not "pure blooded," who "[go] crazy trying to be white." Indeed, a pointed reference to "the black behind the ears" closed each of the six stanzas that followed. In this way, "El negro tras de la oreja"—both the décima and the heritage it referred to—taunted and ridiculed Dominicans who ignore or deny their black ancestry.[3] This book has explored how and why Dominicans came to have the "black behind the ears" and under what circumstances they have as open secrets displayed their blackness.

Historically, Dominican identities developed in counterpoint to Spain, Haiti, and the United States. The first murmurs of a specifically Dominican identity began in the socio-racial interactions between the Creole elite and the Afro-Hispanics of the Spanish part of Santo Domingo. These groups became increasingly self-aware politically, socially, and culturally during the Spanish colonial period. Spanish colonial policy had devastated the economy of Santo Domingo and left impoverished the small Creole community in the seventeenth century. The poor material condition of the colony and weak political condition of the Spanish colonial government, taken together with demographic predominance of the African and Afro-Creole population during the seventeenth century, lead to a more socio-racially incorporative system. Creole poverty taken together with the particularities of cattle ranching, domestic slavery, and manumission rates in the Spanish part of Santo Domingo had created a large, relatively independent rural class of former slaves and their descendants. That group was incorporated into the colonial system through the Catholic church, the military, and kinship system, and its members accordingly came to consider themselves "the whites of the land."

In the French part of Santo Domingo, conversely, the vast majority of the population was neither institutionally nor ideologically incorporated into a Creole identity. Rather, the French Creole elite made continual efforts to draw rigid boundaries between whites and non-whites. At the same time, however, those very efforts betrayed the fact of extensive mixing between master, freed, and enslaved classes. "In 1770 there were about 6,000 emancipated people of color; in 1780, 12,000; and by 1789, 28,000. . . . By 1789, they owned one-third of the plantation property, one-quarter of the slaves, and one-quarter of the real estate property in

Saint-Domingüe, as well as competing in commerce and trade."[4] Thus, by the turn of the nineteenth century, nearly half a million slaves were under the control of roughly 30,000 whites and 35,000 mulattos.[5] Mulattos played an intermediary, rather than an incorporative, role in this socio-racial order. They understood themselves to be a class apart from both whites and blacks. When in the aftermath of the French Revolution the slaves revolted, however, the mulatto elite joined forces with them because the white Creoles had rejected their claims, and the revolutionary Third Estate had excluded them. As these former slaves and mulattos struggled to form an independent nation, they ultimately were allied under the banner of an ideologically Black Republic when Haiti was founded in 1804. Although socially a complex and extensive racial taxonomy and white-supremacist racial order continued after the Haitian Revolution, legally and politically, blackness was conferred on all of its citizens, regardless of ancestry.[6]

In November 1821, seventeen years after Haiti was founded, the Dominican Republic likewise became an independent state when José Nuñez de Cáceres declared the country's independence from Spain. That first independence was short-lived, however. Following its protracted revolutionary war, internecine civil wars, and contested attempts to consolidate the new state, Jean-Pierre Boyer established a United Haiti in 1820 when he succeeded Alexandre Petión as ruler of the south, and Henri Christophe, who had ruled the north, committed suicide. Two years later, Boyer marched on the newly formed Dominican Republic and declared the entire island unified under Haitian rule. This unification was a peaceful and essentially bloodless transfer of power because, as Nuñez de Cáceres put it, "The majority of the Dominican population was mulatto, and many were favorably disposed to the unification with Haiti. To them, the Haitian government promised land, the abolition of taxes, and the liberation of the few remaining slaves."[7]

Over time, however, the negative effects of the Haitian government's economic and public policies materialized for residents of the former Spanish part of the island. In particular, policies intended to generate government revenue to pay France the exorbitant indemnification it had demanded in exchange for granting Haiti diplomatic recognition and trade relations were enforced through military repression and, as a result, generated extensive discontent. Spanish Creole critiques of those policies explained that this discontent was due not only to their political illegitimacy, but also to the inherent (that is, racial) incompatibility between the Haitians and "Dominicans." Thus, when on February 27,

1844, La Trinitaria, a pro-independence group led by Juan Pablo Duarte, overthrew the Haitian Unification government headed by Boyer, it did so under the banner of an integrated Dominican national identity as Hispanic, Catholic, and white. Henceforth, all things Haitian would be ideologically coded as antithetical to all things Dominican, including blackness. The Dominican historian Rubén Silié has aptly put it this way: "The perception of Haitians imposed from the pinnacle of power in the Dominican Republic was totally prejudiced, so that if the Haitians [did] not deny their African origins, the Dominicans [did] not recognize it."[8]

The U.S. government and capitalist elite joined in concert with this emergent anti-Haitianist Dominican discourse through narratives in which they displayed the Dominican Republic as the most "Hispanic, Catholic, and white" of (Latin) American nations against the Haitian Other. Whether they were official U.S. government commissions sent to examine the country as a potential territory, capitalist entrepreneurs, wealthy travelers, academics, or Marines, U.S. observers almost universally displayed Haiti and Haitians discursively as primitive, dirty, animalistic, black, and ugly. Dominicans and the Dominican Republic, by contrast, were presented as clean, courtly, white, and generally welcoming of white Americans.

These discourses about both nations on Hispaniola supported U.S. imperialism in each. U.S. political and economic intervention in Haiti was justified ideologically because Haiti was framed as a backward country in need of (capitalist, patriarchal, and white-supremacist) civilization. The Dominican Republic, although represented as superior to Haiti, could only benefit from further infusions of Anglo industriousness, whether in the form of individual colonists, military governance, customs receivership, or tourism, which would bring it to the maturity these narrators claimed it still lacked. Thus, Dominican identity negotiated the fraught space between Anglo-dominant notions of white patriarchal supremacy that defined Dominicans' racially mixed heritages as degenerative and their self-positioning as "the whites of the land" in relation to Haiti, who they in turn defined as the antithesis of civilization.

An aspect of that discursive and political negotiation was the rise of indigenism as an ideology that allowed Dominicans to stake their claims to the land they inhabited and to resist the expansionist and interventionist designs of Haiti, Spain, and the United States. At the same time, they embraced their Hispanic cultural heritage as distinct from the French and Anglo heritages of the Haitians and Americans, respectively. Thus, Indo-Hispanicity was coupled with anti-Haitianism to give birth to Dominicanidad. In turn, Dominicanidad's ideological code became embedded in official identity displays and discourses of institutions such as the Museo del Hombre Dominicano, which formed part of the ruling relations' conceptual practices of power.

These conceptual practices of power intersected unevenly but saliently with U.S. imperial discourses that ironically supported Dominican nation-building projects through shared anti-Haitianist and indigenist discourses and ideologies. These discourses coalesced during the Trujillato, which organized an extensive propaganda machine that circulated its own auto-ethnographic narratives of Dominican identity. Along with the expansion of Dominican identity displays and discourses abroad, the preservation and institutionalization of public-history projects at home offered Dominicans evidence for their own nation's claims to Indo-Hispanicity.

Following his assassination, Trujillo's leading anti-Haitianist and Hispanophile ideologue, Joaquín Balaguer, assumed power. Yet that power was contested by a New Wave of thinkers and activists who sought increased political and cultural representation of previously marginalized and excluded ideas and populations, as well as the recognition and recovery of African heritages. During both of his extended presidential terms, Balaguer steadily increased the state's diffusion of anti-Haitianist and Hispanophile discourses and displays. Among the venues created for that racial project was the Museo del Hombre Dominicano.

The Museo del Hombre Dominicano created an auto-ethnographic display and discourse that built on the dynamic dialogue between the imperial texts of U.S. travel writers and anti-Haitianist Dominicans by offering tangible evidence of Dominican's Indo-Hispanic pasts. At the same time, the Museo has fostered the development of "techniques of the body" that engender the internalization of its Indo-Hispanic discourse and display. Looking at photographs of South American Indians who stand in for their Taíno ancestors; walking through the exhibit's progressive levels; and hearing docents explain how much of the indigenous past is present in contemporary Dominican culture, Dominican visitors are encouraged to internalize the Museo's display. If the New Wave movement was working to face Dominican blackness, the Museo del Hombre Dominicano's exhibits pushed blackness back behind the ears.

Just as the Museo is a site that fosters internalization, the Dominican beauty shop offers social and technical supports for both the internalization and externalization of Indo-Hispanicity. At shops like New York City's Salon Lamadas, Dominican women's bodies are transformed into active displays of Dominican identity discourses. The shop, in other words, offers techniques of the body that will keep the black behind the ears of Dominicans' "face work."[9] Dominican hair culture centers on the creation of hair that appears naturally "indigenous" out of hair that betrays the blackness of the woman who has it. For hair is fundamental to Dominican identity displays and discourses: It marks the boundaries between Dominicans and Haitians and, in New York, between Dominicans and African Americans.

Despite ideological and cultural imperatives to keep the black behind the ears, however, some Dominicans have displayed their blackness up front. Dominicans in Washington, D.C., have a long history of affirming their black heritage, even as they continue to consider themselves Dominican. Removed from the web of anti-Haitianist, Negrophobic, and indigenist ideological codes woven by cultural institutions in the Dominican Republic and New York City, Dominicans in D.C. have participated in African American social worlds, where they have been encouraged to incorporate U.S. racial ideologies such as hypo-descent, even as they have been shielded from its exigencies because of their status as Latin American immigrants and Latinos. They have traveled both African American and Latin American routes to self-recognition and self-affirmation, carrying their Dominican identities with them along the way.

Previous scholarly observers of Dominican identity such as Paul Austerlitz have argued that Dominicans, like the Haitians Melville Herskovits studied in the 1930s, suffer from "'socialized ambivalence' regarding national and racial identity."[10] For Austerlitz, "Socialized ambivalence" in the Dominican case refers to the schism between "African-derived aesthetic[s]" and "the prevailing Hispanophilism" of the Dominican state and elite. Socialized ambivalence is characterized by "a simultaneous desire to say or do two opposite things."[11] The underlying assumption would seem to be that black and Hispanic are "two opposite things."

Robert K. Merton and Elinor Barber similarly write about "sociological ambivalence" or the "incompatible normative expectations incorporated into a *single* role of a *single* social status."[12] The fundamental cause of sociological ambivalence is an internally contradictory social structure. Although ideologically and institutionally "African" and "Hispanic" have been constructed as oppositional, at the level of Dominican identity discourses and displays such as hair culture, black and Hispanic are much more strategically ambiguous. To be ambiguous is to have "several possible meanings or interpretations."[13] Ambiguity, in other words, allows for equivocation.

Writing about ambiguity in Trinidad, Aisha Khan observed that research on Caribbean ethnic and racial identities has long documented multiplicity and intermediacy as an organizing principle of identity formation. "An important issue to emerge from this literature was that the so-called intermediate categories—that is, combinations lying between the extremes of 'black' and 'white'—signal important questions about the nature of ambiguity and the significance of the relationship between appearance (phenotype) and background in social relations, and more broadly, between social identity and social stratification, and ultimately between ideology and power."[14] Conceptually, ambiguity can be understood as both elusive meaning and systematic multiplicity. Elusive meaning is indeterminate and signals arbitrary identity choices. By contrast, systematic multiplicity of meaning is conditioned by a defining mechanism. It is a strategic response to power and its structures. It is the later conceptualization of strategic ambiguity that holds in my analysis. Ambiguity is invoked in the first place because of the various and competing ideological codes that frame blackness, whiteness, and indigeneity in the Americas.

Through their identity displays, Dominicans make manifest their situated sense of self in discursive, symbolic, and embodied forms. The salience of their identities, as Erving Goffman argued, is heightened in contexts in which the relationships tied to that identity are either extensive or intensive and affective or interactive.[15] Thus, the Dominican women at Salon Lamadas were individually committed to their role-conferring identities as Dominican women because of the number and quality of interactive and affective relationships with other Dominican women and the shop itself that supported those identities. By contrast, the Dominicans in Washington, D.C., had fewer interactive commitments with other Dominicans and Dominican cultural institutions, and they had more extensive and interactive commitments with African Americans, which encouraged the internalization of black identity as a role-conferring identity. Nonetheless, there were sufficient affective commitments generated by their role-conferring identities as "Latins" in Washington, D.C., to sustain their identities as Dominican, as well.

Although I have drawn on Goffman's insights on the presentation of self, I have also viewed identity as being enacted through staged practices and interactions across linguistic and ideological codes. Role identities are not always monolingually scripted and, accordingly, are not always mutually intelligible for the performer and her various audiences. Strategically ambiguous discursive strategies allow both for a coherent display of self and for the equivocal perceptions of others, even as the interaction is structured by power relations. Thus, identity is both internalized and externalized through techniques of the body that are "developed, stored, and transmitted through social organization and social relationships."[16]

Operating in the context of both Latin American and U.S.-framed white, African American, and Latino conceptual practices of power, Dominicans engage in a sort of ideological "code switching" in which both the Dominican Republic's and United States' race systems are engaged, rejected, and sustained at various historical and biographical moments. In so doing, they have forced Anglo Americans, African Americans, and other Latino/as to examine their assumptions about racial categorization, ethnic identity, and nationality, and about whether what is "visible" is "real" outside any given cultural or ideological context.

Notes

Introduction

1 "Descubriendo nuestra identidad," 1.

2 Forbes, "The Evolution of the Term Mulatto," 57.

3 Alix was a well-known poet from Santiago and a master at poetically capturing both the distinctive Cibaeño dialect and national race discourse of his era. He was a prolific writer, and his work appeared in flyers and most of the country's newspapers throughout his life. The popularity and wide public dissemination of Alix's décimas indicate their extensive influence. Indeed, he often used his décimas as currency, trading them for goods in local markets and stores: Alix, *Décimas inéditas*, 8.

4 Alix et al., *Décimas dominicanas de ayer y de hoy*, 15. Unless otherwise noted, all translations from Spanish-language texts and interviews throughout the book are mine.

5 Jenkins, *Social Identity*, 21.

6 I have chosen to use the historically accurate term "Unification" rather than "Occupation" to refer to the period between 1822 and 1844, when the island was under the consolidated governmental rule of Jean-Pierre Boyer and was known as "Unified Haiti." An ideological component of the Dominican Republic's political and governmental separation from Haiti was the nationalist reframing of the Unification as an "occupation." As critical Dominican historians such as Emilio Cordero Michel and Juan Isidro Jiménes have shown, however, this terminology is ahistorical and ideological. See Emilio Cordero Michel, *La revolución haitiana y Santo Domngo* (Santo Domingo: Editora Nacional, 1968) and Juan Isidro Jiménes Grullon, *Sociología política dominicana, 1844–1966* (3 vols.; Santo Domingo: Taller, 1974–75).

7 The myth of Haitian rapacity targeting innocent (white) Dominican virgins was most fully articulated in Cesar Nicolás Pénson's 1891 short story, "Las vírgenes de Galindo," a dramatization of a historic case in which the elite landowner Don Andres Andújar and his three young daughters were murdered in 1822. The trial concluded that the perpetrators were Dominican, but the court of popular opinion insisted that the murderers must have been Haitian soldiers. Pénson's fictional narrative incorporated many of the facts of

the case but disavowed them because they were the product of a Haitian Unification legal system that was incommensurate with the providentially legitimated knowledge of the townspeople who judged unnamed Haitians to be the true murderers. In other words, Pénson's narrative is exemplary of the anti-Haitianist ideological base of nationalist Dominican identity formations: see Venator Santiago, "Las Vírgenes de Pénson."

8 Torres-Saillant, "Introduction to Dominican Blackness," 6.

9 Cambeira, *Quisqueya La Bella*, 102.

10 Ibid., 116.

11 Moya Pons, "Dominican National Identity in Historical Perspective," 16.

12 Frances Robles, "Black Denial," A Raising Voice: Afro–Latin American Series.

13 Christina Violeta Jones and Pedro R. Rivera, "Black Denial Response: Did the *Miami Herald* Have an Agenda?"

14 Cf. "Naturally Curly.Com Forum" at http://www.naturallycurly.com/curltalk/viewtopic.php?p=1201723&highlight=&sid=c4365db5ddf20e de963f61157362f820&PHPSESSID=6e9a409cc058c10d109cde4815ad1c89. Accessed August 9, 2007.

15 Shohat, *Talking Visions*, 47.

16 For a discussion of transnational social fields, see Basch et al., "Theoretical Premises."

17 For an excellent overview of these methods, see Denzin and Lincoln, *Handbook of Qualitative Research*.

18 Ibid., 1–17.

19 Cf. Abrams and Hogg, *Social Identity Theory*; Alcoff and Mendieta, *Identities*; Berger and Del Negro, *Identity and Everyday Life*; Fong and Chuang, *Communicating Ethnic and Cultural Identity*.

20 See Mead, *Mind, Self, and Society*.

21 Cornell and Hartmann, *Ethnicity and Race*.

22 Stryker, *Symbolic Interactionism*.

23 Goffman, *The Presentation of Self in Everyday Life*.

24 Smith, *Writing the Social*, 159; Smith, "The Standard North American Family," 50–64 (the quotation is on 51).

25 Anderson, *Imagined Communities*, 6–7.

26 Jenkins, *Social Identity*, 20.

27 Ibid., 21. See also Mead, *Mind, Self, and Society*; Cooley, *Social Organization*; Goffman, *The Presentation of Self in Everyday Life*.

28 Including, for example, the community located just to the north of Santo Domingo, Mata de los Indios, named a UNESCO World Heritage Site in 2001 for its preservation and display of African diaspora cultural practices, or Boca de Nigua, where the descendants of *cimarrones* continue to practice and celebrate black expressive cultural forms.

29 That is, as migrants who reside, work, or are educated for alternating but extended periods of time both in their country of origin and the host country. They accordingly develop households and social networks in and across both places, creating what Basch and colleagues have called a "social field that crosses national boundaries" (Basch et al., *Nations Unbounded*, 22).

30 Peña et al., "'Racial Democracy' in the Americas."

31 Personal communication with the author, November 15, 2004.

32 Duany, *Quisqueya on the Hudson*, 13.

33 Moya Pons, "Dominican National Identity and Return Migration," 32.

34 Antonio de Moya, "Sobre el problema racial en la República Dominicana: Bosquejo para una aproximación psico-histórica," mimeograph, Santo Domingo, 1986, in Fennema and Loewenthal, *La construcción de raza y nación en la República Dominicana*, 31.

35 See Hoffnung-Garskof, "Nueba Yol," 171–73.

36 Levitt, *The Transnational Villagers*, 107.

37 Ibid., 109.

38 Dore-Cabral, "Encuesta Rumbo-Gallup," 12.

39 Vicioso, "An Oral History," 272.

40 Waters, *Black Identities*, 5.

41 Ibid., 7.

42 Bailey, *Language, Race, and Negotiation of Identity*, 2.

43 Rubiés, "Travel Writing and Ethnography."

44 Pratt, *Imperial Eyes*, 6–7.

45 Brown, "Cultural Representations and Ideological Domination," 658.

46 Guzmán, "Raza y lenguaje en el Cibao."

47 Ibid., 36.

48 Roberts, "The (Re)construction of the Concept of 'Indio' in the National Identities of Cuba, the Dominican Republic and Puerto Rico," 116.

49 Synott, "Shame and Glory," 381.

50 McCracken, *Big Hair*.

51 Earlier researchers of race in the Caribbean have likewise found that hair is a primary criterion in the evaluation and classification of an individual's racial status. See, e.g., Rogler, "The Role of Semantics in the Study of Race Distance in Puerto Rico"; Mintz, "Cañamelar."

52 Carlos Dore-Cabral, "Reflexiones sobre la identidad cultural Dominicana" (*CASA*, January–February 1985), as cited in Fennema and Loewenthal, *La construción de raza y nación en la República Dominicana*, 43.

53 Fennema and Loewenthal, *La construción de raza y nación en la República Dominicana*, 63–64.

54 Roberts, "The (Re)construction of the Concept of 'Indio' in the National Identities of Cuba, the Dominican Republic and Puerto Rico," 99.

55 Itzigsohn et al., "Immigrant Incorporation and Racial Identity," 18.

56 Itzigsohn and Dore-Cabral, "Competing Identities?" 243.

57 Duany, "Reconstructing Racial Identity," 165.

58 Del Pinal and Ennis, "The Racial and Ethnic Identity of Latin American Immigrants in Census 2000," 9.

59 Moya Pons, "Dominican National Identity and Return Migration," 31.

60 Sagás, *Race and Politics in the Dominican Republic.*

61 del Pinal and Ennis, "The Racial and Ethnic Identity of Latin American Immigrants in Census 2000," 11.

62 Smithsonian Institution, *Latino Resources at the Smithsonian.*

63 Corporán, "Building Bridges."

64 Newsome, "Approaches to Material Culture Research and Representation."

65 Torres-Saillant, "The Tribulations of Blackness," 126. It should be noted that Torres-Saillant does not provide disaggregated numbers for each; nor does he indicate the source of his percentages.

66 I conducted another eight single-session in-depth interviews that lasted two to three hours with Dominicans who participated in the exhibit, whether by donating artifacts or by being profiled. I also interviewed a self-described Afro-Puerto Rican participant who has continued to be actively involved with the Anacostia as a result of *The Black Mosaic.* The real names of these respondents and participants are used because they were used in the exhibit, which was a public venue and forum. There is one exception: Sofia Mora is a pseudonym, the use of which was requested by Dr. Mora herself following our interview. The interviews I conducted explored elements of the participants' life histories that I suspected might elucidate how these Dominicans came to their pro-negritude racial consciousness. These interviews were both thematic and life-history compilations.

67 Levitt and Gomez, "The Intersection of Race and Gender among Dominicans in the U.S," 9.

68 Itzigsohn et al., "Immigrant Incorporation and Racial Identity," 28.

69 Oboler, *Ethnic Labels, Latino Lives*; Shorris, "Latinos"; Vicioso, "An Oral History (Testimonio)"; Winn, *Americas.*

70 Vicioso, "An Oral History (Testimonio)," 231.

71 See, e.g., Waters, *Black Identities.*

72 Itzigsohn et al., "Immigrant Incorporation and Racial Identity."

73 Hoffnung-Graskof, "Nueba Yol," 363–64.

74 Duany, "Reconstructing Racial Identity"; idem, "Transnational Migration from the Dominican Republic"; idem, *Quisqueya on the Hudson,* 36–37.

75 See, e.g., the special issue of *Latin American Perspectives* (25, no. 3 [May 1998]); Rodríguez, *Puerto Ricans.*

76 Howard, *Coloring the Nation.*

77 Mejía Ricart, as quoted in Rout, *The African Experience in Spanish America,* 287.

78 Hoetink, *El pueblo Dominicano (1850–1900).*

79 Guarnizo, "One Country in Two."

80 Guarnizo, "Los Dominicanyorks," 82.

81 Surprisingly, Guarnizo did not indicate any data on the racial self-identification of his respondents. Although respondents were asked to what degree the subjective experience of discrimination in the labor market influenced their decision to become entrepreneurs, neither self-perception nor the perception of survey administrators was included in the otherwise finely specified survey instrument. I would have liked to know, for example, the relationship between their status in each country's respective racial-classification system and their economic opportunities and constraints. Were racially or phenotypically privileged Dominicans more likely to benefit than their darker co-nationals from the kinds of social capital Guarnizo argues is fundamental to the binational enterprise? Research with other Latino groups has found that the lighter members of those groups experience higher educational attainment rates and, subsequently, higher upward social mobility than their darker co-nationals: see Murguia and Telles, "Phenotype and Schooling among Mexican Americans"; Baynes, "If It's Not Just Black and White Anymore, Why Does Darkness Cast a Longer Discriminatory Shadow than Lightness?"

82 Guarnizo, "One Country in Two," 308.

83 This is a pseudonym for the actual salon.

84 The entire research design was subjected to intensive review by the Human Subjects Review Board of the cuny Graduate School and University Center, which required the fully informed consent of all human subjects.

85 Badillo and Badillo, "Que Tan Racistas Somos," 61–62.

86 Although *rubia* narrowly means blonde, in Dominican contexts it refers more generally to light-haired, light-skinned, and "fine"-featured individuals.

87 González, "Patterns of Dominican Ethnicity," 113.

88 Rodríguez, *Changing Race*, 107.

89 The Hawthorne effect is the supposed influence of the researcher on the research subjects' behavior and was first documented as a methodological concern in the workplace behavior studies conducted at the Hawthorne plant of the Western Electric Company. Much debate has ensued since then, and though many researchers have decided that their effect on the research is either nonexistent or can be controlled for, others remain convinced that the effect does occur: see Jones, "Was There a Hawthorne Effect?"

90 Harper, "Talking about Pictures," 14.

91 See González, "Giving Birth in America."

92 For more on the effect of pregnancy on fieldwork with other mothers and their children, see Reich, "Pregnant with Possibility."

93 I conducted fifteen extended life-history interviews with regular clients of the salon I was observing. They ranged in age from twenty-one to sixty-two, represented a variety of socioeconomic and residential statuses, and were diverse in regional origin and generation of immigration. Thirteen of the inter-

views were conducted in Spanish; two were conducted in "Spanglish" and translated where necessary for reader comprehension. All of the interviews were conducted in the respondents' homes. Conversations that took place in the beauty shop were reconstructed from field notes, which were taken either in the shop's bathroom or immediately after I exited the shop each day. All interviews were tape recorded, transcribed, and translated by the author. The interviews consisted of two to three separate three-hour sessions following a modified version of the Seidman model: see Seidman, *Interviewing as Qualitative Research Method.*

The first interview was a life-history interview in which the respondent's migrations, labor-market experience, educational experience, family life, and personal history were explored. The second interview inquired into the respondent's experience of Dominican beauty culture, both at Salon Lamadas and more generally. If time permitted, the second interview also included a photo-elicitation component during which respondents were asked to rank and describe men and women of various ethnicities and appearances selected by the interviewer from hairstyle books used at Salon Lamadas. If time was short, a third interview was conducted for the photo elicitation, following the examples set by previous researchers interested in racial self-perception among Latin American communities and among ethnic women in the United States.

94 Conrad Kottak, as quoted in Harris, *Patterns of Race in the Americas,* 57.

95 Hunter, "Mind Games and Body Techniques," 178.

96 Godreau, "Confronting the Panic," 2.

97 Ibid.

1 Traveling Narratives

The quotation in this chapter's title is from Chester, "Haiti," 214.

1 Kaminsky, *Reading the Body Politic,* xv.

2 Tejada Ortíz, *Cultura popular e identidad nacional,* 240.

3 Pratt, *Imperial Eyes,* 146.

4 This is a reference to Pedro Henríquez Ureña's formulation articulated in *Seis ensayos en busca de nuestra expresión* (1927), as quoted ibid., 175.

5 Omi and Winant, *Racial Formation in the United States,* 56.

6 Toussaint Louverture marched on Santo Domingo and declared slavery abolished on January 1, 1801, under the flag of the French government, which had dominion of the entire island, according to the 1795 Treaty of Basel, and which endowed him with the authority to enforce the 1793 abolition of slavery in the French territories.

7 Moya Pons, *The Dominican Republic,* 6.

8 Moreau de Saint-Méry, *A Topographical and Political Description of the Spanish Part of Santo Domingo*.

9 For a more extended biography, see Roberts and Roberts, *Moreau de St. Méry's American Journey (1793–1798)*.

10 Moreau de Saint-Méry, *A Topographical and Political Description of the Spanish Part of Santo Domingo*, 92.

11 Ibid., 94.

12 Ibid., 95.

13 Ibid., 83–92.

14 Ibid., 5.

15 These are improved defense, naval security in times of war, increased subsistence capacity, population increase, improved agriculture, and increased commerce: see ibid., 433–71.

16 For an excellent account of Moreau de Saint-Méry's political biography, see Dubois, *Avengers of the New World*.

17 An interesting firsthand account of this period in Haiti's history from the perspective of a dispossessed white family is the anonymously authored *Secret History*. See also Walton, *Present State of the Spanish Colonies*.

18 Mackenzie, *Notes on Haiti*, 215.

19 Maxime Raybaud published his 1856 account *L'Empereur Soulouque et son empire* in Paris through the Michel Levy Press under the pseudonym Gustave d'Alaux. The text was translated and edited by Emilio Rodríguez Demorizi (Raybaud, *L'Empereur Soulouque et son empire*) and quoted in Hoetink, *The Dominican People, 1850–1900*, 186–87.

20 Hoetink, *The Dominican People, 1850–1900*, 181–84.

21 Tansill, *The United States and Santo Domingo, 1798–1873*, chap. 5.

22 Sheller, "The 'Haytian Fear'"; Dubois, *Avengers of the New World*, esp. chaps. 6–13.

23 Jordan, *White over Black*, 380–86.

24 Montague, *Haiti and the United States, 1714–1938*, 32–33.

25 Inman, "The Monroe Doctrine and Hispanic America"; Weeks, *Building the Continental Empire*.

26 Martínez-Fernández, *Torn between Empires*, 20.

27 For an extended discussion of this, see Tansill, *The United States and Santo Domingo, 1798–1873*.

28 Weeks, *Building the Continental Empire*, 102. See also Hauch, "Attitudes of Foreign Governments towards the Spanish Reoccupation of the Dominican Republic."

29 Nelson, *Almost a Territory*. It is important to note that Cuba was also being considered actively for annexation by the United States during this era, which in part accounts for the U.S. involvement in the War of 1898.

30 Logan, *The Diplomatic Relations of the United States with Haiti, 1776–1891*, 238.

31 Calhoun to Hogan, February 22, 1845, as cited in Tansill, *The United States and Santo Domingo, 1798–1873*, 126.

32 Martínez-Fernández, *Torn between Empires*, 41; Logan, *The Diplomatic Relations of the United States with Haiti, 1776–1891*, 239. Martínez-Fernández notes that the contemporary Spanish observer Antonio López Villanueva estimated the population to be roughly half mulattos, one-third black, and one-eighth white. While Martínez-Fernández credits López Villanueva's assessment with greater accuracy than Hogan's, I would again point to the interests and ideologies of the observer in making his assessment, given that there are in fact no "objective" measures of race.

33 Welles, *Naboth's Vineyard*, 76.

34 Porter, *Diario de una misión secreta a Santo Domingo (1846)*, 24. All translations from this text are my own, as I was not able to access the original English version that is held as a non-circulating item at the Duke University Library.

35 Tansill wrote an extensive history monograph about the U.S. role in the Dominican Republic. *The United States and Santo Domingo, 1798–1873* is considered an unimpeachable resource by Dominican historians. Indeed, it was among the first books translated and published by the Dominican Society of Bibliophiles.

36 Porter, *Diario de una misión secreta a Santo Domingo (1846)*.

37 Tavares K., "La misión secreta del Teniente Porter," 8.

38 Ibid., 5.

39 Ibid., 6.

40 Ibid., 7.

41 Ibid.

42 Logan, *The Diplomatic Relations of the United States with Haiti, 1776–1891*, 247.

43 Martínez-Fernández, *Torn between Empires*, 42.

44 Cf. Nelson, *Almost a Territory*; Welles, *Naboth's Vineyard*; Knight, *The Americans in Santo Domingo*; Martínez-Fernández, *Torn between Empires*, 1994.

45 Hudson, "Jane McManus Storm Cazneau (1807–1878)."

46 Fabens, *In the Tropics*; idem, *Life in Santo Domingo*. *Life in Santo Domingo* was translated and published by the Dominican Society of Bibliophiles as *La Vida en los Trópicos*.

47 Idem, *Facts about Santo Domingo, Applicable to the Present Crisis*; idem, *Resources of Santo Domingo* (1869); idem, *Resources of Santo Domingo* (1871).

48 Martínez-Fernández, *Torn between Empires*, 40.

49 Logan, *The Diplomatic Relations of the United States with Haiti, 1776–1891*, 242–43.

50 Manuel María Gautier to Secretary Fish, July 9, 1869, as cited in Welles, *Naboth's Vineyard*, 369.

51 Torres-Saillant and Hernández, *The Dominican Americans*, 17. Similar rhetoric was deployed during the 1992 and 1996 presidential election campaigns during which Francisco Peña Gómez was accused by Balaguer and his party of a pro-Haitian, Negrophile plot to blacken the country and to concentrate power in black hands.

52 Nelson, *Almost a Territory*, 61, 75.

53 Courtney, as quoted in Torres-Saillant and Hernández, *The Dominican Americans*, 18.

54 Porter offered an account of this second mission to Santo Domingo in "Secret Missions to San Domingo." The article included a short synopsis of his 1846 report, as well. Porter recounted his five-week journey on horseback and on mules over more than 1,000 miles of the Dominican Republic's territory. He had visited every major town, beginning at the capital city, Santo Domingo, and working his way through San Cristobal, Baní, Azua, Cotui, Samaná, La Vega, Santiago, San Pedro de Marcoris, and, finally, Puerto Plata. Throughout, he offered a thumbnail sketch of the country's natural resources, its people, and its culture.

55 Although annexation never took place, the *New York Herald* continued to favor an active U.S. role in the governance of the Dominican Republic as late as 1899, when it called for military intervention: cf. Hoetink, *The Dominican People, 1850–1900*, 93; Nelson, *Almost a Territory*, 75.

56 Hulme, "El encuentro con Anacaona," 88.

57 See Irving, *The Life and Voyages of Christopher Columbus*.

58 Martínez-Fernández, *Torn between Empires*, 249, fn. 106; Logan, *The Diplomatic Relations of the United States with Haiti, 1776–1891*, 247; Keim, *Santo Domingo*.

59 Bejamin Wade was a Whig senator from Ohio who was also a committed abolitionist and co-author of the Wade-Davis Reconstruction Act, a radical alternative to Lincoln's Reconstruction Act, which Lincoln defeated. Andrew Dickson White (1832–1918) was the co-founder and first president of Cornell College. Samuel G. Howe was an antislavery activist, Free Soil Movement leader, educator, and Methodist minister from Massachusetts; he advocated in favor of Dominican annexation. His wife, the renowned suffragist, club woman, and author of "The Battle Hymn of the Republic," Julia Ward Howe (1819–1910), accompanied him on the trip to Santo Domingo and wrote of the experience in her travel narrative: Howe, *Reminiscences, 1819–1899*.

60 Grant, "Message of the President of the United States, Communicating the Report of the Commission of Inquiry to the Island of Santo Domingo," 3.

61 "Hazard's Santo Domingo," 183.

62 Vega, *Imágenes del ayer*.

63 Nelson, *Almost a Territory*, 70–74.

64 Hazard, *Santo Domingo, Past and Present*.

65 Stimson, "The Influence of Travel Books on Early American Hispanism."

66 Hazard, *Santo Domingo, Past and Present*, 215.

67 Ibid., 249.

68 Ibid., 398.

69 Ibid., 111, 459.

70 Ibid., 485.

71 Ibid., 486–87.

72 Haas, *Conquests and Historical Identities in California, 1769–1936*.

73 Cf. Acuña, *Occupied America*, chap. 5.

74 Hazard, *Santo Domingo, Past and Present*, 2.

75 Pedro Franciso Bonó, as quoted in Hoetink, *The Dominican People, 1850–1900*, 188.

76 Ibid.

77 Bhabha, *Nation and Narration*.

78 Sommer, *One Master for Another*, xiii-xiv.

79 Franco, *Historia de las ideas políticas en la República Dominicana*, 29–30.

80 Sommer, *Foundational Fiction*, 251–52.

81 See "La Republique Dominicaine a L'Exposition Universelle de Paris"; "Catálogo de los objetos que presenta la República dominicana á la Exposición histórico-americana de Madrid"; "The Dominican Republic."

82 Hoetink, *The Dominican People, 1850–1900*, 36.

83 Ober, *Our West Indian Neighbors, the Islands of the Caribbean Sea, "America's Mediterranean,"* 183–92.

84 Ibid., 189.

85 Boyce, *United States Colonies and Dependencies, Illustrated*, 566.

86 Ibid., 584.

87 Ibid., 595–604.

88 Ibid., 37.

89 Ibid., 597–603.

90 Internet Speculative Fiction Data Base, Cushing Library Science Fiction and Fantasy Research Collection and Institute for Scientific Computation at Texas A&M University, available online at http://www.isfdb.org/cgi-bin/ea.cgi?A._Hyatt_Verrill (accessed February 27, 2005).

91 Verrill, *Port Rico Past and Present and San Domingo of To-Day*, 227.

92 Ibid., 358.

93 Ibid., 227–34.

94 Ibid., 309–11.

95 Ibid., 311.

96 Ibid., 357.

97 Franck, *Roaming through the West Indies*.

98 Heuttner, "Harry A. Franck."

99 Franck, *Roaming through the West* Indies, 17.

100 Ibid., 106–107.

101 Ibid., 108–109.

102 Ibid., 109–10.

103 Ibid., 116–17.

104 Ibid., 119.

105 Weed, "Hearing the Truth about Haiti."

106 Franck, *Roaming through the West Indies*, 148.

107 Renda, *Taking Haiti*, 171–72.

108 Franck, *Roaming through the West Indies*, 189.

109 Ibid., 197, 209, 215.

110 Ibid., 203.

111 Ibid., 201.

112 Ibid., 234.

113 Ibid., 197.

114 Ibid., 235.

115 Inman, *Trailing the Conquistadores*, 121.

116 Inman, *Through Santo Domingo and Haiti*, 79; idem, *Trailing the Conquistadores*, 122.

117 Foster, *Combing the Caribbees*, 271.

118 Ibid., 282.

119 Ibid., 288.

120 Inman, *Trailing the Conquistadores*, 138.

121 Ibid., 157.

122 Ibid., 167.

123 Roorda, *The Dictator Next Door*, 190–91.

124 Ibid., 88.

125 Burks, *Land of Checkerboard Families*.

126 As an interesting aside, it should be noted that L. Ron Hubbard, the infamous founder of Scientology, was the guild's second president and that he used that post to launch his Scientology project.

127 Pritchett, "The Man Who Reads Unwritten History"; Ruber, "Burks of the Pulps"; Renda, *Taking Haiti*, 216.

128 Renda, *Taking Haiti*, 13.

129 Ibid., 175.

130 Burks, *El país de las familias multicolores*.

131 Burks, *Land of Checkerboard Families*, 17.

132 Ibid., 14–15.

133 Ibid., 122–23.

134 Ibid., 18–20.

135 Ibid., 138–40.

136 Ibid., 43.

137 de Leeuw, *Crossroads of the Caribbean Sea*.

138 Renda, *Taking Haiti*, 237–38.

139 Herskovits, "Journey for Journey's Sake."

140 De Leeuw, *Crossroads of the Caribbean Sea*, 237.

141 Ibid., 270.

142 Ibid., 241.

143 Ibid., 314.

144 Ibid., 318.

145 Ibid., 322.

146 Ernst, *Report and Opinion in the Matter of Galindez*. Ironically, Ernst was a staunch critic of Hollywood censorship, communist baiting, and right-wing conservatism.

147 Walker, *Journey toward the Sunlight*, 8–11.

148 Ibid., 28.

149 Morrison, *Playing in the Dark*, 67; Walker, *Journey toward the Sunlight*, 28, 30.

150 Walker, *Journey toward the Sunlight*, 33.

151 See the UNESCO frontispiece in Galván, *The Cross and the Sword*.

152 El Sistema Nacional de Cultura, *Informe República Dominicana*.

153 Ibid., 262.

154 Campbell, "Travel Writing and Its Theory," 262.

155 Pratt, *Imperial Eyes*, 153.

156 Ibid., 236.

2 Indigenous Displays

1 Pagán Perdomo, interview.

2 Torres-Saillant, "Introduction to Dominican Blackness," 54.

3 Smith, *Writing the Social*, 73.

4 Ibid., 75.

5 Ibid., 158.

6 Bennett, *The Birth of the Museum*, 6–7.

7 Ibid., 47.

8 See del Castillo and Murphy, "Migration, National Identity and Cultural Policy in the Dominican Republic."

9 Rydell, *All the World's a Fair*; King, *Colonial Discourses, Collective Memories, and the Exhibition of Native American Cultures and Histories in the Contemporary United States*.

10 Scheckel, *The Insistence of the Indian*.

11 Borneman, "American Anthropology as Foreign Policy," 665.

12 Deloria, *Playing Indian*.

13 Krech and Hail, *Collecting Native America, 1870–1960*, 1–24.

14 "Aims and Objects of the Museum of the American Indian Heye Foundation," 17.

15 Kidwell, "Every Last Dishcloth."

16 King, *Colonial Discourses, Collective Memories, and the Exhibition of Native American Cultures and Histories in the Contemporary United States*, 8.

17 Veloz Maggiolo, *Arqueologia prehistorica de Santo Domingo*, 7–8. Meriño was a member of the Azul Party, which had engaged in armed resistance against the republic's reannexation by Spain in 1861 and which rejected Baez's attempt to annex the country to the United States in 1871.

18 Mejía, "Plan acerca de la fundación de un Museo Nacional," 513.

19 Archivos General de la Nación, *Obras de Trujillo*.

20 Roorda, *The Dictator Next Door*, 170–71.

21 Pan American Union, *Program and Rules of the Second Competition for the Selection of an Architect for the Monumental Lighthouse*.

22 Roorda, *The Dictator Next Door*, 116–17.

23 Derby, "The Dictator's Seduction."

24 Sang, *La política exterior del dictador Trujillo, 1930–1961*, 833.

25 Austerlitz, *Merengue*, 75–76.

26 Personal communication, Dominican Studies Institute, City College of the City University of New York, October 1998.

27 López Rodríguez, "Presentación," 8.

28 Torres-Saillant, "Introduction to Dominican Blackness," 55.

29 Balaguer, sidebar article in *Primacías de América en la Española*, 5.

30 For a much more comprehensive and critical account of the quincentennial, see García Arévalo, *Santo Domingo en ocasión del Quinto Centenario*.

31 Sagás and Inoa, *The Dominican People*, 208–33.

32 Chester, *Rag-Tags, Scum, Riff-Raff, and Commies*, 3.

33 Ibid., chap. 10.

34 For an excellent dramatized account of these periods, see Sención, *They Forged the Signature of God*.

35 See Martin, *Overtaken by Events*.

36 Larrazábal Blanco, *El negro y la esclavitud en Santo Domingo*, 107.

37 Moya Pons, "Modernización y cambios en la República Dominicana," 244.

38 Jiménez, "Exigencias de un cimarrón," in idem, *Exigencias de un cimarrón(en sueños)*, 22–24.

39 Ibid., 243–45.

40 Deive, *La esclavitud del negro en Santo Domingo, 1492–1844*, 14.

41 Ibid., 17.

42 Deive, "Y tu abuela, ¿dónde está?" 109.

43 Oboler, *Ethnic Labels, Latino Lives*, 128.

44 Hoetink, *The Dominican People, 1850–1900*, 179.

45 Mir, 1984, 199, trans. in Torres-Saillant, "Introduction to Dominican Blackness," 57.

46 Albert Batista, *Mujer y esclavitud en Santo Domingo*; Alejandra Liriano, *El papel de la mujer de origen africano en el Santo Domingo colonial, siglos XVI–XVII*; Deive, *La esclavitud del negro en Santo Domingo (1492–1844)*; Larrazábal Blanco, *El negro y la esclavitud en Santo Domingo*; Silié, *Economía, esclavitud y población*.

47 Pichardo, *Santo Domingo*.

48 Among these works is the establishment in 1997 of the Fundación Cultural Bayahonda, which is dedicated to the recording and distribution of Afro-Dominican *musica raíz* (root music) such as Palos and Gagá. See http://www.artelatino.com/bayahonda/bayahonda.html (accessed March 21, 2005).

49 Torres-Saillant, "El retorno de las yolas."

50 Idem, "Introduction to Dominican Blackness," 57.

51 Ibid.

52 Albert Batista, *Mujer y esclavitud en Santo Domingo*, 109–10. The quotation in this section's subhead is from Jiménez, *Exigencias de un cimarrón (en sueños)*, 27.

53 González Canalda and Silié, "La nación dominicana en la enseñanza a nivel primario."

54 Balaguer, *El centinela de la frontera*; idem, *La isla al reves*; García, *Compendio de la historia de Santo Domingo*; Gimbernard, *Historia de Santo Domingo*; Lugo, *Historia de Santo Domingo (de 1556 hasta 1608)*; Marrero Aristy, *La República Dominicana*; Peña-Batlle, *Historia de la cuestión fronteriza*. In addition to being a Trujillista historian and ideologue, Peña-Batlle was foreign minister during the Trujillato.

55 Balaguer in Gimbernard, *Historia de Santo Domingo*, 134.

56 Ibid., 150.

57 Torres-Saillant, "Introduction to Dominican Blackness," 42.

58 González, "Campesinos y sociedad colonial en el siglo xviii Dominicano."

59 Turits, *Foundations of Despotism*, 49.

60 Ibid.

61 Raybaud, as quoted in Hoetink, *The Dominican People, 1850–1900*, 186–87; Logan, *The Diplomatic Relations of the United States with Haiti, 1776–1891*, 247.

62 Atkins and Wilson, *The Dominican Republic and the United States*.

63 Cf. Schomburgk, "Notes on Santo Domingo," "On the Currents and Tides of La Mona," "On the Currents and Tides of the Southern Coasts of Santo Domingo," "On the Geographical Position of Santo Domingo," "Ethnological Researches in Santo Domingo," "Visit to the Valley of Costanza in the Cibao Mountains of the Island of Santo Domingo and to an Indian Burial Ground in Its Vicinity," "Remarks on the Principal Ports and Anchoring Places along the

Coast of the Dominican Republic," and "The Peninsula and Bay of Samaná in the Dominican Republic."

64 See Weeks, *Building the Continental Empire.*

65 Rydell, *All the World's a Fair,* 235–36.

66 Hulme, "El encuentro con Anacaona," 78.

67 Deloria, *Playing Indian,* 20–21.

68 The Black Legend derived from Bartolomeo de las Casas's denunciations of the cruelties of the Spanish conquest of the Americas and its native peoples recounted in his *An Account, Much Abbreviated, of the Destruction of the Indies, with Related Texts.*

69 Hulme, *Remnants of Conquest,* 21–29.

70 Venator Santiago, "Race, Space, and the Puerto Rican Citizenship."

71 Borneman, "American Anthropology as Foreign Policy," 667.

72 Welles, *Naboth's Vineyard,* 463. Astwoods was a prominent African American reverend who was originally appointed under Hayes.

73 Moya Pons, *The Dominican Republic,* 286.

74 Olsen Bogaert, *Legislación sobre el Museo del Hombre Dominicano,* 8.

75 For an extensive compilation of the legislation, see Espinal Hernández, *Patrimonio cultural y legislación.*

76 Krieger, *Archeological and Historical Investigations in Samaná, Dominican Republic.*

77 Weeks et al., "Herbert W. Krieger y la práctica de la arqueologia 'colonial' en la República Dominicana," 78.

78 Fewkes, *The Aborigines of Porto Rico and Neighboring Islands,* 18.

79 Thompson, "Register to the Papers of Herbert William Krieger."

80 Veloz Maggiolo, *Arqueologia prehistorica de Santo Domingo,* 12. Alberti Bosch, *Apountes para la prehistoria de Quisqueya.*

81 Pagán Perdomo, "Notas sobre el tráfico ilícito de bienes culturales en República Dominicana."

82 Lugo Lovatón, "¿Museo del Hombre Dominicano?" in Olsen Bogaert et al., "Un modelo de administración para El Museo del Hombre Dominicano," 14.

83 Harrington himself had been employed by the Heye Foundation in 1908 when he completed his master's degree in anthropology at Columbia University, where he had worked with Franz Boas. According to Kidwell, Harrington was one of the foundation's "most productive collectors" of artifacts from throughout continental America and the Caribbean: Kidwell, "Every Last Dishcloth," 240.

84 Correspondence between Harrington and Hurst, Museum of the American Indian–Heye Foundation, as cited in Pagán Perdomo, "Notas sobre el tráfico ilícito de bienes culturales en República Dominicana," 3.

85 de Booy, "Pottery from Certain Caves in Eastern Santo Domingo, West Indies."

86   Idem, "Santo Domingo Kitchen-Midden and Burial Mound," 108.

87   Pagán Perdomo, "Notas sobre el tráfico ilícito de bienes culturales en República Dominicana," 3.

88   Moya Pons, *The Dominican Republic*, 337.

89   Ibid., 338.

90   Mejía, "Plan acerca de la fundación de un Museo Nacional," 512.

91   Ibid., 513.

92   Idem, untitled article.

93   Idem, "De la necesidad de un museo en nuestra patria."

94   Idem, "El Museo Nacional."

95   Alemar, "Historia del Museo Nacional" (*Listín Diario*, March 22, 1930), as cited in Olsen Bogaert et al., "Un modelo de administración para El Museo del Hombre Dominicano," 14.

96   Cocco de Filippis, *Madres, Maestras y Militantes Dominicanas (Fundadoras)*, 127.

97   Mejía, "De cómo visitar el Museo Nacional."

98   Instituto Antropológico Dominicano, *Primera exposición de arte indígena autóctono*.

99   Ruffins, "Mythos, Memory, and History."

100   García Arévalo, *Santo Domingo en ocasión del Quinto Centenario*, 266.

101   Idem, *Indigenismo, arqueología e identidad nacional*, 15–18.

102   Kidder, *Latin America and UNESCO*.

103   Ibid., 26, 35.

104   Dato Pagán Perdomo interview, and *Album de Oro de la Feria de la Paz y Confraternidad del Mundo Libre*.

105   Olsen Bogaert, *Legislación sobre el Museo del Hombre Dominicano*, 12.

106   Plinio Pina P., *Legislación dominicana sobre museos y protección del patrimonio cultural, 1870–1977*, 65–67, 96–100.

107   Pagán Perdomo, interview.

108   Vega, interview.

109   Olsen Bogaert et al., "Un modelo de administración para El Museo del Hombre Dominicano," 33.

110   Ibid., 39.

111   *Inaugural Exhibit Catalogue*, 1.

112   Vega, "¿Porque los tres?" 129–30.

113   Rodríguez and Soto-Ricart, *Catálogo General*, 91.

114   Pagán Perdomo, *Programación de proyectos y desarrollo institucional, 1997–98*.

115   The Columbian Lighthouse project began during the customs receivership and ended just before Trujillo's regime with international architectural-design competitions held in 1929. Cf. Pan American Union, *Program and Rules of the Second Competition for the Selection of an Architect for the Monu-*

mental Lighthouse. Dominican lore holds that the plans to honor the famous colonial explorer have been long cursed, as demonstrated by the repeated obstacles and delays to initiating and later completing the project, including the sudden, unexpected deaths of project supporters' family members. When construction of the lighthouse was finally begun in the 1980s in preparation for the 1992 quincentennial celebration, it was amid local, national, and international protests by displaced poor and low-income residents, by the American Indian community, and by progressives worldwide.

116   Olsen Bogaert et al., "Un modelo de administración para El Museo del Hombre Dominicano," 79.

117   Matos Moctezuma, "El Museo del Hombre Dominicano," 21.

118   Vega, *Imágenes del ayer*, 131.

119   Davis, *The Problem of Slavery in Western Culture.*

120   Franklin W. Knight, "Introduction," in de las Casas, *An Account, Much Abbreviated, of the Destruction of the Indies, with Related Texts.*

121   de la Cruz et al., *La resistencia indígena y negra en Quisqueya.*

122   Landers, "Maroon Ethnicity and Identity in Ecuador, Colombia, and Hispaniola," 2.

123   Rodríguez and Soto-Ricart, *Catálogo General*, 21.

124   The Museo's administrative offices are located on the second floor. The potential disruption caused by this intervention is assuaged by the display of a Taíno *areyto* (ritual dance performance and celebration) in the foyer of the second floor. The visitor is guided by the placement of this display toward the ramp leading up to the third floor.

125   "Haití" is the island's actual indigenous moniker. For an excellent discussion on the naming of Haiti, see Geggus, *Haitian Revolutionary Studies*, 207–20. According to the Dominican scholars Apolinar Tejera (1855–1922) and Emilio Tejera (1841–1923), "Quizquella" was invented in the sixteenth century by the court cleric Pedro Mártir de Anglería, the author of a lengthy account of the Columbian voyages entitled *Décadas del Nuevo Mundo* (1504–30). Edmundo O'Gorman has argued that some of Mártir de Anglería's account was based on conjecture and hearsay. Apolinar Tejara and Emilio Tejera have argued that "Quisqueya" was embraced in the mid-nineteenth century by the country's leaders in an explicit attempt to invent a distinct indigenous racial heritage for Dominicans in the aftermath of their separation from Haiti: Tejera, "¿Quid de Quisqueya?"; Tejera, *Indigenismos*. Geggus, however, notes that both "Quisqueya" and "Haiti" were being used from the sixteenth century to the eighteenth century in European texts.

126   *Inaugural Exhibit Catalogue*, 14. Interestingly, the renowned archeologist José María Cruxent donated the Venezuelan artifacts.

127   Ibid., 13.

128   The term "American Indians" is used interchangeably with Native

Americans throughout this work because both have been preferred and critiqued by various nations, theorists, and activists, and a universally acceptable term has not been agreed on.

129 For a more extensive account of this process, see Deagan and Cruxent, *Columbus's Outpost among the Taínos*, 82–93.

130 Deagan, "Colonial Transformation," 146.

131 Ibid., 149.

132 Angel, "The Negotiation of Transatlantic Travel for Sixteenth-Century Spanish Women."

133 Deagan, "Colonial Transformation."

134 Photographs of the Museo's dioramas are currently displayed on the Dominican State Tourism Secretary's website at http://www.domincana.com.do/cultura/epocaprecolombina.html (accessed September 17, 2000).

135 Kirshenblatt-Gimblett, "Objects of Ethnography," 389.

136 Albert Batista, "La tercera raíz."

137 Vega, *Ensayos sobre cultura dominicana*.

138 Vega, interview.

139 See Erdman, "Blake's Vision of Slavery," 245.

140 Pratt, *Imperial Eyes*, 97.

141 Cambeira, *Quisqueya La Bella*, 76.

142 Landers, "Maroon Ethnicity and Identity in Ecuador, Colombia, and Hispaniola,"15.

143 García Arévalo, *Cimarron*.

144 Pagán Perdomo, interview.

145 For example, Deagan's project on La Isabela was sanctioned and funded by the Dominican government through the Museo del Hombre Dominicano. Yet, although Deagan is also an experienced archeologist of maroon societies such as Fort Mose in St. Augustine, Florida, she has not to my knowledge been funded to undertake a similar project in the Dominican Republic: see Deagan and MacMahon, *Fort Mose*.

146 Tannenbaum, *Slave and Citizen*.

147 He is referring to Moreno Fraginals et al., *Between Slavery and Free Labor*. Pagán Perdomo, interview.

148 Sued-Badillo, "Facing Up to Caribbean History."

149 Hernández Soto, interview.

3 Dominicans in Washington, D.C.

1 Torres, "The Legacy of Conquest and Discovery," 168.

2 Ibid., 156–66.

3 Ruffins, "Mythos, Memory, and History," 573–74.

4 Rydell, *All the World's a Fair*.

5 Washington, "Atlanta Exposition Address, September 18, 1895."

6 Lott, *Love and Theft*; Nasaw, *Going Out*; Roediger, *The Wages of Whiteness*.

7 Though each of these cultural practices and institutions had existed even during the slavery era, it was after emancipation that they expanded and increased in number.

8 Ruffins, "Mythos, Memory, and History," 508.

9 Campbell, "Introduction," 1.

10 James, "Building a Community-Based Identity at Anacostia Museum," 34.

11 Ibid.

12 While the Anacostia Museum's location in the community continues to be touted as one of its chief cultural and historic strengths, recent African American efforts at self-representation at the Smithsonian have argued in favor of a permanent and significant presence on the Mall. Representatives John Lewis and Mickey Leland each introduced bills in 1989 to found a national museum of African American history and culture at the Smithsonian. Although the bills were not passed, the public debate they engendered about the nature of African American citizenship, history, and representation at the Smithsonian continue to resonate. Today, the common wisdom at the Smithsonian is that a new African American museum will not be built on the Mall, the last possible location having been selected for the new National Museum of the American Indian, which opened in 2002. Instead, exhibits researched, designed, and curated by Anacostia staff, such as "Speak to My Heart: Communities of Faith and Contemporary African-American Life," recently have been mounted at the centrally located Arts and Industries Building. The offices of the Center for African-American History and Culture have been located there as well.

13 Campbell, "Introduction," 26. The Anacostia also moved from the Carver Theater, in the heart of Anacostia, to its current location on a landscaped park. It is no longer easily accessible to pedestrians and is, instead, primarily accessible by car or public transportation.

14 On Kinnard, see Martin-Felton and Lowe, *A Different Drummer*.

15 James, "Building a Community-Based Identity at Anacostia Museum," 38.

16 Smithsonian Institution Task Force on Latino Issues, *Willful Neglect*, ii.

17 Ibid., iii.

18 Latino Oversight Committee, *Towards a Shared Vision*, 4.

19 Roland Roebuck, an active participant in *Black Mosaic* and a vocal Afro-Latino activist in D.C., became an Anacostia Museum board member in 1998: Newsome, interview; James, interview.

20 Webb, "Anacostia Exhibition Looks at Diversity," 1.

21 Newsome, interview.

22 Smithsonian Institution Task Force on Latino Issues, *Willful Neglect*, 31.

23 Ibid., 30.

24 Webb, "Anacostia Exhibition Looks at Diversity," 7.

25 Davis, *Who Is Black?*

26 Unedited visitor' comments, comment no. 8, March 5, 1995, *Black Mosaic* archives, Education Department collection, Anacostia Museum, Smithsonian Institution, Washington, D.C.

27 Anacostia Neighborhood Museum, *How and Why African People Came to North America*, 4.

28 Meeting notes, Sharon Reinckens files, 1994, *Black Mosaic* archives, Anacostia Museum, Smithsonian Institution, Washington, D.C.

29 Ruffins, "Mythos, Memory, and History," 577.

30 Ibid.

31 Untitled document, Sharon Reinckens collection, *Black Mosaic* files, Anacostia Museum, Smithsonian Institution, Washington, D.C.

32 Lugones, "Playfulness, 'World'-Travelling, and Loving Perception," 396.

33 Schutz, *The Phenomenology of the Social World*.

34 Manning, "Multicultural Change in Washington, D.C.," 11.

35 Repak, *Waiting on Washington*, 49.

36 Manning, "Multicultural Change in Washington, D.C.," v–vi.

37 Ibid., 14.

38 D.C. History Curriculum Project, *City of Magnificent Intentions*, 380–83.

39 Ibid., 361.

40 Ibid., 373.

41 Manning, "Multicultural Change in Washington, D.C.," vi.

42 For a discussion of the relationship between the United States' domestic racism and international relations, see Lauren, *Power and Prejudice*.

43 Davis et al., *Latin American Diplomatic History*.

44 Rowe, *The Pan American Union and the Pan American Conferences, 1890–1940*.

45 Sang, *Caminos transitados*, 97.

46 Several factors account for this fact. First, although the Dominican Republic separated from Haiti in 1844, it did not receive diplomatic recognition from the United States until 1855. Second, from 1844 to 1861 and again from 1865 to 1882, rather than establish formal and normalized diplomatic relations abroad, the country's leading conservative caudillos, Baéz and Santana, were preoccupied with establishing their rule. To that end, they sought foreign protection and annexation by various European states and the United States. Third, from 1861 to 1865, the Dominican Republic was recolonized by Spain. Fourth, although Ulises Heaureaux's dictatorship of 1882–99 did

begin to consolidate the Dominican state and to establish regular diplomatic exchanges with European states and the United States, its various political intrigues and corrupt financial plots undermined any possibility of normal diplomatic relations. Finally, the U.S. occupation of 1916–24 subjected the country to U.S. military governance, and therefore the issue of diplomatic relations was moot: see Sang, *La política exterior del dictador Trujillo, 1930–1961*.

47   Ibid., 126–30.

48   U.S. Bureau of the Census, "Table 23."

49   Lewis, *District of Columbia*, 127, 156–62.

50   Cf. Báez-Evertsz and D'Oleo Ramírez, *La emigración de dominicanos a Estados Unidos*; Black, *The Dominican Republic*; Crassweller, *Trujillo*.

51   Aguilar, "Leyendas de nuestra historia"; Campos, interview (Héctor Corporán); Juana Campos, interview (author).

52   See Sánchez Korrol, *From Colonia to Community*; Bonilla and Campos, "A Wealth of Poor"; Duany, *The Puerto Rican Nation on the Move*; García, *Havana USA*; Pérez, "A Circle of Connections"; Grillo, *Black Cuban, Black American*; Masud-Piloto, *From Welcomed Exiles to Illegal Immigrants*.

53   Rodríguez, *Latin Looks*; González, *Harvest of Empire*.

54   The Washington metropolitan area, which includes suburban counties in Maryland and Virginia, has a much larger number of Dominicans (4,760 in 1990 and 12,471 in 2000): Census 2000 website, Lewis Mumford Center for Comparative Urban and Regional Research, University of Albany, available online at http://mumford1.dyndns.org/cen2000/HispanicPop/HispPopData/8840msa.htm (accessed July 25, 2005). Census data on Dominicans in Washington, D.C., prior to 1990 were not available. Indeed, census data on "Latinos/Hispanics/Spanish Mother Tongue" people in Washington is available only for 1940 and from 1970 onward.

55   Ibid., available online at http://mumford1.dyndns.org/cen2000/HispanicPop/HispPopData/8840cc.htm (accessed July 25, 2005). These numbers include the cities of Washington, D.C.; Arlington, Virginia; Frederick, Maryland; and Fredericksburg, Virginia. They coincide fairly closely, however, with numbers extrapolated at the Zip code level for just Washington, D.C.

56   U.S. Bureau of the Census, "Table 23."

57   Census 2000 website, Lewis Mumford Center for Comparative Urban and Regional Research, University of Albany, available online at http://mumford1.dyndns.org/cen2000/HispanicPop/HispSegData/8840cc.htm (accessed July 25, 2005).

58   Ibid., available online at http://mumford1.dyndns.org/cen2000/HispanicPop/HispSegData/5600cc.htm (accessed July 25, 2005).

59   Ibid.

60   Laó-Montes and Dávila, *Mambo Montage*.

61   Census 2000 website, Lewis Mumford Center for Comparative Urban and Regional Research, University of Albany, available online at http://mum

ford1.dyndns.org/cen2000/HispanicPop/HispSegData/5600cc.htm (accessed July 25, 2005).

62 Lavine and Karp, *Exhibiting Cultures*, 1.

63 This boat and its passengers were spotted by Hermanos al Rescate (Brothers to the Rescue) in July 1992 thirty-five miles off the Miami coast. The passengers and their vessel were recovered by the U.S. Coast Guard, who subsequently gave the vessel, made of Styrofoam, tar, cotton fabric, wood, and shower curtains, to Humberto Sánchez, a Cuban American collector of refugee artifacts. Sánchez lent the vessel to the Anacostia for the exhibit: Freeman, "History of this Object: Cuban Refugee Boat."

64 I undertook my research in 1998, three years after the exhibition had been dismantled. I have relied on archival photographs of the exhibition at the Anacostia, newspaper accounts, exhibit photographs, scripts and documentation, and interviews for data on the look and feel of the exhibit.

65 Since Brazilians in *Black Mosaic* were considered apart from Afro-Latinos although they are Latin Americans, it seems that the designation refers specifically to Latinos from Spanish-speaking communities or Afro-Hispanics.

66 Exhibition script, *Black Mosaic*, 2–3.

67 "Identity," exhibition videotape.

68 Unedited visitors comments, *Black Mosaic* archives.

69 Exhibition script, *Black Mosaic*, 7.

70 Ibid., 9.

71 Ibid., 44.

72 Aguilar, "Leyendas de nuestra historia"; Campos, interview (Héctor Corporán); Campos, interview (author).

73 Enslaved Wolofs from the Senegambia region of African led a successful revolt on Christopher Columbus's son Diego's sugar plantation in 1521.

74 "Building Bridges: African-American and Latino Communities in Washington, D.C.," Internal memorandum, *Black Mosaic* archives.

75 See Torres-Saillant, "Introduction to Dominican Blackness."

76 Ruffins, "Mythos, Memory, and History," 509.

77 Karp, "Other Cultures in Museum Perspective," 375.

78 Ibid.

79 Kirshenblatt-Gimblett, "Objects of Ethnography," 390.

80 Hicks, interview.

81 Corporán, interview; Reincken, interview.

82 Cadaval, *Creating a Latino Identity in the Nation's Capital*, 248, fn. 1.

83 Hernández and Rivera-Batiz, "Dominicans in the United States," 50.

84 Ibid., 51.

85 Washington, "A Final Glimpse of Vapors." I thank Gladys Martínez for sharing this manuscript with me.

86 Medina, interview (author).

87   Bueno, interview (Héctor Corporán).

88   Toruella, interview.

89   Campos, interview (Héctor Corporán). The *Black Mosaic* files were not systematically archived when this research was undertaken in 1998. Instead, the materials were stored in various offices, file cabinets, and boxes throughout the museum's Research Department. As a result, data source citations are descriptive rather than archival.

90   Toruella, interview.

91   Holder, "Racism toward Black African Diplomats during the Kennedy Administration"; Maga, "Battling the 'Ugly American' at Home."

92   Kennedy, "Correspondence, April 13, 1961."

93   Toruella, interview.

94   Similar experiences and negotiations occurred for Latin American and Latino baseball players during the same era in the United States: cf. Burgos, "Jugando en el Norte."

95   Campos, interview (author).

96   The U.S. collected and managed Dominican customs revenues from 1905 to 1941. Since import revenues represented the principal source of currency exchange, the United States was effectively managing the Dominican economy during this period.

97   See Atkins and Wilson, *The Dominican Republic and the United States.*

98   Myrdal, *An American Dilemma.*

99   Omi and Winant, *Racial Formation in the United States.*

100   Campos, interview (author).

101   See Cadaval, *Creating a Latino Identity in the Nation's Capital.*

102   Exhibition script, *Black Mosaic*, 86.

103   The term *"cocolo"* is a highly contested one in that some of the people to whom it refers consider it pejorative while others embrace it. The origins of the word have been debated, with some Dominican scholars arguing that it is a distortion of the name of the "islas Tortolas" (Turtle Islands), and others arguing that it is derived from the name of an African tribe: see Dore-Cabral, "En torno a las críticas de Badillo," 70. *"Ingeleses"* refers specifically to those who are of British West Indian heritage.

104   Hoetink, "'Americans' in Samaná."

105   See, e.g., Purcell, *Banana Fallout.*

106   del Castillo and Murphy, "Migration, National Identity and Cultural Policy in the Dominican Republic," 57.

107   Lara, interview (Héctor Corporán).

108   Repak, *Waiting on Washington*, 56.

109   Quander, interview.

110   This is not to imply that African Americans in Washington, D.C., are universally well off. In fact, African Americans in the capital continue to ex-

perience high poverty rates (22 percent); have median per capita incomes of $12,226, or two-thirds less than the median per capita income of $34,563 for whites; and disproportionately fewer college and graduate degrees: see 1990 U.S. Census data, database C90S5F1A, state-level statistics. That said, however, the presence of a large and visible black middle class is sociologically relevant.

111 Repak, *Waiting on Washington*, 69.

112 Ibid., 57.

113 Luna, interview (Olivia Cadaval).

114 Quander, interview.

115 Medína, interview (author).

116 Ibid.

117 Ibid.

118 Exhibition script, *Black Mosaic*, 86.

119 See Lara, "Reflections: Bridging Cultures."

120 There are, of course, Afro-Mexicanos and large Afro-Latino populations throughout Central America and South America. However, as Lara points out, these groups are generally excluded from or overlooked in their nations' imagined communities: see Gordon, *Disparate Diasporas*; Graham, *The Idea of Race in Latin America, 1870–1940*; Purcell, *Banana Fallout*; Wade, *Blackness and Race Mixture*; Wright, *Café con Leche*.

121 Repak, *Waiting on Washington*, 1.

122 Medína, interview (author).

123 Luna, interview (Cadaval).

124 Quander, interview.

125 Peña et al., "'Racial Democracy' in the Americas," 749–62.

126 Cadaval, *Creating a Latino Identity in the Nation's Capital*, 235–39.

127 Ozuma, interview (Héctor Corporán).

128 Medína, interview (author).

129 Quander, interview.

130 Almarante, interview.

131 "Identity," exhibition videotape, *Black Mosaic*.

132 Medína, interview (author).

133 Almarante, interview.

134 Medína, interview (author).

135 Almarante, interview.

136 Toruella, interview.

137 Chaney and García Castro, *Muchachas No More*.

138 Bonetti, "Causas culturales de la prostitución en Santo Domingo"; Duarte, "Household Workers in the Dominican Republic."

139 Bueno, interview (Héctor Corporán).

140 Toruella, interview.

141 This echoes the experiences of Afro-Puerto Rican men in the United

States documented in Thomas, *Down These Mean Streets*; Perdomo, "Nigger-Reecan Blues."

142 Corporán, interview.

4 Displaying Identity in New York City

1 Coleman, "Among the Things That Use to Be."

2 Furman, *Facing the Mirror*, 47.

3 Bennett, *The Birth of the Museum*, 30.

4 There have, however, been various cases brought by black women against employers who subjected them to discriminatory hiring and promotion practices because of how they styled their hair, as well as against beauty shops that refused to serve black clients: see Caldwell, "A Hair Piece."

5 Taylor, *Disappearing Acts*, 30.

6 Knight, *The Caribbean*, 225.

7 Lancaster, *Life Is Hard*, 142.

8 It is interesting to note that World's Fairs and expositions were central sites of bodily display, both self-structured and imposed. Dominicans participated in at least four World's Fairs: the 1892 Exposición histórico-americana de Madrid, the 1893 Brussells Exposition, the 1889 Exposition Universelle de Paris, and the 1907 Jamestown Tercentennial Exposition. To my knowledge, little if anything has been written about Dominican participation in these fairs, a topic that certainly bears further exploration.

9 Furman, *Facing the Mirror*, 47.

10 Renda, *Taking Haiti*, 17.

11 Smith, *Writing the Social*, 73–75.

12 Willett, *Permanent Waves*, 12–51.

13 Ibid., 200.

14 Schroder, *Engagement in the Mirror*, 193.

15 Goodnough, "Refused a Haircut, an Official in Stamford Closes a Salon."

16 Byrd and Tharps, *Hair Story*, 133–64.

17 Banks, *Hair Matters*; Byrd and Tharps, *Hair Story*, 145–47; Cary, *Black Ice*; Frankenberg, *White Women, Race Matters*; Willett, *Permanent Waves*, 2000.

18 Badillo, "Only My Hairdresser Knows for Sure," 36.

19 A *toobie* is a hair-straightening technique in which the hair is divided into sections that are then wrapped flat around the head and held in place with pins. After a period of time, generally depending on the hair's texture, the hair is let down and is usually fairly straight and smooth. A *toobie* is done with little, if any, use of lotions or oils and is done on many different hair textures, including those that are already fairly straight.

20 Kenyatta and Kenyatta, *Black Folk's Hair*; Rooks, *Hair Raising*; Russell et al., *Color Complex*.

21 Although Dominicans had been migrating to New York City since the early nineteenth century, the Dominican community began to establish itself more permanently after the 1965 revolution and the 1965 Immigration Act. For a discussion of the confluence of these occurrences, see Martin, *Overtaken by Events*.

22 A booth renter pays the shop owner a contracted amount, usually a flat fee, for the use of a particular chair or booth, utilities, receptionist's scheduling services, equipment, and supplies such as shampoo and hair chemicals. She then keeps all her earnings and tips.

23 The United States as a whole experienced a shift from a manufacturing to a service economy. While manufacturing made up 30 percent of the gross domestic product just after World War Two, by 1994 it represented just 17 percent. Services, conversely, rose from 9 percent to 19 percent during the same period. Included in those industries are "transportation and public utilities; wholesale trade; retail trade; finance, insurance, and real estate; and services . . . such as health care, advertising, computer and data processing services, legal services, management and public relations, engineering and architectural services, accounting, and recreation": Meisenheimer, "The Services Industry in the 'Good' versus 'Bad' Jobs Debate," 22.

24 Hernández and Rivera-Batiz, "Dominicans in the United States," 44.

25 Ibid.

26 During the 1990s, the Dominican Republic had the highest rate of annual economic growth (7–8 percent) in the Western Hemisphere, surpassing even the United States: see Wiarda, "Leading the World from the Caribbean." As in the United States, the drive toward professionalization has been accompanied by an increase in public attention to the sector. Thus, while in 1995, there was only one article in the national newspapers profiling beauty shops or the beauty industry, in 1996 there were two; in 1997, there were forty-eight; and by 1998, there were sixty five, including a special insert profiling the industry.

27 Rodríguez, "Lucir bien cuesta caro."

28 Ibid.

29 Ibid.

30 Ibid.

31 See Hernández, *The Mobility of Workers under Advanced Capitalism*.

32 Unlike the *bodegueros*, however, Dominican beauty-shop owners have not yet organized, a point that will be considered later.

33 Guarnizo, "One Country in Two," 121.

34 Schroder, *Engagement in the Mirror*, 219.

35 Guarnizo, "One Country in Two," 359.

36   Ibid., 308; emphasis in the original.

37   Ibid., 237.

38   Goris-Rosario, "The Role of the Ethnic Community and the Workplace in the Integration of Immigrants."

39   Guarnizo argues that Dominican women entrepreneurs are disadvantaged relative to their male peers because of their concentration in the service sector, which is less capitalized and offers lower incomes than the commercial firms men monopolize: Guarnizo, "One Country in Two," 121.

40   Ibid., 106–108. For a detailed discussion of this issue, see Miranda, "The Income Mobility of Puerto Rican Bodegueros in New York City."

41   The calculations of average shop distance are based on data available through http://www.maps.yahoo.com.

42   Williams, "Flak in the Great Hair War."

43   See Sutton and Chaney, *Caribbean Life in New York City*; Kasinitz, *Caribbean New York*; Foner, *New Immigrants in New York*.

44   Steven Hipple, U.S. Bureau of Labor Statistics, unpublished data, Current Population Survey, personal communication with the author, June 1999.

45   Coleman, "Among the Things That Use to Be."

46   This is a pseudonym, which will be explained in great detail later.

47   Luís Guarnizo found that Dominican entrepreneurs generally have longer working hours than their wage and salaried peers: see Guarnizo, "One Country in Two," 223–25. African American communities in New York City likewise have salons that accommodate long and varied working hours, as Lisa Jones reports in *Bulletproof Diva*, 11–15.

48   "Remodeled Beauty Salon," 118. I thank Helen Horowitz for sharing this source with me.

49   Although the pseudonym I have chosen is a fairly good approximation of the salon's name, the actual name is a much more fascinating coding. It is derived from a Mexican colloquialism that is generally unfamiliar to Dominicans that means "women crazy in love."

50   All names have been changed in the interests of confidentiality, and citations will not be provided for direct quotes nor interviews listed in the references as a result.

51   Coincidentally, Gazcue is one of the three sites researched in Howard, *Coloring the Nation*.

52   On maids in the Dominican Republic, see Chaney and García Castro, *Muchachas No More*, chap. 3.

53   Gimlin, "Pamela's Place."

54   Schroder, *Engagement in the Mirror*, 33.

55   Howe, *Pink Collar Workers*, 26–60.

56   James, "Beneath the Beehive Lurks a Cultural Icon."

57 Erickson, *Employment Conditions in Beauty Shops*, 37–44.

58 Weber, "Employment Opportunities in Beauty Shops of New York City," 18.

59 Forte, "Community-Based Breast Cancer Intervention Program for Older African American Women in Beauty Salons."

60 Delgado, "Role of Latina-Owned Beauty Parlors in a Latino Community."

61 The translation of the phrase in this section's subhead is "This salon has to be respected," a comment Chucha made frequently,

62 Oldenburg, *The Great Good Place*. Chucha spoke the words that serve as this section's subhead at Salon Lamadas. The quotation translates, "You can't go to beauty shops or to doctors in a rush."

63 Valdés, "Hair Dominicana." The quotation in this section's subhead translates, "It's just that we help each other here." It is from an interview with Alma.

64 Several of the women recounted not being allowed by U.S. consular officials to immigrate with their children, who were denied the residency visas granted to their mothers.

65 A study of Dominican baby showers has not yet been done, but for a related event, see Bahn and Jaquez, "One Style of Dominican Bridal Shower."

66 For more on this see Candelario and López, "The Latest Edition of the Welfare Queen Story."

67 On Latin American coming-out parties, or "*quinces*," see King, *Quinceañera*.

68 Coleman, "Among the Things That Use to Be."

69 Blackwelder, *Styling Jim Crow*, 145.

70 Forte, "Community-Based Breast Cancer Intervention Program for Older African American Women in Beauty Salons."

71 Blackwelder, *Styling Jim Crow*; Bundles, *On Her Own Ground*; Rooks, *Hair Raising*.

72 Battle-Walters, *Sheila's Shop*.

73 Coleman, "Among the Things That Use to Be."

5 Dominican Hair Culture

1 Mercer, *Welcome to the Jungle*, 100–101.

2 Moya Pons, "Modernización y cambios en la República Dominicana," 238.

3 Hoetink, *Two Variants in Caribbean Race Relations*, 120.

4 Ibid., 167.

5 Ibid.

6   Ibid., 168.

7   González, "Patterns of Dominican Ethnicity," 113.

8   For a comparison of how this plays out in New York City and San Juan, Puerto Rico, see Duany, "Trasnational Migration from the Dominican Republic."

9   Itzigsohn and Dore-Cabral, "The Manifold Character of Panethnicity," 328.

10   The term "*hispano* [Hispanic]" was almost universally used interchangeably with "Latino." It was the more prevalent term, however, and will be used here when paraphrasing or quoting others. "Latina/o" will be used when it is the author's description.

11   I framed the dichotomy in these terms in order not to impose "ugliness" on any of the photographs. Several of the respondents themselves used the term "ugly," however, when describing the individual they found least beautiful.

12   Here the term "Hispanic" is used when it is a translation of the Spanish term "*hispana.*" The term "Latina" is used when it is my voice speaking in the text.

13   del Pinal and Ennis, "The Racial and Ethnic Identity of Latin American Immigrants in Census 2000," 11.

14   Although the books were not explicitly racially classified, they were referred to this way by the salon's clients.

15   Rodríguez, *Latin Looks*, 1.

16   Davis, *Who Is Black?*; Harris, *Patterns of Race in the Americas.*

17   Torres-Saillant, "The Tribulations of Blackness" and "Introduction to Dominican Blackness."

18   Badillo, "Only My Hairdresser Knows for Sure," 36.

19   Ibid.

20   Ibid.

21   Valdez, "Género, discriminación racial y ciudadanía," 240, 256.

22   Krohn-Hansen, "Masculinity and the Political among Dominicans," 119.

23   Torres-Saillant, "Introduction to Dominican Blackness," 51.

24   Dore-Cabral, "Encuesta Rumbo-Gallup," 8–12.

25   Badillo and Badillo, "Que Tan Racistas Somos," 61.

26   The heteronormative bias of this line of questioning is clear. It is possible, and probably likely, that one or more of my respondents were lesbian or bisexual. These questions presume that the respondents are heterosexual; a potentially problematic assumption is that any are not, particularly in terms of ranking attractiveness. However, I assume that whether or not the respondents were in fact heterosexual (and all presented themselves as such), they would be able to assess the relative attractiveness of the men presented to

them. In the case of the respondents who had children, I further felt comfortable asking the question about reproduction, because whether or not they were heterosexual they had already made some reproductive choices. For those who were childless, I assumed that they would understand the question primarily in reproductive terms rather than sexual ones.

27 Gilbertson et al., "Hispanic Intermarriage in New York City," 449.

28 Clark and Clark, "Racial Identification and Preference in Negro Children."

29 See, e.g., Hraba and Grant, "Black Is Beautiful"; Williams and Morland, *Race, Color and the Young Child.*

30 Cross, *Shades of Black.*

31 Maxton, "Race Consciousness in Children in the Dominican Republic."

32 Anángela Molina, Lucy Resumil, and Amire Dabas, "La economía en el sector La Joya," as cited ibid.

33 My study did not include children primarily for logistical reasons—lack of time, financial resources, and appropriate training in early-childhood research. I encourage other scholars to pursue this area of inquiry.

34 Valdez, "Género, discriminación racial y ciudadanía," 254.

35 Ibid., 255.

36 Ibid., 240.

37 Badillo, "Only My Hairdresser Knows for Sure," 35.

38 Recently, however, the plastic-surgery industry in the Dominican Republic has gained international attention—and not entirely positive attention. A proliferation of clinics and barely licensed surgeons are performing surgery for low costs, but often with severe health outcomes, including death. The most popular procedures are liposuction, breast reductions, and nose jobs.

39 Hoetink, *El pueblo Dominicano (1850–1900),* 160.

40 Mercer, *Welcome to the Jungle.*

41 See, e.g., Caputi, "Beauty Secrets"; Chancer, *Reconcilable Differences;* Chapkis, *Beauty Secrets;* Ewen, "The Beauty Ritual"; Freedman, *Beauty Bound;* Wolf, *The Beauty Myth.* See also Jeanne Kilbourne's documentaries *Killing Us Softly* (1979), *Still Killing Us Softly* (1987), and *Killing Us Softly 3: Advertising's Image of Women* (1999).

42 Banks, *Hair Matters;* Blackwelder, *Styling Jim Crow;* Bundles, *On Her Own Ground;* Rooks, *Hair Raising;* Ruiz, "Star Struck."

43 Chancer, *Reconcilable Differences,* 117.

44 Hunter, *Race, Gender and the Politics of Skin Tone,* 27.

45 For a more complete elaboration of this argument, see Scott, *Fresh Lipstick.*

Conclusion

1   Levine, *The Flight from Ambiguity*, 81.

2   Isin and Wood, *Citizenship and Identity*, 20.

3   Alix, *Décimas inéditas*, 9.

4   Dayan, "Codes of Law and Bodies of Color."

5   Wucker, *Why the Cocks Fight*, 36.

6   James, *The Black Jacobains*.

7   Moya Pons, *The Dominican Republic*, 123.

8   Silié, "Aspectos socio-historicos sobre la inmigracion Haitiana a la República Dominicana," 4.

9   Goffman, *Interaction Ritual*, 5–9, 41–45.

10   Herskovits, *Life in a Haitian Valley*, 295–96; Austerlitz, *Merengue*, 149.

11   Austerlitz, *Merengue*, 149.

12   Merton and Barber, "Sociological Ambivalence," 543.

13   *Random House Webster's College Dictionary*, 43.

14   Aisha Kan, "What Is 'Spanish'?"

15   Goffman, *The Presentation of Self in Everyday Life*.

16   Ian Hunter, "Mind Games and Body Techniques," 178.

References

Interviews

Fulami Ahota, by the author, Washington, D.C., July 1998.

Francia Almarante, by the author, Washington, D.C., July 1998.

Daniel Bueno, by Héctor Corporán, interview tapes, *Black Mosaic* archives, Anacostia Museum, Washington, D.C., 1993.

Juana Campos, by the author, Washington, D.C., August 1998.

Juana Campos, by Héctor Corporán, interview tapes, *Black Mosaic* archives, Anacostia Museum, Washington, D.C., 1994.

Héctor Corporán, by the author, Washington, D.C., August 1998.

Carlos Hernández Soto, by the author, Santo Domingo, Dominican Republic, July 2007.

Louis Hicks, by the author, Washington, D.C., June 1998.

Portia James, by the author, Washington, D.C., August 1998.

Julia Lara, by Héctor Corporán, interview tapes, *Black Mosaic* archives, Anacostia Museum, Washington, D.C., 1993.

Juanita Laureano, by Héctor Corporán, interview tapes, *Black Mosaic* archives, Anacostia Museum, Washington, D.C., 1993.

Casilda Luna, by Olivia Cadaval, interview tapes, *Black Mosaic* archives, Anacostia Museum, Washington, D.C., 1993.

Maricela Medina, by the author, Washington, D.C., July 1998.

Maricela Medina, by Héctor Corporán, interview tapes, *Black Mosaic* archives, Anacostia Museum, Washington, D.C., 1993.

Sofía Mora (pseudonym), by the author, Washington, D.C., July 1998.

Steven Newsome, by the author, Washington, D.C, August 1998.

Esperanza Ozuma, by Héctor Corporán, interview tapes, *Black Mosaic* archives, Anacostia Museum, Washington, D.C., 1993.

Dato Pagán Perdomo, by the author, Santo Domingo, Dominican Republic, November 1999.

Carmen Quander, by the author, Washington, D.C., August 1998.

Sharon Reinckens, by the author, Washington, D.C., July 1998.

Rolando Roebucks, by the author, Washington, D.C., July 1998.

Ramberto Toruella, by the author, Washington, D.C, August 1998.

Bernardo Vega, by the author, Washington, D.C., August 1998.

Archival Sources

"Building Bridges: African American and Latino Communities in Washington, D.C." Internal memorandum, Anacostia Museum, Education Department files. March 5, 1995, *Black Mosaic* archives, Anacostia Museum, Smithsonian Institution, Washington, D.C.

Exhibition script. *Black Mosaic: Community, Race, and Ethnicity among Black Immigrants in Washington, D.C. Black Mosaic* archives, Anacostia Museum, Smithsonian Institution, Washington, D.C.

Freeman, Kim. "History of this Object: Cuban Refugee Boat." March 1994. *Black Mosaic* archives, Anacostia Museum, Smithsonian Institution, Washington, D.C.

How and Why African People Came to North America: An Introductory Flannel Board Activity on Black History for the Pre-School and Primary Teacher. Department of Education, Anacostia Neighborhood Museum, Smithsonian Institution, Washington, D.C. September 1979.

"Identity." Exhibition videotape. *Black Mosaic* archives, Anacostia Museum, Smithsonian Institution, Washington, D.C.

Meeting notes. Sharon Reinckens files, *Black Mosaic* archives, Anacostia Museum, Smithsonian Institution, Washington, D.C. 1994.

Unedited visitors' comments. Education Department files. *Black Mosaic* archives, Anacostia Museum, Smithsonian Institution, Washington, D.C.

Primary Sources

"Aims and Objects of the Museum of the American Indian Heye Foundation." Pp. 3–27 in *Indian Notes and Monographs: A Series of Publications Relating to the American Aborigines*, 2d ed. Lancaster, Penn.: Lancaster Press, 1936.

Aguilar, Alfonso. "Leyendas de nuestra historia: Juanita A. Campos, 54 años de vida en D.C." *Foro*, April 28, 1994.

Alberti Bosch, Narciso. *Apuntes para la prehistoria de Quisqueya.* La Vega: El Progreso de R. A. Ramos, 1912.

Album de Oro de la Feria de la Paz y Confraternidad del Mundo Libre. Ciudad Tujillo, 1956, Tomo I.

Alix, Juan Antonio. *Décimas inéditas, with a Prologue by Emilio Rodríguez Demorizi.* Santo Domingo: Impresora Moreno, 1966.

Alix, Juan Antonio, Antonio Zacarías Reyes L., and José R. Heredia P. *Décimas dominicanas de ayer y de hoy.* Santo Domingo: Publicaciones América, 1986.

Archivos General de la Nación. *Obras de Trujillo.* Ciudad Trujillo: Editora Montalvo, 1956.

Before and After: American Beauté. Vol. 2. Freehold, N.J.: Dennis Bernard.

Boyce, William D. *United States Colonies and Dependencies, Illustrated: The Travels and Investigations of a Chicago Publisher in the Colonial Possessions and Dependencies of the United States, with 600 Photographs of Interesting People and Scenes.* New York: Rand McNally, 1914.

Burks, Arthur J. *Land of Checkerboard Families.* New York: Coward-McCann, 1932.

———. *El país de las familias multicolores,* trans. Gustavo Amigó, rev. Diógenes Céspedes. Santo Domingo: Dominican Society of Bibliophiles, 1990.

Cary, Lorene. *Black Ice.* New York: Knopf, 1991.

"Catálogo de los objetos que presenta la República Dominicana á la Exposición histórico-americana de Madrid." Santo Domingo, Dominican Republic, 1892.

Chester, Rear Admiral Colby M. "Haiti: A Degenerating Island: The Story of Its Past Grandeur and Present Decay, an Address to the National Geographic Society." *National Geographic Magazine,* vol. 19, no. 3, March 1908, 200–17.

Coleman, Willi M. "Among the Things That Use to Be." Pp. 221–22 in *Home Girls: A Black Feminist Anthology,* ed. Barbara Smith. New York: Kitchen Table/Women of Color Press, 1983.

Corporán, Héctor. "Building Bridges: African American and Latino Communities in Washington, D.C." Paper presented at the 1997 Inter-University Program for Latino Research Qualitative Methods and Museum Studies Seminar, Smithsonian Institution, Washington, D.C., June 1997.

De Booy, Theodoor. "Pottery from Certain Caves in Eastern Santo Domingo, West Indies." *American Anthropologist* 17 (new series), no. 1 (January–March 1915): 69–97.

———. "Santo Domingo Kitchen-Midden and Burial Mound." Pp. 107–37 in *Indian Notes and Monographs: A Series of Publications Relating to the American Aborigines,* vol. 1, no. 2. New York: Museum of the American Indian–Heye Foundation, 1919.

de las Casas, Bartolome. *An Account, Much Abbreviated, of the Destruction of the Indies, with Related Texts,* ed. Franklin Knight. Indianapolis: Hackett Publishing, 2003.

de Leeuw, Hendrik. *Crossroads of the Caribbean Sea.* Garden City, N.Y.: Garden City Publishing, 1938.

"The Dominican Republic." Department of Promotion and Public Works for the Jamestown Tercentennial Exposition, 1907.

Erickson, Ethel. *Employment Conditions in Beauty Shops: A Study of Four Cities.* Washington, D.C.: U.S. Government Printing Office, 1935.

Ernst, Morris L. *Report and Opinion in the Matter of Galíndez.* New York: Sidney S. Baron, 1958.

Fabens, Joseph Warren. *Facts about Santo Domingo, Applicable to the Present*

Crisis: An Address Delivered before the American Geographical and Statistical Society of New York, April 3, 1862. New York: G. P. Putnam, 1862.

———. In the Tropics, by a Settler in Santo Domingo with an Introductory Notice by Richard B. Kimball. New York: G. W. Carleton, 1863.

———. Resources of Santo Domingo: Revised from a Paper Read before the American Geographical and Statistical Society of New York. Washington, D.C., 1869.

———. Resources of Santo Domingo: Revised from a Paper Read before the American Geographical and Statistical Society of New York. New York: Major and Knapp, 1871.

———. Life in Santo Domingo. New York: G. W. Carleton, 1873.

Family Album III. Auburn, Mass., Worcester Reading Company.

Family Images. Vol. 2. Auburn, Mass., Worcester Reading Company.

Foster, Harry L. Combing the Caribbees. New York: Dodd, Mead, 1929.

Franck, Harry A. Roaming through the West Indies. New York: Blue Ribbon Books, 1920.

Galván, Manuel de Jesús. The Cross and the Sword, trans. Robert Graves. Bloomington: Indiana University Press, 1954.

Goodnough, Abby. "Refused a Haircut, an Official in Stamford Closes a Salon." New York Times, March 20, 1995, B5.

Grant, Ulysses S. "Message of the President of the United States, Communicating the Report of the Commission of Inquiry to the Island of Santo Domingo," April 5, 1871. Pp. 1–3 in Report of the Commission of Inquiry to Santo Domingo. Washington, D.C.: U.S. Government Printing Office, 1871.

Grillo, Evelio. Black Cuban, Black American: A Memoir. Houston: Arte Público Press, 2000.

Hazard, Samuel. Santo Domingo, Past and Present: With a Glance at Hayti. New York: Harper and Brothers, 1873.

"Hazard's Santo Domingo." Nation, March 13, 1873.

Heuttner, Katherine Franck. "Harry A. Franck: A Brief Biography." Available online at http://www.harryafranck.com/books.htm (accessed March 4, 2005).

Herskovits, Melville J. "Journey for Journey's Sake." Nation, April 15, 1936, 489.

Hipple, Steven. United States Bureau of Labor Statistics. Unpublished data from the Current Population Survey, personal communication, June 1999.

Howe, Julia Ward. Reminiscences, 1819–1899. Boston: Houghton, Mifflin and Company, 1900.

Inaugural Exhibit Catalogue. Museo del Hombre Dominicano, Santo Domingo, October 12, 1973.

Inman, Samuel Guy. Through Santo Domingo and Haiti: A Cruise with the

Marines. New York: Committee on Cooperation with Latin America, 1920.

————. *Trailing the Conquistadores,* New York: Friendship Press, 1930.

Instituto Antropológico Dominicano. *Primera exposición de arte indígena autóctono.* Ciudad Trujillo: Galeria Nacional de Bellas Artes, 1948.

Internet Speculative Fiction Data Base, hosted by Cushing Library Science Fiction and Fantasy Research Collection and Institute for Scientific Computation at Texas A&M University, available from http://www.isfdb.org/cgi-bin/ea.cgi?A._Hyatt_Verrill, accessed on February 27, 2005.

Irving, Washington. *The Life and Voyages of Christopher Columbus,* ed. John Harmon McElroy. Boston: Twayne Publisher, 1981.

James, Caryn. "Beneath the Beehive Lurks a Cultural Icon." *New York Times,* April 8, 1990, H1.

Jefferys, Thomas. *The Natural and Civil History of the French Dominions in North and South America: Giving a Particular Account of the Climate, Soil, Minerals, Animals, Vegetables, Manufactures, Trade, Commerce and Languages, Together with the Religion, Government, Genius, Character, Manners and Customs of the Indians and Other Inhabitants: Illustrated by Maps and Plans of the Principal Places, Collected from the Best Authorities, and Engraved by T. Jefferys, Geographer to His Royal Highness the Prince of Wales.* London: printed for Thomas Jefferys, 1760.

Jiménez, Blas. *Exigencias de un cimarrón (en sueños): Versos del Negro Blás III.* Santo Domingo: Editora Taller, 1987.

Jones, Christina Violeta, and Pedro R. Rivera. "Black Denial Response: Did the *Miami Herald* Have an Agenda?" Sunday July 8, 2007. *Clutch Magazine.* At http://clutchmagonline.com/newsgossipinfo/black-denial-response-did-the-miami-herald-have-an-agenda/, accessed August 9, 2007.

Jones, Lisa. *Bulletproof Diva: Tales of Race, Sex, and Hair.* New York: Anchor Books, 1994.

Keim, De Bonneville Randolph. *Santo Domingo: Pen Pictures and Leaves of Travel, Romance and History, from the Portfolio of a Correspondent in the American Tropics.* Philadelphia: Claxton, Remsen, and Haffelfinger, 1870.

Kenyatta, Kamau, and Janice Kenyatta. *Black Folk's Hair: Secrets, Shame and Liberation.* Somerset, N.J.: Shonghai Publications, 1996.

Kennedy, John F. "Correspondence, April 13, 1961." Central files, John Fitzgerald Kennedy Library, Boston. Photocopy on file in *Black Mosaic* archives, Anacostia Museum, Smithsonian Institution, Washington, D.C.

"La Republique Dominicaine a L'Exposition Universelle de Paris." Havre: Imp. Maudet and Godefroy, Quai d'Orleans, 1889.

Latino Oversight Committee. *Towards a Shared Vision: U.S. Latinos and the Smithsonian Institution, Final Report of the Latino Oversight Committee.* Washington, D.C.: Smithsonian Institution, 1997.

Lewis Mumford Center for Comparative Urban and Regional Research, University of Albany. Census 2000 at http://mumford1.dyndns.org/cen2000/HispanicPop.

López Rodríguez, Nicolas de Jesus. "Presentación." Pp. 7–10 in *Primacías de América en la Española*. Santo Domingo: Permanent Dominican Commission for the Celebration of the Fifth Centennial of the Discovery and Evangelization of America, 1992.

Mackenzie, Charles. *Notes on Haiti, Made during a Residence in That Republic*, vol. 1. London: Frank Cass, 1971.

Mejía, Abigaíl. "Plan acerca de la fundación de un Museo Nacional" (*Blanco y Negro*, March 1926). Pp. 511–14 in *Abigaíl Mejía: Obras Escogidas*, ed. Arístides Incháustegui and Blanca Delgado Malagón. Santo Domingo: Secretaría de Estado de Educación, Bellas Artes y Cultos, 1995.

———. Untitled article (*Blanco y Negro*). Pp. 514–17 in *Abigaíl Mejía: Obras Escogidas*, Arístides Incháustegui and Blanca Delgado Malagón. Santo Domingo: Secretaría de Estado de Educación, Bellas Artes y Cultos, 1995.

———. "De la necesidad de un museo en nuestra patria" (*Listín Diario*, October 29, 1926). Pp. 518–20 in *Abigaíl Mejía: Obras Escogidas*, ed. Arístides Incháustegui and Blanca Delgado Malagón. Santo Domingo: Secretaría de Estado de Educación, Bellas Artes y Cultos, 1995.

———. "El Museo Nacional" (*Listín Diario*, November 3, 1926). Pp. 521–22 in *Abigaíl Mejía: Obras Escogidas*, ed. Arístides Incháustegui and Blanca Delgado Malagón. Santo Domingo: Secretaría de Estado de Educación, Bellas Artes y Cultos, 1995.

———. "De cómo visitar el Museo Nacional" (*Bahuruco*, September 30, 1933). Pp. 527–29 *Abigaíl Mejía: Obras Escogidas*, ed. Arístides Incháustegui and Blanca Delgado Malagón. Santo Domingo: Secretaría de Estado de Educación, Bellas Artes y Cultos, 1995.

Moreau de Saint-Méry, M. L. *A Topographical and Political Description of the Spanish Part of Santo Domingo*, trans. C. Armando Rodríguez. Ciudad Trujillo: Editora Montalvo, 1944.

Naturally Curly.Com Forum. At http://www.naturallycurly.com/curltalk/viewtopic.php?p=1201723&highlight=&sid=c4365db5ddf20ede963f61157362f820&PHPSESSID=6e9a409cc058c10d109cde4815ad1c89. Accessed on August 9, 2007.

New York City Department of City Planning. *The Newest New Yorkers, 1990–1994*. New York: Department of City Planning, 1995.

Newsome, Steven. "Approaches to Material Culture Research and Representation." Paper presented at the 1997 Inter-University Program for Latino Research Qualitative Methods and Museum Studies Seminar, Smithsonian Institution, Washington, D.C., June 1997.

Ober, Frederick A. *Our West Indian Neighbors, the Islands of the Caribbean Sea, "America's Mediterranean": Their Picturesque Features, Fascinating History,* and *Attractions for the Traveler, Nature-Lover, Settler and Pleasure-Seeker.* New York: James Pott, 1904.

Pan American Union. *Program and Rules of the Second Competition for the Selection of an Architect for the Monumental Lighthouse, Which the Nations of the World Will Erect in the Dominican Republic to the Memory of Christopher Columbus.* Washington, D.C.: Pan American Union, 1930.

Perdomo, Willie. "Nigger-Reecan Blues." Pp. 91–92 in *Boricuas: Influential Puerto Rican Writings—An Anthology,* ed. Roberto Santiago. New York: Ballantine Books, 1995.

Porter, David Dixon. "Secret Missions to San Domingo." *North American Review* 128, no. 271 (June 1879): 616–31.

———. *Diario de una misión secreta a Santo Domingo (1846),* trans. P. Gustavo Amigo Jensen. Santo Domingo: Society of Dominican Bibliophiles, 1978.

Pritchett, E. Blanche. "The Man Who Reads Unwritten History." *Compleat Aberree,* vol. 8, no. 10, March 1962, 11.

Raybaud, Maxime. *L'Empereur Soulouque et son empire.* Trans. and ed. Emilio Rodríguez Demorizi. Pp. 359–60 in *Documentos para la historia de la República Dominicana.,* vol. 3. Ciudad Trujillo: Impresora Dominicana, 1959.

"Remodeled Beauty Salon." *The Architectural Record, Portfolio of Special Building Types* 77 (February 1935): 118–20.

Robles, Frances. "Black Denial." *Miami Herald.* Wednesday, June 13, 2007. At http://www.miamiherald.com/multimedia/news/afrolatin/part2/index.html. Accessed on August 9, 2007.

Rodríguez, Fausto Arturo, and Humberto Soto-Ricart. *Catálogo General: Museo del Hombre Dominicano.* Santo Domingo: Museo del Hombre Dominicano, 1989.

Rodríguez, Glaydori A. "Lucir bien cuesta caro: Los salones de belleza han pasado de pequeños negocios a grandes empresas." *Listín Diario,* June 14, 1998, D3.

Ruber, Peter. "Burks of the Pulps." *New Yorker,* February 15, 1936, 12–13.

Schomburgk, Robert. "Notes on Santo Domingo." *Proceedings of the British Association* (July 1851): 90–92.

———. "On the Currents and Tides of La Mona." *Nautical Magazine,* vol. 21, 1852.

———. "On the Currents and Tides of the Southern Coasts of Santo Domingo." *Nautical Magazine,* vol. 21, 1852.

———. "On the Geographical Position of Santo Domingo." *Nautical Magazine,* vol. 21, 1852.

———. "Ethnological Researches in Santo Domingo: Report of the 21st Meeting of the British Association." *Journal of the Ethnological Society* 3 (1852): 115–22.

———. "Visit to the Valley of Costanza in the Cibao Mountains of the

Island of Santo Domingo and to an Indian Burial Ground in Its Vicinity." *Atheneaeum*, no. 1338 (1853): 787–99.

———. "Remarks on the Principal Ports and Anchoring Places along the Coast of the Dominican Republic." London, 1853.

———. "The Peninsula and Bay of Samaná in the Dominican Republic." *Journal of the Royal Geographic Society* 3, no. 8 (1853): 264–83.

Secret History, or The Horrors of St. Domingo, in a Series of Letters Written by a Lady at Cape Francois to Colonel Burr, Late Vice-President of the United States, Principally during the Command of General Rochambeau (1808), repr. ed. Freeport, N.Y.: Books for Libraries Press, 1971.

Sención, Viriato. *They Forged the Signature of God*. Willimantic, Conn.: Curbstone Press, 1995.

El Sistema Nacional de Cultura. *Informe República Dominicana*. "Establecimientos e Instituciones Culturales de la República Dominicana." Organización de Estados Ibero-Americanos, Para la Educación, la Ciencia y la Cultura. Website. Available online at http://www.campus-oei.org/cultura/rdominicana/informe8.htm (accessed August 23, 2005).

Smithsonian Institution. *Latino Resources at the Smithsonian*. Washington, D.C.: Smithsonian Institution, 1997.

Smithsonian Institution Task Force on Latino Issues. *Willful Neglect: The Smithsonian Institution and U.S. Latinos*. Washington, D.C.: Smithsonian Institution, 1994.

Tavares K., Juan T. "La misión secreta del Teniente Porter." Pp. 7–13 in David Dixon Porter, *Diario de una misión secreta a Santo Domingo (1846)*, trans. P. Gustavo Amigo Jensen. Santo Domingo: Society of Dominican Bibliophiles, 1978.

Thompson, Anna Z. "Register to the Papers of Herbert William Krieger." National Anthropological Archives, Smithsonian Institution, July 1998. Available online at http://www.nmnh.si.edu/naa/fa/krieger.htm#1 (accessed July 24, 2005).

Ultra World of Hair Fashion. Auburn, Mass.: Worcester Reading Company.

U.S. Bureau of the Census. "Table 23: District of Columbia, Race and Hispanic Origin: 1800–1990." September 13, 2002. Available online at http://www.census.gov/population/documentation/twps0056/tab23.pdf (accessed July 29, 2005).

Valdés, Mími. "Hair Dominicana." *One World* 3, no. 1 (March 1997): 70–72.

Vega, Bernardo. *Imágenes del ayer*. Santo Domingo: Fundación Cultural Dominicana, 1981, 1998.

Verrill, A. Hyatt. *Port Rico Past and Present and San Domingo of To-Day*. New York: Dodd, Mead, 1926.

Walker, Stanley. *Journey toward the Sunlight: A Story of the Dominican Republic and Its People*. New York: Caribbean Library, 1947.

Walton Jr., William. *Present State of the Spanish Colonies; Including a Particular*

Report of Hispañola, or the Spanish Part of Santo Domingo; with a General Sur-vey of the Settlements on the South Continent of America, as Relates to History, Trade, Population, Customs, Manners, with a Concise Statement of the Senti-ments of the People on Their Relative Situation to the Mother Country. London: Longman, Hurst, Rees, Orme, and Brown, Paternoster Row, 1810.

Washington, Booker T. "Atlanta Exposition Address, September 18, 1895." Pp. 217–37 in *Up from Slavery: An Autobiography*. Garden City, N.Y.: Doubleday, 1900.

Washington, Nelson. "A Final Glimpse of Vapors." Unpublished manuscript, Washington, D.C., 1994.

Webb, Jo Ann. "Anacostia Exhibition Looks at Diversity." *Torch*, no. 94–98, August 1994, 1.

Weber, Emily Barrows. "Employment Opportunities in Beauty Shops of New York City." Division of Women in Industry and Division of Junior Place-ment, State of New York, Department of Labor, October 1931.

Weed, Helena Hill. "Hearing the Truth about Haiti." *Nation*, November 9, 1921, 533–34.

Welles, Sumner. *Naboth's Vineyard: The Dominican Republic, 1844–1924*, vol. 1. New York: Savile Books, 1966.

Williams, Monte. "Flak in the Great Hair War: African-Americans vs. Domini-cans, Rollers at the Ready." *New York Times*, October 13, 1999, B1–B8.

Secondary Sources

Abrams, Dominic, and Michael A. Hogg. *Social Identity Theory: Constructive and Critical Advances*. New York: Springer-Verlag, 1990.

Acuña, Rodolfo. *Occupied America: A History of Chicanos*, 3d ed. New York: Harper and Row, 1988.

Albert Batista, Celsa. *Mujer y esclavitud en Santo Domingo*. Santo Domingo: Ediciones CEDEE, 1993.

———. "La tercera raíz." *Estudios Sociales* 25, no. 87 (January–March 1992): 5–13.

Alcoff, Linda Martín, and Eduardo Mendieta, eds. *Identities: Race, Class, Gen-der, and Nationality*. Malden, Mass.: Blackwell, 2003.

Anderson, Benedict. *Imagined Communities*. New York: Verso, 1991.

Angel, Amanda P. "The Negotiation of Transatlantic Travel for Sixteenth-Century Spanish Women." Paper presented at the 2000 meeting of the Latin American Studies Association, Miami, March 16–18, 2000.

Atkins, G. Pope, and Larman C. Wilson. *The United States and the Trujillo Regime*. New Brunswick, N.J.: Rutgers University Press, 1972.

———. *The Dominican Republic and the United States: From Imperialism to Transnationalism*. Athens: University of Georgia Press, 1998.

Austerlitz, Paul. *Merengue: Dominican Music and Dominican Identity*. Philadelphia: Temple University Press, 1996.

Badillo, Américo, and Casandra Badillo. "Que Tan Racistas Somos: Pelo Bueno y Pelo Malo." *Estudios Sociales* 29, no. 103 (January–March 1996): 59–66.

Badillo, Casandra. "'Only My Hairdresser Knows for Sure': Stories of Race, Hair and Gender." NACLA *Report on the Americas* 34, no. 6 (May–June 2001): 35–37.

Báez-Evertsz, Franc, and Frank D'Oleo Ramírez. *La emigración de dominicanos a Estados Unidos: Determinantes socio-económicos y consequencias*. Santo Domingo: Fundación Friedrich Ebert, 1985.

Bahn, Adele, and Angela Jaquez. "One Style of Dominican Bridal Shower." Pp. 131–46 in *The Apple Sliced: Sociological Studies of New York City*, ed. Vernon Boggs, Gerald Handel, and Sylvia F. Fava. New York: Praeger, 1984.

Bailey, Benjamin. *Language, Race, and Negotiation of Identity: A Study of Dominican Americans*. New York: LFB Scholarly Publishing, 2002.

Balaguer, Joaquín. Sidebar article in *Primacías de América en la Española*. Santo Domingo: Permanent Dominican Commission for the Celebration of the Fifth Centennial of the Discovery and Evangelization of America, 1992.

——. *La isla al reves: Haití y el destino dominicano*. Santo Domingo: Editora Corripio, 1990.

——. *La palabra encadenada*, 2d ed. Santo Domingo: Sin Sello Editorial, 1990.

——. *Discursos: Temas históricos y literarios*. Santo Domingo: Sirvenase, 1977.

——. *El centinela de la frontera*. Santo Domingo: Liberia Hispaniola, 1970.

Banks, Ingrid. *Hair Matters: Beauty, Power, and Black Women's Consciousness*. New York: New York University Press, 2000.

Basch, Linda, Nina Glick Schiller, and Cristina Szanton Blanc, eds. "Theoretical Premises." Pp. 21–48 in *Nations Unbound: Transnational Projects, Postcolonial Predicaments, and Deterritorialized Nation-States*. Amsterdam: Gordon and Breach, 1994.

Battle-Walters, Kimberly. *Sheila's Shop: Working-Class African American Women Talk about Life, Love, Race and Hair*. Lanham, Md.: Rowman and Littlefield, 2004.

Baynes, Leonard M. "If It's Not Just Black and White Anymore, Why Does Darkness Cast a Longer Discriminatory Shadow than Lightness? An Investigation and Analysis of the Color Hierarchy." *Denver University Law Review* 75, no. 131 (1997): 159–62.

Bennett, Tony. *The Birth of the Museum: History, Theory, Politics*. New York: Routledge, 1995.

Berger, Harris M., and Giovanna P. Del Negro. *Identity and Everyday Life: Essays in the Study of Folklore, Music and Popular Culture*. Middletown, Conn.: Wesleyan University Press, 2004.

Bhabha, Homi. *Nation and Narration.* New York: Routledge, 1990.

Black, Jan Knippers. *The Dominican Republic: Politics and Development in an Unsovereign State.* Boston: Allen and Unwin, 1986.

Blackwelder, Julia Kirk. *Styling Jim Crow: African American Beauty Training during Segregation.* College Station: Texas A&M University, 2003.

Bonetti, Mario. "Causas culturales de la prostitución en Santo Domingo." Seminario sobre la Prostitución, pp. 39–52, Asociación ProBienestar de la Familia, Santo Domingo, Dominican Republic, 1983.

Bonilla, Frank, and Ricardo Campos. "A Wealth of Poor: Puerto Ricans in the New Economic Order." *Daedalus* 110 (Spring 1981): 133–76.

Borneman, John. "American Anthropology as Foreign Policy," *American Anthropologist* 97, no. 4 (December 1995): 663–72.

Brown, Richard Harvey. "Cultural Representations and Ideological Domination." *Social Forces* 71, no. 3 (March 1993): 657–76.

Bundles, A'Leila. *On Her Own Ground: The Life and Times of Madam C. J. Walker.* New York: Scribner, 2001.

Burgos Jr., Adrian. "Jugando en el norte: Caribbean Players in the Negro Leagues, 1910–1950." *Centro* 8, nos. 1–2 (Spring 1996): 128–49.

Byrd, Ayana D., and Loria L. Tharps. *Hair Story: Untangling the Roots of Black Hair in America.* New York: St. Martin's Press, 2001.

Cadaval, Olivia. *Creating a Latino Identity in the Nation's Capital: The Latino Festival.* New York: Garland Publishing, 1998.

Caldwell, Paulette M. "A Hair Piece: Perspectives on the Intersection of Race and Gender." *Duke Law Journal* 365 (April 1991): 41.

Cambeira, Alan. *Quisqueya La Bella: The Dominican Republic in Historical and Cultural Perspective.* Armonk, N.Y.: M. E. Sharpe, 1997.

Campbell, Mary Blaine. "Travel Writing and Its Theory." Pp. 261–78 in *The Cambridge Companion to Travel Writing,* ed. Peter Hulme and Tim Youngs. London: Cambridge University Press, 2002.

Campbell, Mary Schimdt. "Introduction." Pp. 1–6 in *Black and Hispanic Art Museums: A Vibrant Cultural Resource,* ed. Azade Ardali. New York: Ford Foundation, 1989.

Candelario, Ginetta E. B., and Nancy López. "The Latest Edition of the Welfare Queen Story: Dominican Women in New York City." *Phoebe* 7, nos. 1/2 (1995): 7–22.

Caputi, Jane E. "Beauty Secrets: Tabooing the Ugly Woman." Pp. 36–56 in *Forbidden Fruits: Taboos and Tabooism in Culture,* ed. Ray B. Browne. Bowling Green, Ohio: Bowling Green University Popular Press, 1984.

Chancer, Lynn S. *Reconcilable Differences: Confronting Beauty, Pornography, and the Future of Feminism.* Berkeley: University of California Press, 1998.

Chaney, Elsa M., and Mary García Castro, eds. *Muchachas No More: Domestic Workers in Latin America and the Caribbean.* Philadelphia: Temple University Press, 1989.

Chapkis, Wendy. *Beauty Secrets: Women and the Politics of Appearance*. Boston: South End Press, 1986.

Chester, Eric Thomas. *Rag-Tags, Scum, Riff-Raff, and Commies: The U.S. Intervention in the Dominican Republic, 1965–66*. New York: Monthly Review Press, 2001.

Clark, Kenneth, and Mamie Clark. "Racial Identification and Preference in Negro Children." Pp. 169–78 in *Readings in Social Psychology, Prepared for the Committee on the Teaching of Social Psychology of the Society for the Psychological Study of Social Issues*, ed. Guy E. Swanson, Theodore M. Newcomb, and Eugene L. Hartley. New York: Henry Holt, 1947.

Cocco de Filippis, Daisy. *Madres, Maestras y Militantes Dominicanas (Fundadoras)*. Santo Domingo: Editora Búho, 2001.

Cooley, Charles Horton. *Social Organization: A Study of the Larger Mind*. New York: Shocken Books, 1962.

Cordero Michel, Emilio. *La revolucion haitiana y Santo Domingo*. Santo Domingo: Editora Nacional, 1968.

Cornell, Stephen, and Douglass Hartmann. *Ethnicity and Race: Making Identities in a Changing World*. Thousand Oaks, Calif.: Pine Forge Press, 1998.

Crassweller, Robert. *Trujillo: The Life and Times of a Caribbean Dictator*. New York: Macmillan, 1966.

Cross Jr., William E. *Shades of Black: Diversity in African American Identity*. Philadelphia: Temple University Press, 1991.

Dash, Michael J. *Haiti and the United States: National Stereotypes and the Literary Imagination*. New York: St. Martin's Press, 1997.

Davis, David Brion. *The Problem of Slavery in Western Culture*. Ithaca, N.Y.: Cornell University Press, 1966.

Davis, F. James. *Who Is Black? One Nation's Definition*. University Park: Pennsylvania State University Press, 1991.

Davis, Harold Eugene, John J. Finan, and F. Taylor Peck. *Latin American Diplomatic History: An Introduction*. Baton Rouge: Louisiana State University Press, 1977.

Dayan, Joan. "Codes of Law and Bodies of Color." *New Literary History* 26, no. 2 (1995): 295–97.

D.C. History Curriculum Project. *City of Magnificent Intentions: A History of the District of Columbia*. Washington, D.C.: Intac, 1983.

Deagan, Kathleen. "Colonial Transformation: Euro-American Cultural Genesis in the Early Spanish American Colonies." *Journal of Anthropological Research* 52, no. 2 (Summer 1996): 135–60.

Deagan, Kathleen, and José María Cruxent. "From Contact to Criollos: The Archaeology of Spanish Colonization in Hispaniola." Pp. 67–104 in Warwick Bray, ed. *The Meeting of Two Worlds: Europe and the Americas, 1492–1650. Proceedings of the British Academy*, vol. 81. London: Oxford University Press, 1993.

————. *Columbus's Outpost among the Taínos: Spain and America at La Isabela, 1493–1498*. New Haven, Conn.: Yale University Press, 2002.

Deagan, Kathleen, and Darcie MacMahon. *Fort Mose: Colonial America's Black Fortress of Freedom*. Gainesville: University Press of Florida, 1995.

Deive, Carlos Esteban. "La herencia africana en la cultura dominicana actual." *Ensayos sobre cultura dominicana*. 5th ed; Santo Domingo: Fundación Cultural Dominicana, Museo del Hombre Dominicano, 1997.

————. "Y tu abuela, ¿dónde está?" *Boletín del Museo del Hombre Dominicano* 10, no. 16 (1981): 109–14.

————. *La esclavitud del negro en Santo Domingo (1492–1844)*, vols. 1–2. Santo Domingo: Museo del Hombre Dominicano, 1980.

de la Cruz, Juan, Miguelina Rodríguez, Mayra Taveras, and Roman Batista. *La resistencia indígena y negra en Quisqueya*. Santo Domingo: Publicaciones El Barrio GRIPAC, 1992.

del Castillo, José, and Martin F. Murphy. "Migration, National Identity and Cultural Policy in the Dominican Republic." *Journal of Ethnic Studies* 15, no. 3 (1987): 49–70.

Delgado, Melvin. "Role of Latina-Owned Beauty Parlors in a Latino Community." *Social Work* 42, no. 5 (September 1997): 445–53.

Del Pinal, Jorge, and Sharon Ennis. "The Racial and Ethnic Identity of Latin American Immigrants in Census 2000." Paper presented at the Annual Meeting of the Population Association of America, Philadelphia, March 31–April 2, 2005.

Deloria, Philip J. *Playing Indian*. New Haven, Conn.: Yale University Press, 1998.

Denzin, Norman K., and Yvonna S. Lincoln, eds. *Handbook of Qualitative Research*. Thousand Oaks, Calif.: Sage, 1994.

Derby, Lauren. "The Dictator's Seduction: Gender and State Spectacle during the Trujillo Regim." Pp. 1112–46 in *Latin American Popular Culture: An Introduction*, ed. William H. Beezley and Linda A. Curcio-Nagy. Wilmington, Del.: Scholarly Resources, 1999.

"Descubriendo nuestra identidad." *Estudios Sociales* 25, no. 87 (January–March 1992): 1–3.

Dore-Cabral, Carlos. "Encuesta Rumbo-Gallup: La población dominicana más antihaitiana que racista." *Rumbo*, May 3, 1995, 8–12.

————. "En torno a las críticas de Badillo." *Estudios Sociales* 29, no. 103 (January–March 1996): 67–74.

Duany, Jorge. *The Puerto Rican Nation on the Move: Identities on the Island and in the United States*. Chapel Hill: University of North Carolina Press, 2002.

————. "Reconstructing Racial Identity: Ethnicity, Color, and Class among Dominicans in the United States and Puerto Rico." *Latin American Perspectives* 25, no. 3 (May 1998): 147–72.

————. "Trasnational Migration from the Dominican Republic: The Cultural

Redefinition of Racial Identity." *Caribbean Studies* 29, no. 2 (1996): 253–82.

————.*Quisqueya on the Hudson: The Transnational Identity of Dominicans in Washington Heights*. New York: CUNY Dominican Studies Institute, 1994.

Duarte, Isis. "Household Workers in the Dominican Republic: A Question for the Feminist Movement." Pp. 197–220 in *Muchachas No More: Domestic Workers in Latin America and the Caribbean*, ed. Elsa M. Chaney and Mary García Castro. Philadelphia: Temple University Press, 1989.

Dubois, Laurent. *Avengers of the New World: The Story of the Haitian Revolution*. Cambridge, Mass.: Harvard University Press, 2004.

Erdman, David V. "Blake's Vision of Slavery." *Journal of the Warburg and Courtauld Institutes*, vol. 15, nos. 3–4 (1952): 242–52.

Espinal Hernández, Edwin. *Patrimonio cultural y legislación*. Santo Domingo: Editorial Capel Dominicana, 1993.

Ewen, Phyllis. "The Beauty Ritual." Pp. 3–57 in *Images of Information: Still Photography and the Social Sciences*, ed. Jon Wanger. London: Sage Publications, 1979.

Fennema, Meindert, and Troetje Loewenthal. *La construción de raza y nación en la República Dominicana*. Santo Domingo: Editora Universitaria, Universidad Autonoma de Santo Domingo, 1987.

Fewkes, Jesse Walter. *The Aborigines of Porto Rico and Neighboring Islands*. New York: Johnson Reprint Corporation, 1970.

Foner, Nancy, ed. *New Immigrants in New York*. New York: Columbia University Press, 1987.

Forbes, Jack. "The Evolution of the Term Mulatto." *Journal of Ethnic Studies* 10, no. 2 (1983): 45–66.

Fong, Mary, and Rueyling Chuang, eds. *Communicating Ethnic and Cultural Identity*. Lanham, Md.: Rowman and Littlefield, 2004.

Forte, Deidre A. "Community-Based Breast Cancer Intervention Program for Older African American Women in Beauty Salons." *Public Health Reports*, vol. 110, no. 2, March–April 1995, 179–83.

Franco Pichardo, Franklin J. *Historia de las ideas políticas en la República Dominicana*. Santo Domingo: Editora Nacional, 1981.

————. *Santo Domingo: Cultura, política e ideología*. Santo Domingo: Sociedad Editorial Dominicana, 1997.

Frankenberg, Ruth. *White Women, Race Matters: The Social Construction of Whiteness*. Minneapolis: University of Minnesota Press, 1993.

Freedman, Rita. *Beauty Bound: Why Women Strive for Physical Perfection*. London: Columbus Books, 1986.

Fundación Cultural Dominicana. *Ensayos sobre cultura Dominicana*. Santo Domingo: Museo del Hombre Domincano, 1988.

Furman, Frida Kerner. *Facing the Mirror: Older Women and Beauty Shop Culture*. New York: Routledge, 1997.

García, José Gabriel. *Compendio de la historia de Santo Domingo*, 2 vols. Santo Domingo, 1879–82.

García, María Cristina. *Havana USA: Cuban Exiles and Cuban Americans in South Florida, 1959–1994*. Berkeley: University of California Press, 1996.

García Arévalo, Manuel A. *Indigenismo, arqueología e identidad nacional*. Santo Domingo: Museo del Hombre Dominicano and Fundación García Arévalo, 1972.

———. *Cimarron*. Santo Domingo: Fundación García Arévalo, 1986.

———. *Santo Domingo en ocasión del Quinto Centenario*. Santo Domingo: Colección Quinto Centenario, 1992.

Geggus, David Patrick. *Haitian Revolutionary Studies*. Bloomington: Indiana University Press, 2002.

Gilbertson, Greta A., Joseph P. Fitzpatrick, and Lijun Yang, "Hispanic Intermarriage in New York City: New Evidence from 1991." *International Migration Review* 30, no. 2 (Summer 1996): 445–59.

Gimbernard, Jacinto. *Historia de Santo Domingo*. Madrid: MELSA, 1978.

Gimlin, Debra. "Pamela's Place: Power and Negotiation in the Hair Salon." *Gender and Society* 10, no. 5 (October 1996): 505–26.

Godreau, Isar P. "Confronting the Panic: Troublesome Hispanics." Paper presented at the Latin American Studies Association meeting, Miami, March 16–19, 2000.

Goffman, Erving. *The Presentation of Self in Everyday Life*. Garden City, N.Y.: Doubleday, 1959.

———. *Interaction Ritual*. Garden City, N.Y.: Anchor Books, 1967.

González, Juan. *Harvest of Empire: A History of Latinos in America*. New York: Viking, 2000.

González Canalda, María Filomena, and Rubén Silíe. "La nación dominicana en la enseñanza a nivel primario." Pp. 15–29 in *Eme Eme: Estudios Dominicanos*. Santiago de los Caballeros: Universidad Católica Madre y Maestra, 1986.

González, Nancie L. "Patterns of Dominican Ethnicity." Pp. 113–23 in *The New Ethnicity: Perspectives from Ethnology*, ed. John W. Bennett. New York: West Publishing, 1975.

———. "Giving Birth in America: The Immigrant's Dilemma." Pp. 241–53 in *International Migration: The Female Experience*, ed. Rita James Simon and Caroline B. Brettell. Totowa, N.J.: Rowman and Allanbeld, 1986.

González, Raymundo. "Campesinos y sociedad colonial en el siglo xviii Dominicano." *Estudios Sociales* 25, no. 87 (January–March 1992): 15–28.

Gordon, Edmund T. *Disparate Diasporas: Identity and Politics in an African-Nicaraguan Community*. Austin: University of Texas Press, 1998.

Goris-Rosario, Anneris Altagracia. "The Role of the Ethnic Community and the Workplace in the Integration of Immigrants: A Case Study of Immigrants in New York City." Ph.D. diss., Fordham University, New York, 1994.

Graham, Richard, ed. *The Idea of Race in Latin America, 1870–1940.* Austin: University of Texas Press, 1990.

Guarnizo, Luís Eduardo. "Los Dominicanyorks: The Making of a Binational Society." *The Annals* (AAPSS), no. 533 (May 1994).

———. "One Country in Two: Dominican-Owned Firms in New York and in the Dominican Republic." Ph.D. diss., Johns Hopkins University, Baltimore, 1992.

Guzmán, Daysi Joséfina. "Raza y lenguaje en el Cibao." *Eme Eme* 2, no. 11 (March–April 1974): 3–45.

Haas, Lisbeth. *Conquests and Historical Identities in California, 1769–1936.* Berkeley: University of California Press, 1995.

Harper, Douglas. "Talking about Pictures: A Case for Photo Elicitation." *Visual Studies* 17, no. 1 (2002): 13–26.

Harris, Marvin. *Patterns of Race in the Americas.* New York: Walker, 1964.

Hauch, Charles C. "Attitudes of Foreign Governments Towards the Spanish Reoccupation of the Dominican Republic." *Hispanic American Historical Review* 27, no. 2 (May 1947): 247–68.

Hernández, Ramona. *The Mobility of Workers under Advanced Capitalism.* New York: Columbia University Press, 2002.

Hernández, Ramona, and Francisco L. Rivera-Batiz. "Dominicans in the United States: A Socioeconomic Profile, 2000." Dominican Research Monographs of the CUNY Dominican Studies Institute. New York, October 6, 2003.

Herskovits, Melville. *Life in a Haitian Valley.* New York: Knopf, 1937.

Hoetink, Harry. *El pueblo Dominicano (1850–1900): Apuntes para su sociología histórica.* Santiago: Universidad Católica Madre y Maestra, 1985.

———. *The Dominican People, 1850–1900: Notes for a Historical Sociology.* Baltimore: Johns Hopkins University Press, 1982.

———. *Two Variants in Caribbean Race Relations: A Contribution to the Sociology of Segmented Societies.* New York: Oxford University Press, 1967.

———. "'Americans' in Samana." *Caribbean Studies* 2, no. 1 (April 1962): 3–21.

Hoffnung-Garskof, Jesse. "Nueba Yol: Migration and Popular Culture in Santo Domingo and New York, 1950–1992." Ph.D. diss., Princeton University, Princeton, 2002.

Holder, Calvin B. "Racism toward Black African Diplomats during the Kennedy Administration." *Journal of Black Studies* 14, no. 1 (1983): 31–48.

Howard, David. *Coloring the Nation: Race and Ethnicity in the Dominican Republic.* Boulder: Lynne Rienner Publishers, 2001.

Howe, Louise Kapp. *Pink Collar Workers.* New York: Putnam, 1977.

Hraba, Joseph, and Geoffrey Grant. "Black Is Beautiful: A Reexamination of Racial Preference and Identification." *Journal of Personality and Social Psychology* 16, no. 3 (1970): 398–402.

Hudson, Linda Sybert. "Jane McManus Storm Cazneau (1807–1878): A Biography." Ph.D. diss., University of North Texas, Denton, 1999.

Hulme, Peter. "El encuentro con Anacaona: Frederick Albion Ober y la historia del caribe autócono." *Op.Cit.*, no. 9 (1997): 75–128.

———. *Remnants of Conquest: The Island Caribs and their Visitors, 1877–1998.* Oxford: Oxford University Press, 2000.

Hunter, Ian. "Mind Games and Body Techniques." *Southern Review* 26 (July 1993): 172–85.

Hunter, Margaret. *Race, Gender and the Politics of Skin Tone.* New York: Routledge, 2005.

Ignatiev, Noel. *How the Irish Became White.* New York: Routledge, 1995.

Inman, Samuel Guy. "The Monroe Doctrine and Hispanic America." *Hispanic American Historical Review* 4, no. 4 (November 1921): 635–76.

Isin, Engin F., and Patricia K. Wood. *Citizenship and Identity.* London: Sage Publications, 1999.

Itzigsohn, José, and Carlos Dore-Cabral. "The Manifold Character of Panethnicity: Latino Identities and Practices among Dominicans in New York City." Pp. 319–36 in *Mambo Montage: The Latinization of New York*, ed. Agustín Laó-Montes and Arlene Dávila. New York: Columbia University Press, 2001.

———. "Competing Identities? Race, Ethnicity and Panethnicity among Dominicans in the United States," *Sociological Forum* 15, no. 2 (2000): 225–47.

Itzigsohn, José, Silvio Giorguli, and Obed Vázquez. "Immigrant Incorporation and Racial Identity: Racial Self-Identification among Dominicans in New York City and Providence." *Ethnic and Racial Studies* 28, no. 1 (January 2005): 50–78.

James, C. L. R. *The Black Jacobins: Toussaint L'Ouverture and the San Domingo Revolution.* New York: Vintage, 1989.

James, Portia. "Building a Community-Based Identity at Anacostia Museum." *Curator* 39, no. 1 (March 1996): 19–44.

Jenkins, Richard. *Social Identity.* New York: Routledge, 1996.

Jiménes Grullon, Juan Isidro. *Sociología y política dominicana, 1844–1966.* 3 vols.; Santo Domingo: Biblioteca Taller, 1974–75.

Jones, Stephen R. G. "Was There a Hawthorne Effect?" *American Journal of Sociology* 98, no. 3 (November 1992): 451–68.

Jordan, Winthrop. *White over Black: American Attitudes toward the Negro.* New York: Norton, 1977.

Kallendorf, Hilaire. "A Myth Rejected: The Noble Savage in Dominican Dystopia." *Journal of Latin American Studies* 27, pt. 2 (May 1995): 449–70.

Kaminsky, Amy K. *Reading the Body Politic: Feminist Criticism and Latin American Women Writers.* Minneapolis: University of Minnesota Press, 1993.

Kan, Aisha. "What Is 'Spanish'? Ambiguity and 'Mixed' Ethnicity in Trinidad."

Pp. 180–207 in *Trinidad Ethnicity*, ed. Kevin A. Yelvington. Knoxville: University of Tennessee Press, 1993.

Karp, Ivan. "Other Cultures in Museum Perspective." Pp. 373–85 in *Exhibiting Cultures: The Poetics and Politics of Museum Display*, ed. Ivan Karp and Steven D. Lavine. Washington, D.C.: Smithsonian Institution, 1991.

Karp, Ivan, and Steven D. Lavine, eds. *Exhibiting Cultures: The Poetics and Politics of Museum Display*. Washington, D.C.: Smithsonian Institution Press, 1991.

———. "Introduction: Museums and Multiculturalism." Pp. 1–10 in *Exhibiting Cultures: The Poetics and Politics of Museum Display*, ed. Ivan Karp and Steven D. Lavine. Washington, D.C.: Smithsonian Institution Press, 1991.

Kasinitz, Philip. *Caribbean New York: Black Immigrants and the Politics of Race.* Ithaca, N.Y.: Cornell University Press, 1992.

Kidder, Frederick Elwyn. *Latin America and UNESCO: The First Five Years.* Gainesville: University Press of Florida, 1960.

Kidwell, Clara Sue. "Every Last Dishcloth: The Prodigious Collecting of George Gustav Heye." Pp. 232–58 in *Collecting Native America, 1870–1960*, ed. Shepard Krech III and Barbara A. Hail. Washington, D.C.: Smithsonian Institution, 1999.

King, C. Richard. *Colonial Discourses, Collective Memories, and the Exhibition of Native American Cultures and Histories in the Contemporary United States.* New York: Garland Publishing, 1998.

King, Elizabeth. *Quinceañera: Celebrating Fifteen.* New York: Dutton, 1998.

Kirshenblatt-Gimblett, Barbara. "Objects of Ethnography." Pp. 386–443 in *Exhibiting Cultures: The Poetics and Politics of Museum Display*, ed. Ivan Karp and Steven D. Lavine. Washington, D.C.: Smithsonian Institution, 1991.

Knight, Franklin W. *The Caribbean: The Genesis of a Fragmented Nationalism*, 2d ed. New York: Oxford University Press, 1990.

Knight, Melvin M. *The Americans in Santo Domingo.* New York: Vanguard Press, 1928.

Krech III, Shepard, and Barbara A. Hail, eds. *Collecting Native America, 1870–1960.* Washington, D.C.: Smithsonian Institution, 1999.

Krieger, Herbert William. *Archeological and Historical Investigations in Samaná, Dominican Republic.* Washington, D.C.: U.S. Government Printing Office, 1929.

———. *Aboriginal Indian Pottery of the Dominican Republic.* Washington, D.C.: Government Printing Office, 1931.

Krohn-Hansen, Christian. "Masculinity and the Political among Dominicans: 'The Dominican Tiger.'" Pp. 108–33 in *Machos, Mistresses, Madonnas: Contesting the Power of Latin American Gender Imagery*, ed. Marit Melhuus and Kristi Anne Stølen. New York: Verso, 1996.

Lancaster, Roger. *Life Is Hard: Machismo, Danger, and the Intimacy of Power in Nicaragua.* Berkeley: University of California Press, 1992.

Landers, Jane G. "Maroon Ethnicity and Identity in Ecuador, Colombia, and Hispaniola." Paper presented at the 2000 meeting of the Latin American Studies Association, Miami, March 16–18, 2000.

Laó-Montes, Agustín, and Arlene Dávila, eds. *Mambo Montage: The Latinization of New York*. New York: Columbia University Press, 2001.

Lara, Julia. "Reflections: Bridging Cultures." *First–Generation Students: Confronting Cultural Issues*, special issue of *New Directions for Community Colleges* 20, no. 4 (Winter 1992): 65–70.

Larrazábal Blanco, Carlos. *El negro y la esclavitud en Santo Domingo*. Santo Domingo: Julio D. Postigo, 1967.

Lauren, Paul Gordon. *Power and Prejudice: The Politics and Diplomacy of Racial Discrimination*. Boulder: Westview Press, 1988.

Levine, Donald Nathan. *The Flight from Ambiguity: Essays in Social and Cultural Theory*. Chicago: University of Chicago Press, 1985.

Levitt, Peggy. *The Transnational Villagers*. Berkley: University of California Press, 2001.

Levitt, Peggy, and Christina Gómez. "The Intersection of Race and Gender among Dominicans in the U.S." Paper presented at the Meeting of the American Sociological Association, Toronto, August 8–13, 1997.

Lewis, David L. *District of Columbia: A Bicentennial History*. New York: W. W. Norton, 1976.

Liriano, Alejandra. *El papel de la mujer de origen africano en el Santo Domingo colonial, Siglos XVI–XVII*. Santo Domingo: Centro de Investigación para la Acción Femenina, 1992.

Logan, Rayford W. *The Diplomatic Relations of the United States with Haiti, 1776–1891*. Chapel Hill: University of North Carolina Press, 1941.

Lott, Eric. *Love and Theft: Blackface Minstrelsy and the American Working Class*. New York: Oxford University Press, 1993.

Lugo, Américo. *Historia de Santo Domingo (de 1556 hasta 1608)*. Ciudad Trujillo: Editora Librería Dominicana, 1952.

Lugones, María. "Playfulness, 'World'-Travelling, and Loving Perception." Pp. 390–402 in *Making Soul, Making Face: Creative and Critical Perspectives by Women of Color*, ed. Gloria Anzaldúa. San Francisco: aunt lute foundation, 1990.

Maga, Timothy. "Battling the 'Ugly American' at Home: The Special Protocol Service and the New Frontier." *Diplomacy and Statecraft* 3, no. 1 (1992): 126–42.

Manning, Robert D. "Multicultural Change in Washington, D.C.: The Contested Social Terrain of the Urban Odyssey." Report 91-3, Institutional Studies Office, Smithsonian Institution, Washington, D.C., April 1991.

Marrero Aristy, Ramón. *La República Dominicana*, 2 vols., Ciudad Trujillo: Editorial El Caribe, 1957–58.

Martin, John B. *Overtaken by Events: The Dominican Crisis from the Fall of Trujillo to the Civil War*. New York: Doubleday, 1966.

Martin-Felton, Z., and Gail Lowe. *A Different Drummer: John Kinard and the Anacostia Museum, 1967–1989*. Washington, D.C.: Anacostia Museum, Smithsonian Institution, 1993.

Martínez-Fernández, Luís. *Torn between Empires: Economy, Society, and Patterns of Political Thought in the Hispanic Caribbean, 1840–1878*. Athens: University of Georgia Press, 1994.

Masud-Piloto, Felix. *From Welcomed Exiles to Illegal Immigrants: Cuban Migration to the United States, 1959–1995*. Lanham, Md.: Rowman and Littlefield, 1996.

Matos Moctezuma, Eduardo. "El Museo del Hombre Dominicano." *Boletín del Museo del Hombre Dominicano* 7, no. 10 (May 1978): 19–21.

Maxton, Ashindi. "Race Consciousness in Children in the Dominican Republic." Thesis in Africana studies, Vassar College, Poughkeepsie, N.Y., 1996. On file at the Dominican Studies Institute, City College of the City University of New York.

McCracken, Grant. *Big Hair: A Journey into the Transformation of Self*. Woodstock, N.Y.: Overlook Press, 1995.

Mead, George Herbert. *Mind, Self, and Society: From the Standpoint of a Social Behaviorist*, ed. Charles W. Morris, Chicago: University of Chicago Press, 1934.

Meisenheimer II, Joseph P. "The Services Industry in the 'Good' versus 'Bad' Jobs Debate." *Monthly Labor Review* 121, no. 2 (February 1998): 22–26.

Mercer, Kobena. *Welcome to the Jungle: New Positions in Black Cultural Studies*. New York: Routledge, 1994.

Merton, Robert K., and Elinor Barber. "Sociological Ambivalence." Pp. 540–566 in *Sociological Theory: A Book of Readings*, 4th ed., ed. Lewis A. Coser and Bernard Rosenberg. New York: Macmillan, 1976.

Mintz, Sidney. "Cañamelar: The Subculture of a Rural Sugar Plantation Proletariat." Pp. 314–417 in *The People of Puerto Rico: A Study in Social Anthropology*, ed. Julian H. Steward. Urbana: University of Illinois Press, 1956.

Mir, Pedro. *Tres leyendas de colores*. 3d ed. Santo Domingo: Taller, 1984.

Miranda, Ricardo. "The Income Mobility of Puerto Rican Bodegueros in New York City: A Property Rights Perspective." Master's thesis, Massachusetts Institute of Technology, Cambridge, Mass., 1994.

Montague, Ludwell Lee. *Haiti and the United States, 1714–1938*. Durham: Duke University Press, 1940.

Moreno Fraginals, Manuel, Frank Moya Pons, and Stanley L. Engerman. *Between Slavery and Free Labor*. Baltimore: Johns Hopkins University Press, 1985.

Morrison, Toni. *Playing in the Dark: Whiteness and the Literary Imagination*. Cambridge, Mass.: Harvard University Press, 1992.

Moya Pons, Frank. "Modernización y cambios en la República Dominicana." Pp. 211–45 in *Ensayos sobre cultura dominicana,* 5th ed., ed. Museo del Hombre Dominicano. Santo Domingo: Fundación Cultural Dominicana, 1997.

———. "Dominican National Identity in Historical Perspective." *Punto 7 Review: A Journal of Marginal Discourse* 3, no. 1 (1996): 14–26.

———. *The Dominican Republic: A National History.* New York: Hispaniola Books, 1995.

———. "Dominican National Identity and Return Migration." Occasional Papers no. 1, Center for Latin American Studies, University of Florida, Gainesville, 1981.

Murguia, Edward, and Edward Telles. "Phenotype and Schooling among Mexican Americans." *Sociology of Education* 69, no. 4 (October 1996): 276–89.

Myrdal, Gunnar. *An American Dilemma: The Negro Problem and Modern Democracy.* New York: Harper, 1944.

Nasaw, David. *Going Out: The Rise and Fall of Public Amusements.* Cambridge, Mass.: Harvard University Press, 1999.

Nelson, William Javier. *Almost a Territory: America's Attempt to Annex the Dominican Republic.* Newark: University of Delaware Press, 1990.

Oboler, Suzanne. *Ethnic Labels, Latino Lives: Identity and the Politics of (Re)Presentation in the United States.* Minneapolis: University of Minnesota Press, 1995.

Oldenburg, Ray. *The Great Good Place: Cafés, Coffee Shops, Community Centers, Beauty Parlors, General Stores, Bars, Hangouts, and How They Get You through the Day.* New York: Paragon House, 1989.

Olsen Bogaert, Harold. *Legislación sobre el Museo del Hombre Dominicano.* Santo Domingo: Museo del Hombre Dominicano, 2000.

Olsen Bogaert, Harold, Fanny García, and Mayra de Jesús. "Un modelo de administración para El Museo del Hombre Dominicano." Master's thesis, Universidad Autónoma de Santo Domingo, Facultad de Ciencias Economicas y Sociales, Departamento de Administración y Mercadeo, Santo Domingo, Dominican Republic, 1999.

Omi, Michael, and Howard Winant. *Racial Formation in the United States: From the 1960s to the 1980s,* 2d ed. New York: Routledge, 1994.

Pagán Perdomo, Dato. "Notas sobre el tráfico ilícito de bienes culturales en República Dominicana." Paper presented at Museos: Dinosaurios o Dinamos? Explorando el Futuro de los Museos en el siglo XXI conference, ICAMI-ICOM, Auditorio del Banco Central, Santo Domingo, Dominican Republic, November 16–20, 1999.

———. *Programación de proyectos y desarrollo institucional, 1997–98.* Santo Domingo: Museo del Hombre Dominicano, 1997.

Peña, Yesilernis, Jim Sidanius, and Mark Sawyer. "'Racial Democracy' in the Americas: A Latin and North American Comparison." *Journal of Cross-Cultural Psychology* 35, no. 6 (November 2004): 749–62.

Peña-Batlle, Manuel Arturo. *Historia de la cuestión fronteriza*, vol. 1. Ciudad Trujillo, Editora Luis Sánchez Andújar, 1946.

Pérez, Louis. "A Circle of Connections: 100 Years of U.S.-Cuba Relations." Pp. 161–79 in *Bridges to Cuba/Puentes a Cuba*, ed. Ruth Behar. Ann Arbor: University of Michigan Press, 1995.

Pina P., Plinio. *Legislación Dominicana sobre museos y protección del patrimonio cultural, 1870–1977*. Santo Domingo: Museo del Hombre Dominicano, 1978.

Pratt, Mary Louise. *Imperial Eyes: Travel Writing and Transculturation*. New York: Routledge, 1992.

Purcell, Trevor W. *Banana Fallout: Class, Color and Culture among West Indians in Costa Rica*. Los Angeles: University of California Press, 1993.

Random House Webster's College Dictionary. New York: Random House, 1991.

Reich, Jennifer A. "Pregnant with Possibility: Reflections on Embodiment, Access, and Inclusion in Field Research." *Qualitative Sociology* 26, no. 3 (Fall 2003): 351–67.

Renda, Mary. *Taking Haiti: Military Occupation and the Culture of U.S. Imperialism, 1915–1940*. Chapel Hill: University of North Carolina Press, 2001.

Repak, Terry A. *Waiting on Washington: Central American Workers in the Nation's Capital*. Philadelphia: Temple University Press, 1995.

Roberts, Kenneth, and Anna M. Roberts, trans. and eds. *Moreau de St. Méry's American Journey (1793–1798)*. Garden City, N.Y.: Doubleday, 1947.

Roberts, Peter. "The (Re)construction of the Concept of 'Indio' in the National Identities of Cuba, the Dominican Republic and Puerto Rico." Pp. 99–120 in *Caribbean 2000: Regional and/or National Definitions, Identities and Cultures*, ed. Lowell Fiet and Janette Becerra. Rio Piedras: University of Puerto Rico, 1997.

Rodríguez, Clara. *Puerto Ricans: Born in the U.S.A.* Boulder: Westview Press, 1991.

———. *Latin Looks: Images of Latinas and Latinos in the U.S. Media*. Boulder: Westview Press, 1997.

———. *Changing Race: Latinos, the Census and the History of Ethnicity in the United States*. New York: New York University Press, 2000.

Roediger, David. *The Wages of Whiteness: Race and the Making of the American Working Class*. London: Verso, 1991.

Rogler, Charles C. "The Role of Semantics in the Study of Race Distance in Puerto Rico." *Social Forces* 22 (October 1943–May 1944): 448–53.

Rooks, Noliwe M. *Hair Raising: Beauty, Culture, and African American Women*. New Brunswick, N.J.: Rutgers University Press, 1996.

Roorda, Eric Paul. *The Dictator Next Door: The Good Neighbor Policy and the Trujillo Regime in the Dominican Republic, 1930–1945*. Durham: Duke University Press, 1998.

Rout Jr., Leslie B. *The African Experience in Spanish America: 1502 to the Present Day*. New York: Cambridge University Press, 1976.

Rowe, L. S. *The Pan American Union and the Pan American Conferences, 1890–1940*. Washington, D.C.: Pan American Union, 1940.

Rubiés, Joan Pau. "Travel Writing and Ethnography." Pp. 242–60 in *The Cambridge Companion to Travel Writing*, ed. Peter Hulme and Tim Youngs. London: Cambridge University Press, 2002.

Ruffins, Faith Davis. "Mythos, Memory, and History: African American Preservation Efforts, 1820–1990." Pp. 506–611 in *Exhibiting Cultures: The Poetics and Politics of Museum Display*, ed. Ivan Karp and Steven D. Lavine. Washington, D.C.: Smithsonian Institution Press, 1991.

Ruiz, Vicki L. "'Star Struck': Acculturation, Adolescence, and Mexican American Women, 1920–1950." Pp. 346–61 in *Unequal Sisters: A Multicultural Reader in U.S. Women's History*, 3d ed., ed. Vicki L. Ruiz and Ellen Carol DuBois. New York: Routledge, 2000.

Russell, Kathy, Midge Wilson, and Ronald Hall. *Color Complex: The Politics of Skin Color among African Americans*. New York: Doubleday, 1992.

Rydell, Robert W. *All the World's a Fair: Visions of Empire at American International Expositions, 1876–1916*. Chicago: University of Chicago Press, 1984.

Sagás, Ernesto. *Race and Politics in the Dominican Republic*. Gainesville: University Press of Florida, 2000.

Sagás, Ernesto, and Orlando Inoa. *The Dominican People: A Documentary History*. Princeton: Markus Weiner, 2003.

Sánchez Korrol, Virginia. *From Colonia to Community: The History of Puerto Ricans in New York City, 1917–1948*. Westport, Conn.: Greenwood Press, 1983.

Sang, Mu-kien Adriana. *Caminos transitados: Un panorama histórico, 1844–1961*. Vol. 1 of Mu-kien Adriana Sang, *La política exterior dominicana, 1844–1961*. Santo Domingo: Secretaría de Estado de Relaciones Exteriores, 2000.

———. *La política exterior del dictador Trujillo, 1930–1961*. Vol. 2 of Mu-kien Adriana Sang, *La política exterior dominicana, 1844–1961*. Santo Domingo: Secretaría de Estado de Relaciones Exteriores, 2000.

Scheckel, Susan. *The Insistence of the Indian: Race and Nationalism in Nineteenth Century American Culture*. Princeton: Princeton University Press, 1998.

Schroder, David. *Engagement in the Mirror: Hairdressers and Their Work*. San Francisco: R & E Research Associates, 1978.

Schutz, Alfred. *The Phenomenology of the Social World*. Evanston, Ill.: Northwestern University Press, 1967.

Scott, Linda M. *Fresh Lipstick: Redressing Fashion and Feminism*. New York: Palgrave-Macmillan, 2006.

Seidman, Irving. *Interviewing as Qualitative Research Method: A Guide for Researchers in Education and the Social Sciences*. New York: Teachers College Press, 1998.

Sheller, Mimi. "The 'Haytian Fear': International Narratives and Regional Networks in the Construction of Race." Paper presented at the Annual Meeting of the American Sociological Association, Toronto, 1997.

Shohat, Ella, ed. *Talking Visions: Multicultural Feminism in the Age of Globalization.* Cambridge, Mass.: MIT Press, 1998.

Shorris, Earl. "Latinos: The Complexity of Identity." *NACLA Report on the Americas* 26, no. 2 (September 1992).

Silié, Rubén. *Economía, esclavitud y población: Ensayos de interpretación histórica del Santo Domingo Español en el siglo XVIII.* Santo Domingo: Taller, 1976.

———. "Aspectos socio-historicos sobre la inmigración Haitiana a la República Dominicana." Pp. 1–32 in *La República Dominicana y Haití frente al futuro,* ed. Rubén Silié, Orlando Inoa, and Arnold Antonin. Santo Domingo: FLACSO, 1998.

Smith, Dorothy E. "The Standard North American Family." *Journal of Family Issues* 14, no. 1 (March 1993): 50–64.

———. *Writing the Social: Critique, Theory, and Investigations.* Toronto: University of Toronto Press, 2004.

Sommer, Doris. *Foundational Fictions: The National Romances of Latin America.* Berkeley: University of California Press, 1991.

———. *One Master for Another: Populism and Patriarchal Rhetoric in Dominican Novels.* Lanham, Md.: University Press of America, 1983.

Stepans, Nancy Leys. *"The Hour of Eugenics": Race, Gender and Nation in Latin America.* Ithaca: Cornell University Press, 1991.

Stimson, Frederick S. "The Influence of Travel Books on Early American Hispanism." *The Americas* 11, no. 2 (October 1954): 155–59.

Stryker, Sheldon. *Symbolic Interactionism: A Social Structural Version.* Palo Alto, Calif.: Benjamin Cummings, 1980.

Sued-Badillo, Jalil. "Facing Up to Caribbean History." *American Antiquity* 57, no. 4 (October 1992): 599–607.

Sutton, Constance R., and Elsa M. Chaney, eds. *Caribbean Life in New York City: Sociocultural Dimensions.* New York: Center for Migration Studies, 1994.

Synott, Anthony. "Shame and Glory: A Sociology of Hair." *British Journal of Sociology* 38, no. 3 (September 1987): 381–413.

Tansill, Charles Callan. *The United States and Santo Domingo, 1798–1873: A Chapter in Caribbean Diplomacy.* Baltimore: Johns Hopkins University Press, 1938.

Tannenbaum, Frank. *Slave and Citizen: The Negro in America.* New York: Alfred A. Knopf, 1946.

Taylor, Diana. *Disappearing Acts: Spectacles of Gender and Nationalism in Argentina's "Dirty War."* Durham: Duke University Press, 1997.

Tejada Ortíz, Dagoberto. *Cultura popular e identidad nacional.* Santo Domingo: Instituto de Cultura Dominicana, 1998.

Tejera, Apolinar. "¿Quid de Quisqueya?" *Boletín del Archivo General de la Nación*, no. 8 (1945): 216–21.

Tejera, Emiliano. *Indigenismos*. Santo Domingo: Editora de Santo Domingo, 1977.

Thomas, Piri. *Down These Mean Streets*. New York: Knopf, 1969.

Torres, Gerald. "The Legacy of Conquest and Discovery: Meditations on Ethnicity, Race, and American Politics." Pp. 153–69 in *Borderless Borders: U.S. Latinos, Latin Americans and the Paradox of Interdependence*, ed. Frank Bonilla, Edwin Meléndez, Rebecca Morales, and María de los Angeles Torres. Philadelphia: Temple University Press, 1998.

Torres-Saillant, Silvio. "El retorno de las yolas: La vista desde la diaspora." Paper presented at Congreso Internacional: La República Dominicana en el umbral del siglo XXI, July 2426, 1997, Pontífica Universidad Católica Madre y Maestra, Santo Domingo, Dominican Republic, July 24–26, 1997.

———. "The Tribulations of Blackness: Stages in Dominican Racial Identity." *Latin American Perspectives* 25, no. 3 (May 1998): 126–46.

———. "Introduction to Dominican Blackness." Dominican Studies Working Paper Series 1. City College of New York, CUNY Dominican Studies Institute, New York, 1999.

Torres-Saillant, Silvio, and Ramona Hernández. *The Dominican Americans*. Westport, Conn.: Greenwood Press, 1998.

Turits, Richard. *Foundations of Despotism: Peasants, the Trujillo Regime, and Modernity in Dominican History*. Stanford, Calif.: Stanford University Press, 2003.

Valdez, Claudina. "Género, discriminación racial y ciudadanía: Un estudio en la escuela dominicana." Pp. 231–66 in *Miradas desencadenantes: Los estudios de género en la República Dominicana al inicio del tercer milenio*, ed. Ginetta E. B. Candelario. Santo Domingo: INTEC and FLACSO, 2005.

Vega, Bernardo. "¿Porque los tres?" Remarks at the opening of Taíno and Spanish Heritage in Today's Dominican Culture, March 24, 1981; repr. in *Museo del Hombre Dominicano Boletín 16*, no. 16 (1981): 129–32.

Vega, Bernardo, ed. *Ensayos sobre cultura dominicana*, 5th ed. Santo Domingo: Fundación Cultural Dominicana, Museo del Hombre Dominicano, 1997.

Veloz Maggiolo, Marcio. *Arqueologia prehistorica de Santo Domingo*. New York: McGraw-Hill Far Eastern Publishers, 1972.

Venator Santiago, Charles Robert. "Race, Space, and the Puerto Rican Citizenship." *Denver University Law Review*, no. 78 (2001): 907–20.

———. "Las Vírgenes de Pénson." Unpublished manuscript, 2004. In the author's possession.

Vicioso, Sherezada (Chiqui). "An Oral History (Testimonio)." Pp. 229–35 in *Breaking Boundaries: Latina Writing and Critical Readings*, ed. Asunción Horno-Delgado, Eliana Ortega, Nina M. Scott, and Nancy Saporta Sternbach. Amherst: University of Massachusetts Press, 1989.

————. "An Oral History." Pp. 270–75 in Denis Lynn Daly Heyck, *Barrios and Borderlands: Cultures of Latinos and Latinas in the United States.* New York: Routledge, 1994.

Wade, Peter. *Blackness and Race Mixture: The Dynamics of Racial Identity in Colombia.* Baltimore: Johns Hopkins University Press, 1993.

Waters, Mary. *Black Identities: West Indian Immigrant Dreams and American Realities.* New York: Russell Sage, 1999.

Weeks, John M., Peter Ferbel, and Virginia Ramirez Zabala. "Herbert W. Krieger y la práctica de la arqueologia 'colonial' en la República Dominicana." *Boletín del Museo del Hombre Dominicano* 20, no. 26 (1994): 77–92.

Weeks, William Earl. *Building the Continental Empire: American Expansion from the Revolution to the Civil War.* Chicago: Ivan R. Dee, 1996.

Wiarda, Howard. "Leading the World from the Caribbean: The Dominican Republic," *Hemisphere 2000,* vol. 7, no 4 (July 1999). Available online at http://www.csis.org/americas/pubs/hemvii4.html (accessed December 17, 2006).

Willett, Julie. *Permanent Waves: The Making of the American Beauty Shop.* New York: New York University Press, 2000.

Williams, John, and Kenneth Morland. *Race, Color and the Young Child.* Chapel Hill: University of North Carolina Press, 1976.

Winn, Peter. *Americas: The Changing Face of Latin America and the Caribbean.* Berkeley: University of California Press, 1992.

Wolf, Naomi. *The Beauty Myth: How Images of Beauty Are Used against Women.* New York: Harper, 2002.

Wright, Winthrop. *Café con Leche: Race, Class, and National Image in Venezuela.* Austin: University of Texas Press, 1990.

Wucker, Michelle. *Why the Cocks Fight: Dominicans, Haitians, and the Struggle for Hispaniola.* New York: Hill and Wang, 1999.

Index

Note: f refers to a figure; n refers to a note; and t refers to a table.

Blanco, Carlos Larrazábal, 92, 95

Bodegueras, 186

Bogaert, Harold Olsen, 112

Bonó, Pedro Francisco, 57–58

Booth renters, 183, 199–201, 290n22

Borneman, John, 86, 102

Bosch, Juan, 3, 91

Bosch, Narciso Alberti, 88, 105, 117, 243

Bourdieu, Pierre, 254

Boyce, William D., 61–62

Boyer, Jean-Pierre, 37, 41, 80, 98, 256n7, 258

Brown, Richard Harvey, 16

Brussell's Exposition (1893), 289n8

Bueno, Daniel, 152, 153, 172, 173–74

Buns (children's hairstyle), 218, 251

Burks, Arthur J., 73–76

Burton, A. A., 53

Businesslike appearances (photo elicitations), 242, 244t7, 247–48

Caamaño Deñó, Francisco A., Col., 91

Cáceres, Ramón, 140

Cacos (guerilla forces in Haiti), 67–68, 69, 75, 76

California, colonization of, 56

Cambiaso, Luis, 87

Campos, Juana, 158f17; on African American identification of Latinos, 159–60; arrival of, in Washington, 151; children of, 157, 158f18; on distance between African Americans and whites, 157; on participating in *Black Mosaic*, 160–61; racial self-perception as *India*, 160. *See also* Quander, Carmen; Toruella, Ramberto

Caribbean Archaeology Conference, 109

Casa Identidad Mujer Negra, 92

Catholicism: as characteristic of

Dominican Republic, 37, 47, 80–81; conversion to, of indigenous population, 120; Dominican elites and, 37; Spanish-language masses in Washington and, 151

Cattle-ranching economy, 4–5, 43, 257

Cazneau, Jane MacManus, 43, 49

Cazneau, William, 43, 49, 51, 52

Central Americans in Washington, 141–42, 167–70, 172–73

"Century of Misery," 4

Césaire, Aimé, 146

Chancer, Lynn, 254

Chester, Colby M., Rear Admiral, 36

Children: births of, 212–13; hairstyles for, 218, 227–28, 251–52, 252f38; in photo elicitations, 251–53; presence of, in beauty shops, 205–7; racial self-perceptions of, 135–36, 174–75, 240–41, 249–50; of West Indian immigrants, 12

Christophe, Henri, 258

Civil Rights Movement, 24, 131, 139, 165, 166, 169, 174, 221

Clark, Kenneth, 249

Clark, Mamie, 249

Cocolo, 161–62, 287n103

Coleman, Willi M., 177, 179, 191, 221

Colored population of Dominican Republic, 64–65, 68

Columbian Lighthouse, 88, 112, 280–81n115

Columbian Quincentennial, 133, 134

Columbus, Christopher, 60, 88, 103

Congress of Black Culture in the Americas, 146

Constitutionalistas, 91

Cooley, Charles, 8

Cooper, James Fenimore, 86

Cordero Michel, Emilio, 265n6

Corporán, Héctor, 21, 22, 145, 150, 162

facts and, 87; Dominican Republic and, 44–45; Manifest Destiny and, 44, 49, 57–58, 61–62, 100; racial portrayals of Dominicans and, 46, 47, 48–49, 53; Samaná Bay annexation and, 49–50, 52; U.S. business interests and, 49; U.S. Customs Receivership and, 37, 61, 85, 160, 287n96

Exposition Universelle de Paris, 289n8

Fabens, Joseph, 49, 50, 52
Fair of Peace and Brotherhood, 88–89, 110–11
Fanon, Frantz, 26, 146
Fennema, Meindert, 19
Feria de la Paz y la Confraternidad del Mundo Libre, 88–89, 110
Fewkes, Jesse Walter, 87, 105–6
Fieldwork methodology: author's appearance as influence in, 29–30; language of interviews and, 28, 269–70n93; selection of research sites in, 27–29. *See also* Photo elicitations; Salon Lamadas
Fina (descriptor of social class), 198–99
First Colloquium on the African Presence in the Antilles, 92
"First Exhibit of Autochthonous Indigenous Art," 109
Fitzpatrick, Joseph P., 246
Forbes, Jack, 1
Forte, Diedra, 203
Fortuna, Xiomara, 95
Foster, Harry L., 70–71
Franck, Harry A., 65–69, 74
Franco Pichardo, Franklin, 59, 95
Free population of Santo Domingo, 5–6, 39, 99, 257–58
French expansionism in Santo Domingo, 40–41, 270n6

French San Domingüe: Creole identity in, 257; Dominican Republic's emergence from, 36; mulattos in, 42, 258; slavery in, 4, 99, 257–58; travel narratives of, 39–40
Furman, Frida Kerner, 179, 225

Gabb, William, 53, 105
Gabriel García, José, 87, 96
Galíndez affair, 78
Gálvan, Manuel de Jesus, 58–60, 80–81, 93, 97, 110
García, Fanny, 112
García Arévalo, Manuel, 109, 123–24
Garvey, Marcus, 146
Gautier, Manuel María, 51
Gavilleros (guerillas), 69
George Washington High School (New York), 11, 12
Gilbertson, Greta A., 246
Gimbenard, Jacinto, 96, 97–98
Gimlin, Deborah, 201
Giorguli, Silvio, 24
Girls, Dominican: Dominicanidad of, 32; first visits of, to beauty salons, 217–18; hairstyling of, 218–20, 219f26, 227, 228; socialization of, 173; transition of, to sexualized young womanhood, 218–19, 219f26
Godreau, Isar Pilar, 32–33
Goffman, Erving, 7, 8, 262
Gold Fields of Santo Domingo, The (Courtney), 51–52
Goméz, Christina, 23–24
González, Nancie L., 29, 225
González, Raymundo, 98
González Canalda, María Filomena, 96
Good Neighbor policy, 76, 78, 88, 140, 141
Goris-Rosario, Anneris, 186
Great Migration, The, 147, 202

234f30; *Indio/India* identity and, 5, 17–20, 58, 160, 199–200, 225, 240, 241; of men in photo elicitations, 245–46, 246ff34–35, 247t8; mixed looks (mestizaje) and, 235, 236–37, 239, 248; as preferred look of Dominican women, 231, 232f27, 233f29, 234–35; pretty looks and, 231, 233f29, 234f30; Puerto Ricans and, 32–33; racial self-identification and, 19, 25, 225; of second-generation Dominicans, 12–13, 25; whiteness and, 32–33, 170, 224–25, 253. *See also* Latinas; Latino community in Washington; Latinos

Hoetink, Harry, 26, 223–24, 254

Hoffnang, Jeffrey, 11

Hogan, John, 46

Home: beauty parlors in, 184, 186–87, 191, 198; as center of social networks, 155–56, 173; Dominican beauty culture in context of, 219, 220

How and Why African People Came to North America (educational kit for *Black Mosaic*), 135

Howard, David, 9–10, 11

Howard University, 152, 165–66

Howe, Louise Kapp, 202

Howe, Samuel G., 53

Hudson, Linda, 49

Hughes, Langston, 146

Hulme, Peter, 101–2

Hunter, Margaret, 254

Hurst, Harry E., 106

Imbert, Ramon, 87

Imperialism, U.S.: collection of native America and, 86–87; development of Latin American racial identities and, 147; Dominican identity formation and, 38, 259–60; Dominican nation-building projects and, 14; Monroe Doctrine and, 44, 100; racial projects of, 36, 38. *See also* Trujillo, Rafael, and Trujillato

Indigenism: Dominicans and, 103, 259–60; ethnological museums and, 109; identity imaginaries and, 119–20; *indigenista* discourse and, 38; *La nueva ola* (the New Wave) and, 91, 92–96, 112, 114, 127, 260; preservation of indigenous ideologies and, 109; in Santo Domingo, 40; Spanish colonialism and Caribbean, 102. *See also* Museo del Hombre Dominicano

Indo-Hispanicity, 32, 99

Indio/India identity, 5, 18–21, 58, 160, 199–200, 225, 240, 241

Ingles (British West Indians), 12, 152

Inman, Samuel Guy, 69–71

Insin, Engin F., 256

Intellectual Cooperation Organization (ico), 110

Inter-American Union of the Caribbean, 109

Itzigsohn, José, 19, 24, 225

James, Caryn, 202

James, Portia, 133

Jenkins, Richard, 2, 8

Jim Crow, 66, 138, 139, 157, 169

Jiménes Grullon, Juan Isidro, 265n6

Jiménez, Blas, 92–93, 95

Kaminsky, Amy K., 35

Karp, Ivan, 142, 149

Keim, De Bonneville Randolph, 52–53, 54, 55

Khan, Aisha, 262

Kidder, Frederick Elwyn, 110

Kinard, John, 132, 133

King, C. Richard, 87

King, Martin Luther, Jr., 139

Kinky hair (*greñas*), 227, 228, 250, 251

Kirshenblatt-Gimblett, Barbara, 120, 149
Kottak, Conrad, 31–32
Krech, Shepard, 86
Krieger, Herbert, 105, 106, 107
Krohn-Hansen, Christian, 243

Labor migrations: of African Americans from U.S. South, 147; for diplomatic community in Washington, 139–40; for domestic labor, 151, 152; of Dominican women, 140–41, 147, 160; of Haitians to Dominican Republic, 72, 85; West Indian labor migrants and, 12, 152, 161–62
La Isabela, excavations at, 119, 282n145
Landers, Jane, 114, 123–24
Latin American Festival, 151–52, 161
Latinas: black ancestry of, 236; at Dominican hair salons, 210–11; in photo elicitations, 231, 232f28, 243. *See also* Dominican hair culture
Latino community in Washington, 262; demographics of, 141; Dominicans identification with, 169–72, 175; exclusion of, from Smithsonian staff, 133–34, 135; negotiation of racial identity of, 167–68; "Old Guard" and, 172; origins of, 139–40; patterns of socializing in, 157; settlement patterns of, 141–42, 159
Latinos: African heritage of, 134, 248; Afro-Latinos, 134, 136, 144–45, 146, 150; as clientele of Dominican businesses, 186; discrimination against, 133–34, 135; Dominicans' identification with, 169–72, 175, 262; as indigenous to Americas, 134; media images of, 141, 236; negotiation of racial identities of, 167–68; Spanish language and

Latino identity of, 159; stereotyped looks of, 248; use of term, 293n10
La Trinitaria, 259
Lavine, Steven D., 142
La Virgen de la Altagracia (Dominican Republic patron saint), 151
Law No. 318, 111
Lemba, Sebastián, 114
Levine, Donald Nathan, 256
Levitt, Peggy, 11–12, 23–24
Lighthouse-design contests, 88, 112, 280–81n115
Liriano, Alejandra, 95
Listín Diario, 108
Llenas, A., 87
Loewenthal, Troetje, 19
Loose hair, 237, 238, 250
Lott, Eric, 132
Lugones, María, 137, 151
Luna, Casilda, 151, 165, 168–69
Luperón, Gregorio, 57–58

Mackenzie, Charles, 41–42
Mangache, Francisco, 146
Mangache, Juan, 146
Manicurists, 194, 198
Maniel José Leta (runaway slave community), 123–24
Manifest Destiny, 44, 49, 57–58, 61–62, 100, 101
Manufacturing employment, 183–84
March on Washington (1963), 139
Marine Corps, U.S., 65, 67, 68, 69–70, 72, 73–76, 91
Maroons, 95, 114, 123–24, 237
Marrero Aristy, Ramón, 96
Marriage preferences of Dominicans, 243–44, 245–49
Martí, José, 59
Martínez-Fernández, Luís, 49, 272n32
Masculinity, 68–69, 74–75
Masena Péralte, Charlemagne, 67–68

Mauss, Marcel, 32
Maxton, Ashindi, 249–50
McKay, Claude, 146
Mead, George, 8
Media accounts: *Black Mosaic* in, 145; of Dominican beauty culture, 184–85; Haiti vs. Dominican Republic in, 61–63; images of Latin Americans in, 141, 236; Indian heritage promoted in, 5; of Trujillo's regime, 72–73; U.S. expansionism and pro-annexation debate in, 51–54
Medical system (U.S.), negotiation of, 212–13
Medina, Maricela: on anti-black attitudes of Central Americans, 167–69; birthplace of, 161–62; on black Hispanics, 170; on declaration of racial loyalties, 166–67; education of, 152, 165–66; home life of, 173
Mejía, Abigaíl, 88, 106, 108
Men: children's perceptions of, 250; as marriage partners, 245–46; in photo elicitations, 245–48; as reproductive partners, 248–49, 248f36
Men's hairstyles, 247–48, 248f36, 249f37
Mercer, Kobena, 254
Merengues, 20, 88–89
Merton, Robert K., 261
Mestizos: hair quality of, 237–38; Hispanic identity and, 235, 236–37, 239, 248; Quincentennial commemoration and, 134; in Spanish Santo Domingo, 42, 43; whiteness and, 42, 43, 58–59, 224; women's bodies in narratives of *mestizaje*, 57, 125
Miami Herald, 5–6
Migration: *Black Mosaic* exhibit and, 134–35; forced migration from Santo Domingo, 3–4; girls' first

visits to beauty salons and, 218–19; Great Migration from U.S. South, 202; of Haitian labor to United States, 72; impact of, on Dominican racial perceptions, 11–12; nationalist identity and, 20; of non-elite Dominicans, 9, 266n29; of political dissidents from Dominican Republic, 92; restrictions during Trujillato, 110, 140; return migrants and, 11–12, 25; transnational Dominican identity and, 11; in Trujillo era, 110, 140–41, 160. *See also* Labor migrations
Mir, Pedro, 94–95
Monolithic Room (Museo del Hombre Dominicano), 116
Monroe Doctrine, 44, 100
Montague, Ludwell Lee, 44
Mora, Sofía: education of, 152–53; on negotiation of racial identity, 167; racial self-perception of, 162–64, 163f19
Morales Languazco, Carlos F., 106
Moreau de Saint-Méry, M. L., 14, 39–41, 147
Morrison, Toni, 79
Moya Pons, Frank, 3, 11, 38, 107
Mulattos, 17t1; in French San Domingüe, 42, 258; Haitian revolution and, 37; historical connotations of, 18; racial self-identification of U.S. Dominicans and, 12; white identity of, 42, 43, 78–79, 224
Museo del Hombre Dominicano: African heritage exhibits of, 85, 111–12, 120–26, 127, 282n145; behavior management technology and, 84–85; drawings of the Dominican Republic in, 53; entrance to, 112–13, 113f6; floor plan of, 115, 115f7, 116–17; founding of, 111–12; Monolithic Room of, 116; pen-and-

Museo del Hombre (*continued*)
ink drawings at, 121, 122, 123, 125;
pre-Colombian artifacts in, 14–15,
112; situ displays in, 119–20, 149;
slavery display of, 120–25; statues
at entrance of, 113, 113f6; Taíno
exhibit in, 115–17, 118f9, 119–20;
women in exhibits of, 119, 125. *See
also* archeological artifacts, excavations
Museum of the American Indian–
Heye Foundation, 86, 105

Nasaw, David, 132
National Committee of Intellectual
Co-operation, 110
National Museum: Anthropological
Research Institute of the University
of Santo Domingo and, 106, 109;
authentic Dominican identity and,
107–8; Diego Columbus's fortress
and, 103–5, 104f3; first exhibit of,
109; founding and establishment
of, 103, 108; in post-occupation era,
107–8
Native Americans, 86–87, 102, 281–
82n128
Negritude, 5–6, 92, 225
Negrophobia: in Alix's décimas, 1–3,
265n3; Anti-Haitianism and, 9; of
Central Americans in Washington,
167–70; of Dominicans, 11, 20,
41–42, 229–30, 244–45; in media
accounts of Haiti, 61–62; norma-
tivity of, 93–94; rejection of, by
Black Mosaic participants, 169; in
travel narratives, 44, 47–48, 51,
55–56, 61–65, 66–67
New Negro Alliance, 138
Newsome, Steven, 22, 134–35
New York metropolitan area: beauty
salons in, 186–87, 188–89t4,
190f20; Latino population in, 142;

racial self-perception studies and,
10, 19
Noble Savage, 102
Nouel, Alejandro, Archbishop, 103
Nueva ola, La (the New Wave), 91,
92–96, 112, 127, 260
Nuñez de Cáceres, José, 37

Ober, Frederic Albion, 60–61, 103
Occupation, The (1822–44). *See*
Haiti
Occupation (U.S.) of Dominican
Republic: Americanization of
language and, 107; during Balaguer
presidency, 91; consumption of
U.S. goods and, 107; guerilla oppo-
sition to, 67–68, 69; infrastruc-
ture improvements during, 71–72;
Marine Corps in, 65, 67, 68, 69–
70, 72, 73–76, 91; paternalist dis-
courses on, 37–38, 73; plundering
of indigenous artifacts during, 86
Office of the National Patrimony
(ONP), 110–11
O'Gorman, Edmundo, 281n125
Omi, Michael, 36, 160
One-drop-of-blood rule, 55, 135, 237
Oné Respé (humanitarian association
in Dominican Republic), 31
Operation Bootstrap, 141
Oral-history interviews, 144–45, 150
Owners of Salon Lamadas, 196–97,
197f23, 204; as childbirth advocate,
212–13; hair texture of, 228, 252; on
job of Dominican hair stylist, 254;
as lesbians, 195–96; relations of,
with clients and coworkers, 211–14;
social class of, 198–99
Ozuma, Esperanza, 152

Pagán Perdomo, Dato, 83, 106, 111,
124
Panamanians, 144–45
Pan American Union, 88, 139

Partido Comunista Dominicano (PCD), 92

Partido Reformista Social Cristiano (PRSC), 90

Pelo bueno (good hair), 182, 199, 204, 215, 228, 231, 237–38, 239

Peña Gómez, Francisco, 273n51

Pen-and-ink drawings, 121, 122, 123, 125

Pénson, Cesar Nicolás, 265n7

Pepín, Ercilia, 90, 106

Permanent Dominican Commission for the Celebration of the Fifth Centennial of the Discovery and Evangelization of America, 89

Pesimista intellectuals, 93

Petión, Alexandre, 258

Photo elicitations: aesthetic norms in, 225–27; best potential candidates in, 242–44; businesslike appearances in, 242, 244t7, 247–48; children's racial preferences in, 250; hair-length groupings of, 230–31; heteronormative bias in, 293–94n26; Latinas in, 231, 232f28, 243; of little girls portrayed in hairstyle books, 251–52, 252f38, 253; men as subjects in, 245–49; methods of, 30, 225–27, 230–31; prettiness in, 231, 232f, 233–34ff, 234–35, 235t5; skin color in, 231, 232–34ff. *See also* Hairstyle books (African American); Hairstyle books (white)

Photography: anti-Haitianism portrayed in, 63; in Museo del Hombre Dominicano exhibits, 117–18; of Taínos, 117–18, 118f9

Pichardo, Bernardo, 96

Pinart, Louis Alphonse, 87

Pink (color of salon décor), 15, 195

Plantations, 3, 4, 98–99, 106–7

Plaza de la Cultura, 8–9, 111, 112

Poor People's Campaign, 131

Port au Prince, 76–77

Porter, David Dixon, 46–49, 52

Potential political candidates in photo elicitations, 242–44, 244t7

Pratt, Mary Louise, 15, 35, 123

Pregnancy, 30, 212–14

Prettiness, perceptions of, 231, 232f, 233–34ff, 234–35t5

Price-Mars, Jean, 146

Primacías de América en La Española (1492–1542), 89

Primitivism: of Haitians, 63, 66, 75–76, 97–98; Native Americans as examples of, 86

Professional status of beauty workers, 203–5, 226

Propaganda: Feria de la Paz y la Confraternidad del Mundo Libre and, 88–89; pro-annexationist, in travel narratives, 51–52; of Trujillato, 72, 73, 77–78, 80–81, 260; for U.S. expansionism, 51–52

Prostitution, 39–40

Providence, Rhode Island, 13, 19

Puerto Rican men, and Dominican women, 186

Puerto Ricans: as best potential political candidate, 243–44; on black identity, 240; oral-history interviews of, 144–45; settlement patterns of, in New York City, 142

Pulp fiction, images of Dominicans in, 73–74

Quander, Carmen, 151, 158f18, 164, 165, 169, 170, 173

Quincentennial commemorations, 90

Race, racism: alterability of, 253, 294n38; American perceptions of whiteness in Dominican Republic and, 46–47; assessments of, in travel narratives, 46–48; blanquea-

Race, racism (*continued*)
miento and, 235, 237, 241–42; caricatures in travel narratives and, 62–63, 79; caricatures of Haitians and, 2–3, 46, 62–63, 66, 75–76, 79, 265n7; cédula de identidad nacional and, 19; in censuses, 20–21; colored population of Dominican Republic and, 6, 64–65, 68; Dominican depictions of Haitians and, 2–3, 265n7; of Dominican Republic in annexation debate, 46, 47, 48–49, 50–51, 53; in Dominican Republic study of racial perception, 16–17, 17t1; facial features as signifier of, 229–30, 294n38; framing of living beings as "last of their race" and, 86; Gallup polls on, 11, 243–44; hair and, 16–17, 17t1, 40, 55, 79, 180–81, 215–16, 227–28, 239–40, 254; of Haiti in annexation debate, 51; images of Dominicans in pulp fiction and, 73–74; *Indio/India* identity and, 5, 17–20, 58, 160, 199–200, 225, 240, 241; intermediate categories of, 262; maroons and, 95, 114, 123–24, 237; of marriage partners, 243–46, 247–49; mixed-race identities of Dominicans and, 73–74; one-drop-of-blood rule and, 55, 135, 237; physical features and, 16; in post-occupation Dominican Republic, 70–71; somatic norm images in, 223–25; Spanish language as marker of, 159–60; of Spanish Santo Domingo, 42–43; translations of, 241; in U.S. annexation initiatives of Dominican Republic, 45–46; vocabulary of, 16, 17t1, 31, 32; of West Indians, 162. *See also* Anti-Haitianism; Black identity; Blackness; *Enriquillo* (Gálvan);

Negrophobia; Photo elicitations; Racial self-identification; Racial self-identification of Dominicans in United States; Skin color; Travel narratives; White identity; Whiteness; White supremacy

Racial self-identification: in Dominican census (1960), 20–21; of Puerto Ricans, 32–33; of Santo Domingans as white, 41–42

Racial self-identification of Dominicans in United States: black identity and, 11, 12, 23t2, 25–26, 159, 162–64, 163f19, 171, 174–76, 225, 228; of Dominican community in Washington, 19, 21, 23t2, 24; identification with Latinos, 169–72, 175, 262; return migrants and, 11–12. *See also* Hairstyle books; Photo elicitations; Salon Lamadas

Raybaud, Maxime, 42–43

Raza cósmica, La, 58

Reagon, Bernice Johnson, 136

Red hair (*pelo colora'o*), 204

Reincken, Sharon, 136, 150

Renda, Mary, 73, 76

Repak, Terry, 165

Reproductive partners, selection of, 248–49, 248f36

Republic of Haiti, 41

Roberts, Peter, 19

Rodríguez, Clara, 29–30, 236

Rodríguez Demorizi, Emilio, 96, 106

Rodríguez Urdañeta, Aberlardo, 120

Roediger, David, 132

Roller sets, 182, 203–4, 219, 220

Roorda, Eric, 72

Rubia, 29, 269n86

Ruffins, Faith Davis, 109, 131, 136

Ruling relations (Smith), 84

Runaway slaves, 4, 92, 93, 114, 123–24

Rydell, Robert, 101

Sallaint, Corina (Mamá Corina),
155–56
Salon hierarchy: beauty salon workers
in, 198–200, 202, 207–8; booth
renters in, 183, 199–200, 200–201,
290n22; educational achievement
in, 198, 200; owners, 198–201
Salon Lamadas, 28, 192f21, 201f24;
African American client at, 209–
10; *Angelitos* and, 211, 214; atmosphere of, 193, 208–9; birthday
celebrations at, 213–14; business
hours of, 193; clientele of, 209–11;
customer satisfaction at, 203–7;
Dominican identity discourses in,
261; eating in, 206–7; floor plan
of, 192f22, 193–94; hairstyle books
in, 227–28; hierarchy in, 198–200;
location of, 191, 193; name of, 195–
96, 291n49; prohibition against
children in, 205–7; as social space,
208; staff of, 196–98
Salvadorans in Washington, 167–68,
172
Samaná Bay, 49–50, 52, 87, 105
San Pedro de Macoris, 106
Santana, Pedro, 45, 51, 52
Santiago de los Caballeros, 16, 60
Santo Domingo: African slaves and
slavery in, 3, 4, 114, 148; cattle
ranches in, 5; Commission of Inquiry at, 53; depopulation of, 3–4;
Dominican identity formation
and, 257; free population of, 5, 39;
French expansionism in, 39–41,
270n6; guerilla forces in, 69; Haiti
invasion of, 37; indigenous ancestry in, 40; infrastructure improvements in, 72; plantations in, 3, 4;
relations of, with Spain, 37, 52,
257; socio-racial formation of, 3–4;
Spanish colonialism and, 257; in
travel narratives, 39–41

Saona Island, 106
Schroder, David, 181, 201
Senghor, Leopold, 146
Sheller, Mimi, 43
Shohat, Ella, 6
Silié, Ruben, 95, 96, 259
Skin color: Dominican identity and,
145; *Indio* identity and, 5, 19; of
men in photo elicitation, 247,
248; preferences in reproductive
partners and, 248–49, 248f36;
prettiness in photo elicitations
and, 231, 232–34ff; primitivism
associated with, 75–76; racial
classifications and, 16, 17t1; somatic norm images and, 223–25; in
Spanish Santo Domingo, 42; valorization of white skin, 239–
40. *See also* Blackness; Whiteness
Slavery: abolition of, 41, 43, 270n6;
artifacts of, 122f11, 123–24; cattle-
ranching economy, 4–5; *cimarrón*
(runaway slave) and, 4, 92, 93, 114,
123–24; corporal punishment of,
121, 121–22ff, 123; in Dominican
identity formation, 3; emancipation in Dominican Republic and,
270n6; free property owners and,
5, 257–58; in French San Domingüe, 4, 99; identification of
slaves as black, 5, 67, 124–25; importation of enslaved Africans, 3, 4,
90, 114, 148; maroon communities
and, 123; in Museo del Hombre
Dominicano's exhibits, 121–25;
opposition to annexation and, 50;
plantation-based African slavery, 3,
4; scholarly works on, 95; Tannenbaum thesis on, 124; in travel
narratives, 121, 121–22ff; women
and, 126
Smith, Dorothy, 7, 8, 84, 180

79; Haitian Revolution in, 79–80; Haitians identified with blackness in, 46–48, 58, 66, 67, 79; Haiti vs. Dominican Republic in, 43–44, 61–65, 75–76; of Mackenzie, 41–42; miscegenation in Dominican Republic in, 74–75; negative depictions of Haiti in, 47, 51, 55–56, 62–65, 66, 70, 75, 259; Negrophobic tropes in, 44, 46–48, 51, 55–57, 61–65, 66–67, 70–71; paternalist discourses in, 73; positive portrayal of Haitians in, 76–77; pro-annexationist propaganda in, 51–55; racial identity in, 13, 41–43, 46–47, 78–79; racialized social settings in, 55–56, 62–63, 66–67; slavery in, 60–61, 121–22; Trujilloist propaganda in, 72–73, 77–78, 80–81, 260; U.S. occupation in, 66–67, 71–72; women in, 40, 71. *See also* Expansionism, U.S.

Treaty of Basel (1795), 41, 270n6

Tres leyendas de colores (Mir), 94–95

Trigueños, 224

Trinidad, 262

Trujillo, Rafael, and Trujillato: cédula de identidad nacional and, 19; Domincan census (1960) and, 20–21; Dominican diplomatic corps and, 140, 284–85n46; Marine Corps and, 72, 73; migrations during, 110, 140–41, 160; public-history projects of, 88–89, 108; public-relations propaganda of, 72, 73, 77–78, 80–81, 260

Turits, Richard, 98, 99

UNESCO, 80, 110, 266n28

United States: annexation of Dominican Republic by, 43, 45; Dominican Republic relations with, 36, 60; Good Neighbor policy of, 76, 78, 140; Native Americans and, 86–87, 102, 281–82n128; perceptions of race of, in Dominican Republic, 46; racial identity in, 11–13; shift from manufacturing to service industries in, 183, 290n23. *See also* Annexation initiatives of United States; Imperialism, U.S.; Travel narratives

Universal Negro Improvement Association (UNIA), 146

Ureña, Pedro Henríquez, 58, 59, 96

Valdés, Mimi, 211

Valdez, Claudina, 250–51

Vasconcelos, José, 58

Vásquez, Horacio, 104, 140

Vásquez, Obed, 24

Vega, Bernardo, 53, 111, 112

Verrill, A. Hyatt, 63–65, 87

Vicioso, Chiqui, 12, 24, 25

Vincent, Stenio, 76, 77

Wade, Benjamin F., 53

Walker, Stanley, 78–80

Washington, D.C. *See* Black community in Washington; Dominican community in Washington

Washington Heights, New York. *See* Dominican community in New York City; Salon Lamadas

Waters, Mary, 12

Weeks, William Earl, 44

Wessin y Wessin, Elías, 91

West Indians, 12, 152, 161–62

White, Andrew D., 53

White beauty salon operators, 201, 202

White identity: blanqueamiento and, 235, 237, 241–42; of Dominicans, 15–16, 20–21, 47, 49, 55–57; racial self-perceptions of children and, 249–50; of return migrants, 25;

White identity (*continued*)
of Trujillo, 71; of West Indians as
"white blacks," 162
Whiteness: assessments of, in travel
narratives, 46–47; as beauty, 215,
216–17, 231, 232–33ff; class mobility and, 47; colored population
of Dominican Republic and, 64; as
desired identity, 1–2; in Dominican census (1960), 20–21; Dominican hair culture and, 182, 228,
234, 235t5; Dominican Republic as
whiter than Haiti, 46–47, 51, 70–
71, 259; of Dominican Republic in
annexation debate, 50–51, 55; hair
texture and, 16–17, 180–81, 215,
216, 239–40; Hispanic norms of,
32–33, 170, 224–25, 253; Iberian
variant of, 224, 229; mestizos and,
42, 43, 58–59, 224; portrayals of
Dominicans in travel narratives
and, 46, 47, 48–49, 53, 55, 78;
prettiness and, 231, 232, 235, 236;

racial self-identification of Dominicans in the United States and,
23–24; social mobility and, 5, 23–
24; Spanish Santo Domingo and,
42; in Trujlloist propaganda, 72; in
United States, 253–54
White supremacy, 1–3, 58–59, 61–62,
93, 132, 265n3
Willett, Julie, 180
Winant, Howard, 36, 160
Wood, Patricia K., 256
World Columbian Exposition (1893),
103
World's Fairs and Expositions, 60,
86, 88–89, 101, 103, 110, 131,
289n8
Woss y Gil, Alejandro, 103

Yang, Lijun, 246
Young Dominicans: black identity of,
174–75, 240–41; social space of,
173–74; Spanish language used by,
12–13, 159

GINETTA E. B. CANDELARIO

is an associate professor of sociology and Latin American

and Latina/o studies and a member of the Program Committee

for the Study of Women and Gender at Smith College.

Library of Congress Cataloging-in-Publication Data

Candelario, Ginetta E. B.
Black behind the ears : Dominican racial identity
from museums to beauty shops / Ginetta E. B. Candelario.
p. cm.
Includes bibliographical references and index.
ISBN-13: 978-0-8223-4018-8 (cloth : alk. paper)
ISBN-13: 978-0-8223-4037-9 (pkb. : alk. paper)
1. Blacks—Dominican Republic—Race identity.
2. Ethnicity—Dominican Republic. 3. National characteristics,
Dominican. 4. Dominicans—United States—Ethnic identity.
I. Title.
F1941.F55C36 2007
305.896'07293—dc22   2007017114